A Prelude to the Welfare State

D1546154

**NBER Series on Long-term Factors in
Economic Development**
A National Bureau of Economic Research Series
Edited by Claudia Goldin

Also in the series

Claudia Goldin
*Understanding the Gender Gap: An Economic History of
American Women* (Oxford University Press, 1990)

Roderick Floud, Kenneth Wachter, and Annabel Gregory
*Height, Health and History: Nutritional Status in the United
Kingdom, 1750–1980* (Cambridge University Press, 1990)

Robert A. Margo
*Race and Schooling in the South, 1880–1950: An Economic
History* (University of Chicago Press, 1990)

Samuel H. Preston and Michael R. Haines
*Fatal Years: Child Mortality in Late Nineteenth-Century
America* (Princeton University Press, 1991)

Barry Eichengreen
*Golden Fetters: The Gold Standard and the Great Depression,
1919–1939* (Oxford University Press, 1992)

Ronald N. Johnson and Gary D. Libecap
*The Federal Civil Service System and the Problem of
Bureaucracy: The Economics and Politics of Institutional
Change* (University of Chicago Press, 1994)

Naomi R. Lamoreaux
*Insider Lending: Banks, Personal Connections, and Economic
Development in Industrial New England* (Cambridge
University Press, 1994)

Lance E. Davis, Robert E. Gallman, and Karin Gleiter
*In Pursuit of Leviathan: Technology, Institutions, Productivity,
and Profits in American Whaling, 1816–1906* (University of
Chicago Press, 1997)

Dora L. Costa
*The Evolution of Retirement: An American Economic History,
1880–1990* (University of Chicago Press, 1998)

Joseph P. Ferrie
Yankeys Now: Immigrants in the Antebellum U.S., 1840–1860
(Oxford University Press, 1999)

Robert A. Margo
Wages and Labor Markets in the United States, 1820–1860
(University of Chicago Press, 2000)

A Prelude to the Welfare State

The Origins of Workers' Compensation

**Price V. Fishback and
Shawn Everett Kantor**

The University of Chicago Press

Chicago and London

PRICE V. FISHBACK is the Frank and Clara Kramer Professor of Economics at the University of Arizona and a research associate of the National Bureau of Economic Research. His published work includes *Soft Coal, Hard Choices: The Economic Welfare of Bituminous Coal Miners, 1890–1930*. SHAWN EVERETT KANTOR is professor of economics and public administration and policy at the University of Arizona and a research associate of the National Bureau of Economic Research. His published work includes *Politics and Property Rights: The Closing of the Open Range in the Postbellum South*.

Their work on the battles over state insurance of workers' compensation, discussed in this book, was awarded the Cole Prize for best article in the *Journal of Economic History* in 1996–1997.

The University of Chicago Press, Chicago 60637
The University of Chicago Press, Ltd., London
© 2000 by The University of Chicago
All rights reserved. Published 2000
Printed in the United States of America
09 08 07 06 05 04 03 02 01 00   1 2 3 4 5
ISBN: 0-226-25163-2 (cloth)

Library of Congress Cataloging-in-Publication Data

Fishback, Price Van Meter.
    A prelude to the welfare state : the origins of workers'
compensation / Price V. Fishback and Shawn Everett Kantor
        p.   cm.—(NBER series on long-term factors in economic
development)
    Includes bibliographical references and index.
    ISBN 0-226-25163-2 (cl. : alk. paper)
    1. Workers' compensation—United States.   2. Workers'
compensation—Law and legislation—United States.   3. Workers'
compensation—Law and legislation—United States—States.
4. Insurance, Employers' liability—United States.   I. Kantor,
Shawn Everett.   II. Title.   III. Series.
HD7103.65.U6F535   2000
368.4'1'00973—DC21   99-38648
                                                                         CIP

♾ The paper used in this publication meets the minimum
requirements of the American National Standard for Information
Sciences—Permanence of Paper for Printed Library Materials,
ANSI Z39.48-1992.

Relation of the Directors to the
Work and Publications of the
National Bureau of Economic Research

1. The object of the National Bureau of Economic Research is to ascertain and to present to the public important economic facts and their interpretation in a scientific and impartial manner. The Board of Directors is charged with the responsibility of ensuring that the work of the National Bureau is carried on in strict conformity with this object.

2. The President of the National Bureau shall submit to the Board of Directors, or to its Executive Committee, for their formal adoption all specific proposals for research to be instituted.

3. No research report shall be published by the National Bureau until the President has sent each member of the Board a notice that a manuscript is recommended for publication and that in the President's opinion it is suitable for publication in accordance with the principles of the National Bureau. Such notification will include an abstract or summary of the manuscript's content and a response form for use by those Directors who desire a copy of the manuscript for review. Each manuscript shall contain a summary drawing attention to the nature and treatment of the problem studied, the character of the data and their utilization in the report, and the main conclusions reached.

4. For each manuscript so submitted, a special committee of the Directors (including Directors Emeriti) shall be appointed by majority agreement of the President and Vice Presidents (or by the Executive Committee in case of inability to decide on the part of the President and Vice Presidents), consisting of three Directors selected as nearly as may be one from each general division of the Board. The names of the special manuscript committee shall be stated to each Director when notice of the proposed publication is submitted to him. It shall be the duty of each member of the special manuscript committee to read the manuscript. If each member of the manuscript committee signifies his approval within thirty days of the transmittal of the manuscript, the report may be published. If at the end of that period any member of the manuscript committee withholds his approval, the President shall then notify each member of the Board, requesting approval or disapproval of publication, and thirty days additional shall be granted for this purpose. The manuscript shall then not be published unless at least a majority of the entire Board who shall have voted on the proposal within the time fixed for the receipt of votes shall have approved.

5. No manuscript may be published, though approved by each member of the special manuscript committee, until forty-five days have elapsed from the transmittal of the report in manuscript form. The interval is allowed for the receipt of any memorandum of dissent or reservation, together with a brief statement of his reasons, that any member may wish to express; and such memorandum of dissent or reservation shall be published with the manuscript if he so desires. Publication does not, however, imply that each member of the Board has read the manuscript, or that either members of the Board in general or the special committee have passed on its validity in every detail.

6. Publications of the National Bureau issued for informational purposes concerning the work of the Bureau and its staff, or issued to inform the public of activities of Bureau staff, and volumes issued as a result of various conferences involving the National Bureau shall contain a specific disclaimer noting that such publication has not passed through the normal review procedures required in this resolution. The Executive Committee of the Board is charged with review of all such publications from time to time to ensure that they do not take on the character of formal research reports of the National Bureau, requiring formal Board approval.

7. Unless otherwise determined by the Board or exempted by the terms of paragraph 6, a copy of this resolution shall be printed in each National Bureau publication.

(Resolution adopted October 25, 1926, as revised through September 30, 1974)

To Fran

To Jennifer, Quinn, and Jake

Contents

Acknowledgments

In the course of writing this book we have benefited from the generosity of numerous colleagues, granting agencies, and our families. We owe special thanks to Claudia Goldin for her comments, guidance, and encouragement while we wrote the original journal articles underlying this book and then worked to develop our ideas into a book manuscript. Gary Libecap generously shared his insights on numerous drafts of each phase of the project. We have been truly lucky to have such a great colleague with us in Arizona.

Financial support for the project was provided by the National Science Foundation Grant No. SBR-9223058, the Earhart Foundation, the University of Arizona Foundation, and the Spanish Ministry of Education and Culture. Mark Isaac in his role as department head was helpful in providing funds for travel and data entry when they were needed most.

Presenting our work in numerous forums over the eight years of working on this project helped us to clarify the issues and to understand workers' compensation better ourselves. Colleagues involved in studying the Development of the American Economy under the aegis of the National Bureau of Economic Research endured numerous presentations of various phases of the work. Each discussion helped us improve the work immensely. We have benefited from the comments of workshop participants at numerous universities, including Ben-Gurion, California–Berkeley, California–Davis, California–Los Angeles, California–Riverside, California Institute of Technology, Carlos III de Madrid, Carnegie Mellon, Chicago, Columbia, Cornell, Georgia, Harvard, Hawaii, Hebrew, Hoover Institution, Illinois, Indiana, Kansas, Kentucky, London School of Economics, Maryland, McGill, North Carolina State, Northwestern, Queens (Ontario), Stanford, and Toronto. We presented various components of the research at a number of conferences, including meetings of the Economic History Association, the Cliometrics Conference, All-UC Economic History Conference, the American Law and Economics Association, and the Allied Social Science Associations.

Many colleagues along the way have offered important advice on data, analysis, and interpretation. John Wallis and Sumner LaCroix, who shared the travails of graduate school with Price, continue to be great friends, confidants, and professional colleagues to us both. The following people have given us specific comments that changed the way we thought about some aspect of what we have written about workers' compensation: Lee Alston, Jeremy Atack, Susan Carter, Lee Craig, Barry Eichengreen, Joseph Ferrie, Richard Epstein, Doc Ghose, Edward Glaeser, Avner Greif, Michael Haines, Robert Higgs, Lawrence Katz, J. Morgan Kousser, Jeff LaFrance, Patrick Legros, Dean Lueck, Bob Margo, Joel Mokyr, Roger Noll, Douglass North, Ron Oaxaca, Martha Olney, Sam Peltzman, Stan Reynolds, Jim Ratliff, Joshua Rosenbloom, Barbara Sands, Joseph Sicilian, William Sundstrom, Richard Sutch, Joseph Terza, Robert Topel, Tom Weiss, Paul Wilson, John Wooders, and a host of anonymous referees. All of these people helped improve the book, yet responsibility for any of its shortcomings is ours.

We collected empirical evidence for our research with the help of fine staff members at several excellent archives and libraries: the U.S. Department of Labor Library, the Wisconsin State Historical Society, the Ohio State University Library, the Ohio Historical Society, the Cincinnati Public Library, the Alabama Department of Archives and History, Missouri Historical Society, the Minnesota State Historical Society, the University of Washington Library, and Littauer and Baker Libraries at Harvard University.

We received able research assistance from Joshua Gotkin, Melissa Thomasson, Kari Beardsley, and Sule Balkan. Amanda Ebel and Jeff Taylor entered and checked tremendous amounts of data.

We would like to thank the following publishers for allowing us to reprint material from our earlier articles that have appeared in print in their journals. Small parts of chapter 2 have been reprinted from Price V. Fishback and Shawn Everett Kantor, "'Square Deal' or Raw Deal? Market Compensation for Workplace Disamenities, 1884–1903," *Journal of Economic History* 52 (December 1992): 826–48 (used with the permission of Cambridge University Press); and from Shawn Everett Kantor and Price V. Fishback, "Non-Fatal Accident Compensation Under the Negligence Liability System at the Turn of the Century," *Journal of Law, Economics, and Organization* 11 (April 1995): 406–33 (used with the permission of Oxford University Press). Small parts of chapter 3 and a significant part of appendix D were published in Price V. Fishback and Shawn Everett Kantor, "Did Workers Pay for the Passage of Workers' Compensation Laws?" *Quarterly Journal of Economics* 110 (August 1995): 713–42 (used with the permission of MIT Press). Small parts of chapter 3 and a significant portion of appendix F appeared in Shawn Everett Kantor and Price V. Fishback, "Precautionary Saving, Insurance, and the Origins of Workers' Compensation," *Journal of Political Economy* 104 (April 1996): 419–42 (courtesy of the University of Chicago Press). Parts of chapter 4, appendix H, and appendix I appeared in Price V. Fishback and Shawn Everett Kantor, "The Adoption of Workers' Compensation in the United States, 1900–1930," *Journal of Law and Economics* 61 (October 1998): 305–42 (used with the permission of the University of Chicago Press). A small part of chapter 5 appeared in Shawn Everett Kantor and Price V. Fishback, "Coalition Formation and the Adoption of Workers' Compensation: The Case of Missouri, 1911 to 1926," in *The Regulated Economy: A Historical Approach to Political Economy,* edited by Claudia Goldin and Gary D. Libecap, 259–97 (Chicago: University of Chicago Press, 1994). Parts of chapter 5 appeared in Shawn Everett Kantor and Price V. Fishback, "How Minnesota Adopted Workers' Compensation," *Independent Review* 2 (Spring 1998): 557–78 (used with the permission of the Independent Institute). Parts of chapter 6 and appendix J are from Price V. Fishback and Shawn Everett Kantor, "The Durable Experiment: State Insurance of Workers' Compensation Risk in the Early Twentieth Century," *Journal of Economic History* 56 (December 1996): 809–36 (used with the permission of Cambridge University Press). Parts of chapter 7 and appendix K first appeared in Price V. Fishback and Shawn Everett Kantor, "The Political Economy of Workers' Compensation Benefits, 1910–1930," *Explorations in Economic History* 35 (April 1998): 109–39 (used with the permission of Academic Press).

Price owes special thanks to his family. I owe the largest debt to my wife Pam Slaten. Sharing our lives together has enriched my own life beyond measure. My sister Taylor is warm, generous, and one of the finest people I know. Better yet, she indulges my second childhood, as I play with my nieces Jamie, Erin, and Katherine. I dedicate the book to my mother Fran, who instilled in me the positive attitude that has helped me appreciate just how wonderful life can be.

Shawn's debts to his family are no less. This book is dedicated to my wife Jennifer and boys Quinn and Jake. The best part of a day of writing was coming home. Parts of the book's rewriting and editing took place during a sabbatical leave visit to Universidad Carlos III de Madrid. My friends Diego Moreno and Praveen Kujal made me feel welcome in a foreign land. The fondest memories of working on this book occurred not in an office, archives, or before a computer, but in the course of seeing Europe with $1\frac{1}{2}$ and $3\frac{1}{2}$ year olds. Carrying Quinn on my shoulders up a mountain in Sintra, or riding a camel through the Negev, or watching the boys play amidst the Roman Forum, those are the most precious moments.

Introduction

Why Study the Origins of Workers' Compensation?

Workers' compensation fundamentally changed the nature of workplaces and social insurance in the United States. When introduced by state governments between 1910 and 1920, it became arguably the first widespread social insurance program in U.S. history. Workers' compensation set precedents for government requirements of employment-based social insurance that led to the implementation of unemployment insurance, social security, medicare, and eventually to the entire network of modern social welfare programs in the United States. It was by far the most successful form of labor legislation proposed by the Progressive Movement in the early 1900s. In the legal realm, workers' compensation was the major tort reform of the twentieth century, helping set the stage for the acceptance of no-fault liability rules for automobile accidents and strict liability court rulings for product liability.

Workers' compensation programs are sponsored by state governments to help workers deal with the aftermath of workplace accidents. If an accident arises out of and in the course of employment, the employer is required to pay for nearly all of the medical costs of the accident and to replace up to two-thirds of the workers' lost earnings. Depending on the state, employers can obtain insurance coverage for this responsibility from insurance companies, through state funds, or if solvent enough, through self-insurance. In the 1990s American employers spent approximately 2 to 2.5 percent of their payrolls on costs associated with workers' compensation. The families of accident victims receive over 40 billion dollars in benefits each year, an amount that nearly doubles the payments of benefits to unemployed workers.[1] The programs have been the subject of substantial debate over the past two decades. During the 1980s and early 1990s, workers' compensation costs rose faster than health care costs, and numerous state legislatures have sought various reforms.

Today, workers' compensation is one of a wide range of social welfare programs. The federal government, in various combinations with state and local governments, offers unemployment insurance, social security, aid to families with dependent children, food stamps, medicare, medicaid, supplemental security income, and subsidies for housing and other basic needs. Around 1910 the social welfare landscape was nearly barren in comparison. Help for the poor or those with the ill fortune to incur illness, injury, or unemployment was largely a local responsibility. Various cities and counties, along with charitable organizations, provided some forms of poor relief. State governments provided limited schools and housing for the insane and for disabled children. The federal government provided disability pensions to the aged veterans employed as troops in the Civil War. Workers injured in workplace accidents had some recourse for receiving compensation if they could show that the employer was at fault for the accident. There is also evidence that employers paid higher wages to workers who faced greater risks of accidents or of becoming unemployed, although it is unclear that the higher wages fully covered the expected loss associated with such events. Generally, families took steps to protect themselves against ill fortune by accumulating precautionary savings, by joining mutual societies through fraternal organizations or at work, by purchasing limited amounts of insurance, or by sending women and children to work when bad times hit. Yet these methods offered protection for only a limited period, as families whose breadwinners experienced unemployment or injuries sometimes lost several months of income.

In the early twentieth century, the attitude toward payments to the unfortunate was based on notions of fault and responsibility. There was a general feeling that the vast majority of the poor bore the lion's share of responsibility for their fate. They should receive only a brief helping hand to get them back on their feet. Policymakers feared that generous benefits to the destitute would keep them from assuming responsibility for their own well-being, which in turn would lead to continued reliance on the benefits. For their own good, the unemployed needed to continue seeking work and payments to them would only retard their efforts to search effectively. The elderly poor were generally understood to not have saved enough during their primary earning years, and too much of a handout to this group would encourage current working families to rely on future handouts. The families of workers injured or killed on the job received compensation only if it could be shown that the employer and not the worker or his coworker was at fault.

During the Progressive Era some of these attitudes began to change, as reformers began pressing for governments and employers to accept more responsibility for the ill fortune of the poor. Various employment-based social insurance programs were proposed at the state level, including workers' compensation for the injured, unemployment benefits, sickness insurance, and old-age pension programs. Of these programs, only workers' compensation received widespread support. All but five states adopted workers' compensation between 1910 and 1921. Thus, workers' compensation became the first widespread civilian, employment-based social insurance program. Along with mothers' pension programs, which were established virtually simultaneously, workers' compensation set the stage for the broad network of social programs we have today.[2]

The shift toward workers' compensation established the precedent for governmental aid programs for needy civilians that was not tied to notions of fault. Further, it established the underlying principle that the government should require that employers provide or share in providing for the funds distributed to their workers when injured, unemployed, or retired.

Why did workers' compensation lead the way and not other programs? Many legislative changes are evolutionary rather than revolutionary. Workers' compensation was a much smaller step toward social welfare programs than unemployment insurance or social security would have been. Employers were already required by common law to compensate injured workers when the employer was at fault, while employers bore no legal responsibility to their unemployed or retired workers. Thus, it was easier for employers to swallow the requirement that they compensate their workers for all accidents regardless of fault than it would have been for them to pay unemployment compensation.[3] From the general public's perspective, workers' compensation did not impose a general tax burden outside the employment relationship. Compensation for workplace accidents also was less troubling for those who worried about personal responsibility and the impact of payments on the poor's acceptance of responsibility. The continued mechanization of workplaces raised questions about the assignment of fault for workplace accidents. Many accidents seemed to come from the inherent dangers of work and fault could not easily be assigned to either the worker or employer. If the employer was not at fault under the old system, then the worker and his family bore the brunt of the damage, even though the accident victim might not have been at fault.[4] Payments to accident victims also seemed less likely to cause behavior that led to more accidents, a phenomenon known as "moral hazard," than would payments, say, to workers who were unemployed. Injuries were painful, raising the cost of the accident to the worker well beyond lost earnings and medical expenses. When introduced, the workers' compensation programs also worked to prevent moral hazard by limiting the payments to two-thirds and often much less of lost earnings. Thus, if any social welfare program was likely to be acceptable as a relatively small step in the evolutionary process and a testing ground before further steps were taken, it was workers' compensation. Had workers' compensation not been reasonably satisfactory to employers, workers, insurers, and taxpayers in the 1910s and 1920s, it could easily be argued that unemployment insurance and social security would not have received widespread support. Once unemployment insurance and social security were established, it became easier for the federal government in combination with the states to further develop welfare programs that were not based on employer contributions. Thus, workers' compensation was a key early link in the chain establishing the American welfare state. The programs were truly a prelude to the modern welfare state.

The introduction of workers' compensation involved more than just introducing social insurance. From a legal perspective, the new laws established the leading liability reform of the early twentieth century. The liability rule change is an important issue in modern discussions of the optimal set of liability rules for accidents, whether they occur at work, on the road, in hospitals, or in the use of products. The liability rules, by determining who is responsible for the damage, determine the incentives to prevent accidents for the parties involved in a relationship. At the turn of the century, the liability for workplace accidents was assigned based on fault. In the simplest terms, if the worker could show that the employer's negligence had caused the accident, the worker potentially received his medical costs plus had his lost income replaced. However, if the worker's own negligence caused the accident, the employer was legally required to pay him nothing. Employers could also invoke additional defenses that we will discuss later. The workers' compensation laws shifted the liability to a no-fault rule. Essentially, any worker injured on the job received compensation, although the compensation did not fully replace his lost earnings. This shift in liability helped set precedents for the shifts in liability from fault-based to no-fault systems that we see in many areas today. The courts have implicitly moved away from negligence liability to strict liability for consumer products, while numerous states have adopted various forms of no-fault policies.

The study of the transition from negligence liability to workers' compensation offers an excellent opportunity to compare the actual operations of different types of liability rules. While negligence liability was the basis of the common law treatment of workplace accidents at the turn of the century, the vast majority of accident cases were settled outside the court system. Using the court system was costly enough that there was no guarantee that the payments of damages to injured workers closely followed the strictures of the common law. By examining the de facto compensation system under negligence liability and workers' compensation, we can make more direct comparisons of liability rules in actual settings, rather than focusing on a theoretical comparison of liability rules in a vacuum. Further, the impact of different liability rules are determined in part by the degree to which insurance and labor markets operate smoothly.

We will examine how the change to workers' compensation influenced wages, accident prevention, and insurance purchases with an eye to how employers, workers, and insurers benefited or lost from changes in these systems. The result is a careful empirical comparison of the operations of negligence and no-fault rules in a real-world setting.

Finally, studying the origins of workers' compensation offers an opportunity to learn how politics and economics influence legislation at the state level. Policymakers have increasingly called for a shift in social welfare programs from the federal to the state and local level. They anticipate that the gains from experimentation with different programs and "survival of the fittest" will exceed any losses from uniformity in policies across the country. Workers' compensation is rare among the major social insurance programs in that it was from the beginning legislated at the state level with no federal involvement and has remained a state responsibility ever since. The political strength and the specific interests of employers, workers, insurers, and reformers differed in the various states. The result was substantial variation in the workers' compensation programs with respect to various attributes, including benefit levels, administrative systems, and methods of insurance. In turn, the features of the workers' compensation program influenced the wages paid to workers and likely influenced to some degree employment and the types of industry that developed in each state.

The adoption of workers' compensation is an important case study that offers some insights into what we can anticipate from a focus of policy at the state level. Since the beginning of the Republic, policymakers and scholars have recognized that interest groups are a driving force in our political economic process. With that in mind, we can understand legislation as falling in one of various categories along a continuum. At one extreme, an interest group manages to get the legislature to enact legislation that benefits its special interest at the expense of all other interest groups. At the other extreme is legislation that benefits all of the interest groups. In our numerous conversations with people in the course of writing this book, the vast majority of those with whom we spoke, including many scholars, told us that they believe that workers' compensation was introduced as the result of a major victory scored by workers over their employers. But there seems to be a disconnection between the opinions held by most people and what is found in the scholarly literature. As we show in chapter 1, several scholars have documented that many employers actively supported workers' compensation when it was introduced. In fact, we show that workers, employers, and insurance companies all tended to support the general notion of workers' compensation, although they fought bitterly over the details of the law. Although not every person in each group benefited from the law, we think it clear that the vast majority in each group gained from the new law in each state.

This finding raises some questions about the importance of progressive reformers to the adoption of workers' compensation. Reformers sought a wide range of social insurance programs, including unemployment insurance, sickness insurance, and old-age insurance, yet workers' compensation was the only one that passed because it received widespread support from the economic interest groups. This does not mean that progressives played no role. They contributed to the passage of the general law and had even more impact on specific details of the law in some states. Yet it might well be said that workers' compensation owed less of its success to the progressives than was owed by the progressives themselves to the passage of workers' compensation for their own success.

What explains the general view that workers' compensation was a victory for workers over employers? It may well be that most people base their opinions on their impressions of the current system and have not had the time or inclination to read the scholarly literature. When we talk to employers, they actively complain to us about the costs of workers' compensation programs, which rose faster than health care costs during the 1980s and early 1990s. Workers express some dissatisfaction with benefit levels but seem horrified if we suggest a return to the old negligence liability system. Generally, most people view workers' compensation positively, as a way to force employers to compensate workers for the dangers that they face in the workplace. It is not surprising, therefore, that many people see the origins of workers' compensation as a major victory for workers.

In fact, it is extremely important to understand the origins of workers' compensation and of many of the other forms of legislation and social insurance we have today. As we will see in chapter 8, workers' compensation faces its share of problems today, but many of these problems are different from those that generated the introduction of workers' compensation in the first place. If we understand the origins of workers' compensation, particularly the problems it was meant to resolve, we will be better equipped to overcome today's problems without recreating the problems that brought the program into being in the first place.

Notes

1. U.S. Social Security Administration (1996, 159, 350–51). The government spends approximately $160 billion on public assistance, $23 billion on Aid to Families with Dependent Children, and $22 billion on food stamps.

2. Theda Skocpol (1992) and Jill Quadagno (1988) both emphasize the importance of Civil War disability pensions to veterans as early precursors of modern social insurance. There is a sense in which this is true, because the benefits policies

were increasingly generous over time, covering roughly 18 percent of the U.S. population over age 65 in 1910. In another sense, however, this is just an example of the federal government taking care of former employees. The federal government has often led the way in introducing benefits for its employees.

3. See Skocpol (1992, 296) and Orloff (1993, 239).

4. See Dodd (1936) and Somers and Somers (1954).

Framing the Issues

In 1916 Jim Hurd went to work at the Roda No. 2 mine in Virginia. As he worked to cut and load coal one day, he could hear the roof creaking and rumbling overhead. To prevent roof falls, he typically placed timbers in strategic spots throughout the area of the mine where he was working. Later in the day, Hurd left the area he had been working and met up with Bill Donnelly, whom he stooped down to help move a tie for the coal car tracks. A piece of slate fell out of the roof hitting Hurd and inflicting serious injuries. He died soon afterward, leaving a widow and infant children.[1]

Since Hurd died in Virginia in 1916, any compensation his family received from his employer depended in part on whether it could be shown that the Stonega Coke and Coal Company was negligent. In this case because the fall of slate had occurred in an entryway, where the company had responsibility to keep the roof safe, Stonega's lawyers felt that it was likely that the court would consider the company negligent. Under common law, a court might have awarded Hurd's family a substantial sum that would have paid them the value of his earnings over the rest of his normal life. However, Stonega's lawyers had an array of legal defenses they could invoke to prevent this outcome. For example, they could argue that Hurd knew of the risks of a slate fall when he took the job and that Hurd was already receiving extra compensation in his wages from Stonega to accept these risks. Thus, Stonega could be freed from paying damages by this assumption of risk defense.

Stonega had additional defenses if the cause of the accident had been different. Say Hurd had stayed in his own workplace that day and been killed by a fall of slate there. If Stonega's lawyers could have shown that Hurd's coworker had failed to prop the roof in a timely fashion, then Stonega was freed of liability. They could have argued that Hurd's family should sue his coworker for the damages because the coworker's negligence caused the accident. Finally, say the accident was caused in part by Hurd's own failure to prop the roof effectively. The lawyers could then argue that Hurd's own negligence contributed to the accident, so that Stonega was not required to pay.

Under negligence liability the judicial system had to follow a complicated decision process that determined whether Hurd received compensation from Stonega. If the case went to court, the employer or the insurance company paid legal defense fees, while families like Hurd's typically retained a lawyer who would receive one-fourth to one-third of any payments the family received. If the family won the first round, Stonega's lawyers were likely to appeal the decision. If the family could make a strong case for employer negligence, they could fight it through the appeals court and potentially win a large settlement, but the decision often would be several years away and there still remained the risk of losing on appeal. In fact, the vast majority of cases never reached a court decision. Both sides could benefit by settling the issue quickly. Stonega could avoid their own court costs, while Hurd's family could receive financial assistance to help cover their necessities immediately. Stonega's generosity in settlements was influenced by the cause of the accident. If they felt that they would eventually lose in court, they were likely to make a more generous offer, but one that was well below the potential damages that might be awarded in court. In Hurd's case, where the company feared that they might be found liable, his brother demanded a settlement payment of eight thousand dollars. After protracted negotiations, Stonega settled on a payment to the family of twenty-five hundred dollars, half to the widow and half to Hurd's infant children. In other cases, where the lawyers felt the company was not negligent or that the worker was at fault, Stonega did not pay damages or settled for one or two hundred dollars. On average, the results of several surveys in various states suggest that about half the families of fatal accident victims received a positive payment from employers, and the typical amount was about a year's income. For injured workers, Stonega and other employers sometimes offered benefits like a free use of a company house to the family for a period of time. If Hurd had not died, the coal company might have employed him in a less demanding job until he recovered.

Given the relatively small amounts that Hurd's family might expect to receive, Hurd and his family had to seek ways before the accident of protecting the family against the possibility that he might be injured or killed. Hurd's mining wages were generally higher than in other industries, in part as a reward for accepting the higher risk of mining. Many families tried to increase their savings to have resources available to cover their losses. An accident early in Hurd's career, however, would have led to expenses that easily overwhelmed the savings collected. A number of families bought life insurance with an average payout of about one year's income. The family faced more problems in buying insurance against accidents that disabled him because premiums were expensive and access was limited. Some employers helped workers establish mutual societies to provide a limited level of benefits for families.

Had Hurd been killed in Virginia in 1919, his family would have faced an entirely different legal scenario. All Hurd's family essentially would have had to show was that the accident occurred while he was working. Whether he was at fault, Stonega was at fault, or Hurd's coworker was at fault was irrelevant. The workers' compensation law spelled out the payment that Hurd's family would receive from Stonega based on his weekly earnings. In Virginia in 1919, Hurd's family would have received one hundred dollars for funeral expenses plus a weekly payment of half of his earnings up to a maximum of ten dollars for three hundred weeks. The process was simplified, although the family might have needed to retain legal counsel if Stonega disputed whether the accident occurred on the job, the level of Hurd's weekly earnings, or connections between Hurd and his family. Had Hurd only been injured, there may have been disputes over the extent of the injury and his medical costs. Taking into account all accidents, no matter the cause and results ranging in severity from short-term disability to death, Hurd and his family on average would have received higher payments with the switch to workers' compensation. Under negligence liability there was always the chance of much larger rewards but there were substantial odds that they would receive no payments at all. Under workers' compensation we estimate that employers wound up paying out about one and one-half to three times as much to families of accident victims than under negligence liability.

This transition in the treatment of Jim Hurd's family and other working families not only involved a change in liability rules, it was a central step in the development of the American welfare state. The goal of this book is to answer two central questions: First, how might various groups have gained from the adoption of workers' compensation? Second, what was the process that led so many state legislatures to adopt workers' compensation laws? To answer both questions, we need to examine closely the experiences of workers, employers, insurers, lawyers, and taxpayers during the transition. Close study raises a host of issues: how closely the administration of negligence liability and later workers' compensation followed the liability rules; how the changes in liability influenced accident prevention by employers and workers; the extent to which labor markets rewarded workers for accepting greater risk or penalized them when accident benefits rose; and how well insurance companies could market insurance in light of the problems they had in identifying the risks faced by the purchasers of insurance and controlling changes in accident prevention efforts by the insured. We find that a substantial majority of employers, workers, and insurers gained from the transition. Yet there were no guarantees that the legislation would pass. We therefore examine the political economic process that led to adoption. This involves assessing the strength of unions, manufacturers, lawyers, and insurers in the various states, the extent to which progressive reformers had political clout in each state, and the types of employers in the state. The success of legislation depended on both state and local trends in wages, industrialization, legal rules, and labor laws in each state.

We are not the first scholars to study the origins of workers' compensation. Walter Dodd (1936) and Herman and Anne Somers (1954) offered thumbnail sketches of the reasons for the introduction of workers' compensation as public interest legislation based on their reading of the employer liability reports from various states. They suggested that one reason for the emergence of workers' compensation was the social insurance motive. Reformers decried the common law system of assigning negligence as an anachronism because modern industrial processes created accidents that were neither the fault of the worker nor of the employer, they were simply the outcome of dangerous working conditions. Thus, restricting compensation to cases where the employer was at fault left large numbers of injured workers uncompensated, forced into poverty often through no fault of their own. Further, the way the system worked under negligence liability led to uncertain and greatly unequal payouts for accidents with similar severity. Workers' compensation reduced these problems because all injured workers received some form of compensation.[2] A second reason for the transition away from the negligence-based system was to reduce unnecessarily large transaction and administrative costs. Attorney's fees, court costs, and the administrative costs of insurance left a 40 to 60 percent gap between what employers paid out for postaccident compensation and what workers ultimately received. The largest cost to injured workers probably was the cost of court delays, which could last up to five years. Reformers sought to reduce administrative costs, court delays, and insurance overhead costs by creating a no-fault compensation system that eliminated disputes over negligence or the applicability of the three defenses. Finally, because workers bore the disproportionate share of accident costs under the negligence system, reformers argued that the negligence system gave employers little incentive to reduce accident risk. By shifting the financial burden of industrial accidents onto employers, reformers claimed, accident rates would fall.

In hindsight, it is not clear that workers' compensation settled many of these issues. Total administrative costs for workplace accidents did not necessarily fall with the introduction of workers' compensation. The total costs might even have risen because the number of cases administered rose dramatically after the law was introduced. Further, since most cases under negligence liability were settled outside the courts, it is a very difficult to determine even whether administrative costs per injury and average time to compensation for injury declined.[3] Insurance companies still included significant load factors in the premiums they charged, although the shift reduced problems with adverse selection.

The evidence that workers' compensation improved accident prevention is mixed. Negligence liability gave employers incentive to prevent all accidents where their prevention costs were lower than the expected damages. Employers could obtain discounts in their liability premiums if their accident records improved and could reduce risk premiums in wages by making their workplaces safer (Fishback and Kantor 1992). Reformers also failed to consider moral hazard problems, as better insured workers might have taken less care to prevent accidents. With workers potentially taking less care and employers taking more care to avoid accidents, how overall accident rates would change is theoretically uncertain. As discussed later in chapter 3, empirical estimates vary. The adoption of workers' compensation reduced accident rates in manufacturing (Chelius 1976), but raised them in the coal mining industry (Fishback 1992, 112–25).

Workers' compensation, like most legislation, was not passed simply because it was "in the public interest." Generally, opinions differed across various interest groups, and a political coalition combining all or part of these interest groups had to develop in the legislature for workers' compensation to be adopted. Scholarly descriptions of the composition of this political coalition vary. One of the common accounts of workers' compensation's enactment is that politically influential social reformers of the time helped workers score a significant victory over their employers (see, e.g., Noble 1997, 16). On the surface, this cursory observation rings true. The average postaccident benefits for workplace injuries that workers received under workers' compensation were significantly higher than those under the negligence system. Moreover, in some important states, including California, New York, and Washington, organized labor played a critical role in securing the legislation (Nash 1963; Drescher 1970; Wesser 1971; Tripp 1976; Asher 1983; Pavalko 1989). In some states, labor's influence was even more significant. Robert Asher (1983, 222) claims that the labor unions' successes in strengthening employers' liability laws in New York "frightened employers and forced them to consider workers' compensation as an alternative to a radical employers' liability system." Yet many of these scholars also suggest that employers joined workers in favoring the legislation.

A number of scholars have found that business leaders were the impetus behind the adoption of the legislation. Weinstein (1967) argues that employers saw workers' compensation as a preemptive strike, designed to reduce the necessity for labor to organize politically (see also Bale 1987). Lubove (1967), on the other hand, contends that business supported workers' compensation because of the economic benefits that could be captured by substituting the stability of the compensation laws for the randomness of the negligence liability system. As state legislatures began to strip employers of their common law defenses, the National Association of Manufacturers and many state-level business organizations saw workers' compensation as a way to stem the tide of more frequent and larger jury awards (also see Castrovinci 1976; Kent 1983; Tripp 1976). Workers' compensation therefore did not seem like such a leap to employers given that they were already required by the common law rules of negligence to compensate workers injured in accidents caused by the employers' negligence (Skocpol 1992, 296; Orloff 1993, 239).

Employers were troubled further that insurance companies were only paying out 25 to 40 percent of their liability premiums to injured workers; the remainder went to litigation costs, administrative expenses, and insurance company profits. Buffum (1992), Dodd (1936), and Somers and Somers (1954) argue, for example, that employers supported workers' compensation as a means to reduce the transaction costs of providing remuneration to injured employees. Finally, Dodd (1936) and Somers and Somers (1954) note that employers were becoming increasingly concerned about the animosity that the negligence liability system created between them and their employees. Many employers, therefore, may have viewed workers' compensation as a profit-enhancing strategy because it was expected to cut costs and to enhance productivity. In fact, after many states had already adopted workers' compensation laws, Willard Fisher (1920, 19) wrote in the *American Economic Review* that "by many tokens employers have shown their approval of the system. . . . Much the larger numbers of employers affected have accepted their new obligations cheerfully." Tone (1997, 49) is much more cynical about employers' support of workers' compensation, however. She claims that by "savvily labeling workers' compensation laws as a 'great but uncertain experiment' in social legislation whose long-term impact was unknown, the NCF [National Civic Federation] made its lukewarm support of workers' compensation laws the basis for a full-fledged assault, couched in the vocabulary of prudence and caution, on other social insurance measures."

Workers' compensation was not class-based legislation implemented from the bottom up or from the top down. Workers did not obtain large gains at the expense of employers, nor were recalcitrant workers coerced into accepting the terms of this "uncertain experiment" by their employers. Each group supported workers' compensation in the political negotiations willingly because they anticipated gains from the switch to the new regime. Employers gained a reduction in the uncertainty surrounding their accident costs and saw reduced frictions with their workers, as other scholars have noted. On the surface it appears that they paid too much for these gains because the switch to workers' compensation led to a substantial increase in the amounts they paid for accidents. However, as shown in chapter 3, employers were able to pass on to workers a large portion of the higher costs of postaccident payment through reductions in real wages. Thus, employers gained greater certainty and reduced friction without having to pay for most of the increase in benefit levels. Risk-averse workers, despite "buying" the higher benefits through a drop in their wages, gained because under negligence liability they had problems purchasing their desired levels of accident insurance. The switch to workers' compensation left them better insured against workplace accident risk. Finally, insurance companies willingly supported the legislation, as long as it did not allow the state to write workers' compensation legislation, because they could expand their coverage of workplace accident risk.

If the major economic interests anticipated gains from workers' compensation, what actually facilitated the law's adoption? This question, on the surface, seems rather mundane, but in fact is particularly important in light of recent research that finds that efficiency-promoting institutional changes can be delayed, while inefficient institutions persist. Unraveling this puzzle requires a detailed and comprehensive study of the way in which economic interests are filtered through the political process. Previous work on the development of workers' compensation falls short of this goal. The two quantitative studies of the determinants of the legislation that have been conducted treat the legislative process as in a vacuum, abstracted from the rich differences in compensation laws, and omit a number of potential determinants of the laws (see Pavalko 1989; Buffum 1992). Moreover, the historical studies tend to focus on one particular state and it is difficult to draw broad conclusions without comparing multiple studies. In addition, the previous research on the origins of workers' compensation has not attempted to empirically measure the economic or distributional consequences of the legislation.

We use a blend of quantitative and qualitative studies to develop a comprehensive interpretation of the origins of workers' compensation. Many of the scholars cited here agree with the general statement that workers' compensation legislation was supported by both employers and workers. They did excellent work in identifying the written and oral political stances taken by the various interest groups and the struggles in the legislature to pass the laws in various states. Yet they offer little more than a cursory description of the operations of the negligence liability system, of the changes in the amount of payments received by injured workers under the two systems, and of the impact of the workers' compensation law on wages, accident rates, insurance purchases, and savings. This book offers an in-depth discussion of these issues as well as a quantitative analysis of the speed with which states enacted the legislation and the parameters of the law—such as state versus private insurance of workers' compensation risk and the level of accident benefits—that different states chose. As a result, it complements, deepens, and in some areas contradicts the analysis of earlier scholars. Using empirical techniques and case studies, we are able to identify underlying forces and relationships that help explain some of the puzzles the earlier scholars left behind.

1.1   An Analytical Framework

Institutions are the rules that govern human interactions. They include laws, regulations, customs, mores, religion, and any other sets of constraints that people impose on themselves to structure their social, economic, or political lives. Early research on institutional development held that they were organized in order to maximize economic efficiency (Demsetz 1966, 1967; Davis and North 1971; Alchian and Demsetz 1973; North 1981). On the specific issue of liability for accidents, there is an extensive literature in law and economics that is devoted to discussions of the optimal choice of liability rules (see, e.g., Posner 1972; Brown 1973; Epstein 1973; Shavell 1980, 1987; Veljanovski 1982). In general the discussion has focused on minimizing the sum of accident prevention costs and the expected damages from accidents (probability of the accident times the damage done). If the goal, however, is to provide the optimal amount of social insurance, the problem becomes far more difficult because there are no widely accepted definitions of what that would entail. Under one extreme definition, optimal social insurance requires that all workplace accident victims be fully compensated. Yet such an extreme might not be satisfactory to those who believe in individual responsibility and that workers who do not take simple actions to protect themselves should not be allowed to receive income from employers who do their best to prevent accidents.

There are settings where the sum of prevention costs and expected damages is minimized and workers are fully covered when injured, but this arises only under very extreme assumptions. Say there are zero transactions costs and information can be obtained without cost about the extent of the dangers faced in the workplace and about the workers' and employers' prevention activity. What would happen if the employer bore no liability whatsoever for workplace accidents? Employers with more dangerous workplaces would be forced to pay a wage premium to their workers. In a perfectly functioning labor market where the employer and insurance companies are risk neutral and the workers are slightly risk averse, the wage premium would be equated with the expected damage from accidents. Given that information costs are zero, insurance companies could effectively overcome problems with identifying which workers faced which dangers so that they would not face problems with adverse selection. Further, with zero transactions costs insurance companies could design insurance contracts that gave workers less incentive to keep from adopting more dangerous practices once insured, consequently solving problems with moral hazard. Thus, workers would be able to take their wage risk premium and buy insurance that fully covered their losses.[4]

Even though the employer legally bears no costs of workplace dangers, the worker still receives full compensation when injured through a combination of wage payments and insurance purchases. Employers would have incentives to try to reduce the workplace risks in cases where the reduction in expected damages was greater than their costs of lowering the risks because they can reduce the risk premium that they pay to workers. They would write contracts with workers to get the workers to prevent accidents for which workers had lower prevention costs.

In theory, we might see the same final outcome if the liability were fully shifted to the employer.[5] The employer pays the worker full damages when injured and thus the worker would no longer require a risk premium in wages. The employer could either self-insure or purchase insurance to cover these accident costs. Again, the employer has incentive to prevent accidents where the expected damage exceeds the cost of prevention, either because he can reduce his payments for accidents or he can reduce the size of his insurance premiums. Further, the employer can contract with the worker to have the worker exercise optimal accident prevention.

In such a frictionless world a social insurance program for accident risk is not needed. Injured workers receive full compensation for their expected lost income and medical expenses and thus they and their families no longer become paupers. Workers and employers can write contracts that develop the proper incentives for eliminating the kinds of accidents where the costs of prevention are lower than the expected damages from the accident. In essence, this is an example of the Coase conjecture that through negotiations we can end up at the same optimal point whether we assign the liability to one party or the other (Coase 1960).

Yet frictions do in fact exist and they play an important role in determining the nature of political economic activity and regulation. In fact, Coase's conjecture, like the discussion above, is just a staging ground from which we can identify how transactions costs and information costs get in the way of the operation of markets and try to explore the choice of liability rules. Employers and workers face various costs in writing individual labor and insurance contracts, monitoring the behavior of the other party to the contract, and obtaining information about the risks of jobs. Meanwhile, insurance companies face problems in determining the specific risks faced by the purchasers of insurance and in guarding against the insured taking extra risks once insured. Once a liability rule is established, there are costs to courts or bureaucracies of administering the rules and adjudicating the disputes that might arise. All of these costs are present to varying degrees in every empirical setting, making it nearly impossible to identify "the optimal liability rule" on theoretical grounds.

The correct answer as to what is the optimal liability changes as we focus on different costs. Steven Shavell (1980, 21–22), for example, relaxed only the assumption about the workers' knowledge of the accident risk. His careful analysis shows that if workers have knowledge of only the average risk on the job and not the specific risk they would face for that job, only negligence liability will maximize his measure of social welfare, the sum of the expected incomes of all parties. However, if workers do not have full information about the average risk, then negligence liability will be "inefficient" too. Consider that Shavell relaxed only one of the assumptions. Relaxation of another single assumption leads to a different answer about the optimal liability rule. Once we relax all of the assumptions, there is no theoretical solution to the "optimal" liability rule. The search for optimality becomes an empirical exercise devoted to comparing imperfect rules based on accurate measures of transactions, information, and administrative costs and their impact on the operation of labor and insurance markets. Unfortunately, the size of these costs often defies accurate measurement, so that we are left with inferential techniques.

The adoption of workers' compensation was a move from negligence liability with the legal defenses of assumption of risk, contributory negligence, and fellow servant to a form of no-fault liability where workers were not fully compensated for their lost earnings. Negligence liability offers the employer the incentive to prevent all accidents where his costs of prevention exceed the expected damage for the accident. In this setting workers have extra incentives to prevent accidents because they will not be compensated for any accidents where the employer was not negligent. The contributory negligence defense adds extra incentive for the worker to prevent accidents because the worker receives nothing if he could have prevented the accident at costs lower than the expected damage, even if the employer was negligent. In real-world settings the incentives created by negligence liability are diluted somewhat because the use of the court system is costly and often involves substantial delays. Most of the accident compensation is determined through out-of-court settlements where the liability rule might be only one of several factors that determine the compensation paid. Generally, the operation of negligence rules leads to a large number of accidents where the worker receives no payments from his employer. As a result, workers seek higher pay to accept accident risk and succeed in obtaining a partial risk premium in their wages, but the premium is typically not enough to fully cover their expected losses. A risk-averse worker might use the risk premium in his wages to try to buy insurance, but the insurance company is going to have problems selling him insurance if the insurer cannot obtain reliable information about the risk the worker faces. If insurers have only limited information about the risks faced by individual workers, they will have problems with adverse selection if they just set a rate and offer full coverage. Typically, they will sustain losses if they follow this pricing strategy because only the workers faced with higher risks will purchase insurance. To resolve this problem the companies will limit how much they sell to workers. Further, the insurers will try to limit payouts to prevent against problems with moral hazard. Thus, workers may have to use alternative, more costly methods, like precautionary saving to provide for their families in case of an accident.

The switch to workers' compensation liability, where the employer is liable for all accidents arising out of or in the course of employment, changes the structure of accident prevention. Employers are no longer freed from liability for a wide range of accidents. The total payments they make for accidents might go up or go down. In fact, we show that the switch to workers' compensation in the United States forced them to increase their accident payments. The employers did not bear the full burden of this increase because they were able to pass at least some of the costs back to their workers in the form of wage offsets. Workers essentially paid for an improvement in their insurance. The higher levels of accident payments gave employers more incentives to prevent accidents than before. The no-fault payments also change the prevention calculus for workers, who now have less incentive to exercise care. Insurers may gain in one dimension because now employers have incentive to buy insurance to cover the payments to all of the workers on their payroll. As a result, insurers have fewer problems with adverse selection among the workers in each firm. On the other hand, with the rise in accident payments, the moral hazard problem by workers may become more severe. This problem was partially resolved under workers' compensation because the worker received at most two-thirds of his income when injured, and therefore bore a significant part of the damage of an accident. In the final analysis, the switch to workers' compensation in the United States left workers better insured against workplace accidents than before. They at least partially paid for higher accident benefits. At the same time it is unclear whether prevention efforts rose or fell because the accident prevention incentives went in opposite directions for employers and workers.[6]

In this book we do not try to measure the relative efficiency of the two systems of employer liability and workers' compensation. A comparison of relative efficiency would require us to examine the sum of prevention costs, expected damages, transactions costs, and administrative costs under the two regimes. At one stage we thought we could measure all of the relevant costs and benefits effectively, yet our efforts and the efforts of many others have fallen well short of expectations. Instead, we follow a different tactic. We try to establish information about factors that we can measure. How much were injured workers paid under the two regimes? How well did the actual system of employer liability follow the common law rules on which it was based? When workers' compensation was introduced, how did wages, savings, and accident rates change? What happened to the number of accidents compensated? By answering these difficult questions, we try to establish what employers, insurers, and workers could anticipate they would gain or lose as a result of the transition away from employer liability to workers' compensation. Once we knew what their gain or loss would be, we could then determine whether they would be likely to support workers' compensation legislation. By following this process we have discovered in fact that workers' compensation, with its form of limited no-fault liability, was legislation that benefited a large majority of employers, workers, and insurers. The results do not offer a general prescription for the optimal choice among no liability, strict liability, negligence liability, or the variations and combinations that develop from integrating contributory negligence with other defenses. However, the results do suggest that given the presence of various frictions at the time it was adopted, workers' compensation appears to have been beneficial legislation for a substantial majority of the actors involved. Thus we can learn for general purposes that in a society faced with the sets of constraints that were in place around 1910, workers' compensation might well have been the optimal way to deal with workplace accidents.

If workers' compensation was indeed an institutional arrangement that increased social wealth, should we expect that the program would be adopted? In the early days of the new institutional economics, scholars answered yes (see Demsetz 1966, 1967; Davis and North 1971; Alchian and Demsetz 1973). Since that time, many scholars including the early ones (see North 1981, 1987) have recognized that transaction costs and distributional conflicts are not always easily overcome and often can slow the adoption of income-enhancing institutional change. It is typically when these barriers stand as impediments to institutional change that the relevant interest groups petition the government for a political solution. But once the process of institutional change is politicized, there is no guarantee that relatively beneficial regimes survive while the inefficient ones decay. Indeed, as Gary Libecap (1989b, 7) notes, "the heart of the contracting problem is devising politically-acceptable allocation mechanisms to assign the gains from institutional change, while maintaining its production advantage." But the prospects for such an outcome might not be so bright, for as North (1987, 422) concludes, "one of the most evident lessons from history is that political systems have an inherent tendency to produce inefficient property rights which result in stagnation and decline."

Despite the importance that scholars of economic development attribute to institutions, there are relatively few detailed empirical analyses of the process of institutional change.[7] What causes individuals to seek changes in their institutional environment? What impedes the way of profitable institutional change? How are these barriers overcome? How do the different interest groups with a stake in the new regime translate their economic objectives into political action, if in fact a political solution is called for? What are the economic consequences of the institutional changes; do they lead to the economic improvements that proponents promise? One of the main difficulties that researchers of institutional change have faced is that each individual case has its own set of answers to these questions and generalizing the results of the case studies into a general theory of the process of institutional change has proven difficult. The variables that explain what happened in one instance may do very poorly in predicting what will occur in another.

While this book does not offer a solution to this dilemma, we believe that our approach provides an analytic framework for studying how institutions evolve. Our goal in the book is to trace the process of one particular institutional change from its inception to its conclusion, highlighting the salient ways in which economic interests are filtered into public policy. Our research objective is not only to understand the economic causes and consequences of the adoption of workers' compensation, but also to explain how politics affected the ultimate form of the legislation. The features of workers' compensation laws varied across the United States, and it is this cross-sectional variation that provides the opportunity to study how differences in interest groups' political strengths determine the path and scope of institutional change.

We seek to show how the economic and political environment influenced the passage of complex legislation. Our research methodology has three major components. First, we devote extensive efforts to identifying the gains and losses that various interest groups anticipated from the passage of workers' compensation. While we can learn a great deal from examining the public statements of those groups with a stake in the legislation, understanding how workers' compensation directly affected these groups economically provides us with valuable information about their possible political stance on the law. Our assumption is that political actors could reasonably anticipate the economic consequences of the policies they promoted.[8] Our quantitative analyses of the nature of postaccident benefits before and after workers' compensation and the impact of workers' compensation on wage rates, accident rates, and household choices among consumption, saving, and insurance purchases has established that workers, employers, and insurance companies all received and could anticipate benefits from workers' compensation.

The second major task of our analysis is to determine the context of the transition to workers' compensation. If the major interest groups with a stake in the legislation saw benefits from its adoption, what were the catalysts that sparked the rapid acceptance of the legislation across the United States between 1910 and 1920? We do not claim to provide a comparative analysis of workers' compensation's legislative success relative to that of social insurance programs. The book, however, does provide insights into why compensation legislation was widely accepted during the Progressive

Era, while other programs, such as unemployment insurance, social health insurance, and old-age insurance, were dismissed.

The third strand of our research considers how economic interests were translated into political outcomes. Using a combination of quantitative and qualitative case-study analyses, our goal is to more carefully identify how the political process determined not only the timing of adoption but also the specific form workers' compensation legislation took. These details of the legislation are particularly important because they determined how income would be (re)distributed under the law. While our argument is that employers and workers as a group expected benefits from workers' compensation, we would be remiss to consider the interests of all employers or workers as monolithic. For example, larger or more productive firms may have had a cost advantage in implementing safety equipment and programs that would have lowered their insurance rates. We might conjecture that such firms supported workers' compensation as a means of raising the relative costs of production for their smaller competitors. Employers in industries where they could easily invoke their common law defenses might not have supported workers' compensation because their costs of accident compensation would have risen dramatically under the new system. Similarly, employers in relatively safe industries may not have supported workers' compensation if insurance rates were not fully experience rated because employers with better safety records would end up subsidizing the insurance for employers with worse safety records.

While employers, workers, and insurance companies were the primary groups affected by the legislation, attorneys, taxpayers, farmers, and state bureaucrats had a stake in the outcome as well. Insurance companies, for example, fought against laws that allowed the state to compete in the writing of workers' compensation insurance. Damage suit attorneys stood to lose as workers' compensation would eliminate a part of their practices, and in some states they effectively slowed the adoption of the legislation. On the other hand, some damage suit attorneys and many lawyers with other specialties actively pressed for workers' compensation. Taxpayers in some states opposed the legislation on the grounds that it would create new expensive bureaucracies, raise the costs of paying public employees, or establish state funds that might require taxpayer subsidies. State labor department officials lobbied for workers' compensation legislation on the grounds that it would expand their influence over labor regulation in the state.

Our analysis of the political process blends several general themes from the economics and political science literatures on political decisionmaking. We assume that legislators and other political decisionmakers seek to maximize their own objectives subject to a series of constraints. The constraints are imposed by the demands of voting constituents who have some control over each lawmaker's reelection (Downs 1957; Mayhew 1974; Fiorina 1977), by interest group pressures (Stigler 1971; Peltzman 1976; Hughes 1977; Becker 1983; Olson 1982), by institutional features of the decision process, such as constitutional proscriptions and legislative committee structure (Shepsle and Weingast 1981, 1984; Denzau and Mackay 1983; Weingast and Marshall 1988), and by pressures to maintain their position in a political coalition either for ideological or economic reasons (Poole and Rosenthal 1997). In our detailed empirical studies of the adoption of workers' compensation in various states, we pay close attention to how these constraints that legislators faced influenced the path of institutional change.

1.2   Outline of the Book

The plan of the book generally follows the three major themes highlighted above. Before discussing the adoption of workers' compensation, in the next chapter we provide a detailed description of the legal environment that preceded the legislation. While it is obviously important to understand the historical context out of which workers' compensation emerged, a detailed picture of the negligence liability system serves another purpose as well. In their effort to explain the rationale for workers' compensation, law and economics scholars have analyzed the relative efficiency of the new legal regime relative to its common law predecessor (see, e.g., Posner 1972; Brown 1973; Epstein 1973; Shavell 1980, 1987; Veljanovski 1982). They generally assume that the actual payment of accident compensation followed the de jure rules of the two systems. In their analyses of negligence liability, for instance, injured workers either receive full compensation for their losses when the employer is negligent and cannot invoke one of the common law defenses, or the workers receive nothing. Under workers' compensation injured workers recover up to two-thirds of their lost income for all accidents arising out of or in the course of employment. Because the results of these theoretical models are sensitive to their underlying assumptions, our goal in chapter 2 is to provide a careful empirical assessment of how injured workers in fact fared under the common law. We know that the vast majority of negligence claims were settled out of court to avoid the substantial costs of seeking a court decision. In this setting the common law rules may have had a distorted impact on the actual compensation payments that injured workers received. A better understanding of the de facto operation of the negligence system, therefore, serves as the basis for more accurate theoretical discussions of the relative efficiency of negligence and no-fault legal systems.

In chapter 3 we discuss the major economic changes that resulted from workers' compensation. Our aim is to understand how various economic interest groups fared under the legislation with an eye toward determining what they might have reasonably anticipated would happen. First, however, we establish how workers' compensation changed the nature of postaccident benefits. We show that not only did the percentage of injured workers receiving remuneration increase, but also the average amount they received increased substantially. Our evidence indicates that the average payments to the households of accident victims increased between 75 and 200 percent as a result of the adoption of workers' compensation. We then turn to the economic consequences of this large increase in average postaccident payments. An analysis of wage rates in three relatively dangerous industries shows that nonunion workers experienced a drop in their real wages as a result of the legislation, but unionized workers in the building trades and coal mining confronted much smaller wage offsets. That most workers essentially "paid" for the relatively generous postaccident benefits that workers' compensation mandated helps to explain why employers willingly supported the legislation. What is less clear is why workers were such enthusiastic partners in the push for a new legal regime. An examination of how workers' compensation influenced households' savings and insurance decisions sheds light on this apparent paradox. We show that workers around the turn of the century faced constraints in their ability to purchase private insurance against workplace accident risk. Thus, despite buying workers' compensation benefits through lower real wages, nonunion workers supported the legislation because it left them better insured against workplace accident risk than under the negligence system. Further, as long as the state did not attempt to exclude them, insurance companies thought that the legislation was a good idea as well because it enabled them to expand their coverage of this line of risk.

If the major economic interest groups with a stake in workers' compensation anticipated gains, why did state legislators wait until the 1910s to adopt the law rather than adopting it earlier? In chapter 4 we provide an examination of the changes in the negligence liability system across the United States in the early 1900s that shows that several trends combined to pique the major interest groups' political support of workers' compensation. Workplace accident risk rose, state legislatures adopted a series of laws weakening employers' common law defenses against negligence, and court decisions also began to limit employers' defenses in liability suits. These factors together served to substantially increase liability insurance premiums. Employers, facing an increasingly worsening workplace accident liability crisis, were commonly in favor of workers' compensation by 1910. At the same time, labor unions, which were gaining numerical strength, shifted their focus from reforming the negligence system to fully supporting workers' compensation. Thus, by 1910 politically active employers' groups and labor unions pressed for the enactment of workers' compensation. Analysis of the timing of adoption across the United States confirms our hypothesis that a worsening negligence liability crisis served as a catalyst that brought the major interest groups together in favor of reform.

In chapter 5 we elaborate further on the process by which workers' compensation was enacted. While quantitative analysis of the timing of adoption across the United States provides a useful test of our hypothesis that a liability crisis triggered the movement in favor of workers' compensation, the quantitative analysis treats the political process of adoption within each state as a black box. Therefore, in this chapter we provide a number of synopses drawn from detailed case studies that illuminate the dynamics of institutional change. The studies highlight the difficulty that interest groups have in forming a cohesive coalition in favor of reform. The difficulty is not only in getting employers, insurers, and workers to agree, but also in getting factions within each broad interest group to agree on the type of legislation that they would support.

Given that the major interest groups anticipated gains from workers' compensation, it seems surprising that contemporary accounts sometimes depicted the adoption process as extremely bitter. In exploring this seeming paradox, it is important to consider that the legislation was very complex and involved negotiations over many different specific details of the law, including the choice between private and state insurance of workers' compensation risk and the level of statutory benefits. The details of the law were important because they determined how income would be distributed under workers' compensation.

Probably the most vicious debates were fought over the state insurance issue. Union groups particularly had antipathy toward the insurance companies, seeing them as a key reason why injured workers were unable to receive adequate compensation under negligence liability. Unions, therefore, lobbied vigorously for the replacement of private insurers with state insurance. For their part, insurance companies saw state insurance as an encroachment on their private enterprise and feared the government's further expansion into other forms of insurance. The result was a series of intense disagreements in state legislatures around the country. In chapter 6 we report the results of a quantitative analysis of state legislatures' decisions on the state insurance debate. Further, we conduct detailed case studies of the political debate in Minnesota, Ohio, and Washington. These studies show that a combination of unions and progressive reformers overcame the opposition of insurance companies and agricultural interests to adopt monopoly state insurance schemes in seven states. In ten other states the groups compromised and a state fund was created that competed with private insurers in underwriting workers' compensation. In the remaining states the insurance and agricultural interests won and employers were free to insure their workers' compensation risks with any insurer licensed to do business in the state.

Chapter 7 takes up the question of how the disparities in the political strength of the different groups affected state legislators' choices of benefit levels. We have developed a theoretical model that predicts the optimal benefits from the perspective of workers and employers with different characteristics. We then use these predictions as a basis for understanding the effectiveness of interest groups in politically securing their optimal workers' compensation benefit levels. A quantitative analysis of expected benefit levels from 1910 to 1930 reveals that influential employers in high accident risk industries succeeded in lobbying for relatively low benefits, holding other factors constant, while those in high wage industries succeeded in keeping benefit levels in check. Employers' successes in securing their optimal benefits were tempered in states where organized labor was strong, where political reform movements led to political shifts in the state legislature, and where bureaucratic agencies administered the workers' compensation system.

Comparison of the results from chapters 4 and 5 with those in chapters 6 and 7 reveals an important feature of the adoption of workers' compensation that previous scholars have overlooked. Generally, we have found that progressive reformers had a comparatively small impact on state legislatures' decisions to adopt the general legislation for workers' compensation. In contrast, when it came to the adoption of state insurance or choosing benefit levels, the strength of political reform movements often played a decisive role. The difference stems from the attitudes of the various interest groups. A strong political reform movement was not necessary for the adoption of workers' compensation more generally because the main groups with a stake in the legislation anticipated benefits. On the other hand, when at least two of these interest groups squared off against each other on a particular issue, the political reformers' influence became decisive in a number of cases. These results provide new insights into the political success of workers' compensation during the Progressive Era. Workers' compensation succeeded, while many other relatively "radical" reforms failed, because it received the support of a broad range of interest groups. The social reformers, who had hoped for sweeping social insurance protection for workers, had their greatest influence when the major interest groups agreed to the general principle, but had difficulty reaching a consensus on the details.

Notes

1. This event is described in Stonega Coke and Coal Company, "Operating Report, 1916," from records of Stonega Coke and Coal Company, Hagley Museum and Library, p. 56. The donors of the manuscript collection require that we use pseudonyms to protect the privacy of the families of these men.

2. The American Association of Labor Legislation pressed the argument for workers' compensation as one form of social insurance. See Seager (1910), Rubinow (1913), Moss (1996), and Tone (1997, 32).

3. Whether workers' compensation led to a reduction in marginal transactions costs per case depends on the administration of the new workers' compensation system. Costs per case may have been lower in states with a state insurance fund, but possibly the same or higher in other states. In Ohio, Washington, and West Virginia, where there were exclusive state funds, the processing of claims was almost perfunctory. Carl Hookstadt (1922, 4, 6–7) found that administrative costs per worker were lower than in states with competitive state funds or insurance by private stock companies, in part because state funds were more liberal in compensating workers and challenged fewer claims before industrial commissions. This liberality lowered total legal fees for workers in Ohio, where relatively few workers hired lawyers when going before the industrial commission (Conyngton 1917, 70–71). In Virginia, Colorado, Michigan, Pennsylvania, and Indiana, where private insurance was allowed, administrative costs per case might have been the same as under negligence liability. In these states, compensation was determined through voluntary agreements between the injured miner and the company. The states' Industrial Commissions reviewed the agreement and settled disputes. This process seems very similar to the situation under the negligence system in which most claims were settled out of court. If the costs per settlement were similar under the two systems, the increased number of claims would have raised total administrative costs under workers' compensation above those for the negligence system. The difference in costs may be larger when disputed cases are considered. The Stonega Coke and Coal Company, which self-insured, was involved in approximately ninety hearings of contested cases before the Virginia Industrial Commission between 1924 and 1926. Stonega's lawyers considered each hearing to have required "almost as much legal work done as would have been necessary if there had been a trial at law before a court." Under the negligence system, Stonega's annual reports for 1916–1918 mention only fifty lawsuits, of which thirty-one were settled out of court (operating reports of the Stonega Coke and Coal Co., Report of the Legal Division, 1921, 225, and operating reports for 1916–1926 in boxes 210–212 in the Records of the Stonega Coke and Coal Co., Hagley Museum and Library, Wilmington, Delaware). On the other hand, insurance companies may have seen the costs of offering insurance per dollar paid to injured workers fall with the move to workers' compensation to the extent that a reduction in problems with adverse selection offset any problems with problems in detecting fraud. In the final analysis, we do not know for sure whether the costs per case and/or the total administrative costs fell with the introduction of workers' compensation.

4. Workers would not need to demand higher than the expected damages if they know that they can purchase insurance. However, if there were administrative costs of the insurance, then workers would demand a risk premium large enough to cover the costs of their insurance.

5. This statement is subject to some caveats about the Coase theorem in game theoretic settings.

6. Spillover effects are additional problems that complicate the discussion of liability rules and accident prevention. Spillover effects are most problematic for accidents between strangers, for example, automobile accidents. If a number of motorists are uninsured, problems may arise for insured motorists. If the uninsured motorist causes a serious accident with another automobile, he is likely to be unable to fully compensate the other party for the losses sustained. Thus, the other party either bears the unmet cost of this loss at the time of the accident or is forced to pay higher premiums for insurance to cover this loss. Such spillover

effects are likely to be less problematic in workplace injuries because the employment relationship contains many ties between the worker, the employer, and his fellow worker that are not present in the meeting of strangers. These ties include formal and informal arrangements between the parties for providing appropriate accident prevention.

Under the old negligence system, some of the costs of accidents to uninsured workers were borne by others because families were able to obtain help from charities and meager payments from local governments. These payments were small, however, and the social stigma was large enough that this did not cause a serious mismatch of incentives. Under negligence liability with fellow servant defense, there may have been a spillover problem when a fellow worker caused the accident. According to the fellow servant defense, the fellow worker who caused the accident, and not the employer, was required to compensate the accident victim. Since the fellow worker's wealth was low, the fellow worker would have been unable to compensate the worker fully for his loss. We have not found any evidence that workers were purchasing liability insurance to cover their obligations if they caused an accident to a fellow worker. Nor have we found cases of workers suing fellow workers for damages, possibly because such suits seemed futile. Therefore, there may have been a moral hazard problem with fellow servants taking inadequate care to prevent accidents that would hurt others. This would have increased the problems for insurers of selling accident insurance to workers. Workers' compensation helped reduce this problem since the entire workplace was covered under the employers' insurance premium. On the other hand, under workers' compensation workers had incentives to take less care generally, forcing employers to pay compensation for some accidents that might not have occurred under negligence liability. This gave employers more incentives to prevent accidents. In the final analysis, we do not believe spillover effects to have been nearly so important for the adoption of workers' compensation as they are for modern automobile accident liability. For a good discussion of the political and economic issues related to no-fault liability for automobile accidents, see Harrington (1994).

The payment of medical expenses is one area where spillovers may pose a significant problem in modern workers' compensation, which often offers first dollar coverage with high limits for medical care associated with a workplace accident. A worker whose medical problems potentially could be related to a workplace injury therefore has greater incentives to claim that the condition is work related and therefore obtain repayment of their medical costs. This has led to calls for a merger of employer health insurance with the medical component of workers' compensation to reduce this spillover effect.

7. Shawn Kantor (1998) has made a recent attempt to disentangle the process of institutional change in his analysis of the development of property rights and fencing laws in postbellum Georgia.

8. Alston (1996, 25–26), however, cautions that "the dynamics of institutional change frequently include unintended consequences that take on a life of their own. For this reason I warn against a functionalist approach to institutional analysis whereby the motivations for particular institutions are judged from the consequences of the institutional change." While Alston's concerns are warranted, we do not believe that careful empirical analysis of the effects of institutional change should not be considered a useful starting point in beginning to understand the process of building a political coalition in favor of a particular institutional change. Scholars must use their judgment to assess whether the findings of these empirical studies are consistent with theory and the historical context within which the institutional change is debated.

Compensation for Accidents before Workers' Compensation

Jim Hurd, about whom we wrote in chapter 1, was just one of hundreds of workers killed in workplace accidents in Virginia each year during the early 1900s. Thousands more were seriously injured. The workplace accident toll was staggering when compared with today's much safer workplaces. Between 1890 and 1910 the plight of injured workers and their families drew increasing attention as state governments began to accumulate more accident information. Social reform groups like the American Association for Labor Legislation pressed for the introduction of social insurance, and writers like Crystal Eastman (1910) of the Pittsburgh Survey published stinging indictments of the experiences of many accident victims.

The legal rules governing workplace accident compensation at the turn of the century were based on common law rules of negligence combined with the defenses of assumption of risk, fellow servant, and contributory negligence. In the nineteenth century employers seemed relatively satisfied with negligence liability as the basis for accident compensation. They emphasized the notion of responsibility and felt that they should not be forced to pay for accidents for which they were not at fault. Negligence liability is viewed by some as part of a legal structure designed to promote enterprise and industry (see Friedman 1985, 300–301). Labor leaders, even as late as 1905, were still willing to work within the negligence liability system, seeking to expand liability by limiting the three defenses. Neither the employers' nor the labor leaders' views were fixed. During the first decade of the twentieth century many became increasingly dissatisfied with the operations of the system. Employers were worried about the uncertainties of possible large court awards and dissatisfied that a significant portion of what they paid out for liability insurance never reached the injured worker. Meanwhile, union leaders eliminated some of the defenses in some states, but were still unhappy with the level of payments that were reaching workers and the number who were left with no compensation at all.

Social reformers, like Crystal Eastman and the American Association of Labor Legislation, were dissatisfied with the negligence liability system because they were seeking to establish social insurance programs to aid the families of workers who were injured at work, became unemployed, or were struck down with illness. They argued that social insurance would provide workers with a cushion when ill fortune struck, while giving employers more incentives to prevent such mishaps. They considered the common law employer liability structure to be ill-designed to meet these goals. Since negligence liability based injury payments on fault, reformers argued that too many workers and their families were left uncompensated. Further, they felt that the de facto operation of negligence liability often meant that workers who legally should have received benefits often received nothing or lower payments than that to which they were entitled in theory. Thus, employers had limited incentives to prevent accidents.

In this chapter we examine how the negligence system operated both in theory and in practice. Such knowledge is essential to understanding the pressure for the introduction of workers' compensation. The chapter lays out not only the legal doctrines that were said to determine compensation but also the extent to which these legal doctrines were actually followed in compensating workplace accidents. Most accident compensation was paid out in settlements outside the court system, and we bring together the results of a range of studies that consider those payments. Finally, we address the issue of how well workers were compensated for accepting higher accident risk through the payment of higher wages.

Study of the de facto functioning of the negligence system not only provides historical context for the transition to workers' compensation, it also should inform modern debates over the relative efficiency of different types of liability rules for consumer products, auto accidents, and medical attention. Through theoretical introspection, law and economics scholars have established predictions about the relative efficiency of negligence liability and strict liability using a series of assumptions about transaction and information costs. These studies assume that the de jure rules of the negligence liability system dictated precisely how accident compensation was allocated. Given that there are significant costs associated with adjudicating decisions, it is not clear that the de facto operation of the negligence system actually followed the de jure set of rules. Court costs and other transaction costs were high enough that workers could not expect to receive the levels of compensation that they might have been entitled to under a strict reading of the common law. Moreover, using the court system entailed such costs that most disputes were settled outside the formal legal system, thus raising the question of how well the actual pattern of settlements reflected what would have been generated if the common law were strictly followed. Transaction costs might have prevented many workers with legitimate claims from receiving compensation. Conversely, some workers with better access to legal advice, nonwage income, or capital markets might have received compensation for less "worthy" claims. In other words, the de facto performance of the negligence liability system may have been far from what legal theorists assume. Thus, the study of the negligence system of the early 1900s provides an important set of facts that will enable legal theorists to modify their assumptions and hence their predictions regarding the efficiency consequences of different legal systems in modern discussions.

2.1   The Negligence Liability System

The negligence liability system required an employer to exercise "due care" in protecting his employees against workplace hazards. The employer was legally obligated to hire "suitable and sufficient" coworkers, to establish and to enforce proper rules of conduct within the work environment, to provide a safe workplace, to furnish safe equipment, and to provide employees with warnings and suitable instructions in the face of dangerous working conditions. Relying on Judge Learned Hand's reasoning, Richard Posner (1972, 32) and William Landes and Posner (1987, 85–87) claim that due care required that the employer prevent accidents when his costs of accident prevention were lower than the expected costs of the accident (i.e., losses to the accident victim multiplied by the probability of the accident).

A worker injured on the job bore the burden of proving that his employer had failed to exercise due care in preventing the accident and that the employer's negligence was the proximate cause of the injury. If an injured worker was able to show his employer's negligence, then he was theoretically entitled to compensation up to the amount of his financial losses from the accident (lost wages and medical expenses) plus remuneration for "pain and suffering." Even if an employer failed to conform to the letter of the law, however, he could escape liability by establishing any of three defenses: that the employee had assumed the risks associated with the employment (assumption of risk); that a coworker (fellow servant) had caused the accident; or that the worker himself was negligent or had not exercised due care (contributory negligence).[1]

Under assumption of risk the employer could be freed from liability if the accident was caused by factors that were ordinary for that type of work, or, if extraordinary, if the risks were known and acceptable to the worker when he took the job. A steeplejack, for example, who tripped and fell off of a steeple would likely not have received compensation from his employer because the steeplejack knew and accepted the risks associated with his line of work. The fellow servant doctrine meant that an injured worker was not compensated if the actions of another worker caused the accident. A miner was not likely to be compensated by an employer under the negligence system if a coworker's failure to correctly prop a roof caused injury in a roof fall. Finally, under the contributory negligence defense, workers could not collect damages if they might have avoided the accident by exercising due care themselves to prevent accidents when their prevention costs were lower than the expected damage. For instance, an employer would probably not have been liable for injuries a motorman sustained if he slammed into a wall while driving too fast to make a turn.

Views on why these doctrines were established vary. Posner (1972) and Landes and Posner (1987) claim that the negligence system promoted efficient accident prevention. The negligence standard forced employers to prevent all accidents when their prevention costs were lower than the expected damages of the accident, as measured by the probability of an accident multiplied by the damage done. The contributory negligence defense was added to ensure that workers prevented accidents when their prevention costs were lower than the expected damages. The primary goal of the defense was to save on court costs on the grounds that if both parties were negligent there would be no reason to assign fault to one or the other (Landes and Posner 1987, 89). The assumption of risk defense was justified on the grounds that if workers knew the dangers of their work in advance, then they could negotiate higher wages for accepting the risk (Adam Smith's compensating wage differential) and use this "risk premium" to buy workplace accident insurance. Finally, the fellow servant defense allegedly promoted efficient accident prevention because it gave workers an incentive to report the hazardous actions of coworkers to the employer so that the dangerous behavior could be corrected (Landes and Posner 1987, 309–11).

This theory has led to an extensive literature in law and economics comparing the relative efficiency of various forms of liability systems. Landes and Posner did not formally model the implications of workers' limited information about their workplace accident risk, employers' monitoring costs, transactions costs of negotiating over safety issues, the costs of going to court, or the costs of negotiating settlements. Since Posner's (1972) seminal work, an enormous law and economics literature has developed on the subject (see, e.g., Brown 1973; Epstein 1973; Shavell 1980, 1987; Veljanovski 1982). Theoretical treatments of this issue suggest that the relative efficiency of strict liability and negligence liability with the three defenses depends very strongly on one's assumptions about transaction costs. Since transaction costs are obviously present in a realistic setting, it is not clear that we can predict theoretically which liability system would be optimal in practice.

Even if the negligence liability system had promoted efficient accident prevention, contemporary social reformers viewed the legal system as "unfair" and capricious (Eastman 1910). Lawrence Friedman (1985, 475), in his extensive history of American law, effectively summarizes a common view of the negligence system: "By the beginnings of the Gilded Age, the general features of the new tort law were crystal-clear. . . . Enterprise was favored over workers. . . . Juries were suspected—on thin evidence—of lavishness in awarding damages; they had to be kept under firm control. The thrust of the rules; taken as a whole, approached the position that corporate enterprise should be flatly immune from actions for personal injury." By the turn of the century, however, Friedman goes on to argue (1985, 484), the common law "was wildly nonuniform, full of 'unpardonable differences and distinctions.' This meant that by 1900, the rule had lost some of its reason for being. It was no longer the efficient device for disposing of accident claims. It did not have the courage of its cruelty, nor the strength to be humane. It satisfied neither capital nor labor. It siphoned millions of dollars into the hands of lawyers, court systems, administrators, insurers, claims adjusters. Companies spent and spent, yet not enough of the dollars flowed to injured workmen."

From an injured worker's or his heirs' perspective, proving an employer's negligence before a court and overcoming the three defenses was a formidable task. Describing the British situation under the negligence system, which paralleled the American experience, Bartrip (1985) claims that British workers had little working knowledge of the law and lacked financial means, thus many were precluded from pursuing claims against their employers. Even though lawyers might have accepted strong cases on a contingency basis, injured workers faced relatively high expected costs of pursuing a court claim against an employer. In addition to lawyers' fees and court costs, injured workers faced delays of up to four years before a final court decision was reached (Eastman 1910, 186). After extensive interviews with families of fatal accident victims in Pennsylvania before the state had adopted workers' compensation, Mary Conyngton (1917, 104), a U.S. Bureau of Labor Statistics researcher, summarized how many of the families felt about the negligence system: "The employers were too powerful, they felt; it was useless to try to get anything. The witnesses of the accident were very apt to be in the employ of the man, or company, who had employed the decedent and fear of losing their work would keep them from testifying against their employer. . . . All in all, they thought it better to submit and not to make a bad matter worse by creating for themselves a powerful enemy. Of course for those who took this attitude, there was no delay, no expense, and no uncertainty about the question of settlement."

In her classic study of how accident victims in Allegheny County, Pennsylvania, fared under the common law, Crystal Eastman (1910, 186) concluded that "[t]he immediate need here is so great, the delay of trial so long, that it is not astonishing that most cases are settled out of court." In fact, a study by the Minnesota Bureau of Labor, Industries, and Commerce (1909–1910, 167–87) found that 89 percent of the fatal accident cases, 78 percent of the permanent partial disability cases, and 99 percent of the temporary disabilities were settled without the courts. In addition, of the 994 temporary disability cases studied by the New York Commission on Employers' Liability (1910, 236–37), in only 110 (11.1 percent) did the injured worker receive some compensation through a settlement of a formal legal claim or suit.

Given that so many cases were settled out of court, the de facto operation of the negligence liability system potentially was quite different from the de jure descriptions that the law and economics and legal literatures provide. Legal scholars including Posner (1972), Landes and Posner (1987), and Richard Epstein (1982) have empirically supported their assumptions concerning the operation of the negligence liability system with analyses of court decisions from the turn of the century. In the presence of so many out-of-court settlements, however, court decisions may offer a biased view of how the common law worked in practice. Numerous studies show that modern court decisions are not a random sample of all accident cases (Priest and Klein 1984; Viscusi 1986; Hylton 1993). Legal fees, court costs, and long delays in reaching a final decision gave employers and workers an incentive to avoid the court system and these costs potentially were high enough to distort how the tort doctrines influenced the pattern of accident compensation.

To examine this question more carefully requires the collection of a complete or random sample from the universe of workplace accidents from a specific time and place. Then an analysis can be conducted on how injured workers were compensated, if at all, from court awards or out-of-court settlements. During their deliberations on switching to a workers' compensation system, various state legislatures and governors commissioned investigations into the operation of the employers' liability system in their respective states. In each investigation the commissions sampled workers, or the families of workers, injured or killed on the job and then reported how each accident victim (or heir) was remunerated. In each case they attempted to identify, with varying degrees of success, all accident victims in an area so that information was collected not only on those workers who filed suits but also on the vast majority of workers who remained outside the court system. The commissions generally succeeded in collecting information on the compensation to the heirs of fatal accident victims. The commissions had far less success in collecting full information on nonfatal accidents because they typically had to rely on reports from employers, and there is substantial evidence that employers underreported nonfatal accidents. The commissions expressed little interest in determining how well the patterns of compensation matched the tort doctrines. Yet the raw data they collected are particularly valuable for studying the de facto workings of the negligence system because they provide a sample of all accidents, not just the accident cases that were decided in the courts.

2.2   The Levels of Postaccident Compensation for Fatal Accidents

Evidence drawn from seven studies commissioned in the early 1900s, summarized in table 2.1, reveals that families of married fatal accident victims bore the preponderance of the financial burden of industrial accidents. The studies, which exclude railroad workers, reveal that the percentages receiving no compensation ranged from 22.2 percent of Minnesota families in 1909–1910 to 60.9 percent among men killed in Illinois before 1911.[2] Taking the average value across the samples, about 43 percent of the families of fatal industrial accident victims would have received no compensation at all. If the employers' liability system were operating in strict accordance with the common law rules of negligence, and according to the predictions of Posner (1972) and Landes and Posner (1987), it is not surprising that a large number of injured workers received no compensation. Table 2.2 presents evidence drawn from a variety of sources on the causes of accidents. According to these data, employers were negligent, and thus legally responsible for compensating the injured worker in a well-functioning negligence system, in 0.2 to 47.8 percent of the cases surveyed.[3] Therefore, if the liability system was functioning as legal theory predicts, anywhere from 52 to 99.8 percent of injured workers should have been denied benefits. Given these standards of comparison, the 43 percent of the families of fatally injured workers not receiving compensation possibly might even be considered low.

In order for the liability system to optimize the level of safety and accidents, once an employer's liability has been established, damages must equal the social costs of the accident (Posner 1972, 46). The economic loss of an industrial accident would include medical expenses that the injured worker incurred, the present value of lost earnings, and the monetary value attached to the injured's (or his family's) "pain and suffering." The last column of table 2.1 reports the mean ratio of death benefits to annual earnings; families receiving no compensation are included in this calculation. The mean ratio of employer-provided death benefits ranged from a low of 38.3 percent of annual earnings in Pennsylvania to 119.5 percent in Minnesota.[4] The mean expected compensation (including payments of zero) averaged about 56 percent of one year's earnings. Such low levels of expected compensation clearly created financial hardship for families whose primary wage earners were killed. The amount that families received fell far short of the forgone wages that the fatally injured worker

Table 2.1   Compensation Paid to Families of Fatal Industrial Accident Victims under Negligence Liability

Sample	Number of Usable Observations	Percentage Receiving No Compensation from Employers	Mean Ratio of Compensation to Annual Earnings[a]
Married nonrailroad workers in Erie County, NY, 1907–8	60	35.0	0.69
Married workers in Manhattan, NY, before 1910[b]	48	37.5	0.78
New York State Employers' Liability Commission Report on married workers before 1910	111	—	0.56
All married workers killed in work accidents in Allegheny County, PA, 1 July 1906 to 30 June 1907[c]	165	26.1	0.47
Workers in Virginia coal mines owned by Stonega Coke and Coal, 1916–18	44	29.4	0.41
Married workers in Pennsylvania, 1914	128	53.1	0.34
Nonrailroad workers in Minnesota, 1909–10	45	22.2	1.12
Nonrailroad workers in Illinois before 1911	274	60.9	0.58
Weighted (by sample size) average		44.5	0.56

Sources: Fishback and Kantor (1995, 718). The estimates from New York and Allegheny County, Pennsylvania, are from Eastman (1910, 122, 272–79). Virginia coal mine estimates are from Fishback (1987, 311–12). The Pennsylvania data for 1915 are from Conyngton (1917, 125–45). The Minnesota information comes from the Minnesota Bureau of Labor, Industries, and Commerce (1909–1910, 166–69). The Illinois data are from Hookstadt (1919, 239). In calculating the ratio of expected compensation to yearly earnings, we used the workers' reported wages for the three New York samples, and the samples from Allegheny County and Pennsylvania. Average yearly earnings for the other samples are from Paul Douglas's estimates of annual earnings in U.S. Bureau of the Census (1975, 168). The average yearly earnings for coal miners corresponds to bituminous coal mining and the average for nonrailroad workers is that for manufacturing wage earners in all industries.

Notes: All of the workers in the samples were men. In each sample there are several cases where the payments are unknown. Most of the unknown cases are situations in which lawsuits were pending. We have treated the unknowns as missing values.

[a]The mean compensation includes those families receiving no benefits.

[b]The evidence on compensation was presented as frequency distributions across ranges of dollar amounts. The midpoint of each range was used to calculate the mean levels of compensation.

[c]The sample includes workers employed by Carnegie Steel who received compensation from the Carnegie Fund, which was a relief fund supported solely by the employer. It seems reasonable to include this because the Fund may have reduced the number of suits filed against the Carnegie Company and also was fully funded by the employer. There may be some other payments from other relief funds that were partially funded by employers, so the compensation may be overstated. Eastman (1910) is not clear about whether these are included or excluded in her samples.

Table 2.2 Distribution of Accident Causes (%)

Causes	Germany		U.S. Iron and Steel Plant	Washington State			Pittsburgh Survey[a]
	1887	1908		1913	1914	1915	
Employer negligence	19.8	16.8	4	0.8[b]	0.3[b]	0.15[b]	47.8[b]
Worker negligence	25.6	28.9	7	7.8	7.2	5.3	32.2
Fault of employer and worker	4.45	4.66					
Fellow servant	3.28	5.28	6	2.4	3.2	1.5	13.7
Inevitable risk of work	43.4	42.1	60	69.0	81.7	89.0	28.5
Other			23	19.8	7.4	3.9	
Uncertain	3.47	2.31					
Number of accidents in sample	15,970	46,000	c	c	c	c	410

Sources: From Kantor and Fishback (1995, 412). The German data are reported in Boyd (1912, 359–60), the iron and steel plant and Washington data are from Blanchard (1917, 10–11), and the Pittsburgh data are from Eastman (1910, 86).

Notes: The German and Washington data are reported for a period when workers' compensation was in effect in both jurisdictions. The Pittsburgh data reflect accident causes prior to workers' compensation. The iron and steel plant data cover six years, and the source did not specify the time period or the plant's geographic location.

[a] The survey includes accidents in steel manufacturing, railroading, mining, and unnamed other industries. The percentages sum to greater than one hundred because some accidents were assigned multiple causes. Of the 501 total causes of accidents reported, 37.7 percent were in the steel industry, 18.2 were in railroading, 17.2 were in mining, and 26.9 percent were in the other industries.

[b] Percentage includes accidents caused as a result of the foreman's negligence, as well as the employer's.

[c] Data not reported.

contributed to his family's household income. Depending on the discount rate, the present value of the forgone wages of a deceased worker amounted to ten to twenty times his annual earnings.[5]

The mean levels of compensation often disguise the extent of compensation that most families received. A handful of very large awards potentially could raise the mean well above the levels that most workers received. Table 2.3 shows the frequency distribution of the ratio of fatal accident payments to annual earnings in four of the samples reported in table 2.1. The distributions clearly demonstrate that most families received compensation levels at the low end of the distribution. In the Illinois and Pennsylvania samples, between 70 and 83 percent of the families received less than a half-year's earnings, while firms were more generous in Minnesota where the percentage was just barely over 50 percent. If we focus only on the people who received positive amounts—under the extreme assumption that no payment was a sign the employer was not negligent—the level of benefits still seems relatively meager. Over half of those receiving some positive amount received less than a half-year's earnings in the two Penn-

Table 2.3   Distribution of Postaccident Compensation Relative to Annual Earnings of Fatal Accident Victims (%)

Ratio of Benefits to Annual Earnings	Allegheny County, Pa., 1906–7	Illinois, Coal Mining, 1909	Minnesota, 1909–10	Pennsylvania, 1914
0	26.1	67.9	24.4[a]	53.1
0 to 0.5	44.2	15.2	26.7	27.3
0.5 to 1	15.2	8.9	15.6	10.2
1 to 1.5	7.3	3.6	11.1	2.3
1.5 to 2	3.6	1.8	6.7	3.1
2 to 3	1.2	0.9	0.0	2.3
3 to 4	1.8	0.9	6.7	0.8
4 to 5	0.6	0.0	2.2	0.0
5 to 6	0.0	0.9	2.2	0.8
6+	0.0	0.0	4.4	0.0
Mean (std. dev.)	0.475	0.300	1.184	0.341
	(0.729)	(0.731)	(1.759)	(0.734)
Mean for those with positive compensation (std. dev.)	0.642	0.934	1.567	0.727
	(0.782)	(1.041)	(1.866)	(0.935)
Number of observations	165	112	45	128

Sources: Allegheny County data are from Eastman (1910, 325–31), Illinois data from Illinois Employers' Liability Commission (1910, 131–38), Minnesota data from Minnesota Bureau of Labor, Industries, and Commerce (1909–1910, 166–69), and Pennsylvania data from Conyngton (1917, 152–66).

Notes: As a means of comparison, the benefits to earnings ratio under workers' compensation at the time of each state's adoption (reported in parentheses) was 2.4 in Pennsylvania (1915), 2.3 in Illinois (1911), and 2.4 in Minnesota (1913).

[a]This percentage differs from the percentage reported in table 2.1 because workers were included in this sample only if they reported annual earnings.

sylvania samples, while over half received less than a year's earnings in the Illinois Coal and Minnesota samples. In essence, the system looks somewhat like a lottery where most people received nothing or relatively small amounts that would cover burial expenses, while a few received large awards.

While many workers' families received no compensation, this result could conceivably have matched how the negligence liability system was designed to operate. Many workers' heirs might have received no remuneration because the employer was not negligent or could invoke one or more of the three defenses. The families of eligible workers, however, should have received large enough amounts to compensate them for the lost earnings of the deceased worker. The distributions in table 2.3 imply that a relatively small percentage of workers received large awards, defined as greater than four times annual earnings (roughly two thousand dollars at the time). The percentage who received more than four years' earnings was less than 1 percent in three of the samples, although it reached a high of 8.8 percent in the Minnesota sample. These percentages seem relatively low and suggest that even in cases where employers were clearly negligent, workers' families did not collect anywhere close to the present value of the deceased's lifetime of lost wages.

We can also use the distributions to compare the percentage of workers who would have been better off with the negligence payments than under the workers' compensation benefits that were later adopted. As will be seen later, the fatal accident benefits under workers' compensation provided for streams of payments with present values ranging from two to eight times annual earnings, depending on the state's compensation rules (see table 3.1). The distributions in table 2.3 show that the percentages of families that would have fared better under negligence liability than under workers' compensation was at most 15.5 percent in Minnesota, and approximately 3 percent in Illinois and Pennsylvania. The comparisons therefore imply that the vast majority of families of fatally injured accident victims could anticipate better remuneration under workers' compensation than under negligence liability.

The compensation levels described in tables 2.1 and 2.3 actually overstate the disposable income received by the deceased's family because the legal and medical expenses the families incurred are not subtracted. In the Minnesota sample legal expenses consumed 11.9 percent of the total compensation paid to the heirs of fatal accident victims. Further analysis shows that only eight of the forty-five families paid any legal expenses, and they paid an average of 30 percent of their benefits to lawyers. When medical expenses are considered, some families lost money as a result of the industrial accident. An astonishing 66 percent of the Pennsylvania families had accident-related expenses that exceeded the compensation received from the deceased's employer. Among the Illinois and Minnesota families 18.8 percent and 6.7 percent, respectively, lost money as a result of the accident (no expenses were recorded for the Allegheny County sample). Overall, these data tend to confirm social reformers' claims that the employers' liability system left "well-nigh the whole economic burden of workplace accidents to be borne by the injured workmen and his dependents" (Eastman 1910, 220).

Finally, we should emphasize that the low levels of payments for fatal accidents were not caused by any common law strictures against compensation for fatal accidents. It is true that in England prior to Lord Campbell's Act of 1846 and in the United States in various jurisdictions the common law disallowed recovery of damages where accidents led to death on grounds that "there is no mode of estimating compensation for the death of a man" (U.S. Commissioner of Labor 1908, 85). By 1907, and by the time the foregoing samples were collected, all of the states had enacted laws that gave the personal representatives of the deceased a right of action in negligence cases. These acts often included maximum limits on the recovery of damages. For example, in Virginia and Minnesota the maximum was five thousand dollars, in Illinois the limit was ten thousand dollars.[6] It turns out these limits were not binding in any but the Minnesota samples in table 2.3. For example, the Minnesota maximum of five thousand dollars was roughly eight times the average annual nonfarm earnings in 1910 of $630 estimated by Douglas (U.S. Bureau of the Census 1975, 168), while the Illinois limit was nearly sixteen times annual earnings.

2.3   Nonfatal Postaccident Compensation

Examining nonfatal accident compensation is much trickier than studying fatal accidents. The severity of nonfatal accidents varied a great deal and many of the commissions that collected the data failed to report the types of accidents or only gave broad categorizations of the extent of an individual worker's injury. Further, there is substantial evidence that the reporting of nonfatal accidents under negligence liability was far lower than it was under workers' compensation (for detailed information about the reporting of accidents, see appendix A). If there was little chance of compensation, a worker had little incentive to report an accident under the negligence system because doing so may have jeopardized his job by signaling to the employer that he was either accident-prone or a malcontent. Similarly, employers had little incentive to report accidents for which they did not compensate workers because they might alert factory inspectors and others to dangerous working conditions, which could lead to increased scrutiny and/or fines. Since the samples described here are largely based on information collected from employers, it is likely that the percentage of injured workers compensated is overstated, as would be any calculation of expected benefits.

Table 2.4 presents summary statistics from eleven studies about the amounts of compensation that workers received and the expenses that they incurred from nonfatal injuries reported by employers. In all of the studies considered, there was a group of workers that received no compensation for their financial losses. The percentage receiving nothing ranged from a low of 9.1 percent among workers with serious temporary disabilities in Minnesota to a high of 72.9 percent of the permanent partially disabled in Kansas City, Missouri, in 1912. The weighted average (by sample size) of the percentages receiving no benefits for the group of eleven samples presented in the table is 40.2 percent. Given the reporting problem we have described, the 40.2 percent figure is clearly a lower bound.

Table 2.4 reports the ratio of employer-paid compensation to the reported value of lost wages and medical expenses for those injured workers receiving some positive level of benefits from their employers. Among those workers receiving some positive amount of compensation, the data suggest that many had financial losses exceeding what they received from their employers. Illinois coal miners, Michigan workers, Minnesota workers with nonserious temporary disabilities, and New York workers with both serious and less-serious injuries did not receive enough compensation, on average, to cover their lost wages and medical expenses. The seventeen furniture workers in Michigan who received positive benefits fared the worst among the sampled workers, recovering an average of only about a quarter of their losses.

These findings present two possibilities. First, the relatively low benefits reported in the table might be evidence in support of the social reformers' claims that the negligence system was not compensating injured workers who had reasonable claims against their employers. Even if workers had legitimate cases against their employers, the costs associated with pursuing a claim made full compensation unlikely. Alternatively, the low ratio of benefits to losses for those who received compensation may be an indication that the negligence system functioned as theory predicts, but some legally "undeserving" workers who received small amounts of remuneration pushed the average ratio downward.

The data reported in table 2.4 show that some injured workers received full compensation for their accident losses. A sample of accident victims receiving positive amounts of compensation in Kansas City in 1912 and 1916 and those with permanent partial and serious temporary disabilities in Minnesota were compensated in excess of their reported lost wages and medical expenses on average. The permanently disabled workers in the 1916 Kansas City sample recovered almost 2.3 times the value of their self-reported losses. One way to read these results is to suggest that some injured workers, presumably because their employers were negligent, were remunerated for the economic costs associated with their industrial accidents. Some may have even been compensated in excess of their lost wages

			Ratio of Compensation
		Percentage	from Employers to Losses
		Receiving No	(for Workers with Positive
Sample	Observations	Benefits	Levels of Compensation)[a]
Michigan manufacturing			
workers, 1897–1903	1,532	63.2	Not available
Illinois coal mining, 1908[b]	102	52.0	0.844[c]
Kansas City, Mo., 1912,			
permanent partial disability	85	72.9	1.229
Kansas City, Mo., 1916,			
permanent partial disability	120	29.2	2.274[d]
Kansas City, Mo., 1916,			
temporary disability	130	42.3	1.577[d]
Stonega Coke and Coal Co.,			
Va., 1916–18, serious			
accidents	210	Up to 48.6	Not available
Grand Rapids, Mich., 1910,			
furniture companies[b]	33	48.5	0.240
Detroit, Mich., 1910, various			
companies[b]	26	46.2	0.515
Minn., 1909–10, permanent			
partial disability	20	20.0	1.417
Minn., 1909–10, serious			
temporary disability	22	9.1	1.122
Minn., 1909–10, not serious			
temporary disability	48	29.2	0.695
N.Y., 1907, permanent partial			
disability	60	20.0	0.414
N.Y., 1907, temporary			
disability	902	39.6	0.375

Table 2.4   **Payments to Nonfatal Accident Victims under Employers' Liability**

Sources: Illinois Employers' Liability Commission (1910, 139–45), Kansas City (Missouri) Board of Public Welfare (1912, 15–16; 1916, 8–16), Michigan Employers' Liability and Workmen's Compensation Commission (1911, 99, 106–7), Fishback (1987, 311) summarizing Stonega Coke and Coal Co. Records, Minnesota Bureau of Labor, Industries, and Commerce (1909–1910, 172–87), and New York Commission on Employers' Liability (1910, 244–49). Some of the entries in the table were previously published in Kantor and Fishback (1995, 410).

[a]Compensation from employers might include wages paid during disability, medical expenses, and any employers' liability insurance settlements. Losses primarily include wages forgone during disability and medical expenses that the employee was left to bear. It should be noted that the samples are probably incomplete because they relied on employers' reports.

[b]The sample includes different type of accidents. The data source did not distinguish between them, however.

[c]This estimate is probably biased downward because we excluded five individuals who failed to report the value of their lost wages. Three of these people received relatively large court awards amounting to four thousand, six thousand, and eight thousand dollars, respectively. It seems unlikely that their lost wages would have been substantial enough to offset these large levels of compensation in our benefit to cost estimate.

[d]These measures tend to be biased upward because fifteen accident victims in the permanent partial sample and ten in the temporary disability sample reported that they paid their own medical expenses, but did not provide a dollar value. As a result, in estimating the ratios, we set these workers' medical expenses to zero.

and medical expenses to cover the costs of "pain and suffering." Alternatively, the excess might reflect payments covering the workers' transactions costs of negotiating compensation or a premium reflecting the workers' threatening to pursue their accident claims in the courts.[7]

2.4   The Determinants of Accident Compensation

If there were no transaction costs associated with litigating, then we would anticipate that court decisions would have closely followed the common law doctrines, as long as judges themselves were following the rules. We know, however, that there were substantial costs of going to court and that there were extensive delays, which landed injured workers or their heirs in a world of settlement negotiations, where the courts determined the amount of compensation they received if the negotiations broke down.

The economic literature on settlement negotiations suggests that when the expected court award was below the worker's costs of going to court, the employer would not pay the worker anything. In the case of workplace accidents in the early twentieth century, this scenario might have occurred when the damage suffered was relatively slight, or when the employer was likely to win in court because he could easily defend against the negligence claim and/or invoke one of the three defenses. Once the expected court award exceeds the workers' costs of going to court, however, the bargaining outcome depends on the information available to both workers and employers.[8] If both have the same information about the expected court award, we would anticipate that they would settle out of court. If the employer has information unavailable to the worker, or vice versa, there is no guarantee of a settlement. At the turn of the century, then, we should see a mixture of settlements and court decisions that may or may not reflect the ability to invoke the common law doctrines. In sum, the presence of legal costs makes the link between the common law doctrines and accident compensation tenuous if damages were below legal costs and at higher levels of damages because transaction costs and informational problems may have distorted the relationship between the theory and practice of the common law.

Even if an employer had not been legally liable for a worker's accident, he might have had other reasons for offering accident compensation. Recent research in labor economics suggests that the payment of nonwage benefits potentially can raise productivity or lower turnover.[9] For example, a number of firms, particularly large ones, sought to attract and keep productive workers by enhancing nonwage benefits. Andrew Carnegie and International Harvester both developed private schemes for compensating injured workers prior to workers' compensation, while a number of companies developed model towns to try to enhance the productivity of their workforces. Similarly, firms may have sought to limit turnover of skilled workers by developing a reputation for treating their injured workers well. One signal that employers were making payments for these reasons would be the presence of payments to workers whose expected court costs were higher than their accident costs.

How the common law affected payments to accident victims has been studied in different settings for which information was collected from a population of injured workers, not just those who received a court award. Nearly all the studies show that the common law had an impact on the probability and amounts of compensation received, although the common law was not the only factor determining accident compensation. A study of the Stonega Coke and Coal Mines in Virginia during the years 1916–1918 shows that in settings where Stonega's lawyers felt the company was potentially liable, the probability of paying accident compensation was higher, as was the amount paid.[10] The median payment to fatal accident victims was approximately two hundred dollars higher when the lawyers considered Stonega potentially liable than when they claimed the firm was not liable. Similarly, the company paid a positive amount to each of the fifty-two nonfatal accident victims when the lawyers believed the company was potentially liable. In contrast, they made payments to only thirty-four of the eighty injured workers when the lawyers did not feel that the company was liable (Fishback 1987, 311–13).[11] It is clear that the common law doctrines were not fully decisive. After all, the company did pay forty-six injured workers where the lawyers felt the company was not liable, and two of those workers received fifteen hundred dollars, which was the second smallest payment made to nonfatally injured workers. The company may have made these payments to provide benefits to workers to cut worker turnover, or they may have been paying legally unqualified workers to avoid court costs.

James Croyle (1978) found more mixed results in his study of the operation of the negligence liability system in Minnesota. The Minnesota Bureau of Labor, Industries, and Commerce (MBLIC) collected accident compensation data in 1909 and 1910 in which they attempted to gather information from both employers and injured workers or their heirs. These data therefore include compensation decisions that were made both in and out of a court setting. Croyle found that the common law doctrines were important determinants of fatal accident compensation, although they had much less impact on nonfatal accident compensation. In a regression analysis he found that the employer paid out $1,104 more in compensation to the families of fatal accident victims when the investigators considered the accident to be a result of employer negligence. On the other hand, the assumption of risk defense had little impact; when the investigators considered the accident to be caused by a normal hazard of the workplace, the fatal accident payment fell by only $56. But statistical tests did not reject the hypothesis of no effect (Croyle 1978, 294–97).[12]

Croyle also analyzed data on nonfatal accidents, but we do not believe it to be a random sample of all accidents. The sample for nonfatal accidents was collected from information reported by employers, and it is clear from archival evidence that MBLIC officials were skeptical about employers' accurate reporting of accidents. The MBLIC wrote incredulous letters to numerous employers asking them why no accidents had been reported from their firms. From this incomplete sample of nonfatal accidents, Croyle's analysis shows that employer negligence did not raise the amount paid to nonfatal accident victims, which could be a signal that employers did not report accidents in which they were grossly at fault. On the other hand, where the employers could invoke the assumption of risk defense, the payment fell by $198; when they could invoke the fellow servant defense the payment was $343 lower. There still remains some uncertainty in these estimates, however, because Croyle could not reject the hypothesis of no effect in either case. Croyle did find a difference between court decisions and settlement payments for nonfatal accidents. When he examined court decisions explicitly, employer negligence raised the level of compensation, and in situations where employers could invoke one of the three defenses the average payment to nonfatal accident victims was relatively lower (Croyle 1978, 289–94).[13]

In a study of the probability that nonfatal accident victims received compensation in Michigan between 1897 and 1903, we found that the common law doctrines had a relatively limited impact on the compensation that workers received (Kantor and Fishback 1995).[14] We tested the impact of contributory negligence in two ways. First, in a direct test we found that accidents identified as being caused by worker carelessness lowered the probability that a nonfatal accident victim received compensation by up to 29 percentage points, but in statistical tests we could not reject the hypothesis of no effect. A second, less direct test showed that workers with more experience at their firms were more likely to receive compensation from their employers. It may be that employers had more difficulty invoking the contributory negligence defense against more experienced workers.

To test how the assumption of risk doctrine affected accident compensation, we examined whether a worker who faced greater workplace accident risk was less likely to receive compensation. Employers may have been better able to invoke the assumption of risk defense when workers knew the jobs were riskier. The results show no evidence that greater accident risk raised or lowered the probability that the worker received accident compensation. Finally, we found some evidence that the fellow servant defense might have influenced the probability of payment because injured workers were more likely to receive payments from larger firms. Larger firms would have had more difficulty in invoking the fellow servant defense, all else constant. To the extent that larger firms were more hierarchical, the chances that a supervisor's behavior caused the accident increased; therefore, the firm's ability to invoke the fellow servant defense was limited by the vice-principal doctrine, which considered a supervisor's negligence to be treated as negligence by an employer. Moreover, in larger firms workers were more likely to interact with coworkers from different parts of the firm and the injured worker was likely to have had little working relationships with these people. In these cases, the issue of common employment might have been used to limit the fellow servant defense (Clark 1908, 29–42).

Another implication of the common law is that accident compensation should have borne some resemblance to an injured worker's losses. The Minnesota data show that the level of compensation was clearly influenced by the economic loss a worker or his family incurred as a result of an industrial accident. Croyle's regression analysis shows that families of fatal accident victims with higher annual earnings received more compensation. The increase was roughly $49 for every $1 increase in weekly earnings, which translates to a dollar increase in compensation for each dollar of annual earnings. When we analyzed similar data for Pennsylvania and Illinois coal mining, we found that $1 increases in weekly income raised the compensation by about $36 and $26, respectively, although we could not reject the hypothesis of no effect (Kantor and Fishback 1994b). Croyle's (1978, 290, 294) study of nonfatal accidents shows that payments rose by $1.36 for each $1 increase in income lost from the accident. However, this marginal payment of more than a dollar for each dollar of lost income may not have been true in other states. The Minnesota sample was one of the few samples in table 2.4 where the ratio of nonfatal accident payments to lost income exceeded one.

In summarizing the results thus far, the common law doctrines seem to have influenced the probability and level of accident payments, but they were clearly not the only influence and sometimes not even the dominant influence. Settlements were clearly influenced by institutional features. Families in Minnesota who hired lawyers typically received substantially higher payments that more than offset the cost of legal fees. For every dollar spent on legal expenses, nonfatal accident compensation rose by $2.18, while fatal accident compensation rose by $3.02.[15] Similarly, among the Illinois mining families of fatal accident victims, filing suit seems to have been a major determinant of the amount of compensation a family received. Filing a suit against a mining company raised the fatal accident payments to Illinois coal miners by $1,429. Both results, however, must be approached with caution. It is possible that the only cases that were brought to trial were those in which the employer was clearly at fault and thus the worker was likely to receive a favorable court award.

One reason why the common law might not have been the only determinant of accident compensation is that some employers might have used disability payments as a component of their employees' wage packages. By paying compensation to injured workers, even if compensation was not legally required, some employers may have been able to use this image of relative generosity to reduce turnover among their workers or raise the productivity of the workforce. One way to determine whether employers did so is to examine the probability of paying compensation at very low levels of lost time, which were below any expected measure of legal costs. Table 2.5 shows the percentage of workers who received payments and those who did not receive payments for different levels of days disabled in Michigan between 1897 and 1903. If workers faced legal costs that involved any kind of fixed charge and employers were not using disability payments to raise productivity, we would expect no payments to workers at low levels of days disabled (even if the probability of winning costly litigation was one). However, if the employers received positive productivity benefits from paying workers, then we would expect payments to workers even at very low levels of days disabled. Table 2.5 shows that a similar percentage of workers received payments in the lowest range of days dis-

Table 2.5   **Distribution of Wage Compensation by Days Disabled**

Number of Days Disabled	Number of Workers Not Receiving Wage Benefits	Number of Workers Receiving Wage Benefits
0–5	67 (67.7%)	32 (32.3%)
6–10	117 (65.4%)	62 (34.6%)
11–15	127 (65.1%)	68 (34.9%)
16–20	39 (60.9%)	25 (39.1%)
21–30	234 (64.8%)	127 (35.2%)
31–40	60 (57.7%)	44 (42.3%)
41–50	89 (61.4%)	56 (38.6%)
51–60	76 (57.1%)	57 (42.9%)
61–90	72 (64.9%)	39 (35.1%)
91–120	25 (58.1%)	18 (41.9%)
>120	69 (70.4%)	29 (29.6%)
N	975 (63.6%)	557 (36.4%)

Sources: Michigan Bureau of Labor and Industrial Statistics (1898, 31–55, 72–73, 79–92, 100–101, 108–22, 132–33, 140–51, 158–59, 165–76, 184–85; 1899, 8–37, 58–61, 69–85, 93–94, 102–15, 127–30, 138–52, 156–59, 165–80, 193–96; 1900, 6–37, 46–47, 52–68, 74–75, 83–97, 104–5, 111–27, 132–33, 139–53, 160–61; 1901, 6–37, 52–53, 61–82, 86–87, 95–111, 116–17, 124–46, 152–53, 159–76, 182–83; 1902, 186–251, 268–75, 281–319, 322–23, 328–49, 356–57, 364–83, 386–87, 392–415, 418–19, 426–53, 458–61, 466–95, 504–5; 1903, 34–39, 54–57, 82–85, 110–15, 134–35, 158–65, 184–85, 216–17; 1904, 38–43, 64–67, 96–97, 122–23, 146–47, 176–79, 202–3, 232–35).

abled, in the middle ranges, and the top ranges, which is consistent with the notion that some employers were making payments as implicit fringe benefits and not just seeking to avoid a court award. The evidence is consistent with the view that some, although clearly not all, employers were paying benefits without the threat of court suits.

Although we earlier ascribed the finding that a worker's experience within the firm raised the probability of compensation in Michigan to the employer's difficulties in invoking the contributory negligence defense, there might be two alternative interpretations for this finding. First, since injured workers who had lengthy tenures with their employers were obviously stable employees, firms may have paid disability benefits in order to keep the injured worker financially tied to the firm. Since the average amount of time that workers in the Michigan sample were out of work was about thirty-six days, employers may have used the disability payments as a way to limit turnover and to reduce costs of training new workers. Second, that firms were more likely to compensate more veteran employees is also consistent with labor economists' findings that wages tend to be positively correlated with firm tenure.[16]

Compensating injured workers might also have been a component of an efficiency wage package. Stiglitz (1987) argues, for example, that because monitoring employees is more difficult in larger firms, they will pay above-market wages in an attempt to mitigate employee shirking.[17] The opportunity cost of shirking would be relatively high for these well-paid workers because if they were detected performing substandardly, then they would forgo their above-market wage premiums. This hypothesis implies that larger firms would be more likely to compensate injured workers. In fact, we found evidence in our Michigan study that larger firms were more likely to compensate their nonfatally injured workers.

Since the compensation system involved the decisions of so many different types of people, including employers, lawyers, juries, and judges, noneconomic and nonlegal factors potentially played a role. Various decisionmakers could have sought to show sympathy for families with more dependents. However, Croyle's study of Minnesota found that the number of dependents did not have strong positive effects on the payment of compensation to fatal or nonfatal accident victims. Similarly, we found no evidence that married Michigan workers around the turn of the century were more likely to receive compensation for their nonfatal accidents.

Discrimination was also a potential problem for immigrant workers in the courts. Foreign-born workers might have been less likely to receive compensation due to limited understanding of American law and language or financial constraints that discouraged them from seeking a claim against their employers. In the Michigan nonfatal accident sample we found no evidence of lower probabilities of compensation for immigrants, but it should be noted that 82 percent of Michigan's foreign-born workers were from the United Kingdom, Germany, Scandinavia, or Canada (U.S. Bureau of the Census 1903, 732–35), and McGouldrick and Tannen (1977) argue that such northern European workers faced less discrimination and fewer language and financial barriers than workers from southern and eastern Europe.[18] In a study of fatal accident payments to the families of Illinois coal miners, we also found that nativity had no effect on the levels of payments their families received (Kantor and Fishback 1994b).

Organized labor, in calling for workers' compensation legislation, often saw insurance companies as barriers to compensation and an unnecessary financial burden on limited accident funds. Robert Asher (1969, 464) provides a colorful description of the workers' logic: "The insurance companies had only one motive—profit. Whenever possible, the insurance companies intimidated workers into accepting reduced settlements. In court the insurance companies often won cases on meaningless technicalities. In short, the interest of the casualty insurance companies dictated a policy of opposition to all employee claims. The casualty companies cared little about the suffering of injured workers. But many employers wanted to help injured workers for humanitarian reasons or because they reasoned that contented employees were better workers and were less likely to join unions. Because they could not afford to self-insure, these employers had to let the profit-seeking casualty companies with which they insured handle relations with injured laborers as the insurance companies saw fit." In our analysis of the Michigan data on nonfatal accident compensation, however, we found that 23.7 percent of the firms carried liability insurance, implying that the great majority of firms self-insured. Regression analysis of the probability that a worker received accident compensation contradicts the claims of organized labor. The probability that disabled workers received compensation actually was 3.6 to 6.4 percentage points higher if their firms had liability insurance, although we cannot reject the hypothesis of no difference.

2.5 Preaccident Compensation: Risk Premiums in Wages

Postaccident compensation was not the only form of compensation that workers received for risking bodily injury at work. Studies of recent data suggest that workers often receive higher wages when faced with more dangerous jobs (see Moore and Viscusi 1990). There is also evidence that at least some groups of workers received preaccident compensation in the form of risk premiums in wage rates under the negligence liability system. Recall that a well-functioning labor market and the presence of risk premiums in wages was a key reason why Landes and Posner (1987, 309–11) felt that the assumption of risk defense was not unreasonable or could contribute to efficiency.

We found some evidence of payment of higher wages to workers in more dangerous industries in samples of male workers from several states between 1884 and 1903 (Fishback and Kantor 1992). In a Kansas sample of workers from 1884 to 1887, we found that an increase in the expected income loss from workplace accidents led to a rise in wages that paid for 63 percent of the additional loss. In a Maine sample from 1890, wages rose enough to cover approximately 38 percent of the additional expected loss, while in California the wages rose enough to cover 220 percent of the additional expected loss. We did not find risk premiums in the wages paid to women in Indianapolis in 1892 or to children in New Jersey in 1903, possibly because the level and variation of accident risks were smaller for those groups than for men.[19]

There was also evidence that higher accident risk was rewarded with higher wages in jobs within the same industry. In coal mining in the early 1900s, Fishback (1992, chap. 6) found evidence that work inside the mine where there was greater accident risk paid about 14 percent higher wages than work requiring similar skill outside the mine. In another study of the railroad industry between 1892 and 1909, Kim and Fishback (1993, 811–13) found that railroad workers in jobs with higher fatal and nonfatal accident risk received higher wages. The wages adjusted to changes in fatal accident risk in ways that implied that the railroad labor markets evaluated the life of a railroad workers at roughly thirty thousand to thirty-six thousand dollars in 1967 dollars, which was roughly equivalent to the present value of the lifetime stream of earnings of a railroad worker. The wages adjusted to nonfatal accident risk in ways that implied a market value of a nonfatal accident of slightly more than a year's income.[20]

2.6 Summary

Under the negligence liability system, compensation for fatal accidents was relatively meager. The nature of the liability rules meant that a substantial number of families of fatal accident victims received no compensation. Among those who did receive compensation, the amounts were generally less than a year's income, often little more than payment for burial expenses. Less than 4 percent of the heirs of fatal accident victims received levels of compensation that exceeded the levels they would have received under workers' compensation had that system been in place at the time of their accidents. Similarly, substantial numbers of nonfatal accident victims received no benefits.

Did accident compensation in the early twentieth century, prior to workers' compensation, follow the dictates of the common law system with its three defenses? The fact that numerous injured workers received no benefits could be seen as roughly consistent with the common law doctrines. However, there were substantial delays in court decisions and substantial costs of going to court, thus the vast majority of accident compensation decisions were made outside the courtroom in settlement bargaining. Analyzing how accident victims or their heirs were compensated around the turn of the century suggests that the impact of the common law defenses on accident payments was filtered through a settlement bargaining process that was influenced by legal costs and private information. There is evidence that the common law doctrines guided the de facto system of accident compensation, but other factors clearly influenced who received compensation. Some employers may have used accident compensation as a means of offering nonwage benefits to their workers. Certainly, in some settings they were paying benefits to workers who experienced damages so small that they had no credible threat of taking the employer to court. In other cases, employers paid damages to workers for accidents where they did not consider themselves liable. By offering the implicit promise that they would take care of their injured workers, larger employers may have been able to lower their monitoring costs and reduce turnover among workers who had firm-specific experience.

The presence of legal costs and informational asymmetries made the impact of the common law indirect and complex. For example, analysis of several accident samples shows that the effect of the common law doctrines on the probability and levels of accident payment were not always substantial. The primary role of the common law seems to have been in determining whether the injured worker had a credible threat of pursuing a court case against his employer (i.e., did his expected award in court exceed his legal costs).

Our exploration into the determinants of accident compensation casts some doubt on generally held impressions of the system. We found little evidence that the system was more sympathetic to workers with families. We found no consistent evidence that immigrant workers received less. Nor did we find evidence that workers were less likely to receive payments when insurance companies were involved. On the other hand, workers could enhance the amounts and probability of payment by hiring a lawyer, who effectively served as their advocate in working through the legal system. But hiring a lawyer meant enticing him with a portion of any award that was won or by paying him an upfront fee, which was something most injured workers probably could not easily afford.

Major changes in the common law might have been reflected in a lowering of the worker's legal cost threshold, which would have expanded the range of remunerable accidents. Eliminating the three defenses, for example, presumably would have lowered legal costs by eliminating the debate over the applicability of the defenses in each particular case. The negligence of the employer, the basis for any compensation under the common law, would still require a court decision and some unknown number of workers would still be left uncompensated for their accidents. In fact, it was for this reason that social reformers in the early twentieth century extolled the virtues of workers' compensation and its guarantee of post-accident compensation.

Notes

1. For lucid discussions of the employers' liability system see Clark (1908), Weiss (1966), and Epstein (1982).

2. Interstate railroad workers are excluded from the analysis here, and from consideration in most of the book, because they were covered under the Federal Employers' Liability Acts of 1906 and 1908. Intrastate railroad workers and non-train personnel for interstate lines, such as repairmen permanently stationed in a local workshop, would have been covered under a state's workers' compensation law, however.

3. Since the German and Washington samples reflect accident causes under workers' compensation, the percentages reflecting employer negligence might be biased downward because of the moral hazard (on the part of workers) associated with no-fault insurance.

4. These figures represent gross compensation and ignore the legal expenses that the victim's family often paid. In the 1909–1910 Minnesota study, legal expenses consumed 11.9 percent of the total compensation paid to the families of fatal accident victims. At the higher end of the scale, in forty-six fatal accident cases in Erie County, New York, between 1907 and 1908, the New York State Employers' Liability Commission calculated that 26.3 percent of the gross amount that employers paid to families went to lawyers (Eastman 1910, 290). The introduction of workers' compensation did not completely eliminate the need for lawyers, however. An injured worker or his family may have had to hire a lawyer if the case was contested. Assuming lawyers collected 25 percent of the families' gross compensation in the contested cases, Conyngton's (1917, 110–37) data suggest that lawyers' fees accounted for between 0.9 and 2.7 percent of the total awards under the new system.

5. The present value of the stream of earnings at the time of the accident is the amount of money that would have to be invested at that time to generate the workers' stream of annual earnings. For example, if we put twenty thousand dollars into the bank today at an interest rate of 5 percent compounded annually, we could pay a worker one thousand dollars per year forever. The present value of the stream of one thousand dollars per year forever is twenty thousand dollars.

6. All forty-eight states had such laws by 1907. See U.S. Commissioner of Labor (1908, 85–87). New York, Oklahoma, Pennsylvania, Utah, and Wyoming declared in their constitutions that the amounts recoverable could not be restricted. Maximums were imposed of four thousand dollars in Massachusetts; ten thousand dollars in Illinois, Indiana, Kansas, Missouri, Ohio, Virginia, West Virginia, and Wisconsin; seventy-five hundred dollars in Oregon; seven thousand dollars in New Hampshire; and five thousand dollars in Arizona, Colorado, Connecticut, Maine, Minnesota, and Wyoming. In other states no maximum was named.

7. In a study of modern product liability claims and compensation for bodily injury, Viscusi (1986) found similarly that the amount of the bodily injury payment is often comparable to the size of the loss, although the elasticity of bodily injury loss with respect to the bodily injury payment was below one for the average loss and declined as the loss increased.

8. See Kantor and Fishback (1995). The presence of legal costs has led to a literature on the modeling of settlement negotiations, surveyed by Cooter and Rubinfeld (1989). See also Bebchuk (1984), Daughety and Reinganum (1993), Wang, Kim, and Yi (1994), and Spier (1994).

9. See Lazear (1979), Hutchens (1987), Jovanovic (1979), Altonji and Shakotko (1987), Abraham and Farber (1987), Brown (1989), Topel (1991), and Hersch and Reagan (1990).

10. See Fishback (1987, 311–13). Examples of accidents for which the Stonega lawyers felt the company might be liable include roof falls where an inexperienced miner was working alone, roof falls in haulage ways where the company was responsible for propping the roof, equipment accidents where it was hard to determine who was at fault, and cases where machinery was defective. If an experienced miner was hurt in a roof fall, the lawyers were unlikely to consider the company to be liable. Virginia never passed an employers' liability law that limited the employers' defenses. The Virginia legislature adopted workers' compensation in 1919.

11. The total number of accident victims described in this paragraph does not equal the totals reported in table 2.4 because there were a number of cases where there was missing information about the amount received or the lawyer's opinion.

12. Croyle tried to examine differences between court decisions and settlements, but his sample included only five court decisions, which we feel to be too small a sample from which to derive much information.

13. Croyle included railroad workers in his analysis, which potentially is a problem because the common law doctrines differed for railroad and nonrailroad workers. Railroad workers involved in interstate commerce were covered by the Federal Employers' Liability Act which limited the contributory negligence and fellow servant defenses. Minnesota never passed an employer liability act for nonrailroad workers, but they did have one for railroad workers.

14. Compared to the studies of the negligence liability system reported in table 2.4, the Michigan workers tended to receive accident benefits at a lower rate than their peers. Whereas the weighted average of accident victims receiving no benefits was 40.2 percent in the samples reported in table 2.4, 66.8 percent of the Michigan workers in the Bureau of Labor and Industrial Statistics's data received no wage benefits. The 66.8 percent figure, however, is less than the maximum receiving no benefits found in the table—72.9 percent of the Kansas City workers sampled in 1912 recovered nothing from their employers. Note that 66.8 percent of injured workers receiving no compensation is consistent with the data on accident causes presented in table 2.2. According to those estimates, between 52 and 100 percent of injured workers would have been legally entitled to nothing from their employers under a strict reading of the common law.

15. Croyle found that filing a lawsuit substantially lowered fatal accident payments in Minnesota but raised nonfatal accident payments. However, he also included legal expenses in the analysis, which is highly correlated with litigation. Further, legal expenses are problematic given that many lawyers charged contingency fees. Thus, in Croyle's regression analysis the legal expenses are strongly correlated with the payment because many times they are calculated as a percentage of the payment. We have reestimated the analysis using a dummy variable for the presence of a lawyer and found a positive and statistically significant impact. If the case was decided in court, we found no influence on the amount paid to fatal accident victims.

16. One interpretation of the finding that firms were more likely to compensate their more veteran injured employees is that the disability benefits were a component of a pay-sequencing package. That is, in order to elicit diligent work from their employees, firms may have offered workers less than their marginal revenue

products in the early years of a long-term relationship, and then "overpayment" in later years. See Lazear (1979) and Hutchens (1987). Alternatively, the better fringe benefits associated with longer tenure may simply indicate that these workers were more productive than their coworkers because they had good "job matches," as Jovanovic (1979), Altonji and Shakotko (1987), and Abraham and Farber (1987) argue. Finally, the higher earnings may have been compensation for the worker's investment in firm-specific human capital. See Brown (1989), Topel (1991), and Hersch and Reagan (1990).

17. Brown and Medoff (1989) empirically find a positive relationship between plant size and wages. For general studies of the presence of efficiency wages, see Katz (1986) and Krueger and Summers (1988).

18. The ethnic mix of the sample is representative of the ethnic mix of the Michigan workforce. Foreign-born workers composed 35.1 percent of the workers in the sample compared with 32.4 percent of Michigan's workforce in 1900 (U.S. Bureau of the Census 1904, 306–11).

19. In this same study, we also found evidence that adult workers received higher wages to compensate for longer layoffs (Fishback and Kantor 1992).

20. The evaluation of the value of accidents comes from examining the impact of a change in accident risk (dp) on changes in wages (dw). The change in the wage (dw) would be equal to the change in accident risk (dp) times the value of the loss from the accident (V): $dw = dp \times V$. The analyses cited gave information on dw and dp, which allowed the scholars to solve for V.

The Economic Impact of the Switch to Workers' Compensation

After various state governments tinkered with the negligence liability system by altering some of the common law defenses, the legislatures turned their attention to the more radical reform of introducing workers' compensation. Between 1911 and 1921, forty-three states adopted workers' compensation laws at the behest of political coalitions combining workers, employers, and insurers. To fully understand what each of these groups expected to gain from the legislation, it is necessary to examine the changes wrought by the introduction of workers' compensation. The new laws raised the average accident benefits paid to workers in workplace accidents. The rise in accident benefits, in turn, led to reductions in the wages paid by employers, reductions in savings and insurance purchases by households, and changes in the care taken by employers and workers to prevent accidents.

The switch to workers' compensation eliminated fault as an issue in determining accident compensation. All workers injured in accidents "arising out of or in the course of" employment were compensated. The new compensation rules caused a substantial increase in the percentage of injured workers receiving compensation. Further, the average amount paid to the families of fatal accident victims jumped several-fold. When considering both fatal and nonfatal accidents together, the percentages of wages or payrolls that were paid out in benefits and/or medical expenses to accident victims rose anywhere from 75 to 200 percent with the introduction of workers' compensation.

The rise in postaccident payment led many contemporary reformers to hail workers' compensation as a substantial improvement in workers' welfare, providing them better protection against the financial consequences of workplace accidents. Many observers anticipated an added benefit that employers would take more actions to enhance workplace safety and reduce accident rates. The expectations were reasonable, but changes in social insurance programs often lead to adjustments in labor markets and in the behavior of workers that have consequences that are contrary to what reformers anticipate. Therefore, the de facto redistribution of workplace accident costs associated with the switch to workers' compensation might have been much smaller than what social reformers presumed.

In this chapter we discuss how the introduction of workers' compensation changed the nature of postaccident benefits in the early twentieth century. We then investigate its impact on wages, household saving and accident insurance purchases, and fatal accident rates. In the case of wages, numerous studies of the economic impact of government-mandated benefits find that employers are able to pass at least part of their costs back to workers through reduced wages (see Moore and Viscusi 1990, 24; Gruber and Krueger 1991; Chelius and Burton 1994; and Gruber 1994). A close examination of wages in three dangerous industries when workers' compensation was first introduced suggests that employers were able to pass some of the costs of workers' compensation on to nonunion workers through lower wages, but were less successful in passing the costs on to unionized workers.

Even though many workers may have "bought" the higher benefits associated with workers' compensation through lower wages, we argue in this chapter that they were nonetheless better off as a result of the legislation. We establish that workers were better insured against workplace accident risk under workers' compensation than under negligence liability. Using a large cross-sectional data set of working class households' financial decisions in the period 1917 to 1919, we show that in workers' compensation states households bought slightly less accident insurance and held substantially lower precautionary savings, holding everything else constant. It appears that workers were not able to purchase their desired levels of accident insurance under negligence liability, in part because insurance companies faced significant informational problems in selling workplace accident insurance to individual workers. Instead, many workers were forced to rely on precautionary savings, which were a relatively expensive means of insuring against accident risk. The guarantee of accident benefits from workers' compensation allowed workers to reduce their precautionary saving and, thus, increase their consumption of other goods.

Finally, as long as insurance premiums were experience rated—that is, employers with more dangerous workplaces paid higher insurance premiums—higher workers' compensation benefits imposed higher costs on employers. Since workers' compensation insurance was somewhat experience rated in the early twentieth century, we might anticipate that employers would seek to create safer workplaces if the expected damages they paid for accidents were higher than the costs of preventing the accident. On the other hand, given that they received higher benefits, workers' costs of incurring an accident were reduced, which might have led to their taking less care in preventing accidents or reporting phantom injuries. In this chapter we cite the results of studies that show that workers' compensation was associated with a decline in fatal accident rates in manufacturing industries, but an increase in fatal accident rates in the coal industry. We speculate that differences in the employers' costs of preventing accidents across these industries produced this dissimilar effect on fatal accident rates.

3.1   Accident Compensation under Workers' Compensation

Workers' compensation laws mandated that employers remunerate all workers for their injuries arising "out of and in the course of employment."[1] Accident benefits paid out under workers' compensation were determined by statutory provisions that varied by state and within states over time. The laws typically provided that injured workers (or the families of the deceased) were to be paid a percentage of their weekly wage for a maximum number of weeks, subject to maximum weekly payouts and some maximum total level of compensation. Variations in state patterns are discussed in detail in appendix B. In many states the percentage of the wage replaced varied with respect to the number of family members. In the discussions below we assume that the worker was married with two children, ages eight and ten.

The families of workers killed in workplace accidents typically received benefits under state laws patterned after the New Jersey law of 1911. In New Jersey employers were expected to offer the widow and children of a fatal accident victim weekly payments equal to 45 percent of the workers' wage for up to three hundred weeks. Weekly benefits could not be lower than $5 a week or higher than $10 a week, and the sum of the payments could not exceed $3,000 or be lower than $1,500. In addition, New Jersey offered the family $100 for funeral expenses. Nearly all states focused on paying the money weekly over an extended period of time. Thus the family of a New Jersey worker who was earning a national average wage of $14.83 per week in 1911 could expect to receive $6.67 a week for nearly six years. The present value of this stream of payments using a discount rate of 5 percent was $1,840. This present value reflects how much a family would have had to invest at 5 percent compounded interest at the time payments began to generate the stream of weekly workers' compensation payments. The family would have therefore received a stream of payments with a present value of about 2.5 times the annual income the worker had been earning. New Jersey's initial workers' compensation law was substantially less generous than the laws in Washington, New York, Oregon, West Virginia, and South Dakota, where the present values of fatality benefits exceeded five times annual income. Georgia, Vermont, and Virginia adopted the least generous initial laws with present values of fatality payments that replaced two years' income.

Workers' compensation laws also established benefit parameters for nonfatal accidents, which were far more common than fatal accidents. Nonfatal accidents were separated into three major categories: permanent total disability (e.g., full paralysis), permanent partial disability (e.g., loss of a hand), and temporary disability (e.g., broken leg). In most states, the compensation for nonfatal accidents followed the general pattern of that for fatal accidents. During his disability the worker was paid a percentage of his weekly wage, subject to statutory minimum and maximum payments, for a maximum number of weeks. Each state established a waiting period, ranging from three days to two weeks from the date of the accident, during which time no accident compensation was paid. Injured workers who were out of work for a period less than the waiting period received no compensation. The rules for permanent total disability payments, say for full paralysis, were similar to the rules for fatal accident payments (without the funeral expense payments) in nearly every state.

The relative generosity of the states varied for different types of accidents. We have combined the present values of the accident payments for each type of accident into a summary measure of workers' compensation benefits, the expected benefits. The expected benefits measure takes the present value of the benefits of each of the broad categories of accidents and weights each present value with the probability that such an accident might occur. Rough estimates of the number of manufacturing accidents per thousand workers each year range from 0.14 permanent total disabilities, 2 fatalities, 10 permanent partial disabilities (loss of a hand, finger, or eye), to 120 short-term injuries that disabled the worker longer than the waiting period. In essence, the expected benefit shows what an insurance company might have expected to pay to the families of workplace accident victims earning the national weekly wage during the course of a year. For such workers in New Jersey in 1911, an insurer might have anticipated paying out $8.81 per worker, or approximately 1.19 percent of the worker's annual earnings, in workers' compensation benefits. The expected benefits as a percentage of annual earnings in the first year of operation are shown in table 3.1. Expected benefits ranged from 0.87 percent of annual earnings in Georgia in 1921 and Virginia in 1919 to 2.93 percent of annual earnings in North Dakota in 1919. More details on the calculation of expected benefits are provided in appendix B. The states amended their benefit levels every few years; therefore, the relative generosity of benefits across states varied from year to year. In chapter 7 we discuss the factors determining the choice of benefit levels and table 7.1 compares the expected benefits in each state from the first year of operation through 1930.

Mary Conyngton's (1917) surveys of workers' compensation in Ohio

Table 3.1   **Expected Workers' Compensation Benefits in the First Year**
                 of Operation

State	First Year	Expected Benefit as Percentage of Annual Earnings	State	First Year	Expected Benefit as Percentage of Annual Earnings
Cal.	1911	1.78	Colo.	1915	1.00
N.J.	1911	1.19	Ind.	1915	1.33
Nev.	1911	1.33	La.	1915	1.21
Wash.	1911	2.23	Mont.	1915	1.35
Wis.	1911	2.02	Okla.	1915	0.85
Ill.	1912	1.54	Vt.	1915	1.06
Kan.	1912	1.28	Wyo.	1915	1.08
Mass.	1912	1.72	Ky.	1916	1.63
Md.	1912	1.33	Me.	1916	1.30
Mich.	1912	1.19	Pa.	1916	1.26
Ohio	1912	1.67	N.M.	1917	1.03
R.I.	1912	1.29	S.D.	1917	1.22
N.H.	1912	1.26	Utah	1917	1.43
Ariz.	1913	1.74	Del.	1918	1.01
Minn.	1913	1.21	Idaho	1918	1.47
Neb.	1913	1.34	N.D.	1919	2.93
Tex.	1913	1.91	Tenn.	1919	1.08
W. Va.	1913	1.73	Va.	1919	0.87
Conn.	1914	1.24	Ala.	1920	1.09
Iowa	1914	1.22	Ga.	1921	0.87
N.Y.	1914	2.42	Mo.	1927	1.79
Or.	1914	2.49	N.C.	1929	1.59

Note: See appendix B. The expected benefit is the weighted sum of the present value of fatal accident payments, the present value of hand payments, and the present value of the five-week disability payment. The weights are the probability of this type of accident. The same probabilities were used for all states and are based on averages for manufacturing in Oregon (Oregon Industrial Accident Commission 1919, 28–42). The probability of a fatal accident over the course of a year was 0.001895, for a permanent total disability 0.000136, for permanent partial disability 0.0099, and for temporary total disability 0.1199. We used the fatal accident present value as a measure for the permanent total disability benefits because they were so similar in nearly all the states. We scaled the hand present value down to 21.8 percent of the level listed above because the average value paid for permanent partial disabilities was about 21.8 percent of the hand value (see accident statistics reported in Wisconsin Industrial Commission [1915, 41; 1916, 44; 1917, 6–7] for 1914 to 1917).

and Connecticut in 1915 found that the families of fatal accident victims generally received the benefits to which they were entitled. In Ohio the families' actual death benefits were on average equal to 98.8 percent of the weekly payment that we estimated the families should have received using the statutory rules and each worker's reported weekly wage. In fact, 46 percent of the actual payments were the same as predicted by the statute, 34 percent were slightly higher, and 20 percent were slightly lower. In

Connecticut, the actual payments averaged 99.9 percent of the predicted payments based on the statute. Therefore, cross-state comparisons of estimated workers' compensation payments using the statutory rules should give a reasonable measure of the actual amounts that injured workers and their families received. Note, however, that both Ohio and Connecticut had established state bureaucracies to ensure that workers' compensation benefits were paid to workers and families who were entitled to them. In the states that did not establish a bureaucratic commission and instead relied on the courts to settle compensation disputes between injured workers and employers, the correlation between what workers received and what employers were legally obligated to pay may not have been as strong.

3.2   A Comparison of Postaccident Payments under the Negligence Liability and Workers' Compensation Systems

The primary objective of social reformers and others who lobbied for workers' compensation was to raise the expected benefits that injured workers or their heirs received in the event of an industrial accident. Raising expected benefits meant increasing the percentage of accident victims who received remuneration and/or the average level of benefits they would receive. A priori, we cannot state with certainty whether expected benefits were higher under the old negligence liability system or under workers' compensation. If the old system followed the common law rules to the letter, an injured worker who could show employer negligence and get past the three defenses (assumption of risk, fellow servant, and contributory negligence) was supposed to be fully compensated for the damages, including full replacement of wages. Meanwhile, under workers' compensation all injured workers received at most two-thirds of their lost income. Thus, the properly working common law system compensated fewer workers, but the workers who received payments should have recovered more of their losses than they would have under workers' compensation. It becomes an empirical question whether workers' compensation raised the expected accident payments by sufficiently increasing the percentage of injured workers compensated to offset the lower replacement rate. The potential rise in expected benefits under workers' compensation might have been still larger because, as we point out in chapter 2, it is not clear how well the de facto employers' liability system followed the dictates of the common law. For example, the payments to the families of most fatal accident victims who received some positive amount covered only about one year of the worker's income. Thus, for some types of accidents, workers' compensation might have led to an increase in both the percentage of families compensated and the amounts that they received.

Measuring accident remuneration under the negligence liability and workers' compensation systems is complicated by the various types of accidents. The easiest and most accurate comparisons can be made for fatal accidents. When considering fatal accident payments, there is no question about the severity of the accident because we know that the victims of such accidents had the same fate. Moreover, there are fewer reporting problems when studying fatal accidents because the event was not easily concealed. Comparing nonfatal accident compensation is fraught with difficulty because there exist few data to compare accidents of similar severities across the two legal institutions. In this section we focus first on the payments made to the heirs of fatal accident victims and then turn to comparisons of the two legal systems when all accident types are considered as a whole.

3.2.1   The Rise in Average Compensation for Fatal Accidents

The shift to workers' compensation raised the expected amount of post-accident compensation for fatal accidents in two important ways. First, the percentage of families that received no compensation fell to close to zero. For example, Mary Conyngton's (1917, 109) survey of Ohio and Connecticut families of fatally injured workers in 1915 revealed that only 2.9 and 9.4 percent, respectively, received no benefits under workers' compensation. In those cases where the families received nothing, there was a strong likelihood that the accident did not occur in the workplace or occurred because the worker was intoxicated or had maliciously caused his own accident, either of which barred monetary recovery. The percentages of those not receiving compensation under workers' compensation are substantially lower than even the lowest percentages reported for the negligence liability system in table 2.1.

Second, for those families that received a positive amount of compensation for the death of their primary wage earners, the average payments were significantly higher under workers' compensation than under negligence liability. The information on fatal accident payments under negligence liability in table 2.1 shows that average payments to those families receiving positive amounts ranged from 0.58 of a year's earnings in Virginia coal mines in the period 1916 to 1918 to 1.48 of a year's earnings for nonrailroad workers in Illinois prior to 1911. The average for all the samples was a negligence liability payment of about one year's earnings. By contrast, under workers' compensation the present value of fatal accident payments ranged from 1.94 to 8.26 times annual earnings in most states (see appendix table B.1). The gap between fatal accident payments under workers' compensation and negligence liability is still larger when we factor in the probability of receiving a payment under the negligence liability system. In expected terms, then, the heirs of fatal accident victims could expect to receive only about one-half year's earnings prior to the adoption of workers' compensation.

3.2.2   The Rise in Expected Compensation for All Types of Accidents

When the analysis is expanded to include both nonfatal and fatal accidents, the available data further show that when workers' compensation was introduced, average expected accident benefits increased substantially. Various estimates of the accident compensation paid out under the two systems suggest that the workers' compensation system was, on average, 1.7 to 4 times more generous than negligence liability.

We have attempted to calculate expected benefits under the two systems, holding the underlying risk of a workplace accident constant. We define the expected benefit $E(B)$ as follows:

$$(1) \qquad E(B) \;=\; p_f B_f \;+\; p_n B_n,$$

where p_f is the probability of a fatal accident, B_f is the average benefit paid out for a fatal accident, and the subscript n refers to nonfatal accidents. To make comparisons across time, we then normalized the expected benefits by dividing by average annual income. Thus, the final comparisons are quoted in terms of percentages of annual income or percentages of employers' payrolls. We made the comparisons from two types of sources: workers' reports of the remuneration they received when injured at work and employers' reports of what they paid out to workers.

Comparisons Based on Workers' Reports

To make the calculations based on workers' reports, we used the same probabilities of fatal and nonfatal accidents for both regimes.[2] We then calculated expected benefits under negligence liability using the average amounts of payments reported in the workers' samples. Information on individual workers' remuneration under negligence liability was collected from the New York Commission on Employers' Liability (NYCEL 1910, 246–50), which reported medical payments and wage replacement amounts that workers received from their employers. The data were originally collected from a series of direct interviews conducted on a random sample of workers who had been injured and whose accidents had been reported to the New York Bureau of Factory Inspection in 1907 (NYCEL 1910, 210–11). To calculate expected benefits under workers' compensation, we used the 1914 New York workers' compensation law to determine the present value of the stream of payouts for different types of accidents. In addition, we have limited the comparison to wage replacement only and have ignored how medical payments differed under the two legal systems. Our impression is that medical coverage was better under workers' compensation; therefore, the elimination of medical payments would bias the comparison against finding that workers' compensation benefits were relatively higher.

The New York wage replacement comparisons suggest that the expected wage replacement benefits under workers' compensation were at least 1.75 times as generous as the expected benefit under negligence liability. The estimate that workers' compensation on average paid about 1.75 times as much as negligence liability treats the sample from the NYCEL report as a random sample of the "true" number of accidents under the negligence system. Large numbers of nonfatal accidents that would have been compensable under workers' compensation, however, probably went unreported under negligence liability. In addition, it is likely that the unreported injured workers received little or no compensation; therefore, the average compensation reported for nonfatal injuries under employers' liability in the NYCEL study is likely overstated. By making conservative adjustments for the underreporting of accidents, we have calculated that workers' compensation benefits in New York were 2.5 times as generous as those under the employers' liability system. See appendix C for more details on these calculations.

Even this estimate of a 2.5-fold rise may be understated if we are correct that medical benefits were more generous under workers' compensation. The measured increase in benefits also understates the rise in the net amount that workers received after they paid their legal expenses. Evidence from various sources suggests that when workers hired a lawyer under the negligence system, contingency fees ranged from 20 to 50 percent. Since many workers did not hire lawyers to represent them, the payments to lawyers probably amounted to between 13 and 23 percent of the total amount that workers received under negligence. Some workers also used lawyers to contest claims under workers' compensation, although legal expenses probably consumed less than 5 percent of the total amount that workers received. Thus, after making adjustments for legal payments, the net expected amount an injured worker received might have risen by as much as 300 percent with the introduction of workers' compensation.

Comparisons Based on Employers' Reports

As a second way of comparing the generosity of benefits under the two systems, we examined how much employers reported that they and their insurance carriers paid out in accident benefits, settlements, and medical payments as a percentage of their payrolls. One of the advantages of using employer-reported evidence is that the underreporting of accidents is much less of a problem than for the data collected from workers. Employers reported how much they paid out for insurance and in direct payments to workers, and they did not have to reveal any information about accidents for which they made no payments. Thus, when making their reports about accident compensation, employers did not have to worry about giving factory inspectors specific information about accident problems in their establishments. In fact, to the extent that the generosity of accident benefits enhanced an employer's reputation, firms may have had an incentive to overstate their accident payments.

How much employers paid out for accident compensation conflates both the probability of occurrence and the amount actually paid. Thus, we try to hold the underlying accident risk constant by comparing the same industries in the same state during a period when there would have been little change in accident rates. The Wisconsin Bureau of Labor and Industrial Statistics (WBLIS) in 1906 conducted a survey of employers to determine their accident expenses and how much of this money actually went to workers in the form of wage replacement and medical benefits (WBLIS 1909, 31, 34–35). The WBLIS survey found that employers paid approximately $0.245 in wage and medical compensation for every $100 they paid in wages. Under workers' compensation in 1913, by contrast, the Wisconsin Industrial Commission (1915, 32–38) calculated that workers received wage and medical benefits of $0.82 for every $100 of payroll. This comparison suggests that workers' compensation in Wisconsin was 3.35 times more generous than the negligence liability system.

We were concerned that this Wisconsin comparison might be unreliable because the coverage of industries in 1906 and 1913 differed. To examine this issue more carefully, we matched industries from the 1906 and 1913 listings and found that in all but one of the twenty-three comparisons workers' compensation benefits exceeded those under negligence liability (see appendix table C.1). In fifteen of the twenty-three comparisons, workers' compensation was greater than two times more generous than negligence liability, and in nine of the twenty-three comparisons workers' compensation was more than three times as generous.

As a second measure, we examined the records of the Stonega Coke and Coal Company in Virginia before and after the introduction of workers' compensation on 1 January 1919. During the years 1916 to 1918, Stonega spent roughly $0.97 per $100 on the payroll in compensating injured workers or their families. During the period 1919 to 1923, after workers' compensation was established, Stonega spent approximately $1.70 per $100 on the payroll, which is about 74 percent higher than the payouts under negligence liability.[3] It should be noted that this rise in accident benefits is smaller than those we calculated for Wisconsin and New York in part because Virginia in 1919 had one of the least generous workers' compensation laws in the United States. Virginia's statutory benefit levels in 1919 were roughly half the benefit levels in Wisconsin in 1913 and 40 percent of New York's benefit levels in 1914 (see table 3.1 for a comparison).

The rise in benefits that we have documented for workers' compensation using the employer-reported data may be understated in two ways. The benefits under workers' compensation do not include medical payments or funeral expenses, and we know that employers did pay some medical and funeral expenses under the negligence system that were most likely included in their aggregate expenditure statistics. Furthermore, we did not subtract legal fees that workers paid under the two systems, which would have made workers' compensation look even more beneficent than the negligence system.

3.3   The Impact of Workers' Compensation on Wages

The substantial rise in postaccident benefits led reformers and many social historians to hail workers' compensation as a dramatic improvement in worker welfare. Economists since Adam Smith, however, have suggested that improvements in nonpecuniary benefits are often offset by compensating reductions in wages. In fact, studies of changes in workers' compensation benefits over the past twenty years have shown that increases in benefits are associated with reductions in wage rates (Moore and Viscusi 1990, 24–25; Gruber and Krueger 1991). If labor markets in the early 1900s operated in a similar fashion, the rise in postaccident compensation when states switched to workers' compensation potentially would have been offset by a decline in the risk premium implicit in wages.

At least some employers were aware of this phenomenon when workers' compensation was being discussed. A prominent Washington employer described how a cost-increasing provision in the state's 1911 workers' compensation law would ultimately affect workers: "[T]hey were working a hardship on the laboring man, because this 2 cents that the employer is supposed to pay will not eventually come from the employer, but will come from the laboring man by necessary reduction of wage scale. . . . Competition in all lines in this day is so keen that every employer of labor has to figure his expenses down to the lowest item, and as Washington will have to compete with Oregon, Montana, Idaho, and even California in her productions, eventually the employer is going to take this 2 cents, this small amount to him and a small amount on paper, out of his employee."[4] Of course, most employers who supported workers' compensation were not likely to make these statements very forcefully in public for fear of chilling the support that workers provided the program.

To examine how wages adjusted in response to the introduction of workers' compensation, we constructed three separate panel data sets for relatively dangerous industries in the early 1900s. The first sample covers hourly wage rates from payrolls collected by the U.S. Bituminous Coal Commission. The sample contains state averages for ten jobs from the twenty-three leading coal producing states at the end of each year from 1911 to 1922. The second sample is hourly earnings collected from payrolls by the U.S. Bureau of Labor Statistics for ten different jobs in the lumber industry for the years 1910 to 1913, 1915, 1921, and 1923 in the twenty-three major lumber producing states. The third sample is the wage scales listed in union contracts in the building trades for thirteen occupations in seventy-seven cities for each year between 1907 and 1913.[5] All three data sets allow examination of differences across states and over time during the period when nearly all the workers' compensation laws were adopted.

For each of the three samples we estimated standard wage equations. The equations can be used to assess the impact of changing expected post-accident benefit levels, while controlling for fluctuations in the product market, the skill levels of the workers, restrictions on working time, geographic differences in labor markets, and nationwide changes in the labor market specific to each year. In the coal industry we had enough information to control for several additional factors, including strikes and union strength. A more complete description of the model and the results is presented in appendix D. The wage equations generally confirm relationships found in numerous other wage studies. Wage rates rose when product prices increased and when business was improving. More productive and higher-skilled workers earned higher wages. Strikes and unionization were associated with higher earnings.

The impact of workers' compensation can be assessed in a variety of ways. As a simple starting point, we measured the impact of workers' compensation using a dummy variable with a value of one for states and years in which the workers' compensation law was in effect and a value of zero otherwise. Using this measure, workers' compensation was associated with a decline in wages in two of the three industries. In coal mining the presence of a workers' compensation law reduced hourly earnings by 2.16 percent, while in the lumber industry the reduction was 1.60 percent. In both cases statistical tests reject the view that workers' compensation had no effect on wages. In the building trades, however, the decline was smaller at 0.33 percent, and we cannot reject the hypothesis that workers' compensation had no effect on wages.[6]

The use of a dummy variable provides only a rough estimate of how workers' compensation affected wages across the United States because the laws were associated with more complex changes in accident benefits than a 0–1 variable can capture. A dummy variable fails to represent the substantial variation in accident compensation paid out to workers both under negligence liability and under workers' compensation. The generosity of workers' compensation benefits varied a great deal across states and across time within states (see tables 3.1, B.1–B.4, and 7.1). There also appear to have been differences in the average benefits paid out across states under negligence liability. Inspection of employers' liability insurance manuals shows that rates for this insurance were adjusted depending on a state's liability rules and the outcomes of litigation in the state. For example, holding the type of industry constant, a firm in Ohio under negligence liability would have paid insurance premiums that were 1.8 times larger than the rates a similar firm in Illinois would have paid (DeLeon

1907, 26–27). These differentials presumably correspond to the different amounts of compensation workers in these two states would have received if they were injured under the negligence liability system.

To capture this variation in compensation we have developed a measure of expected benefits in each of the industries. Expected benefits under workers' compensation are constructed by first calculating the gross benefits a worker or his family would have received had he been killed or suffered a permanent total disability, a permanent partial disability, or a temporary four-week disability. We then converted these gross benefit estimates into an expected benefit measure by weighting each of the four types of accident benefits by the probability that each type of accident would occur and then summing the four expected compensation estimates (see appendix B for details of these calculations).[7]

The expected benefits variable measures the monetary value that a risk-neutral worker would place on his expected accident compensation.[8] If workers were risk-averse, however, our measure of expected compensation actually provides a lower-bound estimate of the value that workers would have placed on these postaccident benefits. The expected benefits measure also is strongly correlated with the employers' costs of purchasing workers' compensation insurance because workers' compensation insurance and employers' liability insurance were experience rated.[9] Employers probably would have paid insurance premiums that were about 1.67 times the expected benefit measure, based on administrative load factors quoted by contemporary insurance texts on workers' compensation insurance (see Kulp 1928, 246).

Table 3.2 contains estimates of the sizes of the wage offset from the wage regressions. The letter superscripts mark estimates for which we can reject the hypothesis that workers' compensation had no effect at conventional levels of statistical significance. A coefficient of −1 implies that workers fully paid for increases in the expected benefits that they received, although the worker would not have fully paid for the employer's cost of purchasing the insurance to provide those benefits. Coefficients around −1.67 imply that employers were able to pass on their full insurance costs

Table 3.2	Wage Offsets Associated with the Introduction of Workers' Compensation		
	Sample	Linear	Semilog
	Coal	−1.72[a]	−2.50[a]
	Lumber	−1.04[a]	−0.69[b]
	Unionized building trades	0.02	−0.17

Sources: See table D.1 and Fishback and Kantor (1995, 732).

[a]Statistically significantly different from zero in a one-tailed test at the 1 percent level.

[b]Statistically significantly different from zero in a one-tailed test at the 15 percent level.

to workers. Using modern data, Gruber and Krueger (1991) estimate that workers in the 1970s and 1980s paid for between 56 and 86 percent of their employers' workers' compensation costs. Their results suggest that workers more than paid for the value of the expected benefits that they actually received, but did not fully pay for the insurance costs that employers bore. On the other hand, Moore and Viscusi (1990, 50–51) find wage offsets of approximately 3 times the expected value of the worker's accident benefits and 2.4 times employers' insurance costs.

Our estimates of the wage offsets using the full samples and the most complete set of control variables are listed in table 3.2. Coal and lumber workers in the early 1900s experienced wage reductions that were similar to the ones found in modern studies, while the contractual wages in the unionized building trades barely responded to the increase in postaccident benefits. The estimates in the coal and lumber industries are generally within the range found in modern data. The coal estimate of −1.72 in the first column implies that hourly earnings fell 1.72 cents for each 1 cent increase in the worker's expected accident benefits. Thus, coal workers paid not only for increases in the benefits they expected to receive, but also for the consequent 1.67 cent increase in their employers' insurance costs. Using an alternative semilog specification that is often used in wage analyses, the estimated offset in the second column for the coal industry is somewhat larger at −2.5. In the lumber industry the estimated offset is not as large, ranging from −1.04 to −0.69, but it is still in the range that Gruber and Krueger found in their study of the modern workers' compensation system. By contrast, contractual wages in the unionized building trades did not adjust downward to increases in accident compensation. The coefficient is positive (0.02) and not statistically significant. These results are generally robust to changes in the control variables and time periods covered in the analysis. A complete discussion of the robustness of the results can be found in appendix D and Fishback and Kantor (1995).

The finding of no wage offset in the building trades might be due to the unionization of the industry. Unionization enabled workers to fend off wage reductions in the face of increased employer mandates. We might expect such a result from the building trades, which were the most stable labor organizations in the United States in the early 1900s (Taft 1964, 203). Other studies have shown that workers in unions receive larger compensating differentials for accepting accident risk (Dickens 1984). Moore and Viscusi (1990, 110–20) find that unionized workers experience smaller wage offsets when workers' compensation benefits increase. Dickens (1984) suggests that the union–nonunion variation might arise purely from the differences in the bargaining power of the two sets of workers. Alternatively, Moore and Viscusi (1990) argue that unions obtain better benefits because they represent the preferences of the average worker, whereas the preferences of the marginal worker determine compensating differentials

Table 3.3   **Union and Nonunion Wage Offsets in the Coal Industry**

	1911 to 1922		1911 to 1915	
Sample	Linear	Semilog	Linear	Semilog
Coal nonunion	−2.68[a]	−2.29[a]	−2.46[a]	−2.57[a]
Coal union	−0.44	−2.80[a]	−0.49	−1.94

Sources: See appendix table D.2 and Fishback and Kantor (1995, 735).
[a]Statistically significantly different from zero in a one-tailed test at the 1 percent level.

in competitive markets. Union wages might also be slower to adjust to changes in postaccident compensation because the wages are set in explicit contracts that might be renegotiated every two to three years.[10]

We can further test the impact of unionization on wage offsets by examining the coal sample. In the coal industry the differences in unionization were based on geography, not occupations, because the United Mine Workers of America (UMWA) sought to unionize workers in all jobs into a single union. Using the percentage of workers in the state with paid-up membership in the UMWA as a measure of unionization, we have reestimated the wage offsets for the coal industry allowing for different wage responses for union and nonunion workers. Table 3.3 shows the offsets calculated from the regression equation with the union–expected benefits interaction term included, for both the overall sample and the sample for the period prior to 1916. Under the linear specification, the offset for a worker in a completely nonunion district would have been −2.68. Meanwhile, the offset for a worker in a completely unionized district would have been −0.44, and we cannot reject the hypothesis that unionized workers experienced no wage offset. The effect of unionization is sensitive to specification in the full sample, however. The union offset in the semilog specification in the second column of table 3.3 is slightly larger than the nonunion effect, although the difference between the two is not statistically significant.

The impact of unionization on wages can be explored further by restricting the sample to the years prior to 1916. The differences in the results for the two specifications using the full sample might be driven by measurement error in the union variable during and after World War I. The union membership variable might not fully reflect the long-term strength of the union during and immediately after World War I. The U.S. Fuel Administrator had forced many coal firms to negotiate contracts with the union during the war, thus union membership might understate the union's strength in some areas during World War I. After the war a substantial number of firms repudiated the contracts while union membership was still increasing. When we limit the sample to the pre-1916 years, as reported in the third and fourth columns of table 3.3, the union wage offset is substantially smaller than the nonunion offset under both specifications.

Our analysis of wages near the time workers' compensation was enacted suggests that nonunion workers essentially "bought" a portion of the higher benefits under workers' compensation in the form of lower real wages. Unionized workers, on the other hand, seem to have benefited directly from the higher de jure benefits because they were able to stave off the wage reductions that nonunion workers experienced.[11] The presence of wage offsets for nonunion workers also helps to solve one of the major puzzles in the political economy of the passage of workers' compensation. Even though workers' compensation transferred a significant part of the legal burden of postaccident compensation onto employers, many employers led the way in supporting the legislation (Lubove 1967; Weinstein 1967). Many employers may have supported the legislation in anticipation of passing a substantial portion of their costs onto their workers in the form of lower wages, as the quotation from the Washington employer above suggests.

Politically, workers' attitudes toward workers' compensation may have been influenced by the extent of the wage offset that they could anticipate. In the final analysis both workers and employers might have benefited from the legislation because the wage offsets implied that the employer mandate did not create a large-scale redistribution of income. By supporting workers' compensation, employers could satisfy their workers' demands for better postaccident benefits without having to fully pay for the apparent largesse. Finally, even though their wages might have fallen, risk-averse workers might have benefited from workers' compensation if they were poorly insured against workplace accident risk in the early twentieth century. In the next section, we provide evidence that workers indeed faced difficulty insuring their workplace accident risk privately prior to the adoption of workers' compensation.

3.4   The Impact of Workers' Compensation on Household Saving and Insurance Purchases

By raising the average accident benefits that accident victims or their families received and by making the payment of these benefits more certain, workers' compensation in essence became the first widespread social insurance program in the United States. Since the introduction of workers' compensation, the United States has implemented a number of additional social insurance programs, including social security, unemployment insurance, and subsidized health insurance. Because these programs reduce the uncertainty of future income fluctuations, economists predict that social insurance programs should reduce workers' incentives to hold precautionary savings and should crowd out private insurance purchases.[12] Numerous empirical studies of modern programs confirm these predictions.[13]

One reason precautionary saving would fall as a result of the introduction of a social insurance program, such as workers' compensation, is that workers beforehand could not purchase complete insurance coverage to insure against misfortune's occurrence. In this section we examine how the introduction of workers' compensation affected precautionary saving and insurance purchases using a sample of over seven thousand working-class households canvassed for the 1917–1919 Bureau of Labor Statistics (BLS) cost-of-living survey. We find that workers used precautionary saving to insure against workplace accident risk in the early twentieth century. Because saving was a relatively expensive means of insuring against accident risk, we conclude that workers probably faced limits in the amounts of workplace accident insurance they were able to purchase prior to workers' compensation. Qualitative evidence drawn from insurance industry sources confirms our view that the insurance market around the turn of the century constrained workers' ability to insure their workplace accident risk.

3.4.1   Insuring against Accident Risk

Contemporary evidence suggests that working-class families in the early 1900s insured against workplace accident risk in a variety of ways. Most families saved. Some purchased limited amounts of commercial life and accident insurance. Others insured through employer-based funds or fraternal societies. A number of families sent children or spouses to work, took in boarders, and/or moved in with extended family when an accident occurred.

Various state and federal government surveys prior to the turn of the century give some indication of the extent to which workers purchased insurance prior to workers' compensation. Whaples and Buffum (1991, 102) found that 16 percent of the 5,020 Michigan furniture workers in an 1890 survey purchased some form of life insurance, while 40 percent claimed accident/sickness insurance through membership in a benefit society.[14] Surveys of Kansas nonagricultural workers from 1884 through 1887 show that 26 percent belonged to benefit societies, while 5.5 percent had bought some form of accident insurance (Ransom and Sutch 1989). In an 1890 survey of Maine workers, 22.8 percent claimed to have had life insurance, while 32.6 percent were members of a benefit society (Ransom and Sutch 1990).[15]

Several other surveys provide evidence on insurance coverage just prior to the introduction of workers' compensation. The Minnesota Bureau of Labor, Industries, and Commerce (1909–1910) found that 46.3 percent of the families of fatal accident victims collected insurance that replaced an average of 1.4 times the deceased's annual earnings prior to the establishment of compensation legislation in that state. In Conyngton's (1917) survey of Pennsylvania families of workers killed in workplace accidents in

1915, which was before the state's adoption of workers' compensation, 82.1 percent of the families received payments from some form of insurance, compared with 63 percent in the workers' compensation states of Ohio and Connecticut.

The most comprehensive picture of household purchases of insurance during the early 1900s can be found in the U.S. Bureau of Labor Statistics (BLS) 1917–1919 cost-of-living survey (1986). Table 3.4 shows the percentages of households from the survey that held various forms of insurance. By the early 1910s, families who sought to purchase private insurance against workplace accident risk had several options. The most widely held life insurance was industrial insurance, purchased by 67.6 percent of the households in the BLS sample. The industrial policies were also known as "burial" insurance because the average payout of $138 generally covered only the cost of a burial (Kip 1953, 18; Dryden 1914, 384; Ackerman 1926, 5–12).

About half of the families in the BLS sample sought to replace part of the household head's income if he died through the purchase of old-line insurance or fraternal life insurance. In the BLS sample, 29.2 percent of the households held old-line (or whole life) policies that insured lives and incorporated the accumulation of dividends that could be borrowed

Table 3.4   **Insurance Coverage among Households Surveyed for the BLS Cost-of-Living Study, 1917–19**

Type of Insurance	Percent of Households Claiming One or More Policies
Old-line life insurance	29.2
Industrial life insurance	67.6
Fraternal life insurance	25.9
Establishment life insurance	3.4
Other life insurance	1.4
All types of life insurance	85.2
All types of life insurance except industrial	51.6
Accident insurance	10.0
N	7,475

Source: Fishback and Kantor (1996, 425). The original data are from a survey by the U.S. Bureau of Labor Statistics, Cost-of-Living in the United States, 1917–19, which is available through the Inter-University Consortium for Political and Social Research, No. 8299.

Notes: A number of households held multiple insurance policies. For example, 3.8 percent of the households (or 12.8 percent of the policyholders) held old-line insurance policies on more than one member of the household; 58.4 percent of the households (or 86.4 percent of the policyholders) held industrial life insurance on more than one member of the household; 6.9 percent of the households (26.6 percent of the policyholders) held fraternal life insurance on more than one member of the household; 0.1 percent of the households had establishment life insurance on more than one family member; and 0.6 percent held other life insurance on more than one family member.

against or surrendered. Roughly one-fourth of the households that were interviewed bought life insurance through fraternal societies. These were mostly national organizations bound together by religious, occupational, ethnic, or fraternal ties. Most local societies belonged to a national parent organization that issued "certificates" of membership that entitled members' beneficiaries to death benefits and usually provided for a limited stream of payments in the event of disability (Nichols 1914; Insurance Research and Review Service 1938; Kip 1953). There were no standard death benefits and disability plans, so each worker's access to fraternal insurance varied depending on his religion, occupation, industry, or labor organization (see, e.g., U.S. Commissioner of Labor 1909). Considering all forms of life insurance together, the typical household in the BLS sample seems to have purchased enough insurance to replace about one year's income.[16]

The three types of life insurance discussed above were not directly targeted at workplace accidents because they insured against all causes of death. Mortality statistics for the working-age population suggest that workplace accidents probably accounted for at most 2 percent of all deaths from 1915 to 1920.[17] Insurance companies therefore designed accident insurance that limited their liability to injury and death arising from "external, violent, and accidental means." Precisely defining an accident was an evolving enterprise as insurers and insureds relied on the courts to settle vast differences in interpretation (Cornelius 1920). Accident insurance was clearly written with an eye toward insuring occupational accident risk, as each industry and occupational class was categorized according to its level of danger (Aetna Insurance Company 1919).[18] Evidence offered by Faulkner (1940, 27) suggests that occupational accidents accounted for approximately 63.3 percent of all accidental deaths in 1913, although the percentage had fallen to 28.3 percent by 1938 because of advancements in safety programs and devices.[19]

Although accident insurance represented the most direct way for workers to insure against occupational accident risk, the personal accident insurance business was very limited in the early twentieth century. Only $18.8 million in accident premiums were collected by commercial insurance companies in 1911, compared with $564.7 million in whole life premiums and $750.9 million in industrial life premiums (*Hayden's Annual Cyclopedia of Insurance* 1913, 4, 154–55, 180–81). Among the households that the BLS surveyed in 1917 to 1919, 10 percent had an accident insurance policy.

The commercial accident insurance market was clearly limited by the informational problems of insuring an individual worker's accident risk. With little information on the accident-proneness of the individual, the insurance industry based insurance premiums on occupational averages. But even the information on occupational averages was limited. The national information flows that were useful for experience rating in other lines of insurance were poorly developed in the accident insurance line. The national organization formed in 1914 was described by insurance executive G. F. Michelbacher (1942, 159) as "largely ornamental" with an inadequate staff providing "inconsequential statistical exhibits" compiled with data collected by other organizations. The lack of effective information for setting rates would have led to adverse selection problems, as more accident-prone workers would have purchased the insurance and more careful workers would not. Insurance companies could expect no help from employers in identifying accident-prone workers because negligence liability rules allowed employers to invoke the contributory negligence defense to avoid compensating careless workers. Thus, employers had less incentive to fire irresponsible workers or to impose restrictions on their behavior.

The standard means of reducing problems of adverse selection is to limit the amount of insurance a worker can buy or to establish pricing policies designed to discourage more accident-prone individuals. Accident insurers followed both practices. The Aetna Insurance Company (1919, 96) imposed limits on the risks they would insure, setting death benefit maximums as low as $250 for coal miners, who faced the most dangerous working conditions in the early twentieth century. Physicians, on the other hand, could insure up to $10,000 for accidental death. Further, accident insurance was noted for its high load factors. Even with the high loads, a number of companies writing accident insurance failed over the period 1917 to 1926, while the surviving stock companies suffered a slight underwriting loss (Kulp 1928, 576). The end result was that many workers were unable to purchase complete coverage, and possibly some were shut out of the market altogether.

Workers also tried to obtain insurance through union funds and establishment funds, which were nearly entirely financed by workers' contributions. These funds expanded the range of insurance that workers could obtain, but typically the amount of coverage they provided was small.[20] In 1908, the average death benefit was $109 in establishment funds and $89 in union funds, perhaps enough to cover burial expenses. Many funds offered no temporary disability benefits. In the establishment and union funds where temporary disability benefits were available, the average maximum benefit was about five dollars, and the payments only lasted for an average of fifteen weeks (U.S. Commissioner of Labor 1909, 234–67, 448–87). In contrast, five dollars was typically the minimum payment under workers' compensation and benefits for long-term disabilities lasted up to three to five years.

In general, the BLS survey shows that a wide range of workers purchased at least some form of insurance. In most cases the amount of insurance they purchased was limited either by choice or because there were specific constraints on the amount of coverage insurers or benefit societies offered to workers. Absent full insurance coverage, families could always save against the possibility of an accident. However, saving was a relatively costly means of insurance. At an interest rate of 5 percent, for example, a family that sought to hold a year's income in reserve would have had to forgo consumption of 95 percent of their income in the current year or wait several years to reach its goal. Families could also rely on children to work if the primary wage earner was injured or killed in an accident.[21] Numerous scholars have found that sending children to work was an important means by which families survived hard times and accumulated savings at the turn of the century (see Modell 1979; Goldin 1981; Haines 1985; Keyssar 1986, 158–60; and Rotella and Alter 1993).

3.4.2   The Theoretical Impact of Workers' Compensation on Saving and Insurance

Given that many households had relatively little life or accident insurance coverage in the early twentieth century, families may have relied strongly on precautionary saving to insure against accident risk. The increase in postaccident benefits that workers' compensation guaranteed may have affected households' decisions in two ways. As Cutler and Gruber's (1996) study of the modern Medicaid system implies, households may have reduced their accident insurance purchases, seeing the higher workers' compensation benefits as a replacement for private insurance. Similarly, as Leland (1968) and Kotlikoff (1989, 145–51) predict, if households were using precautionary savings to protect themselves against workplace accident risk, they would also have reduced their precautionary saving as the introduction of social insurance benefits reduced the uncertainty of future income loss from an industrial accident.

In fact, observed changes in family saving patterns in response to changes in postaccident compensation enable us to determine whether workers' access to accident insurance was constrained or not. In appendix E we develop theoretical predictions from a two-period model of saving and insurance choices when workers are faced with a positive probability of a workplace accident. The predictions from the model indicate that if workers were able to purchase all of the insurance that they desired at actuarially fair premiums, then an increase in postaccident benefits would have led to an increase in saving and a reduction in insurance purchases. In other words, workers would have perceived the increase in postaccident benefits as an increase in their expected incomes, which they could have funneled either into saving or consumption. On the other hand, the model suggests that the only condition under which workers would reduce their saving when postaccident benefits rise is when they faced binding limits on the amounts of insurance coverage they could purchase. Faced with such rationing, workers were forced to rely on precautionary saving to help protect themselves against accident risk. The introduction of workers' compensation and its relatively generous postaccident benefits provided better insurance than workers were able to obtain privately, which, in turn, would have allowed them to use income previously targeted for precautionary saving for other purposes. Workers faced with binding limits on insurance availability might still have reduced their insurance coverage when postaccident compensation rose if their desired level of coverage was below the limits imposed by the insurer. That is, workers' compensation might have crowded out private accident insurance consumption under certain circumstances.

The theoretical and empirical research of other scholars suggests that the certainty and generosity of the workers' compensation benefits should have led to a reduction in workers' private insurance, whether through formal or informal channels. At the same time, our theoretical analysis indicates that a decline in precautionary saving as a result of the introduction of workers' compensation might signal that workers had problems purchasing their desired levels of accident insurance prior to the laws' passage. Therefore, risk-averse workers, even if they "bought" the higher benefits through wage reductions, might still have gained from workers' compensation. In essence, they were able to obtain a higher level of protection against accident risk than was available to them under the negligence system.

3.4.3   Empirical Estimates of the Impact of Workers' Compensation on Insurance and Saving Behavior

To examine how variations in expected postaccident benefits influenced precautionary saving and private insurance coverage, we analyzed a cross-section of data on working-class households' financial decisions in both workers' compensation states and negligence liability states around 1918. Between late 1917 and early 1919 the U.S. Bureau of Labor Statistics conducted an intricate survey of the consumption patterns of working-class families in industrial centers of the United States. The study established the budget weights for the consumer price index (U.S. Bureau of Labor Statistics 1924). Agents interviewed 12,817 families of wage earners or salaried workers in ninety-nine cities in forty-two states. From this group we extracted a sample of 7,475 families where the household head was a laborer, operative, or craft worker. For more details on the sample and the analysis, see appendix F and Kantor and Fishback (1996).

We used the information from the cost-of-living survey to examine the impact of workers' compensation on the household's saving and purchases of accident and life insurance. That impact is estimated using an expected benefits measure similar to the one we used in the wage analysis above. In addition, the analysis controlled for other factors that might have influenced saving and insurance decisions.[22]

Table 3.5   Effect of Rising Accident Benefits on Saving and Insurance Purchases

Variable Affected	
Change in probability of purchasing life insurance (%)	0.1
Change in probability of purchasing accident insurance (%)	1.9
Change in savings ($)	
Full sample	−11.58[a]
Full sample (alternative specification)	−8.29[a]
Sample focused on workers' compensation states	−16.06[a]

Sources: See Fishback and Kantor (1996, 432–37) and appendix table F.1.

Notes: The effects reported here show how a one-standard-deviation increase ($7.15) in expected benefits, evaluated at the sample means in the sample, would have affected the variables in the table. The effects reported are based on coefficients from a probit analysis of insurance purchases and ordinary least squares analysis of saving. The assumed $7.15 increase in expected benefits is roughly half the size of the mean level of expected benefits in the sample.

[a]Statistically significant at the 5 percent level.

The effects of an increase in expected postaccident benefits are summarized in table 3.5, which shows the impact of a one-standard-deviation increase in expected benefits ($7.15) from the mean level in the sample ($14.67). We chose to look at the impact of a one-standard-deviation increase because it is close to the change in expected benefits that might have occurred with a shift from negligence liability to workers' compensation.

Life insurance was largely unaffected by changes in expected postaccident benefits. A one-standard-deviation change in the expected postaccident benefits would have lowered the probability of purchasing life insurance by only 0.1 percentage point—from 86.1 percent to 86.2 percent. We cannot reject the hypothesis of no effect on statistical grounds. Workers may not have changed their life insurance coverage much in response to changes in postaccident benefits because they were largely insuring against fatality risks not associated with the workplace. Recall that workplace accidents accounted for no more than 2 percent of the fatalities for the working-age population during this time period.

Changes in expected accident benefits had more influence on the probability of purchasing accident insurance, as a one-standard-deviation change in the benefits would have lowered that probability by 1.9 percentage points. However, we cannot reject the hypothesis of no effect. A change of 1.9 percentage points is relatively large given that only 10 percent of the households in the sample were purchasing accident insurance. As workers' compensation shifted the financial incidence of industrial accidents onto employers, those workers who were purchasing some private accident insurance substituted the guarantee of higher postaccident benefits for their own personal coverage.

The results from the saving regression show clearly that in the absence of complete insurance coverage, working-class families reduced their precautionary saving in response to increases in postaccident benefits. Using the full sample, a one-standard-deviation increase in expected benefits was associated with a reduction in saving of between $8.29 and $11.58, depending on the specification. In all cases statistical tests reject the hypothesis that a rise in expected benefits had no effect.[23] As one example of the impact of a switch from negligence liability to workers' compensation, consider a worker who moved from Virginia, where negligence liability was still in force, to the neighboring workers' compensation state of Maryland. All else equal, his expected postaccident benefits would have risen by approximately $11. Such an increase would have allowed him to reduce his precautionary saving by between $12.88 and $17.82, or between 18 to 25 percent of the mean level of savings in the sample.

To check the robustness of these estimates, we also conducted the analyses by limiting the sample to those states with workers' compensation. One potential criticism of the full-sample estimates is that states without workers' compensation in 1918 tended to be southern states, where saving might have been lower. Further, there may be questions about measurement error in the non–workers' compensation states because we could not rely on explicit laws to estimate the expected accident benefits in such states. Such concerns are unfounded, however. When we estimate the saving equation on a sample that eliminated the non–workers' compensation states, the effect of a one-standard-deviation change in expected benefits was actually larger. For more details on other tests of the robustness of the results, see appendix F.

In general, the regression results show that the higher benefits under workers' compensation were associated with some crowding-out of private insurance purchases and substantially lower saving. The reduction in saving is consistent with the view that workers faced binding constraints on the amount of workplace accident insurance that they could obtain. Therefore, the introduction of workers' compensation may have benefited workers by giving them better protection against the financial losses from an accident. This result also helps to explain why many workers favored the introduction of workers' compensation, even though they may have fully paid for the law's benefits in the form of lower real wages.

3.5   The Impact of Workers' Compensation on Accident Rates

Another metric for comparing the effectiveness of accident liability regimes is the impact on accident rates. Support for workers' compensation legislation among reformers was partially based on the expectation that the new laws would reduce workplace accidents. If employers bore a larger share of the full legal financial burden of workplace accidents, they would have an incentive to increase their accident prevention activities and, thus, lower their costs.[24] This prediction at face value seems reasonable, but it fails to examine the impact of workers' compensation on workers' accident prevention activities. While a rise in postaccident compensation increases employers' incentives to prevent accidents, it reduces workers' incentives because they are able to relax their cautiousness with regard to accidents while keeping the same or even a higher expected income. In the economic literature on safety and insurance, this phenomenon is known as moral hazard.[25] Employers and contemporary lawmakers were well aware of the potential moral hazard problems that might have resulted from workers' compensation. In fact, employers fought vigorously to limit the level of benefits to at most two-thirds of earnings to help reduce incentives that might lead to moral hazard. Limiting benefits, however, does not completely eliminate moral hazard problems. Modern studies suggest that the problem has increased in severity over the past two decades as benefit levels have come close to replacing 100 percent of after-tax income.[26]

Since the rise in postaccident compensation changed accident prevention incentives in opposite directions for workers and employers, it is not clear, a priori, whether workers' compensation would have raised or lowered accident rates. Accident rates tend to fall in settings where employer prevention increases more than worker prevention declines, and vice versa. Empirical studies of modern data on the impact of changes in workers' compensation benefits show that the relative strength of changes in employer and worker prevention efforts vary depending on the particular context. Most studies of the modern era tend to show that increased generosity of benefits leads to increases in nonfatal injury rates.[27] On the other hand, Moore and Viscusi's (1990, 120–35) study of modern fatal accidents suggests that the presence of workers' compensation lowers fatal accidents.

The differences between nonfatal and fatal accident rates could be driven by several possibilities. First, nonfatal accidents typically are much less expensive to the employer than fatal accidents, thus employers may find it more cost effective to focus on fatal accident prevention over nonfatal accident prevention. Second, the moral hazard problem is less severe for accidents that the worker anticipates will lead to more painful disability. The moral hazard problem, therefore, is probably least severe for accidents that lead to fatalities because the worker loses his life and does not share in the postaccident income. The moral hazard problem is exacerbated in settings where the expected disability from the accident is less painful or where it is easier to feign a disability. However, it should be noted that the relationship between the severity of the disability and moral hazard depends on workers' knowledge of the type of disability an accident will cause. In settings where the same type of morally hazardous behavior might lead to outcomes ranging from an ankle sprain to death, we are likely to see death rates and nonfatal accident statistics follow similar patterns. Third, some of the rise in modern nonfatal accident rates might be a result of increased reporting of accidents rather than a rise in the underlying accident rate. As noted in appendix A, the introduction of workers' compensation led to a huge increase in the reporting of nonfatal accidents and much smaller increases in fatal accident reports. All of the modern studies have tried to carefully control for a possible rise in reporting, but all agree that they cannot be certain that the reporting problem is completely eliminated.

Studies of the impact of the introduction of workers' compensation have focused on fatal accident risk. The studies by Chelius (1976), Fishback (1987, 1992), and Buffum (1992) suggest that the introduction of workers' compensation had substantially different effects on fatal accident rates in different industries.

Chelius (1976) examined the impact of workers' compensation laws on deaths using information from the mortality statistics collected by the U.S. Bureau of the Census for twenty-six states during the years 1900 to 1940. The data were collected from a variety of states using standardized death certificates and uniform definitions of causes of death. From these statistics Chelius focused on deaths caused by non-motor-vehicle machinery accidents, which he found to be the only consistent series of data reflecting industrial accident risks. Eighty-seven percent of the deaths in this category occurred in workplaces, while non-motor-vehicle machinery accidents accounted for about 16 percent of deaths. He then created a death rate by dividing the number of fatal accidents by the labor force in each of the states.[28] While controlling for the presence of safety regulations in each state, Chelius found that both employers' liability laws and workers' compensation laws led to reductions in the non-motor-vehicle machinery accident death rate.[29]

Buffum (1992, 102–9, 149–55) reanalyzed the same set of data with more control variables.[30] He reported that when using Chelius's specifications with his control variables he found the same reduction in the death rate that Chelius found. However, using alternative specifications, he found a negative effect of workers' compensation, but the effects are smaller and he could not reject the hypothesis that workers' compensation had no effect on fatal accident rates.[31] Buffum (1992, 101, 143–48) also studied the impact on railroad accidents of the Federal Employers' Liability Act of 1906, which limited the fellow servant and contributory negligence defenses in the interstate railroad industry. Similar to the results reported by Chelius, Buffum found that the federal law reduced accident rates in railroading.

In contrast, the coal industry experienced an increase in accident risk with the introduction of workers' compensation. Fishback (1987; 1992, 116–26) examined the impact of workers' compensation and employers' liability laws on fatal accident rates using a panel data set with information on death rates in coal mining from the twenty-three leading coal states for the years 1903 to 1930.[32] The analysis also controlled for a wide range of state regulations of coal mining, the price of coal, the use of coal cutting machines, the number of days the mines were open, and strike activity. Both employers' liability laws and workers' compensation laws were associated with relatively higher accident rates. The presence of an employers' liability law was associated with a 20 percent increase in the coal death rate, while the presence of a workers' compensation law was associated with a 28 percent increase in fatal accident rates. A 20 percent increase in accident rates meant that an additional man died for every 965 men working an average work year in the mines.[33] Buffum (1992, 86, 140–42) found similar results with a slightly different sample he constructed independently. In his analysis he found that the adoption of workers' compensation increased fatalities by 19 percent and the passage of employers' liability laws increased fatalities by 25 percent.

The rise in accident rates in coal mining is in some ways a perplexing phenomenon. We cannot completely dismiss the possibility that the rise in fatal accident rates reflects better reporting of fatal accidents, but there may have been other forces at work to cause this rise. Coal employers certainly had incentives to enhance safety because the payments they made to injured miners rose with workers' compensation. Furthermore, both state compensation funds and private insurance companies either inspected the mines or reviewed their accident records and rewarded safer mines with lower premiums.[34] Employers responded by adopting safety measures, like first-aid teams and more safety training, that led to lower insurance premiums. This heightened emphasis on safety became more prominent in the operating reports of the Stonega Coke and Coal Company after the Virginia workers' compensation law was implemented.[35]

Yet the rise in accident rates under workers' compensation shows that the employers' increased efforts were either cosmetic or insufficient to resolve the moral hazard problems at each miner's workplace. Since coal loaders and pick miners were paid by the ton of coal they produced, these workers realized that by working a little faster and taking more risks they could earn higher incomes. All too often, a roof fall injured or sometimes killed a miner who tried to finish loading the car before he set new props for the roof. Under negligence liability, the miner had extra incentive to work more slowly and safely because if he was injured in a roof fall, he was likely to get little or no compensation because of the employer's contributory negligence defense. Under workers' compensation, however, he could take more risks to increase his earnings because he was assured injury compensation that was very likely to be higher than what he would have received under negligence liability.[36]

The resulting rise in risk-taking led to more accidents like roof falls. The problem was that roof falls in the miner's workplace, often in remote sections of the mine, were the types of accidents that employers could not prevent at low cost. Effective prevention required constant attention to changing natural conditions; therefore the miner could prevent accidents in his room at much lower cost than the employer could. For the employer to be as effective at preventing roof falls as the miner, the employer had to hire large numbers of supervisors to check the rooms constantly. The costs of hiring supervisors to prevent the extra accidents caused by moral hazard appeared to be higher than the expected cost of paying the workers' compensation benefits to injured workers. Rather than take these costly preventive measures, employers chose instead to pay the extra damages in the form of workers' compensation claims.

The question remains why the results from the coal industry differ from those that Chelius reported for machinery accidents and Buffum found for railroads. When workers' compensation was introduced, it appears that the efforts of manufacturing employers to reduce accident rates more than offset moral hazard problems. The difference between the industries probably can be traced to the differences in employers' costs of preventing accidents. Supervisors could monitor workers' use of machinery more easily in manufacturing than in coal mining. Instead of tramping long distances through a mine to visit sixty men in a day, the manufacturing foreman could probably meet with sixty men in two hours and still had the option, unavailable in a mine, of standing on catwalks above the factory floor and observing overall activity. Further, manufacturing companies discovered that they could eliminate many machinery accidents by putting more footguards and handguards near whirring blades and gears. In general, both manufacturers and railroads were in a position to reduce accidents by improving the safety of machinery. In contrast, many of the accidents in the miner's room in a coal mine were a result of natural conditions that the employer could not fix at low cost.

In sum, the introduction of employers' liability laws and workers' compensation led employers to increase their accident prevention efforts and workers to relax theirs to some extent. The impact on accident rates varied from industry to industry. Employers' increased prevention efforts appear to have dominated in manufacturing and on the railroads, where their costs of accident prevention through changes in machinery and supervision were relatively low. In contrast, in the coal industry where workers had always played a much greater role in accident prevention deep within the mines, accident rates rose. The problems with moral hazard led to the type of accidents that were very costly for the employer to prevent. Therefore, employers chose to pay the extra damages to workers instead of incurring high monitoring costs. Were coal workers made worse off by this increase in accident rates? Certainly not. Given that coal workers were paid piece rates, they relaxed safety precautions only because they were trading safety for higher earnings. The increased benefits offered by workers' compensation allowed workers to increase their current earnings by working faster, while giving them better compensation in case they were injured.

3.6 Summary

The introduction of workers' compensation led to a substantial increase in the benefits workers could expect to receive on average if they were injured at work. The increase in benefits led to a number of individual-level and market readjustments. Wages adjusted in response to employer-mandated accident benefits and workers modified their choices regarding saving and purchasing accident insurance. Further, workers' compensation changed both workers' and employers' incentives to prevent accidents.

Although reformers considered workers' compensation to be a redistribution of income from employers to workers, employers were able to pass at least some of the costs of the higher benefits back to workers in the form of wage reductions. Nonunion workers in the coal and lumber industries "bought" the higher benefits associated with workers' compensation, while unionized workers in the building trades and in the coal industry were more effective at staving off the wage offsets. If these industries are representative, then our analysis suggests that the vast majority of workers who were nonunionized paid for some portion of their increased postaccident benefits in the form of lower real wages.

Even though some workers paid for workers' compensation, they still potentially gained from the legislation because they were better insured against workplace accident risk than before. Under negligence liability workers tried to insure themselves against accident risk in a variety of ways, some through purchases of commercial insurance, others through fraternal societies, still others through employer- or union-based funds. Typically, the insurance that was available offered relatively meager disability benefits and did not completely satisfy workers' desires for income protection against accident risk. Many households therefore accumulated precautionary savings, which was a relatively expensive means of insuring against accident risk. The introduction of workers' compensation reduced the uncertainties of postaccident compensation and raised the level of postaccident benefits. As a result, many households were able to reduce their insurance purchases and were able to free that portion of their incomes targeted for precautionary saving for other purposes.

Although many reformers and even employers predicted that the introduction of workers' compensation would lead to a decline in accident rates, the new legal institution gave workers and employers conflicting incentives for accident prevention. Increased accident benefits gave employers an increased interest in preventing accidents, but some workers were able to relax their attentiveness to accident prevention because the social insurance guaranteed their expected incomes. As a result, in settings where employers could prevent accidents at relatively low cost, accident rates fell. Where the additional accidents from the workers' relaxed prevention were costly for employers to prevent, such as in coal mining, accident rates rose.

In general, the empirical results reported in this chapter suggest that both employers and workers could have benefited from the introduction of workers' compensation. Employers in most settings were probably no worse off because they were able to pass the costs of higher accident bene-fits back to workers. Workers, even if they bought workers' compensation through lower wages, were better insured against accident risk, and could free income used for precautionary saving for other purposes. Even the rise in accident rates in some industries did not imply that workers were harmed by workers' compensation. In the industries where accident rates rose, workers themselves had chosen to relax prevention in order to obtain higher earnings from working faster, knowing that they were financially protected in the unlikely event an accident occurred.[37]

Notes

1. There were many exceptions to this mandate, however. Most states exempted firms with fewer than five workers. In many states, moreover, agriculture, domestic service, casual labor, and public service were excluded from the compensation laws. Sometimes, specific industries were exempted. For example, Maine excluded logging, Maryland exempted country blacksmiths, and Texas excluded cotton gin-ning. The laws also precluded compensation in cases where the worker was intoxi-cated at the time he was injured or if he had maliciously caused his own accident. For a more comprehensive summary of the exemptions across the United States, see U.S. Bureau of Labor Statistics (1918, 58).

2. The probabilities we used in the calculations are the probability of an accident over the course of a year to workers across all industries in Oregon, as reported in Oregon Industrial Accident Commission (1919). The probabilities were calcu-lated by taking the number of compensable accidents in each accident class and dividing by the number of workers covered.

3. See appendix C for more details on the calculations for Stonega.

4. *Seattle Daily Times,* 6 January 1911. The "2 cents" to which the employer referred was a proposed employer contribution to a first aid fund.

5. We have focused the analysis on thirteen occupational classes from the forty specific occupations for which the U.S. Bureau of Labor Statistics reported wage scales by 1923. The occupations chosen reflect a wide and representative character-ization of the important building trades in the early twentieth century.

6. These results are based on using real wages as the dependent variable and our calculations are based on the mean earnings in the sample. When the equations are

run in semilog form, the wage reductions in response to workers' compensation are similar: coal at 1.51 percent, lumber at 1.91 percent, and the building trades at 0.35 percent. See appendix D.

7. For our purposes here, the expected benefit index is calculated using the national average wage for each occupation in each year. We did not use the wage corresponding to each observation because the expected benefits would have been a function of the wage, thus imparting a positive bias to the estimated coefficients of the expected benefits index. Similarly, we could not use the ratio of expected benefits to wages because in some cases maximum allowable benefits became binding and the ratio of expected benefits to wages would have imparted a spurious negative bias. To eliminate these problems, we used the national average wage for each occupation in each year, which allowed the expected benefits index to rise in response to rising wages during the period as well as to reflect differences in expected benefits driven by differences in wages at each skill level. We have also experimented with using the maximum real expected benefits as allowed by law as an instrument for the expected benefits for all observations, and the results suggest a negative and statistically significant wage offset in all cases. We did not focus on these results because the wages in many occupations were not high enough to reach the legal maximums.

8. The concepts of risk-neutrality and risk-aversion are best shown by an example. Say an individual faces a choice between two options: Option A pays him ten dollars for sure, while option B offers him a 50 percent chance of receiving twenty dollars and a 50 percent chance of receiving nothing. A risk-neutral individual would be equally satisfied with either option because on average she would receive ten dollars in option B. A risk-averse person would choose option A, preferring the certain $10.

9. Experience rating forces employers to pay higher premiums if there are more accidents or more severe accidents in their workplaces than the averages on which the basic premium is based. Insurance companies used experience rating across industries and states to set the workers' compensation premiums. The National Council on Workmen's Compensation, the major interstate ratemaker at the time, typically used the national accident experience in each industry to establish a base accident rate and then adjusted the rates for each state to reflect the generosity of benefits there (Kulp 1928, 235–57). Some states were large enough that they could use their own accident evidence to experience rate, while insurance companies used national averages to determine premiums in states with smaller populations. Insurance companies and state funds also adjusted premiums for individual firms based on inspections and some experience rating, but the experience rating at this level was less accurate than the comparisons across industries (Kulp 1928, 258–96).

10. Our experiments with lagged (up to three years) expected benefit terms, however, never showed any signs that the building trades experienced a wage offset.

11. It is possible that union members' compensation packages adjusted along other margins that we cannot measure. For instance, the availability of hours, jobs, working conditions, or other fringe benefits may have responded to higher postaccident payments.

12. Numerous theoretical studies show that when faced with uncertain future income, households may develop a precautionary motive for saving. See, e.g., Leland (1968), Sandmo (1970), Cantor (1985), Skinner (1988), Kotlikoff (1989, 141–51), Zeldes (1989), Kimball (1990), Caballero (1991), Deaton (1991), Carroll (1992), and Hubbard, Skinner, and Zeldes 1994. Skinner (1988) argues that such precautionary saving may account for as much as 56 percent of total life cycle savings.

13. For analyses of the impact of social security on savings, see Feldstein (1974, 1980, 1982), Leimer and Lesnoy (1982), and Hubbard, Skinner and Zeldes (1995). In an empirical study of how increases in social insurance affect private insurance coverage, Cutler and Gruber (1996) find that the expansion of Medicaid coverage from 1987 to 1992 crowded out the purchasing of private health insurance.

14. Unfortunately, Whaples and Buffum provided no estimates of the amount of insurance coverage (even though these data were available), only probability estimates on whether the workers were insured or not.

15. See Ransom and Sutch (1989). The Kansas sample is skewed toward skilled workers and workers in cities far more than the actual distribution of Kansas workers, as reported in the census occupational statistics.

16. This estimate is based on answers to the BLS's questions about the value of insurance. We do not try to use the BLS estimates of the value of insurance further because there seems to be substantial measurement error in the data. It was not clear whether the value of the insurance meant the benefit to be paid upon death or the current cash value of the policy. Further, in the case of accident insurance, the presence of disability benefits makes the evaluation of the policy's value far more complicated. The confusion about the values of policies shows up in the large number of households that offered inconsistent answers to the different questions about insurance. Of the 6,682 households that claimed to have life insurance policies, 1,493 households reported a value of zero for their life insurance. Of the 780 households with accident insurance policies, 521 reported a zero value for their policies. We therefore focus on the question of whether people had insurance or not.

17. This statistic was derived from the U.S. Bureau of the Census, *Mortality Statistics* (1917, 444–45; 1918, 294; 1919, 320; 1920, 296; 1921, 288; 1922, 310). Because the Census did not report which deaths were caused by workplace accidents, we assumed that all accidental deaths from "absorption of deleterious gases," "traumatism by cutting or piercing instruments," "traumatism in mines and quarries," "traumatism by machines," and "railroad accidents and injuries" were work related. Moreover, because railroad deaths also included passengers, we deflated the *Mortality Statistics* figure by the percentage of passenger deaths as reported by the Interstate Commerce Commission (these data are reported in U.S. Bureau of the Census 1975, 740). Although our measure of job-related deaths is very crude, it does suggest that relatively few people died as a result of a workplace accident.

18. Payment of benefits, moreover, followed strict guidelines: benefits were paid provided that the accident did not occur while the insured unnecessarily exposed himself to "obvious danger" or while he was engaged in an occupation more hazardous than that in which he had elected to be classified and insured. If he was employed in a more hazardous occupation at the time of injury, then benefits would be paid according to the insurance his paid premium would have purchased in the more hazardous class (*Hayden's Annual Cyclopedia of Insurance* 1913, 3).

19. Faulkner (1940, 27) reports that the rate of occupational fatal accidents was 45.7 per 100,000 population in 1913 and had fallen to 20.4 by 1938. The death rate from all accidents was 72.2 per 100,000 population in 1938, but Faulkner did not report the same statistic for 1913. Thus, in estimating that 63.3 percent of all fatal accidents occurred on the job, we have assumed that the death rate from all accidents was the same in 1913 as it was in 1938. This assumption seems reasonable given that the overall accidental death rate per 100,000 was 69.6 in 1922.

20. Of the 461 establishment funds surveyed by the U.S. Commissioner of Labor (1909, 339, 538–53) in 1908, 69.2 percent received no funding at all from employ-

ers. Eight percent of the funds received more than 50 percent of their funding from employers. Employers, across the sample, contributed an average of 10.6 percent of the funds' reserves.

21. See Kotlikoff and Spivak (1981) for a theoretical discussion of the use of family members to pool the risk associated with potential income loss.

22. These factors include household earnings, income from other sources, the number of children of various ages, the age of the head of the household, his occupational skill level, the riskiness of his job, possible membership in labor organizations, differences in the cost of living across cities, and geographic characteristics.

23. We have also experimented with other specifications in the saving regression by adding an interaction term between the accident-rate measure and the expected-benefits variable. The magnitudes and t-tests of the expected benefits and accident risk coefficients are similar to the ones reported in appendix table F.1.

24. This statement holds even in the presence of the wage offsets described earlier (see Fishback 1992, 253–54). We can see this by examining the comparative statics of the following maximization problem for an employer. The employer chooses the amount of labor to hire (L) and accident prevention capital to purchase (A) to maximize his profits from production, where profits are

$$A(L, A) = pQ(L) - rA - w[C, d(A)]L - Cd(A).$$

The employer sells output (Q) at a price (p) in the product market. For simplicity assume that output is a function of the amount of labor hired. Costs include the rental price (r) of safety capital, the wage rage $(w[C, d(A)])$, postaccident compensation (C), and accident risk $(d(A))$. Increases in safety capital lead to reductions in the accident rate $(d_A < 0)$ at a diminishing rate $(d_{AA} > 0)$. Output increases with increases in labor $(Q_L > 0)$ at a diminishing rate $(Q_{LL} < 0)$. The theory of compensating differentials implies that wages would decrease with increases in postaccident compensation $(w_C < 0)$ and would increase with increases in accident rates $(w_d > 0)$. Following standard maximization techniques and deriving the comparative statics, it can be shown that the employer will increase his safety capital when postaccident compensation increases as long as wages do not rise at an increasing rate with increases in accident risk, i.e., $w_{dd} \leq 0$.

25. For discussions of this phenomenon, see Viscusi (1992, 84–93, 181–85) and Fishback (1992, 253).

26. When workers' compensation was introduced, hardly any workers paid income taxes because under the tax rate structure prior to 1940 less than 10 percent of households had to pay them. Workers' compensation benefits are exempt from income taxes. As tax rates have risen, workers' compensation benefits have replaced higher and higher percentages of after-tax income. Until the 1970s weekly maximums on benefits still strongly limited the benefits paid out to workers, but a nationwide movement to raise the weekly maximums in the 1970s led to the situation where benefit levels come close to fully replacing after-tax income (see Moore and Viscusi 1990, 54; Kniesner and Leeth 1991, 67–68).

27. See Moore and Viscusi (1990, 28–33, 121–35) for a summary.

28. Lack of accurate definitions of the cause of accidents forced Chelius to use machinery fatalities in the numerator of his accident measure, which might not be a good proxy for all types of fatal accidents. A more serious problem exists in the denominator, which is intended to normalize the number of machinery accidents by exposure to risk from such accidents. The size of the labor force is not a good proxy for hours of exposure to dangerous industrial machinery. In the early 1900s, hours and days worked varied across states and time, as did the mechanization of work. Chelius tried to control for this in the analysis by taking the ratio of the

state death rate to the national death rate, but that does not adequately eliminate the measurement error problem because the changes in hours and use of machinery in each state were not uniform across the nation. The measurement error in Chelius's accident rate may be perverse enough that it outweighs the component of his measure that truly reflects the risk of death by machine.

29. Chelius tried to control for per capita exposure to machinery, the business cycle, and technology of medical care by using the ratio of the death rate in each state to the national death rate for that year as the dependent variable. He also experimented with various controls for fixed effects.

30. His control variables included an alternative measure of resources devoted to safety inspection, employment in mining, employment in railroading, percent female, percent foreign-born, percent illiterate, percent unionized, percent of workers in large firms, and measures of relative manufacturing risk.

31. Buffum (1992, 109–11, 153–55) also examined the impact of workers' compensation using industrial fatalities reported by various states. In this analysis he found that workers' compensation led to an increase in fatalities. Buffum noted, however, that the states had a wide variety of reporting rules, which may have changed over time. These data were not collected in a consistent manner, as the mortality statistics were, therefore we believe that much of the increase found in this data set may be a result of increased reporting.

32. The data for coal mining have fewer problems with measurement error because the U.S. Bureau of Mines and U.S. Geological Survey collected statistics specifically for coal mines, thus all types of accidents in the mines were covered. Further, the measure of exposure to risk in the denominator is subject to less measurement error because the Bureau of Mines and the U.S. Geological Survey collected information on hours worked per day, days worked per year, and average number of workers.

33. In the text we focus on the results from Fishback (1992). The results in Fishback (1987) were very similar, although the control variables differed to some extent and he used a set of dummies to describe different types of workers' compensation systems. In the 1987 paper the analysis showed that employers' liability laws were associated with accident rates that were 17 percent higher. Workers' compensation laws establishing a monopoly state fund were associated with a 23 percent increase in the fatal accident rate, and laws allowing both private and state insurance were associated with 20 percent higher rates. The impact of workers' compensation laws with no state funds was smaller and not statistically significant.

34. The inspections followed schedule ratings that checked the mine against the "ideal" mine. See Graebner (1976, 149–51) and Hookstadt (1922, 53).

35. See Graebner (1976, 151–52) and Stonega Coke and Coal Company, *Operating Reports,* 1916–1925, in Hagley Museum and Library, Wilmington, Del.

36. Since dead miners received no income, there might not be a moral hazard problem for fatal accidents. However, the moral hazard problem arose because miners did not expect each accident to result in death. Roof falls, for example, led to injuries ranging from bruises to crushed limbs to deaths. Only one in fifty to one hundred accidents were fatal. Any regression analysis of fatal accidents implicitly assumes that they are a random sample of all accidents.

37. This argument does not imply that workers were anticipating full compensation for injuries. It suggests instead that workers received, on average, higher postaccident benefits under workers' compensation than under negligence liability, although still less than full compensation. Since the probability of being injured from marginally relaxing accident prevention was still relatively low, the higher earnings workers received from taking more risks would more than offset their expected additional damages from an injury.

The Timing of Workers' Compensation's Enactment in the United States

Workers' compensation fundamentally established an ex ante "contract" between workers and employers, who promised to pay a specified set of benefits for all accidents arising out of or in the course of employment. The legislation raised the expected postaccident payments that workers received as a result of their workplace accidents. In return, workers forfeited their rights to common law negligence suits. Economic theories of government intervention suggest several possible alternative explanations for the adoption of workers' compensation. Interest groups might have competed for legislation that enabled them to redistribute income in their favor at the expense of others (e.g., the "capture" or "rent-seeking" models). Or, faced with some set of market problems, interest groups might have developed a cooperative solution whereby they all gained. Or alternatively, the program might have been enacted as part of the broad-based agenda of a political economic coalition.[1]

The adoption of workers' compensation was not the result of employers' or workers' "capturing" the legislation to secure benefits at the expense of the other. Nor can its adoption simply be attributed to the success of Progressive Era social reformers' demanding protective legislation. Several changes in the workplace accident environment in the early 1900s combined to pique workers' and employers' interests in establishing workers' compensation. The share of the workforce in dangerous industries rose, state legislatures adopted a series of employers' liability laws, and court decisions limited employers' defenses in liability suits. All three changes combined to substantially increase the uncertainty of the negligence liability system. Many employers, facing an increase in the extent of their accident liability and uncertainty about future changes in this liability, favored the adoption of workers' compensation by 1910.[2] Labor unions, growing in strength and increasingly dissatisfied with the results of employers' liability laws, at the same time shifted their focus from reforming the negligence system to fully supporting the transition to workers' compensation. The legislation was enacted so rapidly across the United States in the 1910s because most members of the key economic interest groups with a stake in the legislation anticipated benefits from a shift away from the negligence liability system. One of the major contributions of this chapter, therefore, is to document empirically why, if so many parties anticipated benefits from the legislation, state legislatures waited as long as they did to adopt workers' compensation.

The groundswell to adopt workers' compensation might be seen as a national movement that carried nearly all of the states along with it. It would be a mistake, however, to ignore the activities in each individual state, where legislatures made the actual decision. Analysis of the timing of adoption across the United States supports our contention that the greater uncertainty arising from changes in the negligence system played an important role in the introduction of workers' compensation. The relative strength of major interest groups also played a role, as unions, the manufacturing lobby, and larger and more productive manufacturers helped speed the adoption of workers' compensation. Finally, social reformers played a smaller role in the overall adoption of workers' compensation laws than they did in determining the particular features—such as benefit levels or state insurance of workers' compensation risk—of the legislation in a particular state.

4.1   The Formation of a Coalition in Favor of Reform

Workers' compensation incorporated two key features that help explain why many employers, workers, and insurance companies anticipated gains from the legislation. First, as shown in chapter 3, the transition to workers' compensation increased the amount of postaccident payments that injured workers received. Second, workers' compensation essentially allowed employers and workers to establish an ex ante "contract" in which workers waived their rights to sue in return for a prescribed set of benefits in the event that they were injured on the job.

Given that workers' compensation significantly raised the levels of postaccident compensation that workers received, why would employers support the increase in benefits, which led to such a major de jure redistribution of income? Roy Lubove (1967) and James Weinstein (1967) claim that employers supported the legislation as a means of buying labor peace, as a way to stem the tide of court rulings that increasingly favored injured workers, and as a way to reduce the costs of settling accident claims. David Buffum (1992) argues that employers gained because the new law reduced the uncertainty of their accident payments. Employers also were able to reduce at least some of the burden of higher accident payments by passing the costs of workers' compensation back to workers in the form of lower wages. As seen in chapter 3, the higher expected postaccident benefits under workers' compensation were fully offset by lower real wages for nonunion coal miners and offset to a large degree for nonunion lumber workers. Union workers in coal mining and in the building trades, on the other hand, experienced much smaller wage reductions. Since employers could pass a substantial portion of the increase in postaccident benefits to nonunion workers, they were more likely to favor a no-fault compensation system that was less acrimonious and more certain than negligence liability.

Given that union members experienced relatively small wage offsets, organized labor's diligent lobbying on behalf of workers' compensation is understandable. What is less clear is why nonunion workers, who constituted about 90 percent of the labor force, supported workers' compensation. After all, many could expect to pay for a substantial portion of their new benefits in the form of lower real wages. Workers would have had little desire to "buy" the higher accident benefits under workers' compensation if they could just as easily have used the risk premiums in their old wages to purchase their own workplace accident insurance. We have shown in the previous chapter, however, that workers faced constraints in trying to purchase the levels of accident insurance that they desired in the early twentieth century. Unable to reach their desired level of insurance coverage, families had to rely on household mechanisms, such as saving, to insure against accident risk. Yet saving was a relatively costly means of insurance. Thus, even though their wages might have fallen, risk-averse workers might have benefited from workers' compensation because the laws provided them with a level of expanded insurance coverage against workplace accident risk that they had not been able to obtain privately under negligence liability.

Insurance companies also stood to gain from the passage of workers' compensation, as long as states did not try to displace private insurers through the establishment of state insurance funds.[3] Because of the adverse selection problems associated with selling individual accident insurance, insurers stood to gain if the law compelled employers to insure their entire payrolls. Employers purchased substantially larger amounts of insurance under workers' compensation because they were mandated to provide their entire labor force accident benefits that on average exceeded those of the negligence system. The insurance industry supported the law because the switch from selling accident insurance to workers and liability insurance to employers to selling workers' compensation expanded the scale of their business. The premiums collected by commercial insurance companies for workers' compensation insurance rose from zero in 1911 to $114 million in 1920, despite the presence of compulsory state funds in seven states and competing state funds in ten more. This $114 million rise in workers' compensation insurance nearly tripled our estimate of a decline of $41.5 million in employers' liability premiums.[4]

One group that might have opposed the introduction of workers' compensation comprised attorneys involved in the practice of workplace accident law. In Missouri, for example, these damage-suit attorneys used the political process to slow the adoption of workers' compensation (Kantor and Fishback 1994a). On the other hand, one of the leading personal injury lawyers in the state of Washington, Guvnor Teats, became one of the leading advocates of workers' compensation (Tripp 1976, 543). The transition to the no-fault system did not put workplace accident lawyers out of business. Instead it shifted the nature of their activities. The issues for legal action shifted from negligence to determining whether the accident had occurred at work, the size of the worker's weekly wage, and the extent of the injury. The number of accident cases that received administrative attention also rose sharply, so that many workplace accident attorneys may have seen their business grow. Further, accident attorneys were only a small percentage of the bar. In many states attorneys were actively involved in drafting workers' compensation legislation and a number of state bar associations supported the legislation.

4.2   Why Workers' Compensation?

If employers, workers, and insurers stood to gain from workers' compensation, then we might have expected to see a significant private movement where workers and employers negotiated private contracts that established workers' compensation–like arrangements at the firm level. Under such a private scheme workers would have signed contracts with their employers in which the worker, before any accident occurred, waived his right to a negligence suit in return for a guaranteed set of accident benefits, regardless of fault. Why was a governmental solution chosen?

Part of the answer to this apparent paradox is that the courts did not recognize an ex ante contract in which a worker waived his right to a negligence suit in return for a set of benefits similar to those under workers' compensation. Employers were clearly interested in establishing such contracts. Writing at the turn of the century, Stephen Fessenden (1900, 1203) claimed that it was "customary" at that time for employers to try to create these ex ante contracts, but "it has generally been held by the courts of the United States that a contract made *in advance,* whereby an employee agrees to release and discharge his employer from liability for any injury he may receive by reason of the negligence of his employer, or of his servants, is contrary to public policy and void. This principle has been announced by a Federal court in the following well-chosen language: 'As a general proposition, it is unquestionably true that an employer can not relieve itself from responsibility to an employee for an injury resulting from his own negligence by any contract entered into for that purpose *before* the happening of the injury [emphasis added].'"[5]

In addition, twenty-eight states had codified such court rulings through the passage of laws that held that an ex ante contract did not bar a worker from filing a negligence suit against his employer.[6] The legal environment relating to workplace accidents in the early twentieth century seems very similar to the modern setting pertaining to product liability whereby consumers' agreements to release the manufacturer from potential liability have been routinely ignored by the courts (Huber 1988, 29–30).

In essence, workers' compensation laws established a form of contract between worker and employer that common law decisions and many state statutes would not honor. The preaccident nature of the workers' compensation contract was extremely important in expanding the amount of insurance that employers could offer their workers. Prior to workers' compensation, the courts allowed firms to offer relief contracts in which an injured worker's acceptance of benefits *after* the accident occurred implied his waiver of future negligence claims. This type of ex post contract was acceptable, however, only if the employer had contributed significantly to the firm's relief fund (U.S. Commissioner of Labor 1908, 755). Because the injured workers could always refuse the postinjury payment and file a negligence suit, relatively few employers established funds in which they were the primary contributor. In only 140 of 461 establishment funds examined by the U.S. Commissioner of Labor (1909, 339, 538–53) in 1908 did employers make contributions to the funds, and in most cases their contributions were less than one-third the levels contributed by workers. The employer gained little from contributing to the relief fund because he expanded the number of workers to whom he was paying benefits, while not removing the uncertainty of the negligence system. Injured workers who would have received nothing under the common law could now claim the guaranteed benefits from the employer's fund, while the workers with strong cases could still choose to seek large court awards or settlements.[7]

A final question needs to be answered. Why didn't state legislatures simply pass laws allowing employers and workers to negotiate their own benefit levels in ex ante contracts?[8] Unions and workers pressed hard for the state to set the benefit levels because they could better negotiate accident benefits collectively through the legislature than through individual negotiations with employers. The statutes and court decisions outlawing ex ante contracts were based on the idea that workers, prior to having an accident, might trade away their rights to negligence suits for too low a price (Weiss 1966, 568; *Johnstone v. Fargo,* 184 N.Y. 379 [1906]). Workers and unions were adamant that the workers' compensation laws expand employers' liability, otherwise they would experience no increase in their insurance coverage for workplace accident risk. One sign that workers succeeded in expanding employers' liability under workers' compensation was the choice given to employers in states where workers' compensation was elective. After *Ives v. South Buffalo Ry. Co.* (124 N.Y.S. 920 [1911]) declared the New York compulsory workers' compensation statute for extrahazardous employment unconstitutional, the vast majority of states passed workers' compensation laws allowing employers to elect between workers' compensation and negligence liability.[9] In all of the elective states, however, employers that did not choose workers' compensation were stripped of their assumption of risk, fellow servant, and contributory negligence defenses.

The ex ante nature of workers' compensation contracts allowed the employer to eliminate the uncertainties of large court awards in return for providing his workers with a set of benefits that on average were higher than those under negligence liability. Workers, even if they "bought" the better benefits through wage offsets, still benefited because they received better workplace accident insurance coverage than under the negligence liability system. Meanwhile, insurers found that they could sell more workers' compensation insurance than the combination of employers' liability and private accident insurance. The analysis does not imply that every member of the employer, worker, and insurance interest groups gained from the adoption of the "one-size-fits-all" benefit levels under workers' compensation. The results of our empirical analyses, combined with qualitative evidence indicating wide support among the organizations representing the major interest groups, does suggest however that the median member of each interest group expected to gain from workers' compensation.

4.3   Changes in the Workplace Accident Liability Climate

The first decade of the twentieth century saw dramatic changes in the economic and legal environment surrounding workplace accident compensation, and these changes brought workers, employers, and insurers together in a political coalition favoring workers' compensation. Understanding the timing of the enactment of the legislation requires examination of both national and state-level trends. The workers' compensation movement was national in scope and after 1910 the legislation was adopted rapidly across the United States; therefore, in this section we examine national changes that brought the major interest groups with a stake in workers' compensation together in favor of reform. The legislation, however, was adopted and is administered today at the state level. We further illuminate the factors influencing the passage of workers' compensation in the next section by discussing the results of a quantitative analysis of state legislatures' decisions to adopt.

Between 1885 and 1910 most reform efforts were devoted to broadening employers' liability for workplace accidents. Organized labor pressured legislatures for limitations on employers' common law defenses, anticipating that more injured workers would be compensated and the amount they received would be higher as a result of the laws. They succeeded in obtaining the passage of employers' liability laws in quite a few states, as shown in table 4.1. The number of states with employers' liability laws that restricted one or more of the employers' three common law defenses for nonrailroad accidents rose from seven in 1900 to twenty-three by 1911.[10] The laws acted as precursors to workers' compensation–style legislation because prior to 1910 the passage of the liability laws often increased employers' accident liability, but imposed limits on that liability.

For example, Massachusetts's 1887 employers' liability law was clearly a compromise. Workers gained a limitation on the fellow servant defense, making supervisory workers vice-principals of the employer, which meant that the supervisors' negligent actions could be treated as the negligence of the employer. Employers gained some security because the law imposed a four thousand dollar limit on injury damages and death benefits were limited to a range of five hundred to five thousand dollars. The employers' prorated share of any insurance fund payment was also applied to this amount. Further, workers had to file notice of the accident within thirty days of its occurrence. For the next two decades organized labor pressed for additional expansions in employers' liability without success (Asher 1969). Finally, in 1909 Massachusetts limited the assumption of risk defense and replaced contributory negligence with comparative negligence. Under comparative negligence a worker's own negligence no longer eliminated his claim for damages but instead reduced the share of the damages for which the employer was responsible (U.S. Bureau of Labor Statistics 1914, 960, 987–91).

In New York between 1881 and 1901 various labor groups proposed employers' liability laws with little success.[11] In 1901 the Workingmen's Federation of the State of New York (WFSNY)—later the New York State Federation of Labor—and the New York railroads both submitted bills before the legislature. The legislature passed a compromise measure that was vetoed by progressive governor Benjamin Odell after extensive protest by organized labor.[12] Finally, in 1902 the WFSNY decided that it could succeed in weakening employers' defenses only by passing a relatively weak bill. The WFSNY proposal became law, making employers liable for injuries resulting from the violation of factory laws. Under the law, workers could sue even if they continued working with knowledge of the danger, provided that the employer was responsible for the danger and that workers had assumed only the necessary risks of their occupations. The bill also required notice of suit within 120 days, a sharp reduction from the old three-year limit. A series of court decisions in the next year negated most of the law, and the WFSNY redoubled its efforts to pass new employers' liability legislation. In 1906 the WFSNY helped the railroad

Table 4.1 The Changing Atmosphere of Workplace Accident Liability

Year	State Spending on Labor Issues per Employed Worker (1967 dollars)	Labor Law Index	Number of States with Nonrailroad Employers' Liability Laws That Limit Employers' Defenses[a]	Number of State Supreme Court Cases about Nontrain Workplace Accidents	Total Premiums for Employers' Liability and Accident Insurance (millions of 1967 dollars)	Ratio of Employers' Liability and Accident Insurance Premiums to Life Insurance Premiums
1900		1.69	7	154	63.7	.062
1901		1.89	7	205	78.2	.067
1902		1.97	10	238	90.3	.072
1903	.135	1.52	11	266	95.3	.070
1904	.144	1.49	11	284	106.4	.072
1905	.149	1.48	12	318	120.5	.080
1906	.149	1.50	13	339	134.6	.084
1907	.157	1.56	18	379	147.6	.095
1908	.188	1.58	18	446	159.1	.096
1909	.190	1.69	20	484	165.1	.094
1910	.185	1.75	23	436	202.4	.112
1911	.209	2.05	23	490	225.3	.115

Sources: Fishback and Kantor (1998a, 317). See appendix I.

Notes: The trends displayed by the national aggregates are found in most states. We ran linear trend regressions for each state in each of the categories above. Positive and statistically significant trends were found in thirty-one states for real spending on labor issues, in thirty-five states for court cases, and in thirty-nine states for the ratio of liability to insurance purchases.

[a] This grouping of state laws does not include laws that were focused on railroad workers only or miners only, nor does it include laws that Clark (1908) considered to be restatements of the common law. We focus on laws that dealt generally with the kinds of workers that would have been covered under workers' compensation. If we had included all employers' liability laws of all types, the trend would be similar to the one shown in this column. States with laws that appear to have affected employers' liability for nonrailroad workers prior to 1900 include Alabama, Colorado (an added law in 1901), Indiana (an added law in 1911), Louisiana, Mississippi (1896 ending in 1903 and then a new law in 1910), Utah, and Wyoming. In 1902 Massachusetts (and another law in 1909), New York, and Ohio (with more expansive laws in 1904 and 1910) added laws. In 1903 Kansas (an added law in 1909) and Washington added laws, while Mississippi's law was declared unconstitutional. Nevada added a law in 1905, followed by Wisconsin in 1906, California, Iowa, Oklahoma, Oregon, Pennsylvania in 1907, Idaho and Maine in 1909, Mississippi again, New Jersey and Vermont in 1910, Arizona in 1912, and Arkansas and Nebraska in 1913. For more details about these laws and other employers' liability laws, see appendix G.

brotherhoods pass a liability law pertaining to railroads, after a 1905 scandal weakened Republican dominance of the legislature. However, bills relating to industrial accidents never made it out of committee in 1907 and 1908. The WFSNY's 1909 proposal met the same fate, but the continued pressure by organized labor caused the 1909 legislature to establish an employers' liability commission that was charged with investigating the liability system and the workers' compensation alternative.[13]

Ohio eventually passed employers' liability laws that limited all three defenses, although most of the expansion of liability occurred in 1910 just prior to the adoption of workers' compensation. During Ohio's 1904 legislative session, labor and employers' representatives compromised on an employers' liability reform by passing the Williams Act through a Republican-dominated legislature. Workers gained because the act imposed limits on the assumption of risk defense. In situations where an employer failed to safeguard a machine, the employer could no longer escape liability by claiming that a worker who continued to work with the machine, despite knowing that it lacked protection, had assumed the risk. Employers agreed to the legislation because it limited their risks of paying exorbitant damages by imposing maximums of five thousand dollars for fatal accidents and three thousand dollars for nonfatal accidents.[14] The Metzger Act of 1908 later established similar limits for railroad workers.

By 1909 both the Democratic and Republican platforms in Ohio called for a means of financially protecting workers from injury.[15] When the legislature met again in 1910, the Ohio State Federation of Labor strongly pushed for an expansion of employers' liability. Employers' groups, such as the Ohio State Board of Commerce, bitterly fought the bills and sought instead to establish a commission to study the negligence liability system.[16] After a wild series of amendments and counteramendments in both the House and the Senate, the House agreed to pass the Norris Act as part of a compromise in which the women's hours bill would not come to a vote.[17] The Norris Act established comparative negligence, defined the fellow servant defense more narrowly so that supervisors were not fellow servants, and made employers fully responsible for defects in machinery. Employers found the final version of the bill easier to accept because the limit placed on fatal accident damages was lowered from twenty thousand dollars in the original Norris provision to twelve thousand dollars. In addition, employers succeeded in getting the legislature to establish a commission to study employers' liability and workers' compensation.

While the expansions in employers' liability in some states came through legislation, in others they came through court decisions. The push for reform of employers' liability in Washington had begun by the 1890s. In every legislative session from 1895 through 1909, at least one bill influencing employers' liability for workplace accidents was introduced in the Washington legislature.[18] None of the bills specifically designed to weaken the common law defenses of assumption of risk, fellow servant, and contributory negligence were passed, and many died in committee. The key changes in the compensation of workplace accidents in Washington came about through significant court decisions.

The first landmark decision, *Green v. Western American Company,* came in September 1902 and it sharply limited the assumption of risk defense. Under assumption of risk a worker could report that a safeguard was missing from a machine, the employer could send him back to work, and if the worker was then injured, the employer could escape liability by claiming the worker had known and assumed the risk of working with the machine. Washington State Chief Justice W. H. White eliminated this use of the assumption of risk defense, arguing that it allowed the employer to use the violation of a law to escape liability.[19]

By September 1902 lumber employers were denouncing the courts for their extravagance in negligence cases. The ratio of losses paid to premiums received for liability insurance in Washington rose sharply from 0.39 in 1901 to 0.56 in 1902, while at least one insurance company left the state because it had to pay out twice the sum received in premiums. The insurance companies quickly adjusted their rates, so that by 1903 the loss ratio dropped sharply to 0.30 before stabilizing around 0.40 to 0.47 for the rest of the decade.[20]

Employers in Washington appeared to receive temporary relief in March 1903 with the passage of the Factory Inspection Act. In one sense the act was an employers' liability law because employers were considered negligent for failure to comply with the inspection laws. On the other hand, employers valued the inspection law because they could have their workplaces certified as safe after complying with the Washington Bureau of Labor's recommendations. A number of lower courts in the state began to recognize the assumption of risk defense again for a number of these "safe" firms certified to be in compliance. Meanwhile, in a series of cases known as the "factory act cases," the Washington Supreme Court reaffirmed that unguarded machinery was a violation of the law and could not be used to invoke the assumption of risk defense (Tripp 1976, 535).

Employers anticipated further relief from the implications of the *Green* decision with the passage of the 1905 amendment to the Factory Inspection Act. The 1903 act stated that employers were required to offer the "proper" safeguard, but attorneys said that the courts often held employers liable even in cases where machinery was safeguarded. The 1905 amendment altered the wording to require employers to offer a "reasonable" safeguard. In the 1905 *Hall v. West & Slade Mill Company* decision, however, the Washington Supreme Court ruled that "reasonable" safeguards meant all "necessary" safeguards to prevent accidents (Tripp 1976, 535–37). The court concluded that by virtue of its causing an accident, a tool or machine lacked necessary safeguards. Joseph Tripp (1976, 535–37) claims that the ruling in *Hall* essentially destroyed assumption of risk and turned the factory inspection acts into laws that fundamentally changed employers' liability.

The 1905 ruling initiated a great deal of uncertainty about the extent of employers' liability, which led to a dramatic jump in court activity. The number of employers' liability cases contested in the Washington Supreme Court rose from six in 1904 to thirty-five in 1905 and continued to rise to fifty-three in 1910 and again in 1911.[21] This trend in Washington was matched by similar trends in most states.

One sign of the increased legal uncertainty engendered by shifts in the courts' attitude and the new employers' liability laws is the substantial rise in the number of state supreme court cases related to nonrailroad workplace accident litigation. If the legal environment and court interpretations had remained relatively stable, injured workers and employers typically would have settled out of court, avoiding the high costs of litigating accident claims. As the liability rulings shifted, the increased uncertainty would have led the parties to test the bounds of the law in court more often, as well as to increase appeals to state supreme courts. Evidence on the number of workplace accident court cases appealed to state supreme courts is consistent with the view that uncertainty increased markedly prior to the enactment of workers' compensation. Taking all of the states together, the number of nonrailroad cases in state supreme courts increased steadily from 154 in 1900 to 490 in 1911 (see table 4.1), an almost fourfold jump in workplace accident litigation at the highest judicial level alone.[22]

The expansion of employers' liability and the greater uncertainty of the legal system caused a large increase in the liability insurance premiums that employers paid. In Ohio, for example, the Norris Act of 1910 had an immediate impact on the compensation that workers received. Payments to married men in Cuyahoga County rose approximately 16 percent after the act went into effect.[23] Meanwhile, W. G. Wilson of Aetna claimed that the act led to an even sharper increase in insurance premiums, ranging from 100 to 500 percent. The increase was so sharp that when Wilson testified before the Ohio Employers' Liability Commission, he denied any insinuations that "the liability insurance companies were instrumental in lobbying for the passage of the Norris bill with the obvious purpose of mulcting our patrons for increased premiums."[24]

Similarly, in Washington the series of court decisions limiting assumption of risk caused employers' liability insurance rates to more than triple from $0.45 per $100 on the payroll to $1.50 per $100 in 1910 on a new, model plant with all safety devices installed.[25] In general, between 1900 and 1910, total employers' liability insurance premiums collected in Washington rose more than elevenfold, while premiums for all types of insurance rose only sixfold.[26] These same trends occurred nationally. As shown in table 4.1, the premiums that all commercial insurance companies collected for personal accident and employers' liability insurance rose from $63.7 million in 1900 to $225.3 million in 1911 (constant 1967 dollars), a 354 percent increase. Moreover, this increase in insurers' coverage of employers' liability was not simply an artifact of an ever-increasing insurance industry, because liability insurance outpaced other forms of insurance. The ratio of accident and employers' liability premiums to life insurance premiums increased from 0.062 in 1900 to 0.115 in 1911 (see table 4.1).[27] We should note that the increase in aggregate liability premiums conflates increases in insurance rates with the expanded coverage that employers may have sought. Even if the increase in liability premiums was not completely driven by increases in insurance rates, the figures suggest that the weakening of employers' common law defenses encouraged employers to pay more attention to accident compensation issues than before.

The increasingly unfavorable legal climate added to the consternation of employers because it occurred during a time when industrial accidents were coming to the fore of public attention. In the first decade of the twentieth century, employment in dangerous industries increased, as did public awareness of workplace accidents. Shifts in manufacturing employment toward more dangerous industries between 1899 and 1909 raised the average accident risk that manufacturing workers faced by approximately 13 percent.[28] Meanwhile, the percentage of workers in mining increased from 2.6 percent in 1900 to 2.8 percent in 1910, increasing the number of miners by 300,000 and thus the annual death total by about 600 workers. It is not clear, however, whether the accident risk for specific industries was rising or falling. Measures of fatality rates for mining and railroading have the fewest problems with measurement and reporting error during the period. Table 4.2 shows that fatal accident risk in coal mining rose roughly 20 percent from 1890 to 1910, from a decennial average of 1.43 workers per one hundred thousand man days in the 1890s to 1.71 in the 1900s. On the other hand, fatal accident rates in railroading and in metal and nonmetallic mining appear to have fallen. Even if the true accident rates within industries were constant, the reporting of nonfatal accidents was rising sharply in nearly every state department of labor report of the era, following trends similar to the one displayed for railroad accidents in table 4.2. Although the upward trends in accident risk might have reflected better reporting as opposed to true changes in accident risk, social reformers were able to use the statistics as evidence of a growing workplace accident crisis. The publicity that reformers generated directed substantially more attention to industrial accidents, along with the related financial hardship that they caused.

The worsening workplace accident liability climate in the early 1900s encouraged employer-supported lobbying groups to explore the possibility of a switch to a no-fault compensation system. Between 1908 and 1910

Table 4.2   **Changes in Fatal Accident Risk in the Early Twentieth Century**

Year	Coal Mining Fatality Rates per 100,000 Days Worked	Metal and Nonmetal Mining Fatality Rates per 1,000 Workers	Railroad Fatalities per Million Man-Days	Railroad Nonfatal Accidents per Million Man-Days
1890	1.17	Not available	Not available	Not available
1891	1.43	Not available	Not available	Not available
1892	1.47	Not available	10.4	114.9
1893	1.34	Not available	10.3	119.8
1894	1.50	3.39	7.7	98.8
1895	1.56	4.79	7.6	108.5
1896	1.54	Not available	7.4	119.7
1897	1.42	3.82	6.8	110.6
1898	1.43	3.59	7.5	121.0
1899	1.47	2.87	8.0	126.1
1900	1.62	3.18	8.4	130.6
1901	1.51	3.47	8.7	134.3
1902	1.72	2.74	8.3	141.3
1903	1.57	2.40	9.5	159.5
1904	1.72	2.76	9.12	168.4
1905	1.71	3.41	8.30	165.0
1906	1.62	2.98	9.06	176.9
1907	2.08	2.83	9.28	179.4
1908	1.85	2.37	7.40	179.2
1909	Not available	Not available	5.92	170.2
1910	1.77	Not available	6.80	192.3
1911	1.66	4.19		

Sources: Coal mining fatality rates are the number of bituminous coal miners killed in accidents per thousand employed divided by the average number of days the mines were open in that year (Fay 1916, 10–11). Metal and nonmetal mining fatality rates are reported in Aldrich (1997, 306). The railroad fatality and nonfatality rate divides the number of railroad employees killed (series Q404) and injured (Q405), from U.S. Bureau of the Census (1975, 740), by the total man hours worked by railroad employees from the sample, as reported in Kim and Fishback (1993).

the National Civic Federation, which was composed of leaders from major corporations and conservative unions, devoted substantial time in their meetings to developing and promoting a workers' compensation bill. Meanwhile, the National Association of Manufacturers (NAM) in 1910 called on its members to provide voluntary accident insurance; but then in 1911 the NAM fully endorsed workers' compensation as a solution to the accident compensation problem (Weinstein 1967; Lubove 1967). After forming in 1907, the American Association of Labor Legislation (AALL) became one of the leading advocates for workers' compensation (see Skocpol 1992, 160–204; Moss 1996).[29] The federal government, which often preceded most employers in offering relatively generous workplace benefits, established workers' compensation for federal workers in 1908 as a result of Theodore Roosevelt's strong support (Lubove 1967, 263–64; Johnson and Libecap 1994).

The employers' shift in interest toward workers' compensation coincided with changing sentiments among organized labor, whose ranks were rapidly expanding during this time period. Membership in labor unions increased sharply from 868,000 in 1900 to 2.14 million in 1910, growing nearly three times faster than the labor force (Wolman 1936, 16). The attitudes of major labor organizations went through a substantial change as they gained more experience with the results of employers' liability laws. Around the turn of the century, the American Federation of Labor (AFL) believed that better accident compensation could be achieved by stripping employers of their three defenses (Somers and Somers 1954, 31; Weinstein 1967, 159). Organized labor's reluctance to embrace workers' compensation was part of a more general opposition to government regulation of the workplace. Union leaders theorized that business interests controlled politics and, thus, better benefits for workers could be achieved only through the voluntary organization of workers (Weinstein 1967, 159; Skocpol 1992, 205–47; Asher 1969, 457).

After pressuring state legislatures to pass employers' liability laws, organized labor seems to have become dissatisfied with the results. Large numbers of injured workers were still left uncompensated and a substantial percentage of the insurance premiums paid by employers never reached injured workers. Organized labor harshly criticized insurance companies and lawyers as "parasites pure and simple, absolutely unnecessary in industry, yet demanding a part of its created wealth which they have no part in creating, thereby raising the cost to both producer and consumer."[30] In 1909 the AFL switched its position and passed four resolutions supporting workers' compensation legislation and the organization, at the federal level and through its state affiliates, became a vocal proponent of the legislation.[31]

Increased interest on the parts of employers and workers in workplace accidents coincided with, and may have contributed to, the expansion of states' increasing regulation of the work environment. Table 4.1 shows that state spending (in constant 1967 dollars) on factory inspections, boiler inspections, arbitration and mediation, and publishing labor statistics doubled from $0.09 per employed worker in 1900 to $0.19 by 1910.[32] The increase in spending was often associated with an expansion of state labor department bureaucracies and in many states the state labor department itself became an advocate for the introduction of workers' compensation and further regulation of labor markets.[33] In fact, workers' compensation represented the leading edge of labor legislation during the period. A labor law index (which excludes workers' compensation) in table 4.1 illustrates this point. The index remains roughly constant between 1.5 and 2 until 1911 and only rises coincident with or following the first wave of enactments of workers' compensation laws.

With rising interest by employers and organized labor in workers' compensation, the states began establishing commissions to study the issue.[34] Typically, the commissions included a balance of employers' representatives and representatives of organized labor. In the initial meeting in Washington, when it was discovered that there were few labor representatives, they actually delayed the meeting in order to obtain more representation from organized labor (Tripp 1976). These commissions often served as fact-finding bodies, proposing bills to be considered in the state legislature. In many cases the commissions would agree on the desire for workers' compensation but disagree on the features that should be included; therefore, multiple bills were proposed for legislative consideration.

The support from major employers' groups and organized labor led to the widespread adoption of workers' compensation, after a couple of experiments in Maryland in 1902 and Montana in 1909 were declared unconstitutional.[35] Within the next decade, forty-three states adopted workers' compensation. Table 4.3 shows the years in which state legislatures adopted workers' compensation for the first time, although in some cases the initial laws adopted by legislatures and signed by the governor were struck down by courts or referenda. For example, New York passed two laws in 1910, a compulsory law for extrahazardous employment and a voluntary law for all types of employment. The compulsory law was declared unconstitutional in *Ives v. South Buffalo Ry. Co.* (124 N.Y.S. 920 [1911]) as a constitutional taking without due process of law (U.S. Bureau of Labor 1911, 110).[36] After amending the state constitution, New York established another compulsory law in 1913. By 1930 all the states except Arkansas, Florida, Mississippi, and South Carolina had enacted the legislation. As Harry Weiss (1966, 575) noted, "No other kind of labor legislation gained such general acceptance in so brief a period in this country."

4.4   Lessons from the Timing of Enactment across the United States

Variations in the timing of adoption among the states offer some insights into the political pressures that led to the adoption of the legislation. Economic models of the political process emphasize the importance of interest groups in determining the adoption of new policies. Since we argue that employers, workers, and insurers anticipated gains from workers' compensation, we should expect to see that the law was adopted earlier in states where employers, workers, and insurers were relatively influential. The national trends presented in the previous section suggest that changes in the employers' liability climate led the interest groups to intensify their pressure on state legislatures. Therefore, we should expect to see earlier adoption in response to greater average accident risk in manufacturing, the presence of an employers' liability law, higher employers' liability in-

Table 4.3   **Characteristics of Workers' Compensation Laws in the United States, 1910–30**

State	Year State Legislature First Enacted a General Law[a]	Compensation Elective/Compulsory (private employment)	Method of Insurance[b]	Method of Administration
N.Y.	1910 (1913)[a]	Compulsory	Competitive state[c]	Commission
Cal.	1911	Compulsory[d]	Competitive state[c]	Commission
Ill.	1911	Compulsory[d]	Private	Commission[e]
Kan.	1911	Elective	Private	Courts
Mass.	1911	Elective	Private	Commission
N.H.	1911	Elective[f]	Private	Courts
N.J.	1911	Elective	Private	Commission
Ohio	1911	Compulsory[d]	State	Commission
Wash.	1911	Compulsory	State	Commission
Wis.	1911	Elective	Private	Commission
Md.[f]	1912	Compulsory	Competitive state	Commission
Mich.	1912	Elective	Competitive state	Commission
R.I.	1912	Elective	Private	Courts
Ariz.	1913	Compulsory	Competitive state	Courts
Conn.	1913	Elective	Private	Commission
Iowa	1913	Elective	Private	Arbitration committees
Minn.	1913	Elective	Private	Courts
Neb.	1913	Elective	Private	Commission
Nev.	1913	Elective	State	Commission
N.Y.[f]	1913	Compulsory	Competitive state	Commission
Or.	1913	Elective	State	Commission
Tex.	1913	Elective[g]	Private	Commission
W. Va.	1913	Elective	State	Commission
La.	1914	Elective	Private	Courts
Ky.	1914 (1916)[a]	Elective	Private	Commission
Colo.	1915	Elective	Competitive state	Commission
Ind.	1915	Elective[h]	Private	Commission
Me.	1915	Elective	Private	Commission
Mont.[f]	1915	Elective	Competitive state	Commission
Okla.	1915	Compulsory	Private	Commission
Pa.	1915	Elective	Competitive state	Commission
Vt.	1915	Elective	Private	Commission
Wyo.	1915	Compulsory	State	Courts
Del.	1917	Elective	Private	Commission
Idaho	1917	Compulsory	Competitive state	Commission
N.M.	1917	Elective	Private	Courts
S.D.	1917	Elective	Private	Commission
Utah	1917	Compulsory	Competitive state	Commission
Va.	1918	Elective	Private	Commission
Ala.	1919	Elective	Private	Courts
N.D.	1919	Compulsory	State	Commission
Tenn.	1919	Elective	Private	Courts
Mo.	1919 (1926)[a]	Elective	Private	Commission

(*continued*)

Table 4.3   (continued)

State	Year State Legislature First Enacted a General Law[a]	Compensation Elective/Compulsory (private employment)	Method of Insurance[b]	Method of Administration
Ga.	1920	Elective	Private	Commission
N.C.	1929	Elective	Private	Commission
Fla.	1935	Elective	Private	Commission
S.C.	1935	Elective	Private	Commission
Ark.	1939	Compulsory	Private	Commission
Miss.	1948	Compulsory	Private	Commission

Sources: Kantor and Fishback (1998, 559–60). The details of the laws come from Clark and Frincke (1921), Hookstadt (1918–1920, 1922), Jones (1927), U.S. Bureau of Labor Statistics Bulletin Nos. 126 (1913b), 203 (1917), 243 (1918), 332 (1923), 423 (1926b), and 496 (1929). Information about the late adopters was taken directly from the states' session laws. The methods of insurance, elective versus compulsory, and method of administration are the long-run rules established within the first few years of the passage of the law. Some early states, like California, Illinois, and Ohio, changed their decisions about these issues within two to four years of adopting the law. The method of administration changed in a number of states after the industrial commission movement had developed in the later part of the 1910s.

[a]Some general laws were enacted by legislatures but were declared unconstitutional. The years that the law was permanently established are in parentheses. New York passed a compulsory law in 1910 and an elective law in 1910, but the compulsory law was declared unconstitutional and the elective law saw little use. New York passed a compulsory law in 1913 after passing a constitutional amendment. The Kentucky law of 1914 was declared unconstitutional and was replaced by a law in 1916. The Missouri General Assembly passed a workers' compensation law in 1919, but it failed to receive enough votes in a referendum in 1920. Another law passed in 1921 was defeated in a referendum in 1922 and an initiative on the ballot was again defeated in 1924. Missouri voters finally approved a workers' compensation law in a 1926 referendum on a 1925 legislative act (see Kantor and Fishback 1994a). Maryland (1902) and Montana (1909) passed earlier laws specific to miners that were declared unconstitutional.

[b]Competitive state insurance allowed employers to purchase their workers' compensation insurance from either private insurance companies or the state. A monopoly state fund required employers to purchase their policies through the state's fund. Most states also allowed firms to self-insure if they could meet certain financial solvency tests.

[c]California and New York established their competitive state funds in 1913.

[d]The initial laws in Ohio, Illinois, and California were elective. Ohio and California in 1913 and Illinois later established compulsory laws.

[e]Illinois' initial law was administered by the courts; they switched to a commission in 1913.

[f]Employees have option to collect compensation or sue for damages *after* injury.

[g]Compulsory for motor bus industry only.

[h]Compulsory for coal mining only.

surance premiums, and an increase in workplace accident litigation. Finally, workers' compensation has been considered one of the progressive reformer's leading successes. To the extent that this is true, we would expect states to have adopted earlier in areas where Progressive Era reform groups were relatively influential.

We have examined the impact of these factors in two ways. First, in the discussion that follows, we have divided the states into three groups that are nearly equal in number—those enacting before 1913, between 1913 and 1916, and after 1916. We then compare the mean values for variables circa 1910 that measure the political strength of interest groups, changes in the liability climate, and strength of reform groups. The comparisons indicate the relationship between early enactment and each of these measures, even without holding the other influences constant. These comparisons are reported in table 4.4. It is important to note, however, that the political process was complicated and the various political economic influences may have affected that process in competing and conflicting ways. Second, to examine the impact of each individual factor, controlling for changes in the other variables influencing the adoption of workers' compensation, we performed a discrete-time hazard analysis, which is discussed in more detail in appendix H. The hazard analysis allowed us to incorporate information on the political economic setting for years that the legislatures met between 1909 and the year of adoption in each state. Equally importantly, the hazard analysis allows for multiple factors to influence the enactment decision at the same time; thus, the hazard analysis enables us to isolate the effect of each variable while holding the influences of other variables constant.

4.4.1 Changes in the Legal Environment Governing Accident Compensation

Roy Lubove (1967) and James Weinstein (1967) argue that a key reason why employers supported workers' compensation was the increasingly antagonistic and uncertain legal climate in which accident claims were settled. The passage of employers' liability laws and changes in court interpretations of employers' liability led to higher liability insurance premiums and an increase in legal uncertainty that generated an increase in court activity. All of these factors are associated with earlier adoption of workers' compensation.

When states enacted liability laws that limited an employer's common law defenses, an injured worker's chances of successfully suing his employer for damages increased. This pressure increased the probability that the state would adopt workers' compensation. Among states adopting prior to 1913, 64 percent had employers' liability laws in place in 1910, compared with only 25 percent among the states adopting after 1916. After controlling for all factors in the multivariate analysis, the presence of an employers' liability law for nonrailroad workers that altered one or more of the three common law defenses raised the probability of adopting workers' compensation in any one year by a statistically significant 7.9 percentage points. It should be noted that the employers' liability law had to restrict employers' liability to enhance the chances of adopting workers' compensation. There were some states that established employers' liability laws that simply restated the common law without really changing the

Table 4.4 **Sample Means of Factors Influencing Adoption for States That Adopted Workers' Compensation before 1913, between 1913 and 1916, and after 1916**

| Variables | Means for States Adopting Workers' Compensation | | |
	Early (before 1913)	Middle (1913–16)	Late (after 1916)
Changes in workplace accident liability			
Percentage of states with employers' liability law limiting common law defenses	64.3	55.6	25.0
Percentage of states with employers' liability law restating the common law	0	27.7	18.8
Mean ratio of employers' liability and accident insurance premiums to life insurance premiums	0.126	0.118	0.1
Index of workplace accident supreme court cases (1904–6 = 1) lagged one year	1.52	1.64	1.48
Manufacturing accident risk index	1.35	1.76	1.98
Interest group influence			
Mean percentage of manufacturing workers in establishments with less than 5 workers	5.0	8.5	10.7
Mean percentage of manufacturing workers in establishments with more than 500 workers	29.5	22.1	17.9
Mean manufacturing value added per worker (thousands; constant 1967 dollars)	5.00	5.47	4.18
Mean percentage of labor force employed in manufacturing	35.6	24.1	16.4
Mean percentage of labor force employed in mining	3.0	4.9	2.0
Mean index of unionization	9.7	9.6	8.1
Mean life insurance premiums per worker (constant 1967 dollars)	59.0	42.0	31.9
Mean state spending on labor-related bureaucracy per worker (constant 1967 dollars)	0.24	0.20	0.08
Political climate			
Mean progressive law index	4.57	3.5	2.6
Percentage of states in which party control shifted in the year of adoption in at least one branch of the legislature	14	35	50
Percentage of states in which party control shifted in the year of adoption in both branches of legislature	14	12	33
Mean percentage of presidential vote for socialist in 1912	6.7	7.0	4.2
Mean percentage of presidential vote for progressive in 1912	28.7	25.4	19.8
Share of southern states adopting	0.07	0.28	0.63
N	14	18	16

Sources: See appendix I.

Note: All of the means are 1910 values, unless otherwise stated.

employers' de facto liability. The restatement laws were not associated with earlier adoption of workers' compensation.

The passage of employers' liability laws and changing court interpretations increased the uncertainty with which employers faced their accident liability. When legal interpretations were clearly established, both parties were likely to settle a case out of court to avoid costly litigation. Increased uncertainty about judicial decisions, however, gave at least one of the sides greater incentive to seek a court decision, leading to an increase in the number of cases litigated to a decision. This uncertainty was reflected in a rise in court cases concerning workplace accidents decided at the state supreme court level. By 1910 the typical state that adopted prior to 1916 had experienced a rise in the number of court cases of between 52 and 64 percent since the period 1904 to 1906, while states adopting after 1916 had experienced a slightly smaller average increase of 48 percent. In the multivariate analysis we found that such increases in supreme court activity raised the probability of adoption of workers' compensation.

The changes in the legal environment contributed to an increase in the liability insurance rates that employers paid, which in turn increased the pressure for workers' compensation because employers were uncertain about the future of these rates. As noted earlier, one proxy for higher insurance rates is the ratio of total premiums for employers' liability and accident liability insurance to the premiums for life insurance in the state. In fact, the 1910 value for this ratio was about 26 percent higher in states adopting prior to 1913 than in states adopting after 1916, while the multivariate analysis also shows that higher ratios were associated with a greater probability of adopting workers' compensation.[37]

We had thought that greater average manufacturing accident risk might have led to greater pressure for early adoption. To examine the impact of the shift in manufacturing employment toward more dangerous jobs, we created an accident risk index based on the manufacturing industrial mix in each state. Shifts of manufacturing employment into more dangerous industries did not appear to stimulate earlier adoption of the law. The risk index was higher for states adopting after 1916 than for those adopting earlier. Similarly, the multivariate analysis revealed that the risk index had little impact on the probability of adopting workers' compensation. Thus, it appears that greater public awareness of accident risk was not nearly as important as changes in the employers' liability climate.

In general, the results are consistent with the national-level picture drawn in the previous section. The probability of enacting workers' compensation was significantly higher when employers faced problems with expanding workplace accident liability. These pressures developed as states enacted new employers' liability laws, the legal climate in which accident compensation was adjudicated became more uncertain, and employers' liability insurance rates increased.

4.4.2   Interest Group Influence

In general, manufacturing workers and employers anticipated gains from workers' compensation. Meanwhile, farm interests focused on eliminating farm workers from coverage. Once farm workers were excluded, agriculturalists appear to have been largely indifferent to workers' compensation. As expected, states with more workers employed in manufacturing tended to adopt the law earlier. Manufacturing employed on average 35.6 percent of the workers in states that adopted prior to 1913, compared with 16.4 percent for states adopting after 1916.

Within the manufacturing lobby, larger and more productive firms tended to press harder for workers' compensation. These firms might have benefited more from workers' compensation if they gained a competitive advantage in the product market because higher postaccident benefits raised the costs of accident prevention and insurance coverage more for smaller, less productive firms. Bartel and Thomas (1985) make a similar argument for why larger, unionized firms support modern Occupational Safety and Health Administration (OSHA) regulations. The percentage of manufacturing workers in establishments with more than 500 workers was 29.5 percent in states adopting prior to 1913, compared with 17.9 percent in the states adopting after 1916. Similarly, manufacturing value added per worker in 1910 was 20 to 30 percent higher for states adopting prior to 1917 than those adopting after 1916. At the other end of the size spectrum, firms with fewer than 5 workers tended to seek exemptions from workers' compensation. The exemptions gave the firms the choice of choosing to join the workers' compensation system, while allowing them to retain their common law defenses if they remained outside the system. Although the percentage of workers in establishments with fewer than 5 workers was relatively small in states that adopted earlier, the multivariate analysis suggests that the small firms' opposition to workers' compensation was very weak.

Organized labor joined manufacturing interests in strongly supporting the passage of workers' compensation. The American Federation of Labor (AFL) actively pursued the legislation after 1909. Yet in some states there was substantial disagreement within union ranks whether to lobby for their ideal workers' compensation law immediately or to support a weaker law in the beginning, with the hope of amending the law later (see Castrovinci 1976; Kantor and Fishback 1994a). Although internal disagreements might have slowed the adoption process in some states, in general, a greater union presence in a state substantially raised the likelihood of adoption. We developed a union index for each state to reflect the degree to which the industries represented in the state were unionized at the national level. The index is approximately 20 percent higher in states adopting prior to 1917 than in states adopting after 1916. After controlling for the remaining factors in the multivariate model, the relative impact of the union index on the probability of adopting workers' compensation was greater than that of any other variable.

The insurance lobby favored workers' compensation as a means of expanding their coverage of workplace accidents, as long as the state did not try to establish a state fund to write workers' compensation insurance. One way to measure the general strength of the insurance lobby is to look at the amount of insurance business they did in the state relative to the working population. In this case we use the amount of life insurance premiums paid (in constant 1967 dollars) divided by the number of workers in the state. We focus on life insurance because that was the most common form of insurance sold during the period. Note that this measure is substantially different from the ratio of employers' liability to life insurance discussed earlier. The life insurance measure captures the overall size of the insurance industry, whereas the earlier ratio captures the relative share of employers' liability activity. A comparison of means shows that the life insurance premiums per worker were $59 in the early adopting states relative to $31.90 in late adopting states. It should be noted, however, that the seemingly strong relationship between the insurance lobby and early adoption is eliminated when we control for other factors in the multivariate analysis. The absence of a strong positive effect might have been caused by the connection of the issue of state insurance with workers' compensation in many states. Insurers stood to gain from workers' compensation laws as long as states did not establish their own insurance funds to compete with or replace private insurance of workers' compensation risk. As discussed more fully in chapter 6, seven states created monopoly state insurance funds to fully replace private insurance, ten more set up funds that competed with private insurance carriers, and state insurance was an issue in many of the remaining states that never adopted a state insurance scheme. Even if insurers favored workers' compensation in principle, their opposition to workers' compensation bills that included state insurance diminished the measured impact in the more general adoption equation.

The final interest group that we assess is the state labor bureaucracy. State bureaucrats had several incentives to support workers' compensation. Since both workers and employers sought workers' compensation, regardless of which group more strongly influenced the labor bureaucracies, they had incentive to lobby for the legislation on behalf of their patrons. Further, the state labor bureaucrats' duties and budgets would expand if states created industrial commissions to supervise the operation of workers' compensation. Finally, the labor bureaucrats may have been useful in publicizing the benefits of workers' compensation. In table 4.4 the comparisons of 1910 data show that state spending on labor issues was substantially higher in the early adopting states than in the later adopting states. However, once we control for other factors in the multivariate analysis, the state labor bureaucracies had virtually no impact on the adoption of workers' compensation.

4.4.3   Political Climate

Keith Poole and Howard Rosenthal (1997) find that broad-based political economic coalitions may be as important to the adoption of legislation as narrow economic interests; therefore, we include measures to try to capture the influence of such coalitions. The leading political movement around the time of workers' compensation's adoption was the Progressive Movement, which took different forms in different states. The Progressive Era altered the nature of the political environment in which workers' compensation was debated in many states. Reform-minded legislators became influential in many state legislatures in the early twentieth century. They introduced, along with workers' compensation, such measures as initiatives and referenda, direct primaries, mothers' pensions, state tax commissions, compulsory school attendance, state welfare agencies, merit systems for state employees, minimum ages for child labor, and state commissions to regulate electricity rates. In addition, reformers unsuccessfully sought unemployment insurance, old-age pensions, minimum wages and maximum hours for men, and public health insurance. Potentially, workers' compensation might have been swept along as part of the progressives' broader agenda for socioeconomic reform. We have examined the impact of the Progressive Movement using four measures: the electorate's support for socialist presidential candidates, the support for Theodore Roosevelt's progressive presidential candidacy in 1912, variables that measure shifts in party control of state legislatures, and an index of progressive laws that each state had adopted to date.

The percentage of the vote won by Theodore Roosevelt's presidential campaign offers a rough measure of the extent to which voters in each state supported the nationwide progressive platform in 1912. All three parties expressed their support for workers' compensation in 1912, so the votes for Roosevelt might reflect acceptance of a broader progressive agenda for socioeconomic and political reform. Similarly, the votes garnered by socialist candidates may reflect the intensity of interest in more radical reform. As shown in table 4.4, voters in states adopting prior to 1917 were much more likely to support Roosevelt's progressive presidential campaign than the states that adopted later. Similarly, a higher percentage of voters supported socialist candidates in 1912 in the states adopting prior to 1917 than those adopting after 1917. The multivariate analysis reported in appendix H shows that after controlling for other political economic factors support for Roosevelt's progressive campaign still had a strong effect on the enactment of workers' compensation, while the voting for socialist candidates had virtually no impact on the probability of adoption.

Voting at the presidential level, however, says very little about the impact of reform movements within state legislatures. There is no simple way to measure the impact of the Progressive Movement and other reform movements at the state level. The Democratic and Republican party labels took on different meanings across the states during this time period, as progressive legislators were found in the Republican and/or Democratic parties across the United States in the early twentieth century. One way to capture the effect of reform movements is to measure their success in adopting other forms of progressive legislation. Therefore, we developed an index of progressive legislation that each state had in place at any point in time. The index measures the number of laws from the following list of progressive proposals that the state had passed: ballot initiatives, referenda, direct primaries, a mothers' pension law, a state tax commission, compulsory school attendance legislation, a state welfare agency, a merit system for state employees, a minimum age for child labor, and a state commission to regulate electricity rates. As shown in table 4.4, as of 1910, the states that adopted early had an average of 4.6 of these laws, compared with 2.6 for states adopting after 1917. However, after we control for other factors in the multivariate analysis, the impact of the progressive law index is relatively small and we cannot statistically reject the hypothesis of no effect.

Another way to capture the effect of reform movements is to track shifts in party control within each state legislature. The multivariate analysis revealed that shifts in party control had little impact on the probability of adopting workers' compensation, perhaps because the legislation was widely supported by all political parties and by workers, employers, and insurers. The limited impact of shifts in party control on the adoption of the legislation contrasts sharply with the results using the same legislative shift variables in our study of the battle over state insurance funds. As shown in chapter 6, insurance companies and unions fought bitterly over the state insurance issue, and quantitative analysis reveals that political power shifts were important factors in determining the adoption of monopoly state insurance in a handful of states. In general, it appears that workers' compensation was so widely accepted, while many other Progressive Era reforms were not, because a broad array of interest groups supported the legislation. Other, more controversial features of workers' compensation, like state insurance, did not necessarily have broad support, but reformers who championed a wide range of socioeconomic reforms accomplished their objectives when a political power shift within a state swept them into the majority.

A cursory look at the timing of adoption across the United States shows that southern states tended to adopt much later than northern states. Only 7 percent of the states among the early adopters were southern states, while 63 percent of the states adopting after 1917 were southern states. A question arises about whether there was something "peculiar" about the economic and political environment of the South that led to slow adoption. Gavin Wright (1986) believes that southern labor markets were separate from the rest of the U.S. labor market, while Lee Alston and Joseph Ferrie (1985, 1993) suggest that southern leaders were opponents of social security and other New Deal social welfare programs. However, once we control for the extent of the liability crisis, the influence of economic interest groups, and other progressive measures, the multivariate analysis shows that there was no unmeasured peculiar feature of the South that led to slower adoption.

4.4.4 "Contagion" Effect

When workers' compensation was first being considered, employers raised concerns that the legislation would put them at a cost disadvantage relative to their competitors in neighboring states. Given this attitude, employers may have been more willing to endorse workers' compensation when they were assured that their rivals in other states had similar labor costs. In the multivariate analysis, however, we found no evidence of such a "contagion" effect.

4.5 Summary

Workers' compensation was the leading tort reform and labor legislation of the Progressive Era. It was actively supported by lobbying groups representing employers, workers, and insurers because most of those in each interest group expected to gain from the legislation. Employers anticipated a reduction in labor friction, a reduction in the uncertainty of their accident and court costs, and a reduction in the gap between what they paid for insurance and what injured workers received. In addition, they were able to pass at least some of the additional costs of workers' compensation benefits on to their workers in the form of lower real wages. Workers, on average, anticipated higher postaccident benefits from the new legislation. Even if they "bought" the better benefits through lower wages, they anticipated better "insurance" coverage against workplace accident risk. In essence, workers could reduce their precautionary saving once the law mandated that employers bear the majority of the financial burden of industrial accidents. For their part, insurers believed that the shift to workers' compensation would reduce problems with adverse selection, and thus they could expand their coverage of workplace accidents, as long as the state did not become an insurer itself. These gains could only be realized through the passage of workers' compensation because the courts in the early 1900s did not allow employers and workers to write workers' compensation–style private contracts in which workers waived their rights to negligence suits prior to an accident. Thus, instead of being imposed from the top down or from the bottom up, workers' compensation was enacted because a broad-based coalition of divergent interests saw gains from reforming the negligence liability system.

The catalyst that united these interest groups was an increased awareness of workplace accident problems and substantial changes in the liability system that governed workplace accident compensation. Across the country during the early years of the twentieth century, employers experienced increases in the level and uncertainty of their liability, as employers' liability laws and court decisions altered the traditional negligence system. Even though the changes in employers' liability largely benefited workers, labor leaders were dissatisfied with the results because many workers were still left uncompensated and for those that did receive remuneration, the amount typically did not replace lost income. Criticism of the negligence system was widespread across the United States by 1910, thus resulting in the rapid adoption of workers' compensation legislation across the country.

Some states enacted workers' compensation more quickly than others. In states where employers' liability was increasing relatively sharply, the legislation was enacted more swiftly. In addition, workers' compensation was more likely to be adopted in areas where organized labor and manufacturing employers and workers had more political strength. Larger and more productive employers pressed for adoption even more strongly than other members of the manufacturing lobby. Support for workers' compensation was not limited to narrowly defined economic interest groups, however. Greater support among the electorate for the broad-based program of Progressive Era reformers, as embodied in the support for Theodore Roosevelt in 1912, appears to have contributed to earlier adoption of workers' compensation in a number of states. In general, workers' compensation was *not* the result of one interest group using the political process to extract benefits at the expense of others. Instead, it was legislation that united a broad-based coalition of workers, manufacturing employers, and insurance interests attempting to reform the negligence liability system that all agreed was ill suited for the modern industrial economy.

Notes

1. See Stigler (1971), Peltzman (1976), and Becker (1983) for theoretical treatments of the role of interest groups in shaping regulations. Their models are rich enough to allow for either a "capture" or multiple interest group framework. For the classic work on "rent-seeking," see Tullock (1967). Goldberg (1976) and Williamson (1976) discuss situations in which interest groups might lobby the government to correct a market imperfection and the resulting legislation enhance economic efficiency. Finally, Poole and Rosenthal (1997) claim that broad-based political coalitions have been underemphasized as facilitators of government intervention.

2. Lubove (1967) explains employers' support for workers' compensation in similar terms. He argues that employers sought the legislation because state legislatures and the courts were increasingly favoring injured workers in their efforts to collect compensation. By contrast, Weinstein (1967) argues that employers supported workers' compensation as a way to undermine the growing movement among workers to unionize.

3. For an analysis of states' decisions to enact state workers' compensation funds, see chapter 6.

4. In 1920 the actual level of employer liability premiums was $86 million. Based on the annual growth rate of employer liability premiums between 1905 and 1911, the years prior to the adoption of workers' compensation, we estimated that employer liability premiums would have grown to $129.5 million in 1920. Premium estimates are from *Hayden's Annual Cyclopedia of Insurance* (1906, 4, 161; 1913, 4, 117) and *Annual Cyclopedia of Insurance* (1921, 229–30, 287–88, 465).

5. See also Clark (1908, 13–14).

6. In contrast to the U.S. courts, the English courts allowed ex ante contracts to stand. Clark (1908, 14) found rulings in Georgia (*Western & A. R. Co. v. Bishop,* 50 Ga. 465 [1873]) and in Pennsylvania (*Mitchell v. Pa. R.,* 1 Am. Law. Reg. 717 [1853]) that allowed ex ante contracts that would have barred negligence suits after an accident occurred. However, the Georgia Code of 1895 included specific language that nullified such contracts. Meanwhile, the Pennsylvania Supreme Court in a ruling about acceptance of relief benefits as a bar to a lawsuit stated "that an agreement to accept benefits, the acceptance to operate as a waiver of the right of action was not contrary to public policy, *inasmuch as it was not the signing of the contract prior to the injury (which would not in itself be effective) but the acceptance of benefits after the injury that barred the action* [emphasis added]." See *Johnson v. Philadelphia R. Co.,* 168 Pa. 134, 20 A. 854 (1894). In addition to the common law rulings, Clark and the U.S. Commissioner of Labor (1908) found that twenty-eight states had statutes voiding such ex ante contracts, but many were statutes only pertaining to the railroad industry. States with laws preventing contracts in railroading included Arkansas, Florida, Iowa, Minnesota, Mississippi, Missouri, Nebraska, New Mexico, New York, North Carolina, North Dakota, Ohio, Oregon, South Carolina, South Dakota, Texas, Virginia, and Wisconsin. States with general laws were California, Colorado, Georgia, Idaho (1909), Indiana, Massachusetts, Montana, Ohio (1910), and Wyoming (constitution). Missouri had a law covering railroads and mining and Nevada had a law covering railroads, mines, and mills (we treated these as general laws). Alabama had a similar law in its 1907 Code that Clark missed because he reported on the Code of 1896. Some states later passed additional laws against ex ante contracting.

7. Workers' waiving their rights to a lawsuit prior to an accident was central to workers' compensation's success. When New Hampshire first adopted the legislation, for example, workers had the option to choose between a lawsuit and the workers' compensation benefits after the accident. Employers retained the contributory negligence defense if the worker chose to go to court. The U.S. Bureau of Labor Statistics (1917, 74–75) stated that this feature of the law may explain why only nineteen employers decided to abide by the terms of New Hampshire's voluntary workers' compensation law. Arizona had a similar workers' compensation law but it required employers to join the system. The state completely revamped its law in the 1920s, and this provision was scrapped.

8. The state legislatures in the period 1910 to 1920 never experimented with laws that allowed workers and employers to freely choose their own benefit levels in ex ante contracts. Massachusetts in 1908 and New York (for nonhazardous work) in

1910 established opportunities for workers and employers to sign ex ante contracts, but the benefit levels were controlled by the state board of arbitration and conciliation in Massachusetts and set by the legislature in New York. No one submitted contracts for approval in Massachusetts because the one-year limit on contract duration "rendered it undesirable for employers to formulate plans and to incur the trouble and expense necessary to operate them" (Massachusetts Commission for the Compensation for Industrial Accidents 1912, 14–17). In New York only 38 of 440 employees of one firm had consented to the voluntary system by July 1913. The administrative costs of setting up the New York contracts were prohibitive because the employer and each employee had to sign and submit written agreements to the county clerk, which was a more cumbersome system than the standard methods of election in later workers' compensation laws (Clark 1914, 116–17).

9. The following states eventually adopted compulsory legislation: California, New York, Illinois, Ohio, Washington, Maryland, Arizona, Oklahoma, Wyoming, Idaho, Utah, North Dakota, Arkansas, and Mississippi.

10. States had a wide range of laws specific to the railroad industry, but the focus here is on nonrailroad activity because interstate railroad accidents did not fall under the domain of states' workers' compensation laws. The vast majority of railroad accidents were covered by the Federal Employers' Liability Acts of 1906 and 1908. Some nontrain, noninterstate commerce accidents were handled under state workers' compensation laws, however. In addition, about eight more states in 1900 had laws that restated the common law without changing any of the basic negligence rules. See appendix G for further details on employers' liability laws of the early twentieth century.

11. See Asher (1983) for a complete discussion of the campaign for employers' liability in New York. Many of the bills died in committee. Several passed one chamber of the legislature before dying in the second chamber, but Asher claims that this was a standard tactic used by the legislators to reduce criticism that they were not sensitive to the topic.

12. The proposed bill would have allowed an injured worker to sue if he had warned the employer of defects and then continued working. Organized labor was dissatisfied because the injured worker was required to give notice within sixty days, compared with an earlier three-year limit, and the burden of proof was on the worker to prove that he had given notice of the dangerous condition to his employer (Asher 1983).

13. Asher (1983) suggests several reasons for organized labor's limited success in increasing employers' liability in New York. First, organized labor never represented more than 10 percent of the voting constituency, so their numerical influence in affecting election outcomes was necessarily limited. Second, there were divisions within organized labor ranks. The railroad brotherhoods and many other unions never joined the WFSNY, and even within the WFSNY there was a division between the New York City unions and their more conservative upstate counterparts. Thus, in most years, organized labor was politically ineffective. On a few occasions when politicians felt vulnerable in close elections, however, organized labor was able to mount strong campaigns because they essentially became swing voters in the next election. But these opportunities were limited. In the final analysis employers felt increasing pressure in the early 1900s to consider workers' compensation as a viable option because the 1902 employers' liability law led to more lawsuits and increases in the amounts awarded to workers. Although organized labor was never able to mount a successful campaign, employers feared the threat of more drastic laws.

14. See Mengert (1920, 5–6). In 1904 Republicans had a four to one majority in the House and a seven to one majority in the Senate. The Williams bill passed the Senate twenty-two to four, and the House fifty-seven to twenty-five (Ohio Senate *Journal,* 1904, 710; Ohio House of Representatives *Journal,* 1904, 368). The Williams bill was infamous because it was lost for a period after it was sent to the governor for signing. Mengert mentions gossip that opponents of the bill stole it. The attorney general of Ohio was said to have decided that he could reconstruct the bill from the records, and the public was told the bill had been found folded into another bill. See *Ohio State Journal,* 22 April 1904; *Cleveland Plain Dealer,* 29 April 1904; *Ohio State Journal,* 1, 28, and 30 April 1904.

15. At the same time there were cracks developing in the Republican's conservative hegemony over Ohio politics. In the 1908 election, Democrat Judson Harmon was elected governor, despite the Taft presidential victory and the election of a complete Republican slate for other state offices (Warner 1964, 215, 220; Aumann 1942, 9–10). Harmon was not considered a true progressive, although he sought to make government operate more efficiently. As a consequence, he felt that great improvements could be made in delivering compensation to injured workmen. Most of Harmon's efforts were defeated by a strong Republican legislature in 1909.

16. The same bill was introduced by Norris in the House (House Bill No. 24) and Mathews in the Senate (Senate Bill No. 28) seeking comparative negligence, limits on the fellow servant defense, and further limits on the assumption of risk defense. The political infighting involved a series of attempts at bill-swapping. Representative Brenner in the House led the way for the business groups by proposing a resolution to delay all action on employers' liability and to form a commission to study the issue carefully. His proposal included referring the resolution to himself as a committee of one to be allowed to report it to the floor of the House at the proper time. Despite the efforts of progressive legislators Evans of Cleveland and Ratliff of Cincinnati to get the Brenner resolution referred to the Labor Committee, the House decided instead to refer the resolution to Brenner's committee of one. After the Labor Committee recommended the Norris bill for passage, Brenner sought to amend the bill by fully replacing it with his commission proposal. Brenner's replacement amendment was hotly contested but won by a vote of fifty-nine to forty-one, with seventeen not voting. The House then quickly passed Brenner's version of the Norris bill, which established the commission, without changing the employers' liability law, by a vote of seventy-seven to twenty.

In the Senate the procedure was reversed. Senator Mathews managed to reinstate the employers' liability language into the bill. An attempt by Senator Patterson to replace the employers' liability language with a commission yet again lost by a vote of ten to twenty-two. The Senate then passed the employers' liability version of the Norris Act twenty-six votes to one and sent it back to the House. The House agreed to pass the employers' liability version of the Norris Act, ninety-three to five, but it was a compromise in which the women's hours bill would not come to a vote. This political history is drawn from Foote (1910, 14), Ohio State Federation of Labor (1910, 10), Ohio House of Representatives *Journal* (1910, 253, 537–39, 799–803), Ohio Senate *Journal* (1910, 422–25, 449–50, 479–81), Ohio State Board of Commerce (1910, 60), *Ohio State Journal,* 15 and 31 March 1910; 7, 14, 27, and 28 April 1910, and *Cleveland Plain Dealer,* 15 and 18 March 1910; 5, 7, 27, and 28 April 1910.

17. The women's eight-hour bill was described by the Ohio Manufacturers' Association a year later as a "milker pure and simple" and when passed in modified form was passed "in a spirit of pique because members of the House and Senate had not been paid the amount of money that they expected to make for their

services in defeating it." In the 1911 General Assembly a huge bribery scandal developed over such milker bills. In the words of the secretary of the Ohio Manufacturers' Association, during the session of the General Assembly over the past twenty-five years, "to my personal knowledge, there have been introduced a large number of bills, the sole purpose of which has been to compel persons or interests to purchase their defeat. For very many years, the persons or interests against whom these bills were directed felt and believed that the easiest and cheapest way out was to pay the price demanded, and go on about their affairs" Ohio Manufacturers' Association *Records* (1911).

18. See House Bills (HB) 310 and 526 in 1895; HB 285 and Senate Bills (SB) 212 and 213 in 1897; HB 294 and 336 in 1899; HB 167 and 406 in 1901; SB 34 and 72 and HB 148 in 1903; HB 98, 129, 178, and 385 and SB 169 in 1905; the "Graves bill" in 1907; and SB 171, 205, and 217 in 1909 from volumes *Washington Senate Bills* and *Washington House Bills,* various years. Some of these bills focused on safety regulations, which affected employers' liability by establishing what was considered employer's negligence.

19. The *Green* case was a coal mining case. A miner asked for more timbers to support the roof. His foreman said there were no more timbers, so the miner quit for the day. The next day there were still no timbers, the miner started working and was harmed. See report of the *Green* decision in 30 Wash. 87–116 (1902); see also Tripp (1976, 533).

20. See Washington Insurance Commissioner (1902, 47, 60; 1904, 25, 38; 1906, 32, 47; 1908, 30, 44; 1909, 27, 31; 1910, 28; 1911, 41); see also Tripp (1976, 534).

21. The exception to the rise was a drop in cases to twenty-nine in 1907. The number of Washington Supreme Court cases was compiled from *Washington Reports,* 1904 to 1911. The increase in the cases probably signals an increase in the uncertainty about how the law would be applied.

22. We focused on nonrailroad cases and railroad nontrain cases because these were the types of accidents covered by workers' compensation laws. The trend in table 4.1 is unchanged when railroad cases are included. Including railroad cases, the number of state supreme court cases rises from 220 in 1900 to 640 in 1909, declines to 551 in 1910, and rises to 609 in 1911.

We ran trend regressions for each state and found that in thirty-one states the increased number of cases was statistically significant. In sixteen states there was no statistical trend and in one state there was a statistically significant downward trend. Thus, the pattern for the United States shown in table 4.1 was widespread across the country and not driven by a handful of litigious states.

23. Ohio Employers' Liability Commission (1911, xxxix).

24. Ibid., 204, 210.

25. Washington Industrial Insurance Department (1912, 19).

26. Washington Insurance Commissioner (1902, 47, 60; 1910, 28; 1911, 41).

27. We ran trend regressions for each of the states and found that in thirty-nine states there was a statistically significant increase in the ratio. In seven states there was no statistical trend and in two states there was a statistically negative trend.

28. We created a workplace-accident risk index based on each state's industrial mix and the premiums that employers in each industry paid per one hundred dollars on the payroll into the Ohio State Workmen's Compensation Fund in 1923 (see Ohio Industrial Commission 1923). Ohio had a wide range of industries and the Ohio Industrial Commission sought to price the insurance based on actuarial experiences. We matched the premiums for each industry with the average employment in that industry in each state in 1899 and 1909. The risk index is the weighted average of the insurance premiums across industries using the average employment

in each industry as weights. Changes in the risk index between 1899 and 1909 are caused only by changes in the distribution of employment across various types of manufacturing. The index rose from 1.3 in 1899 to 1.5 in 1909.

29. Weinstein (1967, 162) claims that the AALL represented the interests of large employers, accepting funding from Gary, Rockefeller, and Macy. Moss (1996) claims, however, that the AALL was more independent because it was led by academic economists like John R. Commons, who called for many reforms that employers opposed.

30. Ohio State Federation of Labor (1915a, 23–25).

31. The transition in the attitudes of employers and organized labor are illustrated by Asher's (1969) research on Massachusetts. Although the issue of workers' compensation was broached in the 1903 committee, organized labor's solution was to push for a further expansion in employers' liability. In 1904 organized labor's adamant demand to retain the right to sue for damages as part of any workers' compensation bill destroyed whatever small chance Massachusetts had of passing a workers' compensation bill (p. 457). Annually between 1905 and 1907 organized labor in Massachusetts lobbied unsuccessfully for employers' liability bills that would have limited the assumption of risk and contributory negligence defenses. The failure to achieve their objectives during this period may have caused the labor leaders to change course. In 1907 a committee was formed to consider both employers' liability and workers' compensation bills during the legislative recess. Labor leaders on the committee began to favor workers' compensation, as did leaders from the Massachusetts Civic League. In 1908 the committee endorsed the social principle of workers' compensation and the legislature passed a bill allowing employers to voluntarily establish no-fault accident compensation plans that resembled the workers' compensation programs to come later. No employer created a plan, however. By 1910, the Massachusetts Federation of Labor, the Boston Chamber of Commerce, and the New England Civic Federation all had become interested in a workers' compensation bill, although each group had its own ideas about what the bill should look like. The nature of their compromise is discussed in chapter 5.

32. State-level regressions show that in thirty-one states real spending on labor issues increased at a statistically significant trend. In eight states there was no statistical trend and in four there was a statistically negative trend, primarily because nominal spending remained constant over the period. Five states had no spending on labor issues during the period.

33. For an example of early labor department advocacy for workers' compensation, see Minnesota Bureau of Labor Statistics (1893, 117–55).

34. Commissions were established in Minnesota, New York, and Wisconsin in 1909; Illinois, Massachusetts, Missouri (appointed by governor), Montana (appointed by governor), New Jersey, Ohio, and Washington (appointed by governor) in 1910; Colorado, Connecticut, Iowa, Michigan, Nebraska, North Dakota, Oregon (appointed by governor), Pennsylvania, Texas, and West Virginia (appointed by governor) in 1911; Louisiana in 1912; and Indiana, Maryland (appointed by governor), Tennessee, and Vermont in 1913.

35. The Maryland legislature in 1902 was the first to actually adopt a compensation law that set out to provide guaranteed benefits to injured workers in several hazardous industries. But because the legislation gave the insurance commissioner judicial powers and deprived injured workers of the right to a jury trial, it was ruled unconstitutional two years after its passage. And in 1909 the Montana legislature passed a compulsory compensation law that pertained only to the coal mining industry. Although the law required both employer and employee contribu-

tions into a cooperative insurance fund, it still allowed an injured employee (or his family) to sue for damages under the old liability system. Since the law forced the employer to bear a double burden, the Montana Supreme Court ruled it unconstitutional in 1911 (Weiss 1966, 571).

36. See chapter 5.

37. Recall that total employers' liability premiums may have increased either because rates increased or because more employers chose to insure their accident liability risks. Since the multivariate analysis controls for changes in manufacturing accident risk and for the change in employers' liability laws, the measured impact of the insurance ratio might suggest that employers saw workers' compensation as a means to control their insurance costs.

The Political Process of Adopting Workers' Compensation

There might have been a consensus that no-fault accident compensation would be superior to the erstwhile liability system, but the actual process of enacting workers' compensation involved a complex set of political negotiations both across and within various interest groups and within state legislatures. Because the specifics of the legislation—including benefit levels, state versus private insurance, the administration of the law, the coverage of industries, and the rights of workers to negligence suits—determined how income would be distributed under the new law, reaching compromises on these details were sometimes acrimonious events. In this chapter we use several brief case studies to illuminate how various economic interests were filtered through the political process to shape workers' compensation legislation.[1]

Interest groups typically wrote bills that best expressed politically what they desired; therefore, the bills that were debated within state legislatures were often quite diverse. As would be expected, fights developed between interest groups over the specific features the workers' compensation law would contain. If the groups were far apart the disagreements could delay the process of adoption—by two years in Minnesota and over fifteen years in Missouri, for example. Such delays are consistent with Howitt and Wintrobe's (1995) theoretical prediction that beneficial policies may not even be brought up for legislative consideration because each group fears that it may end up with its opponent's version of the legislation.

The factions that made up broad interest groups—organized labor, employers, or attorneys—did not all share the same views regarding the proper means to achieve better workplace accident compensation in the early twentieth century. In Minnesota and Missouri, for instance, specific unions took opposing sides on the passage of workers' compensation. This fight within the union ranks was not really over the general issue of workers' compensation but over the optimal strategy that unions should employ to secure a law that was closest to their ideal. Typically, one faction believed that in order to secure the enactment of workers' compensation unions had to settle for a basic law without state insurance and relatively low accident benefits. The goal then was to later amend the bill to shape the law more in their favor. Another faction argued that the optimal strategy was to seek what organized labor wanted most when workers' compensation was first introduced because amending the bill later would be more difficult. These internal struggles show that strategic political maneuvering can distort how analysts view an interest group's preferences if we take their support for specific legislation at face value. In addition, it is also important to look at the group's expectations of their future successes in influencing the political process.

The case studies allow us to examine more carefully how political nuances influenced the timing and nature of compensation legislation in the 1910s. Employers, organized labor, insurers, and trial lawyers often had far greater power in legislatures than their numbers would suggest. These groups often framed the public and legislative debates, offered information to legislators, flooded hearings with their witnesses, and generally exerted substantial influence in the legislatures as proposals moved from the employers' liability commission through the House, the Senate, and the governor's office, sometimes to a referendum. In many states multiple proposals came out of the employers' liability commission. Legislators favoring specific bills worked hard to get their favored bills sent to the committees where their allies held sway. Within the committees, compromises were struck, but such compromises were overturned by intricate legislative maneuvers on the floor and battles across chambers. Since at each stage the relative political strength of the different interest groups varied, proposals that carried the day in the House might have faced severe obstacles in the Senate, or faced a governor's veto. In a few states the legislature's decision was then subject to a popular referendum, which sometimes led to complicated strategic moves inside the legislature in anticipation of the referendum. In Missouri, for example, some opponents of workers' compensation voted for union-sponsored amendments to the workers' compensation bill, in anticipation that a more extreme bill would be struck down in the voter referendum. In other states, like New York, the legislation was struck down by the courts as unconstitutional, necessitating a major rewrite of the bill or a constitutional amendment. A closer examination of the adoption process in a variety of states highlights the nuances of the political process that shaped workers' compensation laws.

5.1 Ohio

The adoption process in Ohio illustrates several features that were common to many states. An employers' liability commission was established with balanced representation between organized labor and employers' representatives. Although a majority struck a compromise within the commission, organized labor's discontent with the compromise bill then led to two versions of the legislation being sent to the legislature. While the factions in the House maneuvered the two bills through the committee structure, labor supporters rammed their ideal bill through the Senate. Ohio's governor then exercised his veto threat to craft a compromise that was suitable to all sides.[2]

As part of the political compromise in the passage of the Norris Employer Liability Act of 1910, the Ohio legislature established an Employers' Liability Commission (ELC). As in many other states, the commission included an equal number of employers and labor representatives. The Ohio ELC consisted of five members: W. J. Rohr and W. J. Winans were the labor representatives, George Perks and John Smith represented employers, and J. Harrington Boyd was the nonaligned chair of the commission. The ELC was charged with proposing a bill for consideration by the 1911 legislature. Three main issues became points of contention. The first stumbling block was the issue of how the cost of workers' compensation was to be shared by employers and workers. While in most states there was intense debate over the percentage of wages to be replaced or the maximum weekly benefit, Ohio union officials and employers focused more critically on who would pay the workers' compensation insurance premiums. The second major issue centered on whether a worker, after his accident occurred, would have the right to choose between the guaranteed workers' compensation benefits or suing his employer under negligence liability. Workers wanted the right to choose because if they could prove the employer's negligence, then they could perhaps receive full compensation for their injuries in a court award or settlement. If such a case could not be made, then the worker had the option of selecting the statutory amount of workers' compensation benefits. Employers strongly opposed giving workers this option because it would confront them with the same legal and financial uncertainty from which they were trying to escape. If workers could choose their means of compensation, then employers would be forced to pay damages to all of their injured workers, plus they would still face the possibility of paying very large awards to those workers with strong negligence claims. Thus, under such a legal regime, employers would have gained nothing—their accident costs would have risen and the uncertainty of their payouts would have remained intact. The third issue, and the one that in the years following the adoption of workers' compensation was to became the most contentious of the three in Ohio, was the choice between state and private insurance of workers' compensation risk.

The internal discussions within the ELC foreshadowed the debate to follow in the 1911 legislature. By a four-to-one majority, the commission settled on proposing a compromise bill to the legislature. The commission's bill called for the creation of a state insurance fund and the elimination of private insurance of workers' compensation, which was very satisfactory from the point of view of the Ohio State Federation of Labor (OSFL). Employers were able to secure their own favored provision, however—the ability to pass 25 percent of their compensation insurance premiums onto workers. Further, if a firm joined the state fund, then its workers were automatically enrolled in the system and thus lost their rights to sue for damages under the common law. Employers, particularly the Ohio Manufacturers' Association (OMA), which had formed in November 1910 specifically to address the issues surrounding workplace liability, strongly supported this workers' compensation proposal.[3] Since this bill was to draw the most support from employers, we will henceforth refer to it as the "employer" bill.

The OSFL, while pleased with the state fund proposal included in the majority bill, was deeply disappointed with the remainder of the ELC's bill. They repudiated one of their own representatives to the ELC, W. J. Rohr, for joining the majority after promising his colleague W. J. Winans that he would not.[4] To ensure that the OSFL stance would be included in the official report of the ELC, Winans submitted a minority report that contained a workers' compensation bill that would have required employers to pay 100 percent of their insurance premiums and would have given workers the option of choosing, after their injury had occurred, between workers' compensation benefits and a negligence suit. We refer below to this bill as the "labor" bill.

In the 1911 Ohio legislature a bitter battle developed over the employer and labor bills coming out of the ELC. Employers, organized labor, and insurers lobbied a legislature that included substantially more progressive reformers than the 1910 special session of the legislature. The Democrats had captured a majority in both chambers and progressives from both parties held 47 percent of the House seats and 32 percent of the Senate seats.[5] In the House the labor bill was shepherded to the Corporations Committee, chaired by labor supporter George Nye, which reported the bill out of committee favorably, but, in the words of the OMA, "without giving the matter any consideration whatever."[6] At the same time, the employer bill was sent to the Judiciary Committee, which amended the bill and reported it out of committee without a recommendation. The OMA worried that the OSFL had enough votes to pass the minority bill. Yet the OMA held a trump card because "if the bill had . . . become law it would have had not the least effect, because no employer in Ohio would have insured under it, and the labor leaders and their allies knew this to be a fact."[7]

When the labor bill came up for a vote in the House, the allies of the OMA succeeded in sending both of the ELC's workers' compensation bills to a special committee. Shortly after the House special committee was announced, the political maneuvering in the House became moot. Senate leader William Green, later president of the American Federation of Labor (AFL), shepherded the labor bill through the Senate by a vote of twenty-six to one with only one amendment, which prevented workers from collecting workers' compensation benefits if they chose to sue under the common law.[8] As the House special committee considered the Senate versions of the labor bill and the employer bill, the insurance lobby, operating through the Cleveland Chamber of Commerce, offered up its own workers' compensation bill without state insurance. Despite insurers' claims that a state fund would encourage negligent behavior and increase the level of accidents, their efforts were fruitless because the ELC's employer and labor bills had set the agenda. Hence, state insurance was taken off the table and the focus of the legislative debate was on the share of premiums that employers and workers would pay and on a worker's right to sue for damages.[9] As shown in chapter 6, however, the state insurance issue was hotly contested for several years following the passage of workers' compensation in Ohio.

At this stage Governor Judson Harmon exercised the threat of his veto power, announcing that he favored the employer bill and would veto the labor bill if it were to pass.[10] Harmon, a former judge, then worked closely with the House special committee to craft a compromise that would avoid the constitutional problems highlighted by the New York Supreme Court's *Ives* decision that struck down New York's 1910 compulsory workers' compensation law (see section 5.4). Harmon and the committee wanted to construct a law that was elective technically, but in practice encouraged employers to join the state insurance fund. Their revision penalized employers by stripping them of their three legal defenses if they refused to join the state fund. On the other hand, employers that elected to join the state fund were rewarded in that their workers were prevented from filing negligence suits unless the employer had failed to observe laws requiring the safeguarding of machinery or had caused the worker's injury through a willful act.[11] The special committee also compromised on the percentage of insurance premiums each party would pay. They proposed that employers pay 90 percent of the premiums, workers 10 percent.

When the compromise bill reached the House floor on 26 April 1911, the battle over the two key issues intensified. Republican representative Charles Reid offered an amendment to raise the workers' burden to 20 percent, but it was defeated seventeen to seventy-four, as legislators with strong labor ties voted unanimously against the amendment. The next day progressive representative W. B. Kilpatrick unsuccessfully tried the reverse strategy, calling for an amendment that would have required employers to pay 100 percent of the premiums. The conservative Reid also sought to amend the compromise bill by allowing employers to keep their three defenses in liability suits even if they did not join the state fund. The amendment struck at the very heart of Governor Harmon's attempts to entice employers to join the workers' compensation fund. According to the *Cleveland Plain Dealer,* farmers enthusiastically supported Reid's amendment.[12] As in other states, farm interests were strongly opposed to being included in the workers' compensation scheme and the farm lobby in Ohio was deeply worried that the proposed legislation had not yet excluded them from the law's purview.

Although Reid's amendment lost, legislators attempted to appease agricultural interests and small manufacturers. Special committee chairman Ratliff then amended the bill to exempt employers with fewer than five workers, which became a common provision in most states' laws. Representative Gebhart further appealed to agricultural interests by offering an amendment excluding agricultural workers and domestic servants, which was adopted without a vote. However, on the afternoon that the final vote was taken, Attorney General Timothy Hogan advised the legislature that the amendment excluding agriculture would make the law unconstitutional, and the House rescinded the amendment. The final bill, largely unchanged from the special committee's compromise, easily passed the House in a vote of eighty-three to eighteen. It was then signed into law by Governor Harmon.

While the OMA considered the new law "probably the best law on this subject in the United States today," the association expressed some reservations. As can be seen in table 3.1, Ohio's benefits were relatively generous when compared to other states'. Employers felt that increasing their share of the workers' compensation premiums from 75 percent to 90 percent might have made the difference between success and failure of the new law. Of course, no one would know for sure until the state fund formulated its rates.[13] The Ohio State Board of Liability Awards, the new state bureaucracy created to administer the state's workers' compensation insurance fund, was well aware of this concern. H. R. Mengert claimed that since Ohio's general revenues paid the administrative expenses of the state fund, its workers' compensation rates were below private insurers' employers' liability rates.[14] Indeed, within the next few years, employers agreed to pay 100 percent of the workers' compensation premiums.

5.2 Illinois

The Illinois legislature flirted with a voluntary workers' compensation bill in 1907 before striking it down at the behest of organized labor.[15] By

1910, however, employers' groups and the state federation of labor began pressing for workers' compensation. The Illinois adoption process illustrates the diversity of attitudes that at times developed within the organized labor lobby. Some unions favored workers' compensation while others still sought an expansion of employers' liability instead. As a result, the labor organizations offered competing bills to the legislature. The Illinois experience was also one in which the governor's veto was extremely important. The legislature gave the governor the final choice, as the legislature passed both the workers' compensation bill and an employers' liability bill. To the chagrin of the labor groups that preferred expanded employers' liability, the governor signed the workers' compensation bill into law.

Throughout the period prior to the adoption of workers' compensation, the Illinois Federation of Labor (IFL) pressed for employer liability laws.[16] Employers meanwhile had begun to press for a voluntary system of private insurance. The 1905 legislature established a commission to examine the accident problem and in 1907 it submitted a proposal to establish a voluntary but comprehensive system of private insurance for workplace injuries. The standard plan was for a 50 percent replacement rate for disability and a death benefit equal to the larger of three years' income or one thousand dollars. Employers, however, would pay only half of the premium. Organized labor strongly opposed the plan in the 1907 legislature and instead focused their attention on trying to further expand liability.

Like many other states, Illinois established a commission in 1910 to examine the compensation of workplace accidents and to propose a legislative solution. The commission was balanced with six labor representatives and six employers. While employers and organized labor worked to reach a middle ground on their differences, deep divisions developed within the labor movement. The IFL, with strong internal support from the miners' union, strongly favored workers' compensation. In contrast, the Chicago Federation of Labor (CFL) and the Railway Trainmen's Union (RTU) wanted to modify the negligence system by eliminating the three defenses. They argued that workers' compensation benefits were meager relative to the high awards that could be received under expanded liability, and that expanding employers' liability would force employers to increase their accident prevention activities.

As the workers' compensation commission began to develop a compromise bill, the three CFL representatives on the commission expressed their dissatisfaction with the process and resigned. Governor Charles S. Deneen, a progressive Republican who endorsed workers' compensation, replaced the walkouts with three IFL representatives and the commission sent forward a bill similar to the model bill proposed by the National Association of Manufacturers. The bill offered expected benefits amounting to 1.48 percent of average annual income, which was near the lower end of the scale for early adopters (see tables 3.1 and B.1–B.4). The CFL countered by having representatives introduce an alternative bill to eliminate the three defenses in the 1911 legislature. They then ordered their lobbyists not to waste any time on workers' compensation.

The 1911 legislature passed both the commission's workers' compensation bill and the CFL's liability bill, which led to further jockeying for position on all sides. The Illinois Manufacturers Association (IMA), which was a supporter of workers' compensation, thought the benefit levels were too high, so it urged the governor to veto both bills and then reexamine the workers' compensation bill. The insurance companies also favored workers' compensation on the grounds that expanding employers' liability would make it "manifestly impossible to fix the rates with any certainty," while workers' compensation awards would be more easily predictable (Castrovinci 1976, 89). Although the CFL still opposed workers' compensation, in May 1911 it eventually agreed not to oppose the legislation in exchange for a promise from friends of the governor and his allies that their liability bill would also pass. The governor, however, vetoed the CFL liability bill and signed only the workers' compensation bill because this was the wish of the majority of the compensation commission members. The CFL evidently recovered from this political setback because in 1913 it was actively participating in the process to amend the workers' compensation law to make it more beneficial to injured workers.

5.3   Massachusetts

Massachusetts enacted a workers' compensation law relatively early, as leading employers and organized labor all called for its adoption. These groups overcame efforts to delay the legislation and adopted a compromise measure that offered about average benefits among the early adopters. An attempt by organized labor to eliminate casualty insurance of workers' compensation passed the lower branch of the legislature, but insurance companies effectively fought back in the Senate, so that employers had the option of casualty as well as mutual insurance in the final compromise version of the bill.

In 1908 Massachusetts established opportunities for workers and employers to sign ex ante contracts that seemed to capture the essence of the workers' compensation idea. The benefit levels were to be decided by the state board of arbitration and conciliation in Massachusetts, but the administrative costs to workers and employers of submitting contracts for approval were onerous. The Massachusetts Commission for the Compensation for Industrial Accidents (1912, 14–17) found that no one submitted contracts for approval in Massachusetts because the one-year limit on contract duration "rendered it undesirable for employers to formulate plans and to incur the trouble and expense necessary to operate them."

By 1910 there was widespread interest in workers' compensation in

Massachusetts. The New England Civic Federation, the Boston Chamber of Commerce's Committee on Industrial Relations, and the Massachusetts State Branch of the AFL (MSBAFL) all expressed interest in enacting a workers' compensation bill.[17] They were worried about the gap between what employers were paying in premiums and what workers actually received and the increasing presence of bad feelings between employers and employees. As in other states, however, there was disagreement about the specifics of the legislation. The Boston Chamber's Committee on Industrial Relations drafted its own bill, as did the MSBAFL. Asher (1969) claims that there was substantial disagreement across unions about the precise nature of the bill. Pressure from both the Boston Chamber of Commerce and organized labor forced the legislature to establish a commission to report a bill to the 1911 legislature.[18]

In the commission's hearings the chairman stated that only one in fifteen injured employees received any reasonable award and that employers and employees were unanimously dissatisfied with the current system. They drafted a bill that offered benefits that were in the mid-range of benefits for early adopting states: benefits of 50 percent of the wage, with a minimum of four dollars and a maximum of ten dollars per week, a two-week waiting period, and a death benefit of three hundred times the weekly payment. Labor leaders uniformly approved the bill, although they expressed minor dissatisfaction with the two-week waiting period. Employers objected to specific features of the bill. Some still sought contributory negligence, while small employers in risky industries worried about the cost of the system and employers in low-risk industries sought to reduce the waiting time to allow some of their workers to obtain benefits for their injuries.

In January 1911 the commission argued in favor of postponing legislative consideration of the bill, but Governor and former manufacturer Eugene Foss, the Boston Chamber of Commerce, and organized labor actively pushed for passage of some form of legislation. The major battles fought over the legislation centered on the issue of state insurance, as three bills were sent to the legislature in February 1911. The bill that commission chairman Lowell proposed allowed employers to join a mutual insurance fund or to self-insure. A second bill written by Magnus Alexander proposed mutual insurance, whereby both workers and employers contributed. Organized labor disliked this option and proposed through representatives Saunders and Parks to establish a single mutual insurance company, the Massachusetts Employers Insurance Association (now Liberty Mutual), which would operate privately after receiving some initial financing from the state. All three bills barred casualty insurance. After several hearings a joint Senate-House committee endorsed the Saunders-Parks bill in the House. The bill passed the House on July 10 without a recorded vote.

In the Senate the bill met with strong opposition from "cautious" senators and an effective insurance lobby. In a seventeen-to-sixteen vote the Senate refused to table the bill. Senators under pressure from the casualty insurance lobby amended the bill by a vote of twenty-nine to nine, allowing employers to insure with any stock or mutual insurance company, despite strong opposition to the amendment from labor unions. Asher (1969, 471–72) claims that the insurance lobby would have blocked any further action if the amendment had not been included. After the *Ives* case in 1911 had declared New York's 1910 hazardous workers' compensation bill unconstitutional, legislatures were sensitive to the courts' treatment of workers' compensation legislation. The legislature stayed in session long enough to receive the Massachusetts Supreme Judicial Court's favorable opinion on the bill.

Asher (1969) claims that the 1911 Massachusetts legislature enacted more labor legislation than in any previous period, including an eight-hour act for public employees, a fifty-four-hour law for women and minors, and a moderate anti-injunction law. Organized labor, in tandem with the relatively progressive legislature, was able to reach a compromise with employers so that the workers' compensation law would offer about the average benefits for the period. On the other hand, labor's attempts to eliminate casualty insurance were overcome by a relatively strong insurance lobby.

5.4   New York and the Role of the Courts

Robert Wesser (1971) and Robert Asher (1971) show that the process of adopting workers' compensation in New York involved political infighting and compromise both within and across interest groups. Such a finding is common for most states, so rather than summarize their discussions here, we focus our attention on the role the New York Court of Appeals played in influencing workers' compensation across the nation.

New York led the way for broad-based workers' compensation laws. In 1910, after substantial debate, New York adopted two versions of workers' compensation: a compulsory law for extrahazardous occupations and a voluntary law for all firms. In January 1911 a lower court decision had supported the constitutionality of the compulsory law. On 23 March 1911, however, New York's highest court unanimously declared the compulsory law for hazardous employment to be unconstitutional in *Ives v. South Buffalo Ry. Co.* (124 N.Y.S. 920 [1911]). The court held that "compulsory compensation for all injuries, regardless of fault, imposed on employers a 'liability unknown to the common law,' which 'constituted a deprivation of liberty and property' under the due process clauses of the New York Constitution and the Fourteenth Amendment" (Asher 1971, 361; see also U.S. Bureau of Labor 1911, 110).

New York still had the voluntary law in place after the court decision. Workers and employers could sign workers' compensation contracts with benefit levels similar to those established under the compulsory law. Few employers and workers seemed interested in the voluntary law, however, partly because there were high costs to registering the contracts and partly because they anticipated that a compulsory law might soon be enacted. By July 1913 only one firm had consented to a voluntary agreement and only 38 of their 440 employees had signed contracts. The administrative costs of setting up the voluntary contracts were prohibitive because the employer and each employee had to sign and submit written agreements to the county clerk, which was a far more cumbersome system than the standard methods of election in later workers' compensation laws (Clark 1914, 116–17).

The supporters of workers' compensation focused their efforts on obtaining a constitutional amendment to allow a compulsory workers' compensation law. They tried to pass an amendment in 1911 after the *Ives* decision was announced, but with the limited time available the various supporters could not agree on an amendment before the end of the session. By 1912, the leading labor, employer, and insurance groups were pressing for a constitutional amendment. Five bills were proposed to the legislature. The New York State Federation of Labor (NYSFL) pressed for an amendment that would have required employers to insure through a state fund and that would have also established state old-age and sickness insurance plans. Insurers, the New York Manufacturers' Association, and other employers, in contrast, pressed for the Bayne-Phillips compromise amendment, which would allow the state to make workers' compensation compulsory but did not require employers to insure with a state fund. The New York Association for Labor Legislation (NYALL) decided not to support the NYSFL amendment because they believed that an amendment requiring state insurance and old-age and health insurance would not be supported by the electorate. The Bayne-Phillips amendment passed the legislature in 1912 and in 1913 and was overwhelmingly approved by the electorate in fall of 1913 (Asher 1971, 565).

Throughout 1913 there had been substantial debates about other details relating to workers' compensation. As in other states, labor pressed for state insurance and high benefits, while employers and insurers pressed for lower benefits and the inclusion of private insurers in the system. An attempt at a compromise during May's regular session failed. Finally, after the compulsory amendment was passed in fall 1913, a special session was called. Democrats who had lost their majority for the upcoming legislature wanted to insure the passage of workers' compensation. Governor Martin Glynn strongly supported the more liberal workers' compensation, and the NYSFL and the NYALL had decided that it was futile to bar the insurance companies from the system. As a result, the compromise legislation with high benefits and allowing for both state and private insurance was passed in December 1913 (Asher 1971, 565–93).

Although the *Ives* decision slowed the ultimate adoption of a compulsory law in New York, it did not slow the adoption of workers' compensation in most other states. The decision in the case was handed down in the middle of the legislative sessions for a number of states that adopted workers' compensation in 1911. After *Ives,* Washington went ahead and adopted its own compulsory workers' compensation law, which the Washington Supreme Court later declared constitutional on the grounds that the law was a reasonable regulation that corrected an existing "evil" (U.S. Bureau of Labor Statistics 1913b, 78). In Massachusetts the 1911 legislature submitted the bill to the supreme court for a ruling before passing it (ibid., 76). The solution to the problem in the vast majority of states was the same as that followed by the Ohio legislature, described above. Most states altered the proposed workers' compensation bill to allow employers to choose whether to join the workers' compensation system. Those that did not elect workers' compensation, however, gave up the assumption of risk, fellow servant, and contributory negligence defenses in negligence liability suits. States like Ohio and California later adopted constitutional amendments that allowed them to move from elective to compulsory statutes.

5.5 Minnesota

In Minnesota there was early agreement among employers, workers, and lawyers on support for workers' compensation. However, disagreements between the interest groups over the details of the legislation led Minnesota's employers' liability commission to follow other states in proposing multiple bills to the legislature. The disagreements across interest groups were matched by disagreements among the factions within each interest group. The internal disagreements slowed the adoption of workers' compensation by two years. Within the labor movement the battle was over whether to try to obtain labor's optimal bill on the first try, or to try to establish the principle of workers' compensation and then work on amending the key features later. After extensive legislative struggles, the Minnesota State Federation of Labor (MnSFL) followed the latter strategy. They agreed to support a bill that favored employers, on the grounds that it was important to obtain workers' compensation. They then proceeded to press for amendments over the next decade.[19]

By 1909 workers, employers, and lawyers began to unite in their efforts to adopt workers' compensation legislation. In December 1908 a group of eleven employers met to form the Minnesota Employers' Association (MEA) because of the increased threat of their losing the common law defenses in personal injury lawsuits.[20] The MEA set a favorable tone for the coming debate, arguing that workers' compensation would provide injured workers with quick remuneration without expensive litigation, while keeping the employers' accident costs stable. The MEA suggested that organized labor, the Minnesota State Bar Association (MSBA), and employers join together in presenting a unified argument before the legislature.

In January 1909 the central players in the effort to enact workers' compensation met for five hours in the Commissioner of Labor's office to decry the "inhuman method" of accident compensation that prevailed in Minnesota.[21] George M. Gillette, president of the MEA, William McEwen, Minnesota's Commissioner of Labor and Secretary-Treasurer of the MnSFL, representatives of various railroad brotherhoods, and Hugh Mercer, the chairman of the MSBA's special committee on workers' compensation, developed a united course of action during the meeting. They filed a formal petition with Governor John A. Johnson, requesting him to seek legislation to establish a nonpartisan, three-person commission to investigate the employers' liability system and to present workers' compensation proposals to the 1911 legislature.[22] Gillette of the MEA and McEwen of the MnSFL agreed that all efforts to secure workers' compensation would be channeled through the proposed commission. McEwen made a "gentleman's agreement" with Gillette that organized labor would discontinue their efforts to amend the employers' liability laws. The MnSFL's unambiguous goal was now workers' compensation.[23]

After some debate over who would select the three-man commission, the 1909 legislature granted the governor's request for a commission and legislation requiring employers to report industrial accidents to the Department of Labor and Industries.[24] The governor made the obvious choice of William McEwen, George Gillette, and Hugh Mercer, who were clearly the leaders of the workers' compensation movement in Minnesota.[25] Translating their mutual dissatisfaction with the traditional negligence system into a workable compensation system proved more difficult than the three commission members had originally thought. The commission members' interests split, with labor leader McEwen and attorney Mercer agreeing on one form of legislation while Gillette formulated his own plan. Furthermore, whatever mutual respect McEwen and Gillette had for one another at the beginning of the commission's work had by late 1910 become strained.[26]

Gillette refused to join the majority for three primary reasons. First, the majority bill would have made workers' compensation compulsory for all employers. Gillette (1911a) argued that the compulsory feature of the law was likely to be unconstitutional; therefore, he offered the same alternative adopted in Ohio and many other states, making the law elective in fact, but nearly compulsory in practice because any employer who opted out of the system would have been stripped of the three common law defenses.

Second, the majority bill required employers to pay full medical coverage for the first two weeks of injury, up to one hundred dollars. Gillette claimed that no matter how minor the accident, hospitals and doctors would prescribe treatment in order to extract the full one hundred dollar benefit. Therefore, his bill specified that an employer was only required to furnish "reasonable medical and surgical first aid." Third, Gillette sought to reduce employers' insurance costs. His bill offered the same waiting period, the same percentage of wage replacement, and the same time frame for disbursement as the majority bill. However, he sought to cap an employer's liability for a single accident, like a mine explosion, at fifty thousand dollars. To reduce employers' insurance costs, Gillette further recommended that employees contribute 20 percent of the cost of the insurance, not exceeding 1 percent of the workers' wages.[27] With such widespread disagreement among the interest groups that supposedly wanted workers' compensation the most, the legislature failed to pass any compensation law in the 1911 session.[28]

It was not only because of divisions among interest groups that workers' compensation did not fare well in the 1911 legislature, but also because of disagreements within the respective interest groups. On the employers' side, the MEA decided not to support Gillette's version of the bill because of "diversity of opinion on the subject."[29] A similar split developed within organized labor. McEwen discovered that his own advisory group of fifty labor leaders was dissatisfied with the benefits in the bill that he and Mercer had proposed.[30] McEwen argued that the best strategy was to get some form of workers' compensation and amend it later to obtain higher benefits, but the MnSFL refused to support McEwen's bill unless the benefits were raised. The railroad brotherhoods, in both 1911 and 1913, wanted the negligence liability status quo since they were doing relatively well under the common law.[31] Yet another bill, pertaining to dangerous industries, was proposed by organized labor's legal counsel, Minnesota Supreme Court justice Thomas D. O'Brien. O'Brien's bill gave a worker the choice, after a workplace injury had occurred, between accepting workers' compensation or pursuing a negligence claim against his employer, who could not invoke assumption of risk and fellow servant defenses and was allowed only a modified version of the contributory negligence defense.[32] Employers ardently opposed this bill because, as we note in chapter 4, it defeated one of the primary purposes for employer support of workers' compensation.[33] They still would have to pay workers' compensation benefits to the vast majority of injured workers, no matter who was at fault. Meanwhile, they also would be forced to pay large sums to defend against the negligence suits filed by workers who thought they could get higher benefits through a negligence claim.

With such widespread disagreement among and within the key interest groups, the legislature failed to pass any compensation law in the 1911 session. By late 1912, however, employers and labor representatives had agreed upon a course of action for the 1913 legislative session. The MEA proposed a law that closely resembled New Jersey's law, which had been enacted in 1911 and declared constitutional.[34] The Bar Association continued its support of the commission's majority bill from 1911 which made coverage compulsory, but organized labor was willing to join the employers in supporting the New Jersey law because it was seen as "a fair law and guarantees adequate protection at the minimum of cost."[35] Although the New Jersey law was elective in nature, 90 to 95 percent of the employers were choosing the new system because if they refused the law, they would have been stripped of their common law defenses in a negligence suit.[36]

While employers and labor representatives had agreed on a bill in principle, several aspects of the bill that employers had written posed serious threats to its passage. Various factions within organized labor adamantly opposed four provisions: authorizing employers to pass 20 percent of the insurance costs directly onto workers; a clause allowing for compensation only if the worker was not "willfully negligent" at the time he was injured; a lower set of benefits for the dependents of injured workers living outside the United States; and a provision allowing benefits to be paid in a lump sum without court supervision.[37] Labor was also dissatisfied with the level of benefits offered in the MEA-sponsored bill, suggesting instead that maximum weekly benefits for death and permanent disability be increased from ten to fifteen dollars, the length of benefits increased from 300 to 333 weeks, and the overall maximum benefit boosted from three thousand to five thousand dollars.[38]

Internal conflicts within organized labor continued as the employers' proposed law, which mimicked the low benefits from the New Jersey law of 1911, worked its way through the 1913 legislature. While the MEA and the MnSFL had essentially agreed to set aside their dispute with one another in order to enact a workers' compensation law, a feud within the labor movement grew more heated as the bill reached a final vote in the Senate. The MnSFL and the St. Paul Trades and Labor Assembly (SPTLA) took the position that in order for the principle of workers' compensation to be introduced in Minnesota, sacrifices had to be made. Without compromising their principles—such as having industry bear the de jure full cost of the insurance and the removal of all notions of negligence—the MnSFL was willing to accept lower benefits in the short term, but with the full expectation of amending the law in future legislatures.[39] The low benefits that the MnSFL was willing to accept, however, incited calls that they were "selling out the cause of the workers to their employers."[40] The two most vocal opponents of the compensation bill were the railroad brotherhoods, who were concerned that the new law would preempt their rights under the Federal Employers' Liability Acts of 1906 and

1908, and the Minneapolis Trades and Labor Assembly (MTLA).[41] The MTLA called the proposed bill the "most outrageous piece of legislation attempted to be passed against the interests of the working people of the state" and they "deplore[d] the fact that certain representatives of labor seemed to be satisfied with anything the employers handed them."[42] The SPTLA scolded the MTLA for favoring the "upper class of workers" with its attempt to secure very generous benefit levels immediately: "Shame on such selfishness! If this is unionism and fraternity the less we have of it the better." Like the MnSFL, the SPTLA believed that "half a loaf is better than no bread at all."[43]

The marked-up bill that emerged from the Senate Labor Committee eliminated farm labor and domestic servants from coverage, raised the minimum weekly benefit from five to six dollars, guaranteed foreign and domestic dependents the same schedule of benefits, eliminated any insurance contributions by workers, and removed the "willful negligence" clause. As a compromise, the MEA agreed to the minimum compensation and worker contribution amendments, but not the others.[44] Instead of allowing the labor committee's amendments to delay the passage of workers' compensation any further, however, the MEA decided to take no further action to hinder the bill's progress in the legislature. Gillette finally conceded that the Senate bill was "a satisfactory one and the best that could be obtained."[45]

Despite the opposition of some labor groups, some employers, and "ambulance chasing lawyers," workers' compensation passed the Senate unanimously.[46] As the bill moved to the House, "one of the most interesting fights ever witnessed in the legislature" ensued.[47] For six hours Representative Ernest Lundeen, a Republican and avid supporter of labor issues, cheered on by labor representatives and socialists sitting in the gallery, proposed a litany of labor-supported amendments that effectively served as a filibuster.[48] "Isn't it a travesty on justice to ask you to pass this measure ostensibly for the benefit of the workingmen but urged by the big employers of the state?" Lundeen asked rhetorically.[49] Lundeen and representatives from districts that were more heavily unionized were able to secure five amendments to the Senate's bill, but only two significantly affected the compensation that workers would have received if injured: (1) if workers were disabled for more than thirty days, they were to be retroactively compensated for the first two weeks of not receiving benefits because of the waiting period, and (2) an increase in the medical benefits from $100 to $195. In fact, the House had rejected an amendment to raise the medical benefits to $200, but in an effort to shutdown Lundeen's attacks on the bill, labor leader McEwen was able to orchestrate support for the $195 maximum. Two other important amendments failed to pass—an increase in the weekly benefits from $10 to $15 and the exclusion of all (not just interstate) railroad workers from coverage.[50] The House passed the workers' compensation bill, with its amendments, by an overwhelming 102 to 6.[51]

The benefit levels established by Minnesota in 1913 were relatively low, ranking near the bottom among the states that had adopted workers' compensation by that year (see tables 3.1, B.1–B.4). Because the law provided such minimal benefits, the MTLA concluded that "the compensation law really is a joke, if a pathetic one."[52] McEwen admitted that the "new Workingmen's Compensation law falls far short of our ideal . . . yet . . . it was the very best that could have been passed."[53]

Although the MnSFL (1913, 68) officials were pleased to finally establish workers' compensation as the first phase of their long-term strategy, they soon began phase two. They sought and eventually succeeded in obtaining amendments to the law that would raise Minnesota's benefit levels over the next few years.[54] Meanwhile, they stated emphatically that "no satisfactory solution to the question of workingmen's compensation can be had except through the medium of state insurance."[55] The debates over state insurance are described more fully in the next chapter.

5.6 Missouri

The sixteen-year struggle for the adoption of workers' compensation in Missouri vividly illustrates the importance of political institutions to the successful enactment of public policy. The referendum and initiative mechanism that existed in Missouri created an additional institutional hurdle that the workers' compensation law had to clear. Not only did the relevant interest groups have to agree on a legislative outcome, but so did the electorate. Thus, opponents of workers' compensation, anticipating that whatever emerged from the legislature would have to meet the approval of voters, sought to saddle the legislative bills with amendments that would undermine their chances of success in a referendum. The adoption process in Missouri illustrates how the details of even very popular legislation can be shaped by the political process. Finally, as in Minnesota, disagreements internal to broad interest groups also contributed to the delay in adoption of the law. In fact, the internal struggle within organized labor over the details of workers' compensation in Minnesota pale in comparison with what happened in Missouri.[56]

The impetus for workers' compensation in Missouri came in 1910 when the governor appointed a commission to investigate the workings of the employers' liability system and the feasibility of a workers' compensation law. The commission prepared an employers' liability measure for the 1911 session, which was subsequently killed in the House judiciary committee, and requested that the legislature create its own investigative commission. The General Assembly's 1911 commission, with the mandate to report a bill to the 1913 legislature, included legislators from both chambers and citizens representing organized labor, manufacturing, insurance, and financial interests. Since employer and labor representatives could not strike a compromise—labor asking for unlimited benefits and state insurance and employers asking for the exact opposite—no serious legislation was introduced in 1913. The Senate therefore appointed another commission that was to report to the 1915 legislature. The commission held months of hearings and traveled to several states. In the end they proposed that Missouri enact an elective workers' compensation act, establish an industrial commission, provide for private mutual insurance, and impose a 5 percent tax on insurance premiums to support the industrial commission (Missouri Bureau of Labor Statistics [MBLS] 1918–1920, 206). Although the Senate proposal received a favorable recommendation from the insurance committee, the whole chamber never acted upon the bill. The Missouri State Federation of Labor (MoSFL) and manufacturing interests could agree that workers' compensation in principle was worth pursuing, but the groups could not agree on the particulars of a law. The 1915 session ended with no legislation because the parties disagreed on the levels of accident payments, waiting periods, whether occupational disease should be covered, and organized labor's central goal, state insurance (MBLS 1918–1920, 206).

After two legislative sessions without a compromise with employers, Missouri's main unions began to split. In 1917 both the MoSFL and the St. Louis Building Trades Council (SLBTC) presented separate bills before the legislature and a third measure presented by a group of employers was "refuted by organized labor" (MBLS 1918–1920, 187). With divisions deepening between organized labor and employers and within labor, the session ended with the legislature far from a compromise compensation law.

Realizing that their efforts to adopt a workers' compensation law favorable to them were diminished if they did not present a united front, the two major organized labor groups tried to reach a consensus at the MoSFL's annual convention in 1918. After three days of negotiations with no settlement, the MoSFL, the SLBTC, and the Kansas City Building Trades Council (KCBTC) empowered a special compensation committee to draft a bill for the 1919 legislature (MBLS 1918–1920, 188). The special committee not only included representatives from the SLBTC, the KCBTC, and the MoSFL, but also the Commissioner of the Missouri Bureau of Labor Statistics William H. Lewis and his Supervisor of Statistics A. T. Edmonston (MBLS 1918–1920, 188). What became known as the "Labor Bill" contained organized labor's main objectives: a monopoly state insurance fund and generous maximum benefits, in this case they asked for no ceiling (MBLS 1918–1920, 204).[57]

In 1919 the House passed an amended version of the Labor Bill, imposing an eighteen-dollar weekly maximum, but keeping the state insurance feature intact. The House bill was subsequently killed in the Senate Workmen's Compensation Committee and two efforts by senators sympathetic to the MoSFL to place the bill on the calendar failed. The Senate then passed its own bill (actually a committee substitute bill), which was later adopted by the House and signed by the governor. The Senate bill was much more amenable to employers' interests, placing a maximum of fifteen dollars on weekly benefits and eliminating public insurance.

MoSFL president R. T. Wood claimed that when the Senate bill arrived in the House "if the bill had been amended by the dotting of an 'i' or the crossing of a 't' it would have been killed by an adverse committee upon its return to the Senate. The only possible chance to pass a compensation law at this session was to pass the substitute through the House without amendment." Wood reasoned that if state insurance and high benefits were not politically feasible, then the goal should be to get the best workers' compensation bill possible and to seek prolabor amendments in subsequent legislation. He assured the SLBTC and the KCBTC that "we [MoSFL] stood by the building trades people in a last-ditch fight which almost resulted in the defeat of all compensation measures by the Legislature. We could at any time have obtained the passage of a bill acceptable to the other labor interests of the State, but we fought with the building trades to the last. After the fight had failed and we began a last desperate struggle to get compensation on the statutes, they deserted us instantly and made an open fight on the floor of the House against the passage of the Senate substitute. They were defeated and the bill was passed almost unanimously."[58]

The building trades adhered to an all-or-nothing strategy, either workers' compensation with state insurance and high maximum benefits or no law at all. The building trades and some other union elements, in fact, joined damage-suit attorneys, who clearly had an interest in striking down workers' compensation, in circulating a petition to put the legislative act before the voters in a November 1920 referendum.[59] The strategy was successful. Voters rejected the 1919 workers' compensation law by a close 52.2 to 47.8 percent margin.[60]

By 1921 in Missouri, the MoSFL, the Associated Industries of Missouri (AIM), and other employer organizations were cooperating for the passage of another workers' compensation law.[61] The act that was ultimately adopted had many similarities to the one enacted in 1919, but it added a state fund to compete with private insurance and raised the weekly maximum benefit from fifteen to twenty dollars. The damage-suit lawyers in concert with the building trades councils again forced a referendum. Missouri voters once again struck down workers' compensation by a comfortable margin, 55.2 to 44.8 percent. The lawyers also added an initiative to the ballot that would have abolished the fellow servant defense, substituted comparative negligence for contributory negligence, and left assumption of risk up to the jury.[62] Moreover, if accepted, the initiative would have repealed the 1921 legislative act if both measures passed in the November 1922 referendum (MBLS 1921–1922, 936). Voters, however, soundly defeated the lawyers' alternative (79.9 to 20.1 percent).

The inclusion of state insurance, which helped kill the law in the referendum, was actually a last-minute floor amendment that was widely supported by opponents of workers' compensation. By 1921 legislators could expect that any legislative act would be challenged in a referendum. Thus, by saddling workers' compensation with state insurance, which voters opposed, the opponents hoped to ensure the law's defeat at the polls. In an analysis of the roll-call voting on the state insurance amendment in the House of Representatives, we found that members of the Committee of Commerce and Manufactories, which was dominated by agricultural interests, and representatives whose districts supported the damage-suit attorneys' initiative were more likely to support the state insurance amendment (see Kantor and Fishback 1994a, 288–91).

By 1923 the AIM was claiming that employers' liability was reaching a crisis, with some insurance companies actually pulling out of Missouri. Despite the impetus for workers' compensation, the General Assembly failed to enact new workers' compensation legislation in the 1923 session.[63] Lindley Clark (1925, 602) reported in the *Monthly Labor Review* that the chances of legislation were wrecked by organized labor's demands for an exclusive state insurance system. Despite its losses in the legislature, the MoSFL managed to put an initiative on the November 1924 ballot that included organized labor's demands without compromise: an exclusive state insurance fund and maximum weekly benefit levels of thirty dollars, double the maximum benefits in neighboring Illinois and Kansas.[64]

The AIM and other industry groups actively opposed labor's proposal, sending out two million pieces of literature and placing advertisements in five hundred newspapers and magazines.[65] Opponents urged support from a wide range of interests. Since benefits were set so high, they argued that manufacturers would leave St. Louis and Kansas City for neighboring states.[66] Since labor's proposal would have required firms with as few as two employees to insure, AIM gained support from small business owners who otherwise might not have been directly involved in workers' compensation. Finally, and probably with most success, opponents appealed to the taxpayer since organized labor proposed setting up an expensive commission of five members with salaries of $6,000 each, creating a monopoly state insurance fund, and appropriating more than $4 million to start it.[67] Not surprisingly, the initiative was soundly defeated, 72.6 to 27.4 percent.

Organized labor's resounding defeat in 1924 and employers' increasing urgency to adopt a workers' compensation law led to a compromise in the 1925 legislative session (Clark 1925, 602).[68] The 1925 act was among the more liberal laws at the time. No other state's accident benefits exceeded the 1925 act's two-thirds of the wage, and its twenty dollars per week payment ceiling was higher than ceilings in neighboring Kansas and Illinois. The generous benefit ceiling put Missouri fifth (tied with six others) among all workers' compensation states, while its three-day waiting period tied Missouri for third among the states (U.S. Bureau of Labor Statistics 1926a, 23, 26). Without state insurance, the bill also gained support from the insurance industry. The bill was designed to build a winning coalition on other margins as well. The number of commissioners was cut, as were their salaries, and public employees were covered under the law only if individual municipalities decided so (U.S. Bureau of Labor Statistics 1925b, 1329–30). Thus, the general public's worries about paying more taxes for a larger bureaucracy or an insolvent state insurance fund were assuaged. With these concerns addressed, the electorate supported workers' compensation in Missouri by a more than two-to-one margin.

5.7 Summary

Looking at the details of how workers' compensation was actually adopted in a few representative states illustrates several common themes that emerged in the cross-state quantitative comparisons in the previous chapter. Employers, workers, and insurers all supported the general concept of workers' compensation, but harsh debates developed over specific features of the law. Employers and workers battled over the level of benefits in the law and the issue of whether workers could retain the right to choose to sue under negligence liability after they had been injured. As will be shown in the next chapter, organized labor and insurers fought harsh battles over the issue of state insurance of workers' compensation risk, with employers taking both sides of the issue.

The case studies provide some general lessons about how public policy is actually transformed from ideas into legislation. First, most legislation is complex with multiple attributes, each of which might determine a group's support or opposition to the bill. Because workers' compensation involved a complex set of parameters, opposition to legislation was usually directed at specific benefit levels or the choice between private and state insurance, and not opposition to the general concept of switching to no-fault liability. Although it is possible that interest groups might have disguised their opposition to the general concept of workers' compensation in the form of opposition to specific features of the bill, it seems unlikely that this was true. In the vast majority of states, opposing interest groups compromised relatively quickly in passing a workers' compensation law.

Second, the choices that state legislators made were framed by special interest groups in ways that cannot be determined by just examining the final version of the law. Lobbyists representing unions, employer groups, or insurers offered their ideal bills to the states' liability commissions and legislatures, but at the same time each group was staking out a claim that served as an initial point in forthcoming legislative negotiations. It was the legislators' task to then work out a series of compromises. The compromises were determined in part by the political strength of the various interest groups, but as the case studies illustrate, there were other more subtle aspects of the legislative process that dictated the ultimate shape workers' compensation would take.

Third, legislative institutions were extremely important in determining how the law emerged from the political process. The membership of the committee to which the bill was initially assigned determined not only what type of bill would come out of the committee, but also more importantly whether the bill would be passed on for the whole chamber's consideration. Both houses of the legislature and the governor all had veto power over bills, which was important during the Progressive Era because one chamber might have been more "progressive" than the other and willing to pass legislation that more aggressively reformed workplace accident compensation. For example, the Ohio Senate in 1911 and the Minnesota House in the late 1910s tended to be more supportive of the union's agenda for workers' compensation, while in the other chambers employers and insurers carried much more influence. The bills that were proposed by each of the houses reflected their respective agendas, but in order for workers' compensation to succeed politically a compromise was necessary between the two chambers. In some cases the threat of a governor's veto kept legislators on middle ground between the various interest groups. In Illinois, in fact, the governor made the ultimate choice between expanding employers' liability and establishing workers' compensation.

Fourth, although workers' compensation was widely supported because of its anticipated benefits to a broad group of interests, sometimes disputes between these very same interest groups over specific features of the legislation caused delays in its adoption. Such a finding lends support to Howitt and Wintrobe's (1995) prediction that socially beneficial legislation may not even come up for legislative consideration because each side fears it may get stuck with its opponent's favored policy. Thus, if interest groups' initial proposals were meant as a starting point in the political negotiations, these proposals may have seemed relatively "radical" and a fear that the other side was unwilling to compromise may have caused either side to push for a delay in the law's adoption. Such delays slowed the adoption of workers' compensation by two years in Minnesota and by eight in Missouri. The Missouri case is particularly unusual because even after the interest groups were able to negotiate a compromise in the legislature in 1919 (after having begun the process in 1911), the need to satisfy the electorate led to another set of delays that lasted another seven years.

Finally, the case studies caution against thinking that seemingly cohesive interest groups have the same set of objectives. In Illinois, Minnesota, and Missouri labor unions took opposing sides on the passage of workers' compensation even though all agreed that the overall idea behind the legislation was an improvement on the status quo. Closer inspection shows that the fight among unions was not truly over the general issue of workers' compensation, but actually over the optimal strategy to secure the features of the law that the unions most desired. Typically, one group took the stance that passing a basic bill without state insurance and lower benefits was necessary to get workers' compensation enacted and then it would be relatively easy to amend the bill to obtain the better benefits. The other side argued that the optimal strategy was to seek every desired feature when workers' compensation was first introduced on the grounds that amending the law would be extremely difficult later. The case studies therefore show that in examining the positions of interest groups it is often not enough to show that the new legislation is better than the status quo. It is also important to look at the groups' estimates of the feasibility of amending the legislation later. The adoption of legislation only starts the process of change in that public policy arena, as interest groups with a stake in the legislation continue to apply pressure to shape the intricate details of the law to fit their own demands. For example, when Minnesota enacted its workers' compensation law in 1913, it was among the stingiest in terms of accident benefits. Organized labor, however, was highly successful in lobbying to increase the benefits through amendments of the law later in the decade, and by 1921 the state was guaranteeing workers accident benefits that were among the most generous in the country. Because the features of the workers' compensation law were relatively controversial when the legislation was first proposed, researchers must be cautious in ascribing success or failure to particular interest groups because the law took one form or another. The initial version of the law was simply a starting point for future political wrangling and compromise.

Notes

1. We have benefited tremendously from a series of other scholars' strong case studies. See Tripp's 1976 study of Washington; Asher's 1971 study of Massachusetts, Minnesota, New York, Wisconsin, and Ohio; Reagan's 1981 and Mengert's 1920 studies of Ohio; and Castrovinci's 1976 study of Illinois.

2. For additional descriptions of the introduction of workers' compensation in Ohio, see Fishback and Kantor (1997), Asher (1971, 541–58), Reagan (1981), and Mengert (1920).

3. The OMA originated in Columbus on 10 November 1910 when a group of manufacturers met to discuss the first workers' compensation proposal in the state. Members included B. F. Goodrich, Youngstown Sheet and Tube, Republic Steel, Goodyear Tire, Jeffrey Manufacturing, Dayton Manufacturing, Mosaic Tile, Owens-Illinois Glass Co., and Columbus Iron and Steel. Ohio Manufacturers' Association *Records,* p. 2.

4. Winans (1910, 291–92) and Rohr (1910, 307–8). On organized labor's repudiation of Rohr, see *Ohio State Journal,* 23 March 1911; *Toledo Union Leader,* 24 March 1911; Byrum and Ohio State Federation of Labor, 6. Winans had been the legislative representative for the OSFL and it was discovered later that the OSFL was paying him while he was on the commission. The rest of the commission was not being compensated because the authorizing law for the commission called only for the payment of expenses. In fact, Governor Harmon had contributed five thousand dollars of his own money to pay the commission's expenses. See *Ohio State Journal,* 11 May 1911, and Nichols (1932, 145).

5. In the Senate the progressives had 11 certain votes (9 Democrats, 2 Republicans) and conservatives had 17 (5 Democrats, 12 Republicans). The remaining 6 were middle of the road. In the House there were 68 Democrats and 48 Republicans. Of this group there were 55 progressives (44 Democrats, 10 Republicans, and 1 independent), 43 conservatives (12 Democrats, 31 Republicans), and 12 Democrats and 7 republicans affiliated with neither wing. Speaker of the House Vining was a compromise candidate. The logjam of progressive legislation was broken on 1 May 1911 when bribery charges were filed against some of the most conservative members. See Warner (1964, 266–75, 282–83).

6. Ohio Manufacturers' Association *Records,* Secretary's Report, November 1911; Ohio House of Representatives *Journal* (1911, 399).

7. Ohio Manufacturers' Association *Records,* Secretary's Report, November 1911; Ohio House of Representatives *Journal* (1911, 541).

8. *Ohio State Journal,* 23 March 1911, and Ohio Senate *Journal* (1911, 288).

9. *Ohio State Journal,* 18 April 1911, and *Cleveland Federationist,* 20 April 1911.

10. *Ohio State Journal,* 29 March and 18 April 1911, and *Cleveland Federationist,* 30 March 1911.

11. Mengert (1920, 12) claims that Harmon wrote these clauses. See also Ohio House of Representatives *Journal* (1911, 797–800); *Toledo News-Bee,* 19 April 1911; *Ohio State Journal,* 20 and 28 April 1911; and *Cleveland Plain Dealer,* 28 April 1911.

12. *Cleveland Plain Dealer,* 28 April 1911. See also Ohio House of Representatives *Journal* (1911, 846–52); *Ohio State Journal,* 28 April 1911; and *Toledo News-Bee,* 28 April 1911.

13. Ohio Manufacturers' Association *Records,* Secretary's Report, November 1911.

14. Mengert (1920, 14).

15. For a detailed description of the adoption process in Illinois, see Castrovinci (1976).

16. In 1905 the Illinois railroad safety appliance law restricted the railroads' assumption of risk and contributory negligence defenses. More specifically, if a worker was injured because the employer did not comply with the safety law, and the employee knew of the violation, the employer could not invoke the assumption of risk defense. This law was only applicable to railroad workers (Clark 1908, 60).

17. The Chamber of Commerce committee was led by Edward Filene and other leaders from Boston and Maine Railroad, Simplex Electrical Co., Boston Consolidated Gas, and the Chase and Harriman Bank. Support was not uniform within the Chamber. Frederick Fish opposed workers' compensation and sought to delay the Chamber of Commerce's endorsement of any specific proposal (see Asher 1969).

18. The material on Massachusetts summarizes Asher's 1969 research.

19. For more detailed descriptions of the adoption process in Minnesota, see Kantor and Fishback (1998) and Asher (1971, 1973).

20. The stated goals of the MEA were threefold: to work for the prevention

of workplace accidents; to work toward the adoption of accident compensation legislation that would benefit both employer and employee; and to oppose class legislation. See MEA, 14 December 1908, and *Minneapolis Journal,* 18 December 1908.

21. Minnesota House of Representatives (1909, 13–14).

22. They also requested that the governor propose a bill to require all employers to submit accident statistics to the state Department of Labor so that the commission could have as much information as possible about the industrial accident situation in the state. For a first-hand account of the momentous meeting, see Minnesota House of Representatives (1909, 13–14). See also MnSFL (1909, 20–21); MEA, 11 January 1909; *Minneapolis Journal,* 25 and 28 January 1909; and the "Petition." The signatories to the petition (p. 3), both employer and labor representatives, believed in the superiority of workers' compensation: "shifting the financial risk as a certainty upon the employer, like other expenses of the business, and relieving him of the hazardous uncertainties and expenses incident to present methods of defense, would leave both parties and the State in reasonably satisfactory condition without imposing upon the employer that degree of taxation which would either tend to drive industries from, or keep them out of, this State as a result."

23. Minnesota House of Representatives (1909, 20). Both Gillette and McEwen gushed about their pathbreaking agreement. Testifying before the Labor Committee of the Minnesota House of Representatives in February 1909, Gillette boasted that for "the first time in any state in the Union . . . representatives of employers and representatives of employes . . . have come together and in calm, fair, dispassionate discussion, have attempted to solve a problem which, to my mind, is the most pressing problem before the people of Minnesota." McEwen was no less sanguine: "For the first time in human history . . . the representatives of the employing and the working classes met together in full, free and fair conference . . . and came to a harmonious and unanimous conclusion concerning what was the best thing to do toward removing prevailing hardships and existing evils" in the common law rules governing workplace accident compensation. Minnesota House of Representatives (1909, 29–30) and MnSFL (1909, 20).

24. Letters between the Labor and Industries Department and Minnesota employers show conclusively that the Department took its responsibility of investigating accidents in the state very seriously. A clipping department within the Department scoured the state's newspapers looking for evidence of industrial accidents. If they found a mention of the accident, without receiving notification from the company, a letter of inquiry was generated. In some cases if a firm did not send any information about accidents, an incredulous letter was sent out. For example, on 29 September 1911 Labor Commissioner Houk sent a letter to the Parker and Topping Foundry asking "Can it be possible that no accidents have occurred in that length of time [year ending 31 July 1911] to the people in the employ of said company?" See Minnesota Department of Labor and Industries, Insurance Compensation Correspondence.

25. Although Gillette (1911c, 174, 180) worried about "the danger of injecting . . . a paternalistic and socialistic feature" into the workers' compensation system, he believed that "laws properly framed and intending to do equal justice will probably do more good than breaking down of precedents will do harm." As the president of the MEA, Gillette saw accident reduction as one of the motivating factors producing the mutual cooperation between employers and their workers. As the spokesman for labor interests, McEwen (1911, 168) stood on relatively conservative ground by today's standards: "True progress will consist in the equilibrium

between obtaining the greatest benefits for the largest number of injured workingmen and affecting the least injury to industry." "You must never kill the goose that lays the golden egg; don't do anything to injure capital," McEwen warned Minnesota's workers. See Minnesota House of Representatives (1909, 15) and MnSFL (1910, 22).

26. Speaking before the Minnesota Academy of Social Sciences in December 1910, Gillette (1911c, 175) indicated the fractionalization occurring within the commission and set the tone for the debate to occur in the 1911 legislature: "My own conclusion . . . is that it will be impossible to frame an act in a fair degree satisfactory to the employers and providing reasonably adequate compensation to injured employes or they dependents. . . ." See also *Minneapolis Journal,* 3 December 1910.

27. See Gillette (1911b) for his view of how the Gillette bill differed from that of his colleagues. See also *Minneapolis Journal,* 12 and 17 February 1911, and *Labor World,* 24 February 1911. F. G. Winston, the "head of one of the largest railroad and stripping [sic] contract concerns in the west," argued that a one hundred dollar medical allowance would "create a class of 'ambulance-chasing physicians' to take the place of lawyers." See *Minneapolis Journal,* 24 February 1911. See also *Minneapolis Journal,* 1 February 1911.

28. *Minneapolis Journal,* 2 April 1911.

29. MEA, 14 December 1911.

30. *Labor World,* 4 March 1911; MnSFL (1909, 21); and *Minneapolis Journal,* 5 February 1911.

31. *Labor World,* 25 March 1911.

32. *Labor World,* 8 February 1911, and *Minneapolis Journal,* 23 February 1911.

33. *Minneapolis Journal,* 24 February 1911.

34. MEA, 2 and 16 August 1912, and *Minneapolis Journal,* 14 October 1912.

35. *Minneapolis Journal,* 1 December 1912. Reports from William E. Stubbs, secretary of New Jersey's Employers' Liability Commission, heartened labor leaders. Stubbs concluded that his state's law was functioning relatively smoothly as 94 percent of the workers entitled to benefits were receiving them. See letter from Stubbs to Houk, 21 March 1912, in Minnesota Department of Labor and Industries, Insurance Compensation Correspondence.

36. *Minneapolis Journal,* 14 October 1912.

37. *Minneapolis Journal,* 3, 8, and 31 December 1912; *Labor World,* 28 December 1912 and 18 January 1913; *Minnesota Union Advocate,* 10 January 1913; and MnSFL (1913, 36, 67–68). See also MEA, 2 December 1912.

38. *Labor World,* 18 January 1913, and MnSFL (1913, 68).

39. *Labor World,* 19 April 1913; MnSFL (1913, 36–37); and Railroad Brotherhoods (1912–1913, 22). The *Minneapolis Journal,* 10 April 1913, made the same plea to its readers: ". . . pass the bill and get the system started. It can be perfected better after it is in operation than by laying aside the whole matter for another two years, while the extremists on both sides quarrel about terms."

40. MnSFL (1913, 19).

41. *Labor World,* 15 March 1915.

42. *Labor Review,* 11 and 18 April 1913.

43. *Labor Review,* 14 March 1913. For a summary of the internal fight within the labor movement, see Lawson (1955, 217).

44. MEA, 28 February 1913. See also *Labor World,* 1 March 1913.

45. MEA, 17 March 1913 and 7 April 1913.

46. MnSFL (1913, 19); *Minneapolis Journal,* 4 April 1913; and Minnesota Senate *Journal* (1913, 1156–61).

47. *Labor World,* 19 April 1913.

48. Biographical information on Lundeen is from Minnesota Secretary of State (1913, 664).

49. *Minneapolis Journal,* 12 April 1913.

50. Minnesota House of Representatives *Journal* (1913, 1624–31) and *Minneapolis Journal,* 12 April 1913.

51. Minnesota House of Representatives *Journal* (1913, 1630–31). The Senate did not agree to the House's amendments and a conference committee was organized. Of the two most important amendments that the House enacted, the House agreed to recede from the retroactive benefits for injuries lasting longer than thirty days and a revised medical benefits amendment was written. Instead of providing workers with a maximum of $195 in medical benefits over an extended time period, the new amendment provided up to $100 during the first ninety days of the injury, but the courts could order an additional $100 of medical benefits. See Minnesota Senate *Journal* (1913, 1649–53).

52. *Labor Review,* 25 April 1913.

53. MnSFL (1913, 36; 1914, 27).

54. For more details on this process, see Kantor and Fishback (1998).

55. MnSFL (1913, 68).

56. For more details and statistical analysis of the adoption process in Missouri, see Kantor and Fishback (1994a).

57. Rube T. Wood of the MoSFL claimed that the monopolistic insurance and no maximum payment limit was insisted upon by the SLBTC (*St. Louis Post-Dispatch,* 29 April 1919). The SLBTC's opposition to private insurance is best summarized in statements made by Maurice Cassidy, the Secretary of the SLBTC: "Inexperienced persons who would be entitled to compensation will have to deal with trained insurance claim agents, whose reputations for dishonorable dealings are world-wide. After they brow-beat the claimants into accepting what they have to offer, these claim-adjusters, posing as the employers, will get the claimant to sign the settlement papers" (*Trades Council Union News,* 29 October 1920). For the MoSFL's views regarding how state insurance cut transactions costs, see MoSFL (1918).

58. *St. Louis Post-Dispatch,* 29 April 1919.

59. After the petition was filed, the Missouri Secretary of State, MoSFL president R. T. Wood, other labor leaders, insurance men, and corporation lawyers who favored the new law instituted court proceedings in the Jefferson City Circuit Court to have the referendum set aside. The lower court sustained their motion. However, the referendum supporters appealed to the state supreme court, which reversed the lower court and ordered the referendum to proceed (MBLS 1918–1920, 892).

60. The workers' compensation law was supported by the Republican candidate Hyde, who won the election (*St. Louis Post-Dispatch,* 31 October 1930). The Republicans also achieved the "impossible," their first majority in the Senate (*Kansas City Star,* 4 November 1920).

61. *Kansas City Star,* 6 November 1922; *St. Louis Post-Dispatch,* 25 March 1921.

62. *St. Louis Post-Dispatch* 6 November 1922, and *Trades Council Union News,* 13 October 1922.

63. Associated Industries of Missouri, Bulletin Nos. 150, 169, 185.

64. Kansas had a weekly maximum of fifteen dollars, while Illinois' weekly maximum was fourteen dollars (U.S. Bureau of Labor Statistics, 1926b, 23, 26). Clark's view on the issue is supported by statistical analysis of the referendum voting. See Kantor and Fishback (1994a, 276–87).

65. Associated Industries of Missouri, Bulletin Nos. 191 and 197.

66. Associated Industries of Missouri, Bulletin No. 177.

67. See Clark (1925, 602); *St. Louis Post-Dispatch,* 29 October 1924; and *Kansas City Star,* 2 November 1924.

68. Views on the probability of ever passing a workers' compensation law varied widely at the beginning of 1925. A state labor official saw no reason why a workable workers' compensation law could not be enacted. On the other hand, the *Monthly Labor Review* received reports that the difference of opinion over the nature of the bill was so great that it would be difficult to agree upon a measure to get sufficient support for passage (Clark 1925, 602).

The Fractious Disputes over State Insurance

In adopting worker's compensation, the greatest political turmoil developed over the issue of private versus state insurance of workers' compensation risk. Although workers' compensation is often described as "social insurance," it is actually an employer mandate that a specific set of benefits be paid to the victims of workplace accidents. Employers could purchase insurance to provide these benefits, and an enormous struggle arose over the issue whether employers should purchase the insurance from private insurance companies or through a state-run fund. Union leaders pushed strongly for state insurance on the grounds that private insurers were profiting from denying benefits to many deserving injured workers. Insurers fought to save their business and charged that state insurance was a sign of creeping socialism. The choice between state and private insurance made by various state legislatures established the existing system today and set the stage for later debates over the government's underwriting of unemployment, health, and disability risks.[1] Most states allowed employers to contract with private insurers to underwrite this workplace accident risk. Seven states, however, established monopoly state insurance funds and ten more states created state funds that competed with private insurers.[2] In this chapter we examine the decision to establish state funds to underwrite workers' compensation risks at the time the legislation was first adopted.

Quantitative analysis of the legislative decisions to adopt state insurance shows that monopoly state insurance was an unlikely outcome of the general workers' compensation debate. In most states opposition from insurance companies and farmers overcame the labor unions' demands for state insurance, causing legislatures to choose private insurance. In some states the competing interest groups compromised by allowing private insurers to compete with a state fund. Monopoly state insurance was implemented if either of two conditions occurred: (1) strong labor unions were able to enact state insurance in the face of relatively weak insurance interests and agricultural interests, or (2) monopoly state insurance was swept into place when a strong political reform movement—for example, progressives in the early 1910s and nonpartisans in the late 1910s—incorporated unions' demands for state insurance into a broader program of socioeconomic changes.

The richness of the state insurance debate is captured more fully by examining the decision process in three states: Washington, Ohio, and Minnesota. In all three states narrow interest groups set the terms of the debate and influenced decisions. Meanwhile, progressive political coalitions played a major role in determining the fate of monopoly state insurance during the period from 1910 to 1920. Washington chose monopoly state insurance when workers' compensation was originally adopted in 1911, as progressive reformers within the Republican party played the predominant role in establishing monopoly state insurance. Following the implementation of a monopoly state fund in 1911, Ohio union leaders and insurance companies fought over the issue throughout the decade. After a series of court battles, referenda, administrative decisions, and subsequent legislation, the ultimate decision on the state fund's monopoly depended on the success of the Democratic party, which was the progressive reform party in Ohio. When Minnesota first enacted workers' compensation in 1913, organized labor's efforts to obtain state insurance failed because it held too little political power to overcome conservative Republicans' rejection of the idea. The Non-Partisan League, a populist coalition of farmers and organized labor, developed enough strength to reopen the issue in 1919, but without a majority in the legislature, their efforts to adopt state insurance failed by one vote in the Senate. In general, the importance of progressive reformers in establishing state insurance in several states should not be underestimated.

The chapter helps illuminate a central issue in the empirical political economy literature. Political scientists and economists have long debated whether broad-based political coalitions, such as political parties, or narrowly defined economic interest groups are the determining factor in the development of legislation. The recent analyses of the enactment of the Interstate Commerce Commission (ICC) in 1887 exemplify the polar positions that scholars have taken in their explanations of the origins of regulation. Thomas Gilligan, William Marshall, and Barry Weingast (1989) argue that the ICC was enacted as the result of a compromise between economic interest groups—the short-haul shippers and the railroads—that had a direct economic stake in the issue. Keith Poole and Howard Rosenthal (1993, 1994) claim, by contrast, that the ICC was passed by a broad political economic coalition, and that the argument for narrow economic interests as the catalyst for ICC enactment is overemphasized. The story of how state workers' compensation insurance funds came to be adopted in the 1910s emphasizes that both narrow economic interests and broader political interests determine legislative outcomes, but the importance of each factor varied from state to state. Indeed, as our research suggests, when we must take into account the importance of a political reform movement, our preconceived notions of how different interest groups stood on the issue of state insurance is upset. Thus, instead of disagreement among scholars, our analysis suggests that cooperation among the two intellectual camps will provide a much richer understanding of the growth of government over the last century.

6.1   The Debate over State Insurance

One feature of the workers' compensation system that caused bitter dispute across many states was the method by which the insurance system would be administered. In many states there was a strong movement for state insurance, in which all risks associated with the new law would be insured through newly created state funds and bureaucracies. Social reformers and labor leaders vilified the casualty insurance industry because insurers were seen as contributing to the negligence liability system's debacle. Crystal Eastman (1910), one of the leading proponents of the switch to workers' compensation in the United States, found two major faults with the insurance industry: the presence of liability insurance lowered the chances of an injured worker's receiving compensation, and the insurance industry was profiting at the expense of workers' suffering. According to Eastman (1910, 194), when an employer insured his risk through a third party, the injured worker was sure to be the loser because "the insurance company contracts only to assume the employer's legal liability, not to underwrite his moral responsibilities, or carry out the promptings of his sympathy." Further, since the insurance company was "equipped with system, money, skill, and experience," the chances of successfully suing an insured employer for damages were "formidable." We have already quoted in chapter 2 the similar conclusions reached by historian Robert Asher (1969, 464).

Reformers and historians were in fact mistaken, however, in assuming that workers always fared poorly at the hands of liability insurers. Our analysis of Michigan Bureau of Labor and Industrial Statistics data from 1897 to 1903 found that those workers who were employed by firms that carried liability insurance were just as likely to receive accident compensation as those workers whose firms had no insurance (Kantor and Fishback 1995, 429). Indeed, some companies clearly influenced how their liability insurance carriers settled claims by injured workers or their families. Consider the case of Joseph Garsaw, who was killed while working for the Northern Lumber Company (owned by the Weyerhaeuser Company) of

Cloquet, Minnesota. Northern Lumber's liability insurance company found that "[t]he case was a pure accident. There was no defect whatever in the apparatus and it would hardly seem that under the [common] law that any damage could have been collected." Thus, the insurance company offered Garsaw's widow $250 to settle the case. Northern Lumber, however, "desired an adequate payment to be made for the benefit of the widow and children," so Northern offered the deceased's family $1000 plus funeral expenses and the insurance carrier, in turn, was to raise its contribution to $500. "After talking the matter over with the widow," Northern Lumber paid $1100 plus funeral expenses and the insurance company paid $600.[3] Although Northern Lumber's insurer was not willing to fully back the company's "moral responsibilities," this case suggests that influential clients may have been able to pressure the liability insurance companies into providing the families of workers killed in industrial accidents with relatively better settlements, even though the families may have received nothing if their cases were to have gone to trial.

The insurance industry certainly understood that it had a perception problem. The "blame for the odious conditions affecting the relations between employer and employe [*sic*] under the liability laws," according to insurance industry spokesmen, lay "solely in the law. The insurance was proper. The conduct of the insurance companies usually was proper."[4] J. Scofield Rowe, vice president of the Aetna Life Insurance Company in 1912, reasoned that "[t]he Liability Insurance Companies were brought into existence by reason of the crystallization of public opinion in support of claim making, and are merely the *result*—not the *cause,* of the conditions complained of."[5]

While the insurance industry could certainly defend against claims that the meagerness of accident compensation offered to injured workers was entirely of the insurers' own making, the industry was more susceptible to charges of profiteering. Social reformers and labor leaders criticized the insurance industry because workers received less than half of the premiums that employers paid to liability insurance companies. In Washington from 1910 to 1911, for example, insurance companies typically paid out less than 50 percent of the employers' liability premiums they collected.[6] Similar statistics were cited by employers' liability commissions in Ohio, New York, and Illinois (Ohio Employers' Liability Commission 1911, lxxxiii; Asher 1971, 286; Castrovinci 1976, 85). Such statistics, reformers contended, were clear evidence that insurers were profiting from injured workers' misfortunes. By granting the state a monopoly on the writing of such insurance, reformers continued, both workers and employers could be made better off. By reducing the transaction costs and profits associated with private insurance, employers allegedly would have been able to offer more attractive accident benefits, while paying less for the insurance to provide such generous benefits.

Even after the adoption of workers' compensation laws, private insurance companies were chided for undermining the spirit of cooperation between employers and employees that the new laws were designed to foster. George M. Gillette, the president of the Minnesota Employers' Association and a central figure in the state's adoption of workers' compensation, issued an ultimatum to the insurance companies just after the law was adopted in Minnesota in 1913: "My belief is that it would be good policy on the part of the liability companies not to try to make too much money during the earlier stages of the operation of this law, for I believe such a course would kill the goose." If complaints against insurers accrued or rates became exorbitant and unreasonable, then Gillette warned that "not only in my opinion will Minnesota have state insurance, but it ought to have it."[7]

Contrary to the rhetoric of social reformers and labor leaders, the standard by which they judged the profitability of employers' liability and workers' compensation insurance suggests that their claims were overdrawn. Although it is certainly difficult to assess the profitability of different lines of insurance, we can tentatively use the ratio of losses to premiums as a proxy, which is what advocates of state insurance used to justify their position. Using Minnesota as a representative case, the insurance companies writing workers' compensation in the state paid out between 49 and 56 percent of their premiums a few years after the passage of the law.[8] Fifteen years after the enactment of the law, and seven years after the state insurance issue had been politically resolved in Minnesota, insurance companies were paying out to injured workers approximately 60 percent of their annual workers' compensation premiums.[9] These workers' compensation loss ratios were certainly unimpressive when compared to other lines of insurance. From 1900 to 1927, for example, commercial fire insurers paid out 57.3 percent of their annual premiums.[10] And in the latter part of the 1910s, carriers of industrial life insurance (which had no saving component like ordinary life insurance) only paid out between 24 and 35 percent of their annual premiums.[11]

Opponents of state insurance questioned the reformers' claim that insurance companies were earning excess profits by pointing out that the loss ratio was a flawed measure of profitability. Testifying before the Minnesota legislature's Joint Workmen's Compensation Commission in 1920, Minnesota Insurance Commissioner John B. Sanborn and H. R. Phillips, actuary of the State Insurance Department, explained that state law required insurance companies to retain 50 percent of their premiums as an unearned premium reserve. When policyholders paid in advance for insurance protection at some future date, the insurance company was required to put 50 percent of the premium into reserve.[12] Further, insurance companies were required to keep a loss reserve, which was a pool of funds able to compensate pending claims against the insurer. David McCahan (1929, 76) argued that private insurers also set aside funds for a catastrophe reserve in order to ensure their ability to pay for unforeseen disasters. Also included in the premiums that insurers collected, of course, were administrative expenses and profits.

The complicated accounting of the insurance industry could even confuse practitioners in the field. For example, George D. Smith, chairman of the Nevada Industrial Commission, which administered the state's monopolistic insurance fund, gushed that "our administrative expense is but 8% of premium income, as compared to 40% on an average for private insurance companies."[13] But such comparisons were deceptive in light of the fact that after the first sixty days of a new policy, Nevada employers were billed the month's premium at the end of the month. In other words, the Nevada state fund did not have to set aside an unearned premium reserve because premiums were determined ex post (McCahan 1929, 67). Thus, contrary to reformers' rhetoric, simply observing what percentage of premiums were paid out in claims provided very little information about how efficient, profitable, or exploitative private insurance companies were.

Proponents of state insurance presented little evidence to suggest that the state could save dramatic sums of money by reducing the overhead associated with writing workers' compensation insurance. Critics pointed out that it was the insurance industry, and not the state, that had vast experience in setting rates and processing claims and, thus, could offer insurance most cost effectively.[14] While some monopolistic state funds claimed to have had relatively low administrative expenses, they were criticized for poor service. A 1919 study of the Ohio state fund showed that workers had to wait an average of thirty-seven days before receiving their first payment after an accident. A Special Massachusetts Investigating Commission, on the other hand, found that injured workers in that state, which had no state fund, waited an average of nineteen days.[15] E. H. Downey, actuary for the Pennsylvania State Insurance Department, pointed out that "the monopolistic state fund does not have the inducement of competition to keep itself up on its toes."[16] The very fact that the state granted itself a monopoly was prima facie evidence of its inefficiency, according to J. V. Paterson (1913, 15), president of the Seattle Construction and Dry Dock Company: "If the State has a superior insurance scheme it needs no monopoly." In the final analysis, reformers' hopes for translating efficiency gains from state insurance into more generous benefits for workers were largely illusory. As E. H. Downey explained, "The form of insurance has nothing to do with the scale of benefits. That is a matter of compromise between the employer interests and the employee interests, it depends upon the distribution of political power in the state to be perfectly, brutally frank about it."[17]

Opponents of state insurance pointed to the inevitable politicization of not only the bureaucracy administering the law but also the financial aspects of the state fund. Rowe (1912, 12), the Aetna vice president in 1912, cautioned that it would be impossible for a "state insurance administration to be divorced from politics." W. W. Kinnard, chairman of the Massachusetts Industrial Accident Board, warned the Minnesota Workmen's Compensation Commission in 1920 that "[i]f the [monopolistic] Ohio state fund went up Smoke City they would have to call on their legislature."[18] Such fears ring true today as eight of the twenty-two state-sponsored workers' compensation insurance funds are insolvent because political pressure has forced legislators to keep rates below actuarially sound levels.[19]

At the core of the state insurance debate in the early twentieth century was simple private enterprise philosophy. State insurance supporters like Minnesota representative Thomas J. McGrath "recognize[d] no legitimate function that the private insurance carriers perform under a workmen's compensation scheme that cannot be adequately and properly performed by a state department."[20] The opponents of state insurance questioned why the government should step in to provide a service that could just as easily and cost effectively be provided by private parties. They worried that government intervention into insurance would lead to expansions in the state role: "If insurance is a proper field for the State to enter, why is not manufacturing, or merchandising . . . ?"[21] Ludwig O. Solem, a Minnesota state representative from Minneapolis in 1919, mocked his colleagues who believed the state could offer lower workers' compensation premiums than private concerns: "They say that the rate will be less. My meat, grocery and insurance bills and office rent would be less if the State paid part. They say Insurance Companies are unnecessary. Grocerymen would be useless too if the State took over the grocery business. If the State undertakes this where is it going to stop? Where is there any limit?"[22] Clearly the issue of state insurance raised questions about state intervention that went well beyond the issue of economic efficiency.

Several states chose a compromise solution by establishing a state fund while allowing private insurers to compete with the state. The compromise led to disadvantages and advantages for both the state fund and private insurers. Although insurers preferred the compromise to the establishment of a monopoly state fund, they argued that the state fund would have a substantial advantage in the competition. In a number of states, the state fund's administrative costs were covered by the taxpayer and not employers' premiums. Further, if the state fund became insolvent, it had the option of going to the state treasury for a bailout, allowing the state fund to hold smaller reserves and then charge lower rates. Private insurers, on the other hand, had the advantage of not being required to insure all employers. Members of the Ohio Manufacturing Association noted that private insurers could "come in and pick the gilt edge risks, leaving all the hazardous ones to the state . . . and bring about its disorganization and insolvency."[23]

In the final analysis there is no well-established notion of whether the state or private firms were the optimal agents to insure workers' compensation risk. Claims that state funds could cut administrative costs were offset by problems with the possible politicization of rates and the possibility that inadequate reserves might lead to taxpayers' subsidizing the funds. As discussed below, the choices relating to state insurance depended more on the strength of interest groups and political reformers than on any well-established notion of what was the optimal form of insuring workers' compensation risk.

6.2   The Alignment of the Interest Groups

The dispute over the state's insuring workplace accident risk was particularly bitter. Union leaders blamed insurance companies for many of the problems of the negligence system and sought to eliminate them from workers' compensation entirely. Insurers, who favored workers' compensation because it would have enabled them to expand their coverage of workplace accident risk, suddenly found themselves fighting to stay in this market altogether. Employers split over the issue of state insurance. Those that believed they would be adequately insured at lower rates in the state fund, such as lumber and mining interests in Washington, often supported the idea. But for every industry that anticipated favorable premiums from the state fund, there were others that would have paid relatively higher rates to subsidize the lower rates offered to their counterparts in other industries. One of the salient worries that employers faced was that the state might turn its sights onto other enterprises if the state were allowed to supplant private insurers. Minnesota employers, for example, were reluctant to embrace state insurance on these grounds.[24]

Agricultural interests had a great deal of influence over state politics in the early twentieth century and were very successful in their efforts to be exempted from the workers' compensation system. Yet, even after they had been excluded from the law's purview, farmers opposed certain features of the legislation. Farmers may have opposed state insurance, in particular, because they anticipated that taxpayers might be called upon to bail out insolvent state funds.[25]

While competing interest groups shaped the issues and put pressure on legislators to act on their behalf, the political environment in which legislators made their choices clearly influenced whether state insurance was successful or not. State insurance was considered radical by early-twentieth-century standards, and opponents consistently invoked images of creeping socialism. The union leaders and reformers who sought state insurance typically did not have the political clout to determine the outcome of the state insurance debate. To succeed, they often had to form a coalition with political groups seeking far-reaching socioeconomic reforms that transcended labor issues. Thus, the adoption of state insurance often depended on the electoral successes of the major political reform movements of the time, including the progressives within the Democratic and Republican parties between 1911 and 1913 and the populist Non-Partisan League in the midwest in the late 1910s.

We have performed a cross-state statistical analysis of the decision between monopoly state funds, competitive state funds, and private insurance during the years in which the legislatures made their long-range choice. The results, which are discussed in detail in appendix J, support our characterizations of the attitudes of the various interest groups. The probability of adopting a monopoly state fund was substantially lower in states where agriculture employed more of the labor force and insurance companies sold more life insurance per capita. There were also signs that large firms may have opposed state insurance, as the probability of adopting a state fund was somewhat lower in states where a larger percentage of manufacturing workers were employed in operations with more than five hundred workers. Thus, with the right combination of strong unions and weaker than average agricultural and insurance interests, it was possible to obtain the passage of state insurance, even without a political power shift in the legislature. We found statistical evidence that this confluence of events may have occurred in Nevada and Wyoming.

The empirical analysis also shows that progressive reform movements were important to the adoption of state insurance. In states where the legislature experienced a party shift that favored reform in both houses of the legislature, the probability of choosing a state fund jumped markedly. A reform shift in only one house of the legislature was apparently not enough to strongly raise the probability of adopting a state insurance fund, because the legislative house that had not experienced a reform shift could still block the introduction of the legislation. In fact, of the four states in our sample that experienced a power shift in both branches of the legislature, Ohio adopted a monopoly state fund, and Colorado, Idaho, and Utah adopted competitive state funds. Meanwhile, in states where there was more support for Theodore Roosevelt's progressive presidential campaign in 1912 and where there were a broader range of progressive laws, state insurance had a relatively better chance of being enacted.

The statistical analysis, taken as a whole, indicates that the adoption of monopoly state insurance was relatively unlikely. Some states may have adopted it because of an unusual combination of strong unions and relatively weak insurance interests. If the proper combination of narrow economic interest groups did not exist, then monopoly state insurance was unlikely to be enacted unless union leaders melded their demands with the broader socioeconomic agenda of a strong political reform movement.

Because the decision to implement a state insurance fund involved complex coalitions across economic and political groups, an econometric analysis only begins to capture the richness of the battles over monopoly state funds. In the rest of this chapter we offer detailed case studies of the struggles over the state insurance issue in Washington, Ohio, and Minnesota. Studying these three states has shown that the role of political progressives we found in the regression analysis is actually a lower-bound estimate of their influence over the state insurance debate.

In Washington the progressive reform movement that strongly contributed to the adoption of a state fund in that state occurred *within* the dominant Republican party. In the absence of such a reform movement, our regression analysis suggested that it was unlikely that Washington would have adopted a state fund.[26] The debate over state insurance in Ohio was a drawn-out process that took the form of legislation, court fights, referenda, administrative decisions, and subsequent legislation. The power shift to the Democratic party in Ohio clearly played a role in the initial adoption of a monopoly state fund in 1911. The econometric analysis suggests that in the absence of the power shift Ohio would not have adopted the monopoly state fund. Close analysis of the Ohio case, however, reveals that nearly biennial shifts in the political power of the Democratic and Republican parties led to policy swings favoring and harming the monopoly state fund, respectively. Finally, our examination of Minnesota reveals that efforts to enact a state fund did not cease after a state implemented its first workers' compensation law without a state fund. The statistical analysis predicts that Minnesota would not have adopted a monopoly state fund when it enacted workers' compensation in 1913, although it probably would have if Minnesota had experienced a power shift in both legislative houses. Yet the final choice in Minnesota was in doubt for another six years. The populist Non-Partisan League gained enough strength in Minnesota by the late 1910s to bring the monopoly state fund issue to a serious legislative vote, but it never gained a majority in both legislatures and therefore did not ultimately succeed in adopting a state fund. Supporters of state insurance, however, fell one vote short in the Senate. These case studies illustrate how narrow interest groups set the terms of the debate and influenced decisions at various levels of state government, but it was the political strength of progressive reformers that tipped the scales in favor of relatively radical policy reform.

6.3   The Adoption of State Insurance in Washington

Washington lumbermen, mine operators, and labor unions sought ways to streamline the delivery of accident compensation to injured workers by establishing a compulsory state insurance fund for extrahazardous jobs. Dissatisfaction with the negligence liability system in Washington was widespread by 1910. Employers worried about the sharp rise in their liability insurance rates and the increasing number of court suits, as shown in chapter 4. Workers complained of long court delays, shabby treatment by insurance companies, and the low likelihood of winning a court suit. Both sides blamed attorneys and insurance companies for the inefficiency of the negligence system and the large gap between what employers paid in insurance premiums and what workers received.

In July 1910 Governor Marion Hay, like many other governors during that year, designated a commission to investigate the employers' liability system and to prepare a workers' compensation bill. The commission, which was dominated by representatives from the lumber and coal industries, the two industries most dangerous for workers in the state, wrote a bill that would have guaranteed fixed monthly benefits to workers injured in extrahazardous employment. The most controversial features of the bill were two state insurance funds: a fund that would have collected up to four cents per man-day, half from workers and half from employers, to insure medical expenses from industrial accidents (known as the "first-aid fund"); and a fund to compensate workers' lost earnings. The funds were to be state monopolies and contributions were compulsory, while the state was expected to pay the costs of administering the funds. The Washington State Federation of Labor (WSFL) was the strongest supporter of state insurance, unalterably opposing "any bill that permitted casualty insurance to continue as a disturbing factor between employer and employee by the prevention of quick and just settlements of all questions of compensation."[27]

Many groups expressed general support for a workers' compensation bill but opposed specific features of the commission's bill. Insurers supported the general notion of workers' compensation, but opposed the state fund bill because it "gives absolutely no alternative to the employer or the employee whether they shall insure with the state or an insurance company." The Washington insurers rallied support for their position through the Chamber of Commerce but were relatively inactive compared to the opposition to state insurance in other states in later years. The insurers themselves claimed that "not one liability insurance company has raised a hand to defeat this bill. The liability companies held a meeting in New York and agreed to permit Washington to be the 'dog' on whom the medicine should be tried, and they argued that this would be a lesson to other states who contemplated crazy legislation."[28]

Manufacturers who opposed the commission's bill complained that the state fund's insurance rates were not adequately experience rated. Aware of the dominance of coal and lumber representatives on the commission, other manufacturers believed that the proposed state fund insurance rates would force them to bear a disproportionate share of the coal and lumber industries' accident costs.[29] The commission bill set up funds for thirty-one separate industries, but opponents of the bill worried that the fund in one industry could be tapped to pay for accidents in other industries. The House Committee on Labor and Labor Statistics was able to eliminate much of this objection by adding an amendment to create forty-seven separate funds such that "no class shall be liable for the depletion of the accident fund from accidents happening in any other fund."[30]

Many lumbermen, led by Speaker of the House Howard Taylor, opposed the first-aid fund on the grounds that they were already providing adequate medical care at their mills. Others opposed the first-aid fund as a source of patronage, as an opportunity to build "the greatest political machine ever constructed under the sun. All this money is to be expended by appointees of one man who will build $2.5 million worth of hospitals and employ thousands of men and women to keep them going."[31]

The House fought the battle over the first-aid fund, while the Senate later fought over the state fund to replace lost earnings. The labor committee in the House, chaired by Guvnor Teats, a leading personal injury attorney who helped draft the commission bill, pushed for passage of the amended state insurance bill. Antiprogressives fought to amend the bill to eliminate the first-aid clause and the initial vote ended in a tie of forty votes to forty votes, with sixteen absentees. Speaker Howard Taylor, who opposed the first-aid fund, then directed that all members of the House be found and a vote taken to reconsider the amendment. After ten more members were located, the House voted sixty-four to twenty-six to reconsider the earlier vote, and then proceeded to eliminate the first-aid fund by a vote of fifty-five to thirty-five. The House then passed workers' compensation with the compulsory state insurance provision, but without the first-aid fund, by a vote of sixty-nine to twenty-four.[32]

The House state insurance bill, stripped of the first-aid fund, faced stiff competition in the Senate from a workers' compensation bill without state insurance. Senator Ralph Metcalf, chair of the Senate Labor Committee, proposed the alternative bill on the grounds that compulsory state insurance was likely to be ruled unconstitutional because a New York court had struck down a compulsory workers' compensation law for extrahazardous employment in that state. The New York law, however, did not involve compulsory state insurance.[33]

With the House threatening to kill all Senate bills if state insurance did not pass, the showdown came in a roll-call vote on whether to replace the House's state insurance bill with the Metcalf alternative.[34] The Metcalf proposal lost eighteen to twenty-two. Opponents of state insurance failed again when they tried to reduce support for the final bill by saddling it with the first-aid clause that the House had already rejected and with high salaries for the commissioners who would administer the new workers' compensation system. The House's bill prevailed in the Senate thirty votes to ten.

The various interests clearly framed the debates on the first-aid fund and the state insurance fund. The political climate in the legislature, however, may have been the decisive factor that led to the adoption of the state insurance fund. The 1911 Republican legislature was one of the most reform-minded in Washington's history.[35] Workers' compensation was just one platform of the progressive reformers' agenda, as the legislature also ratified the federal income tax, passed women's-hours legislation, and expanded voter participation in government by establishing the initiative, referenda, and recall processes and judicial nominations by primary. An econometric analysis of the various roll-call votes concerning the first-aid fund in the House and the state insurance fund in the Senate confirms that the impact of interest group politics on the voting was overwhelmed by the activities of progressive reformers with a broader agenda than just workers' compensation (see Fishback and Kantor 1996, 819–24). The predominant influence in all the votes was the legislator's voting record on other progressive legislation. Progressives strongly supported both the first-aid fund in the House and the state insurance fund in the Senate. Thus, without the strong progressive reform movement within the Republican party in the 1911 legislature, state insurance probably would not have been enacted.

6.4   The Extended Fight over Monopoly State Insurance in Ohio

The development of the state fund in Ohio differed from the experience in Washington in that Ohio's struggle over state insurance was extended over a number of years after enactment of workers' compensation. When workers' compensation was first adopted in Ohio in 1911, state insurance was packaged as part of the overall legislation. Once the state fund was established, however, insurers and organized labor fought several contentious battles over the issue. Ohio resembled Washington in one major way, however: who won the battle over state insurance was largely determined by changing political coalitions in state government.

As part of a political compromise to pass the Norris Act in 1910, which sharply limited employers' defenses against negligence suits, the Ohio legislature charged the Employers' Liability Commission (ELC) with the responsibility of proposing a workers' compensation bill. The ELC consisted of five members: two labor representatives who followed the Ohio State Federation of Labor's (OSFL) lead in supporting monopoly state insurance; two employers' representatives who made no mention of the issue in their published statements; and Chairman J. Harrington Boyd whose public statements imply that he accepted the OSFL's argument for a monopoly state fund.[36]

Whether it was the commission's agenda-setting or the insurance companies' lack of interest, only one insurance executive testified before the ELC.[37] Without additional testimony to sway their prior beliefs, the commission proposed two workers' compensation bills, both requiring employers to insure their accident risks through the state. The Democrats captured a majority of both chambers of the 1911 legislature, and progressives from both parties held 47 percent of the House seats and 32 percent of the Senate seats. Given this political environment, the ELC's relatively radical plan for state insurance passed without serious controversy.[38] Although employers were required to insure through the state fund, as a compromise the law made employers' participation in the workers' compensation system voluntary. Those employers who opted out, however, waived their right to invoke any of the three common law defenses—assumption of risk, fellow servant, and contributory negligence—in a negligence suit.

The insurance companies tested the new state insurance system at every turn over the next several years. They initially attacked the new state fund on the grounds that the law was unconstitutional. After the Ohio Supreme Court validated the law in January 1912, insurers attempted to cast aspersion on the state fund's ability to protect employers against situations in which injured workers filed lawsuits claiming that their accidents were caused by an employer's willful act or disregard of a safety law.[39] The insurers claimed that such suits were increasingly likely because the courts were failing to draw a clear distinction between a negligent and willful act. The Ohio State Board of Liability Awards (the state fund administrator) responded with a pamphlet that reassured employers that the workers' compensation law was constitutional and gave full protection, that the distinction between willful acts and negligence was clear, and that the attorney general had ruled that private insurers could not sell liability insurance to indemnify employers against willful acts.[40]

The OSFL, the Board of Liability, and progressive leaders worried that because of the confusion regarding the state fund's insurance of some risks, many employers elected not to participate in the workers' compensation system.[41] At the 1912 Ohio Constitutional Convention, therefore, they proposed a constitutional amendment that would strengthen the monopoly state fund by allowing the legislature to make workers' compensation coverage compulsory. After almost no floor debate the proposal passed the convention unanimously. Despite the public opposition of the Ohio Board of Commerce and many manufacturers, Ohio voters approved the workers' compensation amendment in the November 1912 election, 60 to 40 percent.[42] An econometric analysis of the referendum results suggests that progressive reformers strongly supported the amendment. Voters who supported Roosevelt's progressive presidential run were more likely to support the amendment. Voters in areas with a higher percentage of immigrants also supported the measure. The amendment received strong opposition in agricultural areas, although the vote against workers' compensation may have just been part of a general opposition to amending the Ohio Constitution. Agricultural areas voted against nearly all the constitutional amendments that year.[43]

With a larger Democratic majority and a true progressive governor in James Cox, the 1913 legislature was fertile ground for enacting the compulsory law allowed by the constitutional amendment.[44] As a compromise to employers, however, the compulsory bill was crafted to allow employers to self-insure their workers' compensation risks. Thus, while workers' compensation coverage was compulsory in Ohio, employers now had only two options for insuring their risk—the state fund or self-insurance. A labor-sponsored amendment in the Senate sought to prohibit employers from maintaining mutual benefit associations with other employers in lieu of their participation in the state fund. The amendment lost nineteen to thirteen, leaving open the possibility that insurance companies could sell reinsurance to self-insuring employers, thus allowing them some access to insuring workers' compensation risk. The compulsory bill then passed both houses unanimously.[45]

During the summer of 1913 the insurance companies unsuccessfully tried to use the newly created initiative and referendum process to repeal the compulsory workers' compensation law. After the strategy failed, the insurance companies then focused their efforts on the 1914 governor's race, supporting Republican Frank Willis. Governor Cox proudly stated to the OSFL that he would continue his policy of preventing liability insurers from writing workers' compensation insurance. Willis, on the other hand, sought support from the OSFL by stating his desire to raise benefit levels.[46]

Willis defeated Cox in the 1914 election and conservative Republicans reclaimed both legislative chambers, while the number of labor representatives fell to its lowest in years. Seizing their chance, the insurers had House Bill No. 1 introduced, which would have allowed private insurers to compete with the state fund in the writing of workers' compensation insurance. Opponents argued, however, that private insurers would "pick the gilt edge risks, leaving all the hazardous ones to the . . . Fund . . . and bring about its . . . insolvency."[47] The bill was sent to the Labor Committee which recommended that it be indefinitely postponed, to which the whole House agreed by a vote of seventy-five to twenty-five.[48]

The insurers also failed in their attempt to have the workers' compensation law amended to allow injured workers to sue under the common law without affecting their claims under the compensation law. Insurers hoped that once the amendment passed they could obtain authority to write insurance against that liability. The goal was to offer workers more benefits in hopes of obtaining their support so that the state insurance idea could ultimately be undermined. Both the OMA and the OSFL excoriated these proposals to their membership, and the amendment failed.[49]

The insurance industry then tried to obtain an administrative ruling on their behalf, asking the Industrial Commission to modify its rules to allow the industry to sell workers' compensation insurance. The request was denied and the insurers finally turned to newly appointed Republican insurance commissioner Frank Taggert for a license to sell mutual insurance to employers who chose to self-insure their workers' compensation risks. Taggert granted the license and also gave the private insurers an advantage over the state fund by allowing them to sell insurance against common law suits in which workers claimed that their employers' willful act or failure to honor safety laws had caused their accidents.[50]

The OSFL battled back by aiding Attorney General Edward Turner in filing suit in the Ohio Supreme Court against over twenty insurers. While the court deliberated, the state fund again became an issue in the gubernatorial race of 1916. In a rematch of the 1914 race, James Cox announced his support for a labor union petition to expel private insurance from workers' compensation altogether. The court then handed down its final decision on 31 January 1917, holding that employers had the right to self-insure and that insurance companies could reinsure self-insuring employers.[51]

Although the OSFL was dissatisfied with the court decision, the 1916 election results largely made the debate over private insurance in Ohio moot. Cox returned as governor, the Democrats recaptured both houses, sixteen OSFL members held seats in the legislature, and gone were "quite a few senators and representatives who had tried to impair the Workers' Compensation law in the interests of the liability insurance companies." The OSFL introduced House Bill No. 1, which would have outlawed the private insurance of workers' compensation risks. The bill sailed through the House by a vote of 118 to 2, the Senate 28 to 2, and was quickly signed into law by Governor Cox on 19 February 1917. The insurance companies issued yet another court challenge on the grounds that the new law canceled contracts, but the Ohio Supreme Court sustained the new law.[52]

The Ohio case demonstrates how the relative success of the competing economic interests depended on the structural political changes that were occurring at the state level in the 1910s. Unions, employers, and insurance companies framed the debate over state insurance by establishing the menu of choices available to legislators. Throughout the short period during which state insurance was debated in Ohio, the relative strength of the various interest groups changed very little, but substantial changes in public policy occurred. The key factor that produced these changes was the undulating political power of the progressive coalition that favored state insurance. Progressive Democrats established the state fund and continued to strengthen it, but when conservative Republicans recaptured the majority, the door was opened for private insurance. Finally, when progressive Democrats returned to power in 1917, they slammed the door shut on private insurance.

6.5   Minnesota's Failed Attempt at State Insurance

Minnesota failed to enact compulsory state insurance by one Senate vote in 1919. The Minnesota State Federation of Labor (MnSFL) lobbied strongly for state insurance in 1913, when workers' compensation was first adopted, and throughout the 1910s. They had little success until 1918 when reformers from the Non-Partisan League seriously threatened the dominant Republican party. Although the Non-Partisans did not capture a majority in either chamber, they wielded enough political strength to pass a weak state insurance bill in the House, and they barely failed in the Senate.

The Minnesota Employers' Association (MEA) and the MnSFL agreed to a compromise workers' compensation bill without state insurance in 1913, but the MnSFL stood firm in its belief that "no satisfactory solution to the question of workingmen's compensation can be had except through the medium of state insurance."[53] A bill to amend the state constitution to allow for state insurance died in the 1913 legislature, as insurance companies and employers lobbied against it. But George Gillette, president of the MEA, issued an ultimatum to the insurance industry: if workers or employers complained about bad treatment or high premiums, then "not only . . . will Minnesota have state insurance, but it ought to have it."[54] Gillette's rhetoric, combined with organized labor's insistence on state insurance and Ohio's and Washington's recent enactment of monopoly insurance funds, posed a serious threat to insurance companies and independent agents operating in Minnesota. Accordingly, in September 1914, a "few stalwart insurance men" met in Minneapolis to form the Insurance Federation of Minnesota (IFM) to act as the industry's lobbying group against state workers' compensation insurance and other state intrusions into the insurance industry.[55]

State insurance supporters won a significant victory in the 1917 legislature when the Senate's Employers' Liability Committee recommended passage of a state insurance bill. However, the committee suggested that the bill be referred back to the Judiciary Committee for a report on its constitutionality. After the Senate successfully voted to recall the bill from Judiciary, the committee reported that the law would have been constitutional, but the bill nonetheless lost forty-two to twenty-one.[56] The House did not consider the bill after the Senate defeat.

As the IFM presciently advised its members at the close of the 1917 legislative session, "the fight against state insurance in Minnesota has really just begun." Secretary E. A. Sherman admitted that he did not know "[w]hat new influences they [MSFL] will bring to bear in later contests . . . but I mention for your earnest consideration—the Non-Partisan League."[57] Perhaps the most important influence that organized labor brought to the 1919 legislative session was their numbers. Between 1918 and 1920 union ranks soared 75 percent, from fifty-one thousand members to over eighty-nine thousand.[58] But certainly the most threatening political force in the state, from the IFM's perspective, was the emergence of the Non-Partisan League.

The first plank of the League's labor platform was the implementation of a state monopoly on the writing of workers' compensation insurance. Although the Non-Partisan League failed to win the governor's seat in 1918, it was quite successful in building a coalition that altered the balance of political power in Minnesota, pitting a newly formed coalition of grain farmers, organized union members, and radical progressives against the Republican party. Although the Non-Partisans were able to secure twenty-four seats in the House and eight in the Senate, hardly a majority in either chamber, the animosity generated in the 1918 elections was carried into the 1919 legislative session. As Carl Chrislock noted, the Republicans' "compulsion 'to beat' the Nonpartisan League dominated the legislature of that year [1919]."[59] State-run workers' compensation insurance proved to be one of the battlegrounds.

Organized labor described its struggle for state insurance in 1919 as "one of the hottest fights ever waged in the state legislature."[60] The IFM called their fight to suppress the legislation "the most closely fought legislative contest Minnesota has ever known."[61] After four hours of floor debate in the House, during which time an amendment was passed to allow nonprofit mutual companies or interinsurance exchanges to compete with the state fund, a bill creating a state insurance fund won by a comfortable seventy-eight to forty-eight margin.[62] An econometric analysis of the roll-call vote on this issue suggests that a coalition combining the efforts of organized labor and the Non-Partisan League were key supporters of state insurance (see Fishback and Kantor 1996, 828–33). Representative Asher Howard, who opposed state insurance in the 1917 legislature but supported it in 1919, captured the feeling that many legislators no doubt shared: "If you want to prevent the seats of this House from being filled by Socialists and Nonpartisans you have got to play fair with the workingmen and the farmers."[63]

The House's state insurance bill moved to the Senate, where the "legislative contest was very intense and the feeling engendered was extremely bitter."[64] The Senate Committee on Workmen's Compensation, by majority report, substituted the House's bill for the Senate's and recommended passage. Three senators, however, offered a minority report that would have allowed private insurance subject to regulation by a workers' compensation board.[65] The Senate rejected the minority report by a vote of thirty-one to thirty-five. The majority report—to substitute the House's state insurance bill for a Senate state insurance bill—failed passage when the vote deadlocked at thirty-three.

The House bill came up for direct consideration the next day. Senator

Charles R. Fowler, a lawyer sympathetic to the insurance interests, introduced an amendment allowing employers to insure their workers' compensation risks with licensed, for-profit insurers.[66] The Fowler amendment passed thirty-four to thirty-two. The amended bill was unsatisfactory to organized labor because the primary reason for allowing the state to dominate the writing of workers' compensation insurance was the belief that the state insurance could be offered at lower cost than private insurance. At the urging of the MnSFL, the amended bill was defeated by a vote of nine to fifty-seven.[67]

Empirical analysis of the major votes on state insurance in the Senate revealed no statistically significant patterns, which might be attributable to the substantial logrolling within the 1919 Senate. The IFM suggested that state insurance "was made a political issue, and the interests of the insurance men were used as trading stock for political expediency, or to secure votes in favor of or against other measures pending in the legislature."[68] Labor claimed that a "two percent beer bill was used as a club" against them in the Senate.[69] Further, Asher (1973, 29–30) suggests that there was a logroll between Republicans who wanted an iron ore tax killed and legislators who wanted state insurance.

The debate over state insurance in Minnesota continued as interim committees from both chambers investigated workers' compensation and state insurance in 1920. The stated objective of the committees was to make the workers' compensation system more responsive to injured workers and to lower employers' insurance costs. After an exhaustive investigation in which the committees heard from the MnSFL, MEA, IFM, and workers' compensation officials in ten other states, the majority of each committee concluded that their objectives could best be achieved by encouraging competition in the field of workers' compensation insurance and by regulating insurance rates. A minority in each committee continued to propose state insurance as the solution, but the weakening strength of the Non-Partisan League led to the demise of monopoly state insurance in Minnesota.[70] The 1921 legislature overwhelmingly followed the committees' majority opinion to raise benefits, allow competition among mutual and stock companies, and establish an industrial commission to administer the system and regulate insurers.[71] Thus, while the 1921 legislators were willing to augment the state's regulation of private industry, they stopped short of substituting public for private enterprise. Had the Non-Partisan League been as strong as the progressives in Ohio and Washington in earlier years, Minnesota would have enacted state insurance in 1919.

6.6 Summary

Union leaders pushed strongly for state insurance of workers' compensation risk while insurance companies just as strongly opposed it, and agricultural interests (and other taxpayers) worried about the possibility of paying higher taxes if the state fund was actuarially unsound. In the majority of states the countervailing political influences of these groups were enough to keep most states from establishing monopoly state funds. In ten states, however, a compromise position was reached in which private insurers competed with a state insurance fund. The extreme position of establishing a monopoly state fund occurred in only seven states. In some states an unusual combination of strong organized labor and weak agricultural and insurance interests led to the adoption of monopoly state insurance. In others, however, organized labor only succeeded because a progressive political reform group with a broader social and political agenda came to power and aided in adopting a state fund. Moreover, the political reformers in some states not only garnered support from organized labor but also co-opted agricultural interests, who at times chose to support state insurance as part of the broader political agenda proposed by the reformers.

The adoption of state insurance of workers' compensation risk contrasted sharply with the enactment of workers' compensation legislation generally. Because employers, workers, and insurers saw that they could gain from the adoption of the legislation, workers' compensation was enacted relatively quickly in the 1910s. Because of this broad support from the major economic interests groups with a stake in workers' compensation, the progressive movement in the early twentieth century actually played a smaller, more indirect role in the law's overall adoption than it did in the enactment of state insurance. State insurance was so controversial, polarizing the same groups that came together to support workers' compensation generally, that progressive politics often played a pivotal role in the state insurance decision by forging a coalition with organized labor and neutralizing farmers' traditional opposition.

Our quantitative and case-study analyses suggest that in order to properly explain the growth of government, both narrow economic interests and broad-based political coalitions must be considered carefully. Whereas some scholars of political economy have argued that one or the other explanation is sufficient to explain why public policy is enacted, we find that both are important and that both forces sometimes interact in complex ways. Examining the adoption of monopoly state insurance across the United States clearly shows that narrow economic interests and broad political coalitions played significant, but sometimes unequal, roles. The importance we attribute to either explanation will always depend on the specific case under consideration.

Notes

1. For example, the federal government collects the premiums and acts as the single payer for Unemployment Insurance, Social Security, Medicare, and Medicaid. Alternatively, reformers have proposed that the government mandate the benefits and allow private insurers to underwrite the insurance required to deliver them.

2. The monopoly state funds were established in Ohio (1911), Washington (1911), Nevada (1913), Oregon (1913), West Virginia (1913), Wyoming (1915), and North Dakota (1919). The competitive state funds were established when workers' compensation laws were initially adopted in Michigan (1912), Maryland (1914), Colorado (1915), Pennsylvania (1915), Montana (1915), Idaho (1917), and Utah (1917). New York (1913), California (1913), and Arizona (1925) established competitive state funds when amending or replacing workers' compensation laws that had been passed earlier.

3. See the letter dated 9 February 1910 from the Northern Lumber Company to William McEwen, in the Minnesota Department of Labor and Industries, Insurance Compensation Correspondence.

4. Vorys (1914, 9).

5. Rowe (1912, 2).

6. Washington Insurance Commissioner (1902, 47, 60; 1904, 25, 38; 1906, 32, 47; 1908, 30, 44; 1909, 27, 31; 1910, 28; 1911, 41).

7. Letter dated 23 April 1919 from Gillette to Minnesota's liability insurance companies in Minnesota Employers' Association (MEA) *Minute Book* (vol. 1).

8. These data represent losses to premiums for the years 1915 and 1916, respectively. See Minnesota Commissioner of Insurance (1917, 180–81).

9. The loss ratio in 1926 was 0.607 and 0.603 in 1927. See Minnesota Commissioner of Insurance (1927, 93; 1928, 85).

10. Minnesota Commissioner of Insurance (1928, 20).

11. Minnesota Commissioner of Insurance (1920, 184, 194–95).

12. Minnesota Department of Labor and Industries, Workmen's Compensation Commission Hearings (hereafter "Hearings").

13. Chancellor (1919, 8).

14. See, for instance, Rowe (1912, 12). In testimony before the Joint Committees of the Minnesota Legislature on the State Fund Plan of Workman's Compensation, Thomas J. Duffy, chairman of the Industrial Commission of Ohio, admitted quite candidly to what opponents of state insurance feared would happen if inexperienced bureaucrats took over an industry that set its prices based on scientific methods: "In making our first schedule of rates we simply guessed at it. We put down a dollar for this and a dollar and a quarter for that, and fifty cents here and twenty cents there, and we didn't know whether we were anywhere near the correct amount or not" (Minnesota State Federation of Labor [MnSFL] 1919, 5).

15. See McCahan (1929, 56). The waiting period (the amount of time out-of-work before compensation commenced) in Ohio in 1919 was seven days and it was ten days in Massachusetts. See also Driggers's (1913, 15) claim that the Washington state insurance fund was woefully understaffed to handle the influx of workers' compensation claims.

16. Comments of E. H. Downey, actuary of the Pennsylvania State Insurance Department, in "Hearings," 24 February 1920 file, pp. 2–3.

17. Ibid.

18. Comments of W. W. Kennard in "Hearings," 7–8 April 1920 file, p. 26. While state funds incurred no losses up to 1934, Dodd's (1936, 551–52) descriptions of

state funds suggest that voters had reason to worry that tax revenues would be tapped to support bankrupt state insurance funds. Washington and West Virginia, for example, sometimes found it necessary to make loss payments in warrants rather than in cash. Many funds were not on a safe actuarial basis, and deficits developed in funds for a number of industries. Dodd (1936, 552) claimed that no injured employee would be denied benefits from a state fund because "if a state fund . . . were unable to meet its obligations, the interested groups in the community would almost certainly have sufficient political strength to obtain payment from the public treasury."

19. *Wall Street Journal,* 24 July 1992, A3B.

20. McGrath offered the minority opinion of the Minnesota House of Representatives Special Interim Committee (1921, p. 1846).

21. Rowe (1912, 16).

22. *Minneapolis Labor Review,* 14 March 1919.

23. Minutes of Executive Committee Meeting, 15 July 1916, Ohio Manufacturers' Association *Records,* pp. 8–9. See also Mengert (1920, 31).

24. See MEA, *Minute Book,* 2 August 1912.

25. See Kantor and Fishback (1994a) for a discussion of farmers' rejection of state insurance in Missouri during the 1920s.

26. In fact, the measures of political power shifts in our econometric analysis miss the reform movement in Washington. As shown in appendix J, without the power shift, the analysis predicts that Washington probably would not have adopted a monopoly state fund. Once the power shift that took place within the Republican party is incorporated into the calculations, Washington's predicted probability of adopting a monopoly state fund rises to a nearly 93.7 percent probability.

27. *Seattle Union Record,* 4 March 1911.

28. *Seattle Daily Times,* 7 and 31 January 1911.

29. See *Argus,* 18 February 1911, and *Seattle Daily Times,* 17 January 1911, 13 February 1911, and 7 March 1911.

30. Washington Industrial Insurance Department (1912, 23) and Washington House of Representatives *Journal* (1911, 438–43). The amendment went a long way toward solving the experience-rating problem across industries, but it did not eliminate worries within industries that safer employers would be forced to pay higher rates to subsidize unsafe competitors. The problem arose soon after the state fund was established when a small powder mill exploded, killing six girls, and the state fund fought with Dupont over whether Dupont should contribute the bulk of the funds to compensate a competitor's accident victims. See Paterson (1913, 9–10).

31. *Seattle Daily Times,* 2 February 1911. See also Pacific Coast Lumber Manufacturers' Association (1911, 4).

32. Washington House of Representatives *Journal* (1911, 443–50, 459–60); Washington Industrial Insurance Department (1912, 19–25); *Seattle Daily Times,* 22 February 1911; *Seattle Post-Intelligencer,* 22 February 1911; *Seattle Union Record,* 25 February 1911; *Argus,* 25 February 1911; and Tripp (1976, 544).

33. The Washington Supreme Court later took a position diametrically opposed to the one of the New York court when it declared the Washington compulsory state insurance law constitutional. See *Seattle Daily Times,* 7 March 1911, and Tripp (1976, 72–73).

34. *Seattle Union Record,* 4 March 1911; *Seattle Daily Times,* 3 March 1911 and 7 March 1911; and *Seattle Post-Intelligencer,* 4 March 1911.

35. The Progressive Movement developed a strong following within the Republican party. See Schwantes (1979, 193–99) and Kerr (1963, 1–10).

36. For the OSFL's position, see the testimony of Voll and McNamee, Ohio Employers' Liability Commission (1911, vol. 2, 414, 417). For Boyd's views, see Ohio Employers' Liability Commission (1911, vols. 1 and 2); *Ohio Journal of Commerce*, 15 October 1910, 246–48; and Ohio State Board of Commerce (1910, 214–55).

37. Aetna executive W. G. Wilson fully endorsed the concept of workers' compensation with the employer paying the premiums and the state regulating the insurance industry. He challenged Boyd's depiction of insurance costs as including all liability premiums for every type of accident. The average employers' liability loss payments were between 50 and 60 percent of the premiums. Nor did Boyd mention that the insurance company expenses included inspection departments, which played a major role in thwarting accidents. Wilson claimed that the cost of selling liability insurance was lower than any other form of insurance and that the administrative overhead of workers' compensation would be about 16 to 17 percent. Finally, he attacked the general notion that the government should be involved in the insurance industry: "Why not suggest the State forming a fund to protect this small manufacturers' property in case of its loss by fire, or to protect against the calamity of the death of the employer and, if we may do these things, why may not the State enter the coal mines and bring forth the fuel to warm the people and engage in the manufacturing of clothing and the raising of crops to feed them? This subject of workmen's compensation is so attractive in itself, that it may very easily and subtly lead us upon dangerous ground" Ohio Employers' Liability Commission (1911, pt. 2, 204–11).

38. Warner (1964, 266–75, 282–83).

39. Ibid. (336).

40. Ohio State Board of Liability Awards (1912). See also the speech by Thomas J. Duffy, head of the Board, in Ohio State Federation of Labor (1913a, 101–2).

41. See Ohio State Federation of Labor (1912, 16) and Ohio Manufacturers' Association *Records,* Secretary's Report, 19 November 1912.

42. See Ohio State Federation of Labor (1912, 16, 22); Ohio Manufacturers' Association *Records,* Secretary's Report, 19 November 1912; Mengert (1920, 15); and Foote (1912, 42–43).

43. Warner (1964, 341) argues that nearly all of the referenda issues received strong support from the urban areas and counties closest to them. However, when we include urban areas in the voting analysis, the impact is small and statistically insignificant, while the remaining variables stay strong.

44. The Democratic majority in the Senate was twenty-six to seven and the House majority was eighty-seven to thirty-six. See Warner (1964, 386–87).

45. Mengert (1920, 20).

46. Ibid. (23–24), Warner (1964, 393–94), and Ohio State Federation of Labor (1915a, 25–27).

47. Ohio Manufacturers' Association *Records,* Minutes of Executive Committee Meeting, 15 July 1916. See also Mengert (1920, 31).

48. Ohio State Federation of Labor (1915b, 7) and Donnelly (1915, 42).

49. Ohio Manufacturers' Association *Records,* Secretary's Report, 28 April 1914.

50. Ohio State Federation of Labor (1915a, 18) and Mengert (1920, 29).

51. Mengert (1920, 32–34).

52. Ohio State Federation of Labor (1917, 1–10) and Mengert (1920, 34–36).

53. MnSFL (1913, 68). See also *Labor World,* 2 February 1913 and 7 June 1913.

54. Letter dated 23 April 1919 from Gillette to Minnesota's liability insurance companies in MEA, *Minute Book.*

55. The Insurance Federation of America was formed in 1911, in response to the adoption of the state fund in Ohio, to ensure that workers' compensation laws allowed for private insurance. See Insurance Federation of Minnesota (IFM) (1989, 1).

56. Minnesota Senate *Journal,* (1917, 766–70, 957, 1091–92).

57. IFM, Report of the Secretary (1917, 6–7).

58. Minnesota Department of Labor and Industries (MDLI) (1917–1918, 167; 1919–1920, 172).

59. Chrislock (1971, 185), quoting from the *Minnesota Mascot,* 18 April 1919.

60. *Labor World,* 5 April 1919.

61. IFM, Report of the Secretary (1919, 42).

62. *Minneapolis Labor Review,* 14 March 1919.

63. Ibid. Howard was understood to represent the interests of the Chamber of Commerce.

64. Lawson (1955, 353).

65. Minnesota Senate *Journal* (1919, 972–75).

66. *Labor World,* 15 April 1911, and Minnesota Senate *Journal* (1919, 1147–48).

67. Lawson (1955, 353), and Minnesota Senate *Journal* (1919, 1148–49).

68. IFM, Report of the Secretary (1919, 45).

69. *Labor World,* 12 April 1919:

70. Asher (1973, 39–40).

71. Minnesota Senate, Interim Commission (1921, 10) and Minnesota House of Representatives, Special Interim Committee (1921).

The Battles over Benefit Levels, 1910–1930

During the legislative session in 1919 when Alabama adopted workers' compensation, a major debate erupted over the benefit levels proposed in the bill offered by Senator M. L. Leeth. His bill called for injured workers to receive 60 percent of their earnings up to a maximum of $17.50 per week. Ben Stroud, the manager of the Alabama Manufacturers and Operators Association, wrote to the *Birmingham News* that if such benefits were adopted "it becomes perfectly clear that the burden on Alabama industry will be excessive and force them to decline to come under the bill or to assume a heavy handicap in the approaching struggle for industrial existence." Pressure from employers led Senator Acker to amend the Leeth bill by reducing the replacement rate to 50 percent with a weekly maximum of $12.00 per week. Senator Leeth responded: "If the employers would only study the proposed act they would find that it is fair and reasonable. The maximum doesn't amount to so much. It only guarantees to the man . . . that if he is making $200 a month his wife and little children may get $72 of that per month. How degrading it is for a man to be so hardhearted and selfish that he will say to the employe's [*sic*] family, that we will not allow you but $48 per month to educate your children, to pay house rent, and support your family." Despite Senator Leeth's efforts, Acker's amendment became the basis for benefit levels in Alabama. The rhetoric in Alabama typifies the discussions over benefit levels in nearly every state. Whether the employers' proposed benefit levels or the proposals of labor leaders carried the day was determined by the relative political strength of employers and organized labor, by the nature of industry in the state, and by the extent of political reform movements.[1]

Benefit levels were particularly important because they determined the share of the rents that each group expected to receive from the legislation. Employers sought to limit benefits by imposing maximums on weekly and overall accident payments or by trying to force workers to pay a share of the employers' insurance premiums. Meanwhile, organized labor consistently fought for accident benefits that paid higher percentages of lost earnings, with no ceilings on weekly benefits and short waiting periods. Our sense is that insurance companies were generally not a central player in the benefit debates because the range of benefits discussed would not have led to significant moral hazard problems that would have affected their ability to underwrite workers' compensation insurance. The political negotiations over benefit levels did not stop with the introduction of workers' compensation. Unions continued to apply pressure to raise benefit levels in most states in most legislative sessions throughout the 1910s and 1920s.

The benefit levels sought by various groups of employers and workers were influenced by their wage rates, accident risk, factors determining the insurance premiums for workers' compensation, and the extent to which workers shared in paying the costs of those premiums through wage offsets. After considering the demands of lobbying groups, state legislatures, subject to the governor's veto, ultimately made the final choice. This chapter explores both the economic and political factors that influenced how workers' compensation benefit levels were determined in the political process. Did state legislators focus their attention on the demands of workers, who were far more numerous than employers and, thus, constituted the majority of interested voters? Alternatively, were legislators heeding the demands of organized employer groups, as many labor unions claimed at the turn of the century? What role did Progressive Era reformers play? And finally, after workers' compensation was established, how did the agencies administering workers' compensation influence the level of benefits?

The results of both quantitative and qualitative analyses suggest that benefit levels were influenced by all three groups: employers, workers, and reformers. How workers' compensation benefits varied across states depended on the relative strength of the interest groups and the economic factors that influenced their demands. Workers succeeded in securing relatively higher benefit levels, all else constant, in states where unions had a strong following, where political reforms led to party shifts in the state legislature, and where the workers' compensation system was administered by a bureaucratic agency. On the other hand, employers in more dangerous industries managed to hold benefit levels down, while employers also held benefit levels in check in states where high-wage workers had demanded substantial increases.

7.1   The Large Variation in Workers' Compensation Benefits

Since workers' compensation benefits were determined by state-level legislation, there was potential for substantial variation in the benefit parameters that the different state governments chose. To show how the legislative parameters that determined workers' compensation benefits differed across states and over time, we developed a measure of expected workers' compensation benefits for each state from the first year the state adopted a general workers' compensation law through 1930. For each year and state we computed the present value of the stream of payments a worker or his family would have received for each of the four categories of industrial accidents given the particular rules governing workers' compensation in each state. The index is calculated assuming that the hypothetical worker in each state earned the national average manufacturing wage and a discount rate of 5 percent. We then calculated a weighted average of the benefit levels across the four types of accidents where the weights, which are the same for all states and years, are the probabilities that the broad category of accident might occur. Thus, the numbers in table 7.1 represent the expected accident compensation (in constant 1967 dollars) for the hypothetical worker at the end of the year listed. Appendix B provides a detailed description of the benefits calculations and of the variables used to construct our estimates.

When we make comparisons across states in a particular year, the expected benefits index summarizes how the workers' compensation parameters differed across states because the wage used to calculate each state's measure is the same. However, cross-time comparisons of the index for the same state varied from year to year either because of a change in the state's workers' compensation law, a change in the national average manufacturing wage, or changes in the price level used to deflate the nominal figures. We used the national average weekly wage in each year to calculate the expected benefits index because there was a substantial rise in nominal wages during this period. If we had used a constant wage throughout, the expected benefits index would not have fully shown the impact of changes in many of the workers' compensation parameters in various years. For example, if we had used the low wages of around 1910 to calculate expected benefits for the 1920s, the expected benefits measures for those years would be well below the actual levels. If we had used the high wages circa 1930, some of the states without maximums in the early 1910s would have had extraordinarily high benefit levels that would not reflect the actual payments that workers received during the earlier period.[2]

Expected benefits varied widely across states within any year. In 1920, for example, the expected benefits ranged from a low of $22.90 to a high of $48.70 (in 1967 dollars). The relative position of each state also fluctuated from year to year. Washington and Oregon's benefits were relatively

Table 7.1   Expected Workers' Compensation Benefits (constant 1967 dollars), by State, 1910–30

State	1910	1911	1912	1913	1914	1915	1916	1917	1918	1919	1920	1921	1922	1923	1924	1925	1926	1927	1928	1929	1930
Ala.											30.67	34.33	36.66	36.01	35.94	35.05	34.72	35.39	35.87	35.87	36.81
Ariz.		47.02	46.97	46.37	45.81	45.23	45.59	42.61	39.29	36.23	33.93	65.04	68.30	68.23	68.09	71.75	71.29	74.11	76.56	76.96	76.43
Cal.				46.70	41.40	40.84	42.88	41.24	44.73	46.62	45.80	49.15	50.13	52.96	53.57	52.46	51.97	53.01	53.77	57.02	56.56
Colo.						25.96	24.46	23.32	19.86	22.93	19.80	22.16	23.66	29.01	28.95	28.24	27.97	28.51	28.90	33.63	34.50
Conn.					32.75	34.09	35.20	33.84	34.72	39.33	38.53	40.69	42.26	43.40	43.68	45.44	45.15	47.36	48.95	49.22	48.83
Del.									26.99	36.41	34.58	38.71	40.50	40.61	40.53	39.52	39.15	39.90	40.45	40.45	41.50
Ga.												25.03	36.40	36.99	36.92	36.00	35.66	36.35	36.85	36.85	37.80
Iowa					31.98	31.55	32.57	31.40	26.83	34.84	30.08	33.67	35.95	35.31	35.44	34.57	34.24	34.90	35.37	35.37	36.29
Idaho									39.15	34.08	29.43	32.02	44.86	44.07	43.99	42.90	42.49	43.31	43.90	43.73	44.86
Ill.			40.67	39.42	38.96	38.43	39.71	41.47	39.45	38.78	33.48	38.44	41.04	40.32	40.24	43.92	43.50	44.64	45.25	49.59	50.88
Ind.						34.64	35.77	37.80	38.77	36.09	31.16	34.88	37.24	36.58	36.51	35.61	35.27	44.84	45.45	45.45	46.63
Kan.			33.77	33.99	33.59	33.14	34.29	37.74	38.82	34.57	29.85	33.41	35.67	35.05	34.98	34.11	33.79	41.65	42.22	42.22	43.32
Ky.							43.83	39.13	36.50	31.78	31.34	35.08	37.45	36.79	36.72	35.81	35.48	36.16	36.65	36.65	37.60
La.						31.55	35.79	34.41	38.79	38.85	39.61	42.78	46.59	46.71	49.93	48.69	48.23	49.16	51.64	51.64	52.98
Mass.			45.36	45.32	59.14	58.53	57.11	52.87	46.37	42.42	37.00	41.23	49.49	50.40	54.08	52.77	52.27	55.65	57.45	57.46	58.88
Md.			35.05	35.28	36.21	35.72	36.91	35.50	34.13	30.02	41.54	46.50	49.65	48.78	48.68	47.48	47.03	47.93	48.59	48.59	49.85
Me.							34.83	33.56	29.44	36.88	32.79	41.26	43.77	43.45	43.45	45.42	45.01	46.01	46.77	46.81	47.79
Mich.			31.47	31.68	31.30	30.88	31.95	30.78	26.37	35.38	30.55	34.95	37.32	36.66	36.59	35.69	35.35	46.10	46.73	46.73	47.94
Minn.				32.36	31.98	32.92	34.00	39.82	34.11	38.30	33.07	45.87	48.95	55.95	56.12	54.98	54.52	56.00	56.84	56.85	58.05
Mo.																		57.33	58.11	58.11	59.62
Mont.						35.15	36.32	34.93	29.93	32.50	28.06	31.60	33.74	33.14	33.08	38.71	38.35	39.08	39.62	47.42	48.66
N.C.																				52.67	54.04
N.D.										78.20	75.40	82.45	85.69	87.06	87.18	85.28	84.54	82.45	84.02	84.15	85.55
Neb.				35.57	35.15	34.68	35.81	45.21	38.50	41.99	36.26	40.58	43.33	42.57	42.49	41.43	41.04	41.83	42.40	42.40	43.51
N.H.			33.37	33.59	33.20	32.75	33.89	32.65	29.16	26.33	24.09	26.22	27.62	38.64	38.68	37.82	37.49	38.38	39.08	39.13	39.84
N.J.			31.41	31.59	31.22	30.80	31.80	30.57	27.36	30.12	26.00	29.11	31.08	40.52	40.64	39.81	41.12	42.22	43.11	49.71	50.45
N.M.		31.47						26.57	25.12	28.53	25.66	30.28	32.01	31.76	31.70	30.92	30.63	31.21	31.64	35.80	36.74
Nev.				39.47	42.15	44.69	46.15	44.37	60.72	69.01	62.64	68.43	72.25	72.28	72.39	70.81	70.20	71.94	73.31	73.42	74.65

(continued)

Table 7.1 (continued)

State	1910	1911	1912	1913	1914	1915	1916	1917	1918	1919	1920	1921	1922	1923	1924	1925	1926	1927	1928	1929	1930
N.Y.[a]	47.23	47.60	47.06	49.91	63.68	62.82	64.93	62.48	62.61	58.82	54.61	59.75	70.48	73.15	73.55	76.77	76.17	80.44	82.78	83.13	83.09
Ohio			44.26	47.09	48.57	47.92	49.48	43.35	41.58	38.97	33.64	39.33	42.00	41.26	52.04	50.75	50.27	51.24	51.94	51.94	53.29
Okla.						19.52	20.19	19.45	16.67	26.47	27.93	28.45	29.01	31.91	31.85	31.06	30.76	31.36	31.78	31.78	32.61
Or.					65.59	64.87	62.37	53.55	45.60	41.64	35.95	47.69	49.92	50.63	50.84	49.64	49.17	50.12	50.80	50.80	52.12
Pa.							33.82	32.51	27.85	24.25	24.66	27.60	29.47	28.95	28.90	28.18	27.92	28.45	39.20	39.20	40.22
R.I.			34.05	34.28	33.88	33.42	34.58	39.61	35.12	31.52	32.77	37.55	38.86	40.13	40.40	39.50	42.11	43.10	43.86	43.91	44.74
S.D.								31.59	30.33	28.15	24.47	31.55	33.64	33.12	33.07	32.26	31.96	32.59	33.05	33.06	33.89
Tenn.										28.73	24.81	27.77	29.65	38.51	38.43	37.48	37.13	42.81	43.39	43.39	44.52
Tex.				50.93	50.31	49.67	50.78	43.41	44.66	40.48	34.95	39.12	41.77	51.90	52.51	51.83	51.50	53.59	54.50	54.50	55.25
Utah								37.12	36.09	43.70	37.73	42.23	45.10	44.30	44.21	43.12	42.71	43.53	44.13	44.13	45.28
Va.										23.36	24.13	27.01	28.84	28.33	29.88	29.14	28.86	29.42	29.82	29.82	35.63
Vt.						27.49	28.39	27.30	30.11	28.02	27.23	33.14	34.39	35.07	35.16	34.43	34.14	35.04	35.69	35.70	36.34
Wash.		58.93	56.90	55.56	54.82	54.28	50.46	54.41	38.66	48.67	42.02	47.03	50.22	56.00	55.89	54.50	53.99	55.22	55.97	55.97	57.43
Wis.		53.39	51.69	43.10	42.53	42.10	39.36	41.69	35.73	31.23	27.10	51.27	54.64	58.17	58.09	56.68	56.15	61.14	62.04	62.04	63.56
W. Va.				46.19	45.60	44.82	42.93	37.85	32.28	37.83	32.66	36.56	39.04	52.78	52.82	51.51	51.03	52.01	52.72	52.72	54.09
Wyo.						28.06	26.09	27.73	23.61	26.73	27.18	36.33	38.79	38.11	38.04	37.09	36.74	38.25	38.78	38.78	39.78
Real wage	52.6	53.0	52.9	53.3	52.6	51.9	53.7	51.7	53.2	53.4	56.4	57.4	58.5	61.9	62.6	61.8	61.4	63.9	66.1	66.4	65.9
Weekly wage	14.72	14.83	15.34	15.82	15.84	15.79	17.57	19.87	24.01	27.67	33.81	30.77	29.39	31.62	32.05	32.44	32.54	33.23	33.89	34.08	32.94
CPI 1967 = 100	28	28	29	29.7	30.1	30.4	32.7	38.4	45.1	51.8	60.0	53.6	50.2	51.1	51.2	52.5	53.0	52.0	51.3	51.3	50.0

Sources: Fishback and Kantor (1998b, 118–19) and appendix B. The real weekly wage is the national average manufacturing weekly wage in 1967 dollars.

Notes: Expected benefits are those in effect at the end of the year listed. Empty cells indicate no workers' compensation law was in effect at the end of the year. Some states adopted workers' compensation or changed benefit levels in one year, but the change was not effective until the next year. The figures in this table report the benefit levels actually in effect on 31 December of each year, regardless if changes were expected to take place the next day, for example.

[a] New York passed both a compulsory and a voluntary law in 1910. The compulsory law was declared unconstitutional, and the voluntary law was hardly used. New York passed a new law in 1913 that went into effect in 1914.

high when the states first introduced their laws, but the states provided fixed benefits to all injured workers, regardless of their wages, so the states' rankings fell sharply through the latter half of the 1910s as inflation eroded the value of the fixed amounts. In most states the rapid increase in wages during World War I often caused benefit levels to hit statutory maximums, thus causing the weekly maximum benefit to fall to as low as 25 to 33 percent of the weekly wage.[3]

After some delay most states raised their maximums between 1919 and 1923. The pattern of benefits in Texas provides a typical example of the inflationary effects on expected compensation when the states were slow in raising the benefit ceilings. When the law was first adopted in 1913 it provided expected benefits valued at $50.93 (in constant 1967 dollars) and by 1920 inflation had caused expected benefits in that year to fall to $34.95. Texas did not change the maximum allowable benefit until 1923, and that legislative change only brought the expected benefits to approximately the 1913 level, in real terms.

7.2 The Political Economy of Benefit Levels

What explains such a wide variation in benefit levels across states and over time in the early period of workers' compensation? Although the passage of workers' compensation generally was due to the cooperative efforts of the various interest groups, contentious disputes nevertheless persisted between workers and employers over the level of accident benefits. There was a range of benefit levels within which both workers and employers could gain from the legislation. Benefits had to be high enough that workers were better insured against workplace accident risk than under negligence liability. On the other hand, employers demanded an upper limit on benefit levels, in part, to avoid the moral hazard problems that might undermine their basic reason for shifting to workers' compensation—to reduce accident cost uncertainty. Public testimony and the bills proposed both by employers' and workers' groups in various states show clearly that workers sought workers' compensation parameters that led to higher benefit levels, while employers proposed parameters associated with much lower levels. The pressure from employers and workers was then filtered through the legislative process. In this section we describe the factors that influenced the benefit levels that workers and employers lobbied for and lay out the potential legislative outcomes.

7.2.1 The Employers' Choice of Benefit Levels

While employers generally lobbied for lower benefit levels, their choice of benefit levels varied in response to a variety of economic constraints. When employers decided on the benefit levels for which they lobbied state legislatures, they had to balance the costs of providing such insurance for their workers against the gains in the form of increased productivity. The costs of higher benefit levels were based largely on the insurance premiums that employers had to pay to obtain workers' compensation coverage.[4] Employers also anticipated some gains from higher benefit levels because better nonwage benefits have often been associated with higher productivity and lower turnover among workers. Further, employers generally did not bear the full economic burden of higher benefit levels even though the employer was required by law to pay all insurance premiums in nearly every state.[5] Nonunion workers often implicitly shared in paying the insurance costs associated with higher benefit levels because employers were able to pass a portion of the insurance costs on to workers through wage offsets (see chap. 3).

The preferred benefits of profit-maximizing employers potentially varied in response to a number of factors: the inherent danger of their workplaces, the productivity of their establishments, their size, the nature of their product market, their ability to pass their insurance costs on to workers through lower wages, and other factors influencing the premiums they paid for workers' compensation coverage.[6]

Employers generally sought to reduce the costs of their insurance premiums for workers' compensation coverage. Essentially the portion of the insurance premium that an employer actually paid could be written as

Premium $=$ (Accident probability) $\times$ (Benefits) $\times$ (Load factor)

$\times$ (Experience-rating parameter)

$\times$ (1 $-$ Share workers paid through wage offsets).

Higher benefit levels meant higher premiums. In more dangerous industries the higher accident risk raised premiums, holding benefit levels constant; therefore, employers had incentives to seek lower benefit levels to reduce the impact of higher accident risk on their insurance premiums. Another determinant of the premium was the load factor charged by insurers to cover administrative costs, to earn a profit, and to limit problems with adverse selection.[7] In states where insurance regulators allowed workers' compensation insurers to charge higher loads, employers tended to seek lower benefit levels to reduce the effect of these higher load factors on their insurance premiums.

The premiums paid for workers' compensation insurance were also influenced by the effectiveness of experience rating, which was the insurers' practice of making the employer's workers' compensation premium a function of the number and severity of accidents in that industry and in his workplace. If the premiums were not accurately experience rated, then the premiums that employers with more dangerous workplaces paid would be subsidized by payments from less dangerous workplaces. In these cases, employers with more dangerous workplaces might allow for higher benefit levels because they would not pay the full share of their insurance premium. Meanwhile, employers with less dangerous workplaces would have more incentive to push for lower benefit levels.[8] Our sense from cross-industry comparisons of workers' compensation insurance premiums, however, is that differences in accident risk across industrial classifications were reasonably well captured by adjustments in the manual rates set for each industry.[9] Within industries, however, experience rating across firms was less complete (McCahan 1929, 100–118). Studies of modern workers' compensation and examination of experience-rating formulas in the 1920s show that within industries, larger firms are more likely to be experience rated than smaller firms (Worrall and Butler 1988; Aldrich 1997 99–100, 153). Thus, if the same sort of relationship held eighty years ago, then larger firms may have had incentives to keep benefit levels lower than did smaller firms.

On the other hand, larger firms may have had an incentive to raise benefit levels to the extent that there were economies of scale in preventing accidents or in obtaining coverage of workers' compensation risk. In such a setting higher benefits would have raised the workers' compensation costs of smaller firms relatively more than for larger firms, giving larger firms a competitive advantage in the final product market. Such an anticompetitive strategy was most effective in settings where the industrial competitors were largely located within the same state. It was much less effective in settings where most of the competitors were located in other states with different workers' compensation laws.

Since employers potentially experienced higher productivity gains from providing workers relatively generous fringe benefits, some employers might have lobbied for higher benefit levels if they in turn led to higher productivity and profits. These employers were likely to be in industries with higher product prices, higher profit margins, or in industries where greater worker effort and reduced turnover had more of an effect on productivity.

Theoretically, employers generally tended to oppose changes in benefit levels and benefit maximums simply because wages changed. If the focus was on the benefit level, for example, when setting weekly maximums, the employers' choice of benefit levels was typically not influenced by the wage rate because the wage rate does not appear in the premium calculation above. Thus, both high-wage and low-wage employers would have opposed workers' efforts to obtain increases in benefit levels based on arguments that wages had changed.[10]

7.2.2   Factors Influencing the Workers' Choice of Benefit Levels

The workers' choice of optimum benefit levels depended on the balance between the benefits of higher compensation when they were injured and any costs they paid for obtaining the higher benefits. Workers clearly benefited from higher statutory benefit levels because this would have increased their payments if they were injured. Yet savvy workers could have anticipated that the higher benefits would come at some cost because employers were able to pass on at least part of their insurance costs related to higher benefits to nonunion workers through wage reductions. The wage offsets meant that workers were essentially paying for at least part of any increase in workers' compensation benefits and the "price" they paid was determined by the size of the premiums employers paid for workers' compensation coverage and the extent of the wage offset.

Economic analysis of the workers' optimal choice of benefits suggests that the level of benefits that they sought was determined by their wages, the dangers of their job, and a variety of factors influencing the insurance premiums paid by employers for workers' compensation coverage.[11] Workers with higher wages tended to demand higher benefit levels in settings where the weekly maximum was the focal issue. In economic terms benefit levels might be described as a normal good since workers with more income could "afford" to pay the costs associated with higher benefit levels.[12]

It is not clear whether workers in more dangerous jobs were more likely to demand higher benefit levels. If there were no wage offsets, these workers would clearly have sought higher benefit levels because they were more likely to face situations in which they were injured. On the other hand, the presence of the wage offsets meant that workers in more dangerous jobs would share in paying the higher premiums required to help pay for the higher benefits. Thus, workers in more dangerous jobs had to balance both the gains and losses from higher benefits and would not necessarily demand higher benefit levels.

The presence of wage offsets also meant that factors that might influence the employers' insurance premiums would influence the workers' optimal choice of benefits. Increases in the workers' share of the premiums through wage offsets would have tempered workers' efforts to secure higher benefit levels. Higher insurance loads raised the insurance premiums, which in turn would have caused workers to seek lower benefit levels to lower their implicit share of the premium costs. The extent of experience rating also influenced workers' choices. If the premiums were not experience rated very accurately, then the premiums paid for more dangerous workplaces would be subsidized by the premiums paid by employers for less dangerous workplaces. In these cases, workers in more dangerous workplaces might seek higher benefit levels because the insurance premiums would not fully reflect the greater danger and thus the worker and the employer would not fully pay the cost of raising the benefit levels.

Table 7.2 compares how workers' and employers' benefit level choices would have been affected by the various economic factors discussed above. Increases in insurance load factors and more accurate experience rating would have caused both workers and employers to reduce the benefit levels

Table 7.2   **How Economic Factors Influenced the Employers' and Workers' Demands for Benefit Levels**

Changes in the Optimal Level of Benefits with Respect to Increase in	Employer	Worker
Workers' implicit share of insurance costs (extent of wage offset)	Increase	Decrease
Accident rate	Decrease	Increase or decrease
Experience rating of premiums	Decrease	Decrease
Insurance load factor	Decrease	Decrease
Wage[a]	No effect	Increase
Product price	Increase	—
Number of workers	Increase or decrease	—
Labor productivity	Increase	—

Source: Fishback and Kantor (1998b, 115).

Notes: Dashes imply no prediction. These predictions are derived from economic models of the benefit decisions for workers and employers. The full derivations are reported in Fishback and Kantor (1998b, app. A). The predictions above assume that both workers and employers share in paying the workers' compensation insurance premium, which implies a partial wage offset. When the worker completely pays the insurance premium in the presence of a full wage offset, the accident rate and the insurance load would have no impact on the employers' choice of benefit levels. When the employer pays the full insurance premium because there is no wage offset, the workers would demand higher benefits when the accident rate rises, but none of the other factors would affect their choice of benefit levels.

[a]This is the prediction when employers and workers are choosing levels of benefits. If they are choosing the replacement percentage of wages, the employer will seek lower benefit percentages when the wage rate increases, while workers might seek higher or lower benefit percentages.

they sought. There are three types of changes, however, that might have led workers and employers to seek conflicting changes in benefit levels. First, increases in wages would have led workers to demand higher benefit levels, while employers would have sought no changes in benefit levels. Thus, the absence of any effect on benefit levels when wages changed might have been a signal that employers had significant influence over the benefit-setting process in state legislatures. Second, in areas where there was more inherent danger, high-risk employers would have pressed for lower benefit levels, while workers in high-risk industries might have sought either lower or higher benefit levels. Finally, when the wage offset increased, causing workers to pay a larger implicit share of the workers' compensation insurance premiums, employers would have allowed higher benefit levels while workers would have sought lower benefit levels, holding other factors constant.

7.2.3   Potential Legislative Outcomes

While groups of workers and employers lobbied for their optimal benefit levels, state legislators made the final decision subject to the governor's veto. As in the other chapters, we suggest that legislators chose benefits using a political calculus in which they maximized their own objectives, subject to pressures from the electorate and from competing economic and political interest groups. Employers and workers were able to exert influence on the legislators' choices based on their relative strength in the political arena. Employers' political strength was derived largely from their ability to organize effectively, which enabled them to apply political pressure on legislators, provide legislators with relevant information on the issue, and offer reelection contributions and support. On the other hand, their large numbers gave workers political strength because they were the vast majority of the electorate. Such strength was more effectively wielded when there was a strong union presence that could organize the workers' lobbying efforts. Workers' efforts were boosted further in states where there was a strong progressive reform movement, as shown in the previous chapter's analysis of state insurance funds. Once workers' compensation had been enacted, bureaucratic agencies established to administer the law potentially influenced benefit levels because they played a major role in providing legislators with information about how the system functioned. The workers' chances of raising benefits or employers' opportunities to determine benefit levels were enhanced if they could influence the bureaucratic agency administering the law.

Legislators may have responded to the lobbying of workers and employers in several ways. If legislators' political successes were tied to satisfying the median voter interested in the workers' compensation issue, then they were likely to focus on choosing the optimum benefit level from the workers' perspective because workers were far more numerous than employers.[13] If the key to political success was pleasing interest groups that could provide significant resources to aid in reelection campaigns, for example, then legislators may have focused on satisfying the demands of the most influential interest groups, or at least reaching a middle ground between those demands and the wishes of median voters. During the early 1900s, many unions claimed that employers' interests dominated state legislatures, which would have meant that employers' demands would have dominated in legislators' decisionmaking. On the other hand, in states where organized labor was strong, unionized workers wielded significant political power, as unions served as the mechanism that helped workers overcome the free-rider problem in voicing their political views (Olson 1965).

7.3 Lessons from a Quantitative Analysis of Workers' Compensation Benefit Levels

What specifically motivated legislators' choices is an empirical question. We examined how various political economic factors influenced the large variation in workers' compensation benefit levels across states and time. In our regression analysis we simultaneously examined how states' benefit levels were affected by such factors as the extent of union strength, average accident risk, the extent of wage offsets, firm size, manufacturing productivity, broad-based political coalitions, and the workers' compensation bureaucracy. We also controlled for the influence of events associated with specific years that would have affected all states in the same way, as well as the influence of specific features of each state that did not change over time. The quantitative results are reported in further detail in appendix K and in Fishback and Kantor (1998b).[14]

The statistical findings suggest that the legislatures heeded the demands of both employers and workers. While workers had an advantage because they accounted for a larger share of the voters in elections, employers still wielded significant political clout in the legislatures through their organized lobbying efforts and their financial support of legislators in elections. Workers were more successful at raising benefits in states where organized labor was stronger and thus could come closer to matching the concerted lobbying efforts of employers. Benefit levels were higher, ceteris paribus, in states with greater unionization, where political upheaval led to shifts in party control of the state legislature, and where bureaucracies, as opposed to the courts, administered the workers' compensation system.

One sign that state legislatures responded to the demands of high-accident-risk employers is that benefits were lower in states where more workers were employed in dangerous industries. Employers in those industries preferred lower benefit levels, while their workers might have chosen either higher or lower benefits. Both measures of accident risk led to economically significant reductions in benefit levels. A 10 percent increase in average accident risk in manufacturing was associated with roughly a 5 percent reduction in benefit levels. Similarly, a 1 percentage point increase in the percentage of workers in mining, one of the most dangerous industries during this time period, was associated with a 2.4 percent decline in benefit levels.[15]

Another sign that legislators were attentive to the demands of employers is the absence of a strong positive effect of higher wages on benefit levels. When wages were higher, workers generally would have demanded higher benefit levels. Meanwhile, optimizing employers had incentives to oppose raising benefit levels in response to higher wages.[16] The quantitative analysis could not reject the hypothesis that benefit levels were unaffected by changes in wages. Thus, employers appear to have been successful in limiting the benefit increases that workers sought simply because their wages rose.

We anticipated that firms with more employees, that received higher product prices, or that had higher labor productivity would have been more likely to support higher benefits. When we tested these relationships, however, we could not reject the hypothesis of no effect. The results cast some doubt on the notion that larger and more productive firms could have used higher workers' compensation benefits to gain a product market advantage over their smaller and less-productive competitors.

Benefit levels received a relatively strong boost from the presence of stronger unions. Workers gained more political clout in areas where organized labor was relatively stronger. In addition, unionized workers also had relatively strong incentives to push for higher benefit levels because they were more effective at preventing wage offsets (see chap. 3). On the other hand, the lower wage offset meant that employers had an incentive to lobby for lower benefit levels. The quantitative analysis indicates that in states dominated by industries where organized labor had a greater national presence, organized labor was successful in overcoming the pressure from employers for lower benefit levels. When our union measure rose by 1.0 percent, the benefit levels rose by 0.97 percent.

Legislators often have broader agendas than simply pleasing narrowly focused economic interest groups. To ensure reelection they also had to pay at least some attention to the demands of the electorate, which may have meant balancing workers' compensation issues with other social, political, or economic issues. Reform movements played a small role in determining the timing of adoption of the law and a larger role in the choice between private and state insurance (see chaps. 4 and 6). They also played a role in determining the level of benefits.

Shifts in the party composition of state legislatures had economically and statistically significant positive effects on benefit levels. Strong political reform movements during the Progressive Era often caused the party composition of state legislatures to shift dramatically around the time of the introduction of workers' compensation. Thus, during these initial upheavals, we might expect to see higher benefits in settings where political control of the legislature shifted from one party to the other. Further, when the reformers' opponents attempted to retake the legislature, they may have competed to obtain the support of the reform-minded sectors of the electorate by proposing even higher benefits. For example, in the 1914 gubernatorial race in Ohio, Republican gubernatorial candidate Frank Willis called for higher benefits in his efforts to unseat progressive Democratic governor James Cox and to lead the Republicans in their efforts to retake control of the legislature from the Democrats.[17] In the quantitative analysis a shift in party dominance in at least one branch of the legislature was associated with a 5.1 percent increase in benefit levels.

Once workers' compensation was adopted, workers appear to have been joined in the struggle for higher benefits by the bureaucratic agents that administered the new system. States typically chose to administer their workers' compensation programs in one of two ways. By 1930, ten states administered the laws through the courts, with employers and workers establishing agreements regarding accident compensation subject to the statutory guidelines and the courts settling disputes. Thirty-eight states administered workers' compensation with a bureaucratic commission, which directly oversaw the disbursement of accident compensation.[18] The state commissions had the potential to act as advocates for changes in the workers' compensation laws because they were often a key source of information for legislators, although their attitudes could have been influenced by either employers or workers. The quantitative analysis shows that when a state had a workers' compensation bureaucracy in place during the previous year, the benefit levels were about 7.3 percent higher. Thus, it appears that workers benefited more than employers from the lobbying by administrative agencies.

7.4   Lessons from Three Case Studies of the Political Struggle over Benefit Levels

The quantitative analysis highlights the important roles played by workers, employers, and reformers, yet it does not offer a full picture of how benefits were determined in the political process. Information from cases studies in Ohio, Missouri, and Minnesota adds more depth to the analysis. The case studies confirm many of the findings in the quantitative analysis, while illuminating how workers and employers compromised on their original demands. In a number of cases each interest group had to settle internal disputes regarding their willingness to compromise in choosing the final benefit levels.

7.4.1   Proposed Benefit Levels and the Nature of Compromise

In all three states the benefit levels proposed by employers were clearly lower than the benefit levels sought by workers. As a result, the legislative process involved a series of compromises in which various different parameters of the workers' compensation law were subject to simultaneous negotiation.

In Ohio when workers' compensation was being discussed in 1911, the key parameter that distinguished the benefit packages proposed by organized labor and employer groups was the de jure percentage of workers' compensation premiums that workers would pay. The Ohio Manufacturers' Association (OMA) actively supported a proposal requiring workers to pay 25 percent of the insurance premiums to provide workers' compensation benefits. The Ohio State Federation of Labor sponsored an alternative proposal that called for employers to pay the entire premium. The law that was enacted struck a compromise between these two positions that also involved other features of the legislation. Workers were required to pay only 10 percent of employers' insurance premiums, but in return they gave up the option of choosing between filing a negligence suit or a workers' compensation claim after an accident occurred. Early in the process organized labor obtained their key demand that the state, and not private companies, insure workers' compensation risk. Although the OMA worried that paying 90 percent rather than 75 percent of the insurance premium might have led to the failure of the new law, their fears were unjustified, because within several years employers accepted the entire legal burden of workers' compensation premiums (Fishback and Kantor 1997, 12, 16–17).

In Minnesota during the 1910s the legislature made a series of changes in benefit levels. In each case the benefits proposed by workers exceeded the benefits proposed by employers. In 1913 when workers' compensation was enacted, the employers' initial proposal was to pay the same benefits as in New Jersey, which offered the lowest benefits of any state at the time (see table 7.1), while requiring workers to pay 20 percent of the insurance premiums. Organized labor, on the other hand, was adamantly opposed to paying any of the insurance costs and proposed raising the maximum weekly death benefits from the employers' proposal of ten dollars to fifteen dollars, the number of weeks workers would receive permanent disability or death benefits from 300 to 333, and the maximum total benefit from three thousand to five thousand dollars. The final result largely favored employers. Despite several attempts to improve benefits through amendments in the House and Senate, the legislature essentially followed the New Jersey low benefit structure. Workers managed to force employers to pay the entire insurance premiums, but they traded away the option to choose between negligence suits and workers' compensation claims, as Ohio workers had.

After both employers and workers in Minnesota agreed to slightly improve benefit levels in the 1915 legislature, they waged a major struggle over benefits in 1917. Organized labor, with the help of the Department of Labor and Industries, proposed a substantial increase in the wage replacement rate from one-half to two-thirds, a substantial rise in the maximum weekly benefit, a reduction in the waiting period from two weeks to one week, and a requirement that employers pay all medical costs. During the legislative session, labor's representatives in the legislature compromised at a replacement rate of 60 percent, a weekly maximum of twelve dollars, and a reduction in the waiting period of one week. During the course of the 1910s, the continued pressure from organized labor raised benefits from near the bottom of benefits in 1913 to a ranking among the top quartile of the states with workers' compensation in 1921 (see table 7.1).

In Missouri, where the battles over the passage of workers' compensation lasted nearly fifteen years, the gap between the employers' and organized labor's proposals was often quite large. For example, in 1919 the labor proposal called for a wage replacement rate of two-thirds along with no weekly maximum. The bill that passed the 1919 legislature more closely matched the employers' demands by lowering the weekly maximum to fifteen dollars. After voters struck down the 1919 act in a referendum, organized labor continued to propose substantially higher benefits than those offered by employers both inside the legislature and in proposals to be voted on in referenda. Finally, in a 1925 act employers and workers compromised, the employers allowed relatively high benefits in return for the elimination of state insurance, and voters approved the law in a 1926 referendum. In the first year of operation in 1927, Missouri's benefits ranked sixth among the forty-three workers' compensation states (see table 7.1).

7.4.2   Organized Labor's Support in the State Legislatures

In the regression analysis of benefit levels across states and time, we found that areas where organized labor had more strength tended to have higher benefit levels. Similarly, studies of roll-call voting within state legislatures show that legislators with strong ties to organized labor consistently voted to amend legislation to include higher benefits. Legislators that could be identified as having strong union ties nearly unanimously voted in favor of higher benefits. In addition, legislators from districts with higher unionization rates consistently supported higher benefits.[19]

In Ohio in 1911 there was a series of House votes on amendments to the compromise bill that required workers to pay 10 percent and employers to pay 90 percent of the workers' compensation insurance premiums. When the compromise bill reached the House floor on 26 April, Republican representative Charles Reid offered an amendment to raise the workers' burden to 20 percent, but it was defeated seventeen to seventy-four, as legislators who had strong labor ties voted unanimously against the amendment. The next day progressive representative W. B. Kilpatrick tried the reverse strategy, calling for an amendment that would have required employers to pay 100 percent of the premiums. After Speaker of the House Samuel Vining, at Reid's behest, ruled the amendment out of order because the issue had already been voted on, Kilpatrick appealed the decision and lost by a close vote of forty to thirty-eight. Again, legislators with strong labor ties unanimously voted against the speaker's decision; progressives and representatives from districts with relatively high accident rates also tended to vote against the speaker's ruling.[20] Kilpatrick then tried again in the afternoon, moving that the vote on Reid's original amendment be reconsidered and amending Reid's amendment so that employers would be required to pay the entire workers' compensation premium. This time his amendment was voted down thirty-five to seventy.[21] Labor representatives again supported this amendment.[22]

In 1913 the Minnesota House voted on a series of amendments related to benefits. These included attempts to raise the weekly maximum benefit payment from $10 to $15, the maximum level of medical benefits from $100 to $195, and the payment of retroactive benefits to workers after thirty days of disability to cover the benefits they had not been paid during the two-week waiting period. Roll-call analysis of the voting on the each of these amendments showed that legislators from districts where union members constituted a greater percentage of the population tended to vote in favor of the amendments. Although union members accounted for a relatively small fraction of a representative's total constituency (averaging 1.5 percent), a change of 1.8 percentage points (one standard deviation) in union membership in a legislator's district would have increased the legislator's probability of voting for the amendments by 20 to 34 percentage points.[23]

In Missouri in 1919 the battle over benefits included a roll-call vote in the House on raising the weekly maximum from eighteen to twenty-one dollars. The amendment was struck down by a vote of forty-seven to seventy-five. Analysis of the voting shows again that legislators from districts where union members constituted a larger percentage of the population strongly supported the measure (Kantor and Fishback 1994a).

7.4.3   The Effects of Differences within Interest Groups

In several states there were differences in attitudes within groups about the proper benefit levels. As discussed in chapter 5, in some states internal strife within labor groups and employer groups actually led to perverse effects, delaying the adoption of workers' compensation in Minnesota by two years and in Missouri by nearly fifteen years.

In Minnesota the internal struggle over the proper parameters of the law developed early in 1911. The 1909 Employers' Liability Commission fractured as the organized labor and state bar representatives offered a majority report while a minority report was written by the employers' representative. The division in the commission paled, however, in comparison with the divisions within the interest groups themselves. The membership of the Minnesota Employers' Association (MEA) was not willing to support their own representative's bill because they could not agree on the proper parameters of the bill (MEA, 14 December 1911). On the labor side, the labor representative found that his own advisory group of fifty labor leaders thought the benefits he had proposed were too low. The disagreement within each group stifled effective compromise between the groups and prevented the adoption of workers' compensation in 1911.

Internal conflicts within organized labor continued as the employers' proposal, which mimicked the low benefits in New Jersey, worked its way through the 1913 legislature. The Minnesota State Federation of Labor (MnSFL) and the St. Paul Trades Assembly were willing to accept the relatively low benefit levels, as long as they imposed the full de jure cost of insurance on employers and worker negligence would never bar the payment of benefits. To establish workers' compensation in 1913, they were willing to accept the low benefits in the MEA proposal with the full expectation of amending the law in future sessions of the legislature.[24] The low benefits in the proposed bill led some members of the MnSFL, the railroad brotherhoods, and the Minneapolis Trades and Labor Assembly (MTLA) to accuse the MnSFL of "selling out the cause of the workers to their employers." They argued for pushing for higher benefits in the initial law on the grounds that the law could not be easily amended later.[25] To some extent, the MnSFL's prediction that they would be able to amend workers' compensation to increase the benefits in later legislatures proved prescient. Over the next several legislatures they were able to obtain higher benefits and move from a ranking among the lowest benefit levels in the nation in 1913 to one among the upper quartile by 1919 (Kantor and Fishback 1998).

The struggle over the details of workers' compensation legislation that delayed adoption in Minnesota was minor in comparison to what occurred in Missouri. Missouri was one of the many states to establish a workers' compensation commission in 1910. However, the failure on the part of organized labor and of employers to compromise effectively over the level of benefits, waiting periods, the coverage of occupational diseases, and state insurance led to stalemates in the legislature throughout the 1910s. By 1917 a divisive split had developed within organized labor. The Missouri State Federation of Labor (MoSFL) was ready to compromise with employers so that workers could finally receive the benefits of workers' compensation. They planned to seek amendments to the law later. The building trades unions, on the other hand, were interested in securing their desired bill at the time of adoption, on the grounds that amending the law later would be difficult politically. The divisions within organized labor delayed the adoption once again in 1917 (Kantor and Fishback 1994a).

In 1918 the MoSFL and building trades unions came together and proposed a bill for the 1919 legislature that called for relatively generous benefits—two-thirds of the wage and no maximum weekly benefit—and state insurance. It is clear that legislators focused more fully on the demands of employers because the bill enacted by the 1919 legislature imposed a maximum weekly benefit of fifteen dollars per week and eliminated state insurance. Once again, the MoSFL agreed to the changes, arguing that if state insurance and high benefits were not politically feasible, then the goal should be to get the best workers' compensation bill possible and to seek prolabor amendments in later years. The building trades unions disagreed, demanding a law with state insurance and high maximum benefits or no law at all. The building trades and some other union elements then joined damage-suit attorneys in seeking a referendum to strike down the legislative act. The strategy was successful, as voters rejected the 1919 workers' compensation law by a close 52.2 to 47.8 percent margin.

The intransigence of the building trades continued for several more years. In 1921 the MoSFL, the Associated Industries of Missouri (AIM), and other employer organizations cooperated to pass a new workers' compensation law that added a state fund that would compete with private insurers and raised the weekly maximum benefit from fifteen to twenty dollars. The building trades council remained dissatisfied with this compromise and again joined the damage-suit lawyers in forcing a referendum that struck the act down. In 1923 the legislature could come to no compromise, freeing organized labor to place their dream initiative with state insurance and high weekly maximums of thirty dollars on the ballot. The initiative's resounding defeat at the polls finally convinced the building trades that compromise was necessary. In 1925 the legislature passed another workers' compensation law, which was approved in a 1926 referendum, that eliminated state insurance but gave Missouri workers their relatively generous benefits.

7.4.4   The Significance of Political Institutions

The case histories also show how the original proposals were altered and shaped into legislation by the political process. The interest groups tried to frame the debates over their proposals, but the debates were often reframed as the proposals moved from the employers' liability commissions through the House, the Senate, the governor's office, and even voter referenda. Since at each stage the relative political strength of labor and employers varied, proposals that carried the day in the House might face severe problems in passing the Senate, while the compromises struck in the legislature might not satisfy the electorate. The case studies, therefore, show the importance of veto power at each stage of the political process in shaping the ultimate form of workers' compensation laws. The importance of this veto power is also illustrated by the party shift coefficients in the quantitative analysis. A party shift in one house of the legislature raised benefit levels to some degree by reframing the debate in the other house, but the benefit levels rose still higher when the party shift occurred in both houses of the legislature.

In Ohio a key event that shaped the final law occurred in 1911 when labor leader and Senate president pro-tem William Green rammed a modified version of the labor proposal through the Senate. The Senate action established a benchmark for further discussion but was not decisive. Governor Harmon, who was less progressive than the legislature, immediately announced that he would veto the labor version of the bill, and then worked with House members to develop a compromise that eventually was enacted (Fishback and Kantor 1997, 12–17).

In Minnesota in 1913 and again in 1915 the veto power of one house of the legislature is effectively illustrated by the struggles over the waiting period before benefits would be paid. In both years the House passed bills that called for shorter waiting periods than those proposed in bills passed by the Senate. The bills then went to conference committee where the Senate's rejection of the shorter waiting period stood.[26]

Missouri's experience offers a final example of the impact of veto power by the voters in referenda. In 1919 the Missouri House passed a bill with a weekly maximum of eighteen dollars, which also included a state insurance provision. The Senate then lowered the maximum to fifteen dollars and eliminated state insurance. As described above, the interest groups dissatisfied with the legislation, albeit for different reasons, forced a voter referendum that vetoed the legislation. Once the potential for a veto by referendum was established, more strategic behavior was practiced in legislative deliberations. In 1921 a state insurance fund to compete with private insurers was added by floor amendment at the last minute. The amendment was widely supported by opponents of workers' compensation as a means of ensuring the law's defeat at the polls (Kantor and Fishback 1994a, 288–91).

7.5 Summary

The general concept of workers' compensation included a range of benefits under which both employers and workers could benefit. Yet, adjustments of benefit levels within that range could lead to a significant redistribution of the gains available from enacting the legislation. Thus, even though employers and workers might have gained with any benefit level within the range when compared to the status quo, significant disputes erupted as both employers and workers sought to increase their share of the gains from passing the law. The disputes ultimately were settled by state legislators.

The state legislators paid substantial attention to the demands of several interest groups. Employers in high-risk industries succeeded in pressuring legislatures to keep benefit levels low. Further, they succeeded in convincing legislatures to hold the line on benefits despite wage increases. The employers' push for low benefits was tempered in areas where organized labor was strong. In states with a greater share of manufacturing employment in unionized industries, benefits were substantially higher. Furthermore, once agencies were established to administer workers' compensation, organized labor succeeded in enlisting the efforts of state administrators to help raise benefit levels in the years after workers' compensation was adopted.

Another key factor in determining benefit levels was the presence of political reform movements, like that of the progressives, within state legislatures. Political power shifts, as measured by shifts in the party dominance of state legislatures, played a stronger role in the determination of benefit levels than they did in the adoption of workers' compensation more generally. In chapter 6 we find a similar result when examining the struggles over state insurance. We believe the reason is that all sides expected to benefit from the adoption of workers' compensation, but their interests differed on the issue of benefit levels. Employers typically opposed high benefits, but in states where political reformers forged a coalition with organized labor, the benefit levels were higher and relatively radical features such as state insurance were more likely to have been included in the workers' compensation law.

Case histories offer several additional insights into the determination of benefit levels. They confirm that workers initially proposed higher benefits than employers were willing to offer. Organized labor and employers played important roles in framing the debates over benefit levels, which involved a range of parameters including the wage replacement percentage, the weekly maximums, waiting periods, and the de jure share of the insurance premiums paid by employers. The case studies show that the legislative compromises over benefit levels often involved adjustments along these different margins. In Ohio and Minnesota, for example, employers increased their de jure share of the cost of insurance premiums to ensure that workers did not retain their rights to sue under negligence liability. Finally, the studies of Minnesota and Missouri show that the struggle over benefits could sometimes lead to perverse results. Even though employers and workers both anticipated gains from workers' compensation, their struggle to increase their share of the gains through adjustments in benefit levels actually led to delays in the adoption of workers' compensation by two years in Minnesota and nearly a decade in Missouri.

Notes

1. Stroud's argument was printed in a letter to the editor of the *Birmingham News* under "Manufacturers on Compensation Act," 9 February 1919, 6. Senator Leeth's statement appeared in "Senator Leeth Explains Why Compensation Bill Was Delayed," *Labor Advocate*, 8 March 1919, 1.

2. We also used the national average wage, as opposed to each state's specific wage, to avoid a spurious positive relationship between wages and benefits in the quantitative analysis that we summarize later in the chapter and in appendix K.

3. In nearly all states employers were required by statute to pay all of the insurance premiums required to provide the workers' compensation benefits. However, the issue of whether workers would share in paying the premiums was actively discussed in some states. In the initial Ohio law workers were required to pay a share of the premium, which in essence reduced their expected benefits from the law. We have adjusted the expected benefits in Ohio downward.

4. The employer might pay these premiums to a separate insurer, either private or state, or he might self-insure and just pay out the workers' compensation premiums directly.

5. The exceptions were Ohio and Oregon just after they passed workers' compensation. Both states joined the remaining states in forcing employers to pay 100

percent of the workers' compensation insurance premiums within a few years of their initial passage.

6. The employer's demand for workers' compensation benefit levels can be derived from the maximization of the following profit function:

$$A(C) = RQ(zL,C) - WL - (1 - k)e(1 + h)pCL,$$

where L is the number of workers employed, R is the product price, z is a labor productivity parameter, and $Q(zL,C)$ is output, which rises at a diminishing rate with increases in labor and benefits (Q_L, $Q_C > 0$; Q_{LL}, $Q_{CC} < 0$). We assume that the derivative of the marginal product of labor with respect to benefit levels is positive ($Q_{LC} > 0$). Generally, efficiency-wage models predict that improvements in workers' nonwage benefits can lead to greater labor productivity. Further, increased compensation when injured would allow workers more freedom to increase productivity because the worker's net loss from an accident is reduced. The representative employer would then choose C to satisfy the first-order condition for a maximum:

$$(2) \qquad A_c = RQ_c - ep(1 - k)(1 + h)L = 0,$$

leading to the following demand function for benefit levels:

$$C^e = C(R, z, e, p, k, h, L).$$

When there is less than a full wage offset, an employer would seek higher benefit levels in settings where the wage offset (k) is higher, in industries where the accident rate (p) is lower, there is less experience rating (e is lower), insurance loads (h) are lower, the product price (R) is higher, and labor productivity (z) is higher. The employer's choice of the optimal benefit level will be the same whether wages rise or fall. In other words, the employer's optimal benefit level is independent of the wage, as the first-order condition suggests. A discussion of the derivation of these results and how they might be influenced by other assumptions can be found in Fishback and Kantor (1998b).

7. In a world where there were no information costs or costs of administering insurance, the insurance premium would have been "actuarially fair." An actuarially fair premium is equal to the benefits paid when an accident occurs multiplied by the probability the accident would occur. Given the administrative costs of selling insurance, companies would then add a load factor into the premium to cover their administrative costs. Load factors were sometimes included to reduce problems associated with adverse selection, which arise because insurance companies cannot always tell the difference between customers with high risks and those with low risks. Without such information, if they set the premiums based on the average risk, only high-risk customers will buy, and the insurance companies will lose money. By setting the premiums higher, under some conditions the insurance company can make money selling insurance to the high-risk customers even though they sell no insurance to the low-risk customers.

8. Experience rating is important because incomplete experience rating offers high-risk groups the opportunity to obtain subsidies from low-risk groups. Baicker, Goldin, and Katz (1998) view problems with experience rating as a central factor in explaining the introduction of unemployment insurance in the United States in the 1930s.

9. Workers' compensation appears to have been more fully experience rated than unemployment insurance later became, in part because private insurers played a much larger role in determining workers' compensation insurance premiums. McCahan (1929, 100–118) suggests that private insurers were relatively effective at experience rating across industries because they pooled information through the

National Council on Compensation Insurance. He suggests that state funds had less success at experience rating, although many state funds tried to experience rate across industries by maintaining separate funds for each industry grouping.

10. On the other hand, in situations where benefits were set as a percentage of the wage, that is, the maximums were not binding, the wage rate played a role in determining the benefit level. Consequently, higher-wage employers tended to press for lower benefit percentages to reduce their insurance premiums. Workers' compensation benefits can be discussed in terms of the level of benefits or in terms of replacing a percentage of the wage. We focus much of the discussion on benefit levels here because a large share of the battles fought were over the maximum weekly payment to workers. Generally, our discussions of how the choice of benefits is influenced by the dangers of the job, load factors, productivity, wage offsets, and so on are the same whether we focus on benefits as levels or as percentages of the wage. The prediction of how wage rates would influence benefits is the only predicted effect to differ. For further discussion, see Fishback and Kantor (1998b, app. A).

11. The optimal benefit levels from the standpoint of the individual worker can be determined by examining the maximization of the following expected utility function:

$$E(C) = (1 - p)U[W - ek(1 + h)pC] + pV(C),$$

where p $(0 \le p \le 1)$ is the probability that the disabling accident would occur. The worker's net income if he remains uninjured is the term $[W - ek(1 + h)pC]$, where W is the workers' annual wage not accounting for any potential wage offset from employer-provided accident insurance, k is the share of the cost of the benefits that workers pay through wage offsets $(0 \le k \le 1)$, e is the extent to which insurance premiums are experience rated to reflect industrial differences in accident risk $(e < 1$ implies that the worker's industry was subsidized by other industries), h is the insurance load factor, which reflects administrative costs, including the monitoring costs associated with moral hazard problems, and pC represents the actuarially fair insurance premium that would provide C dollars worth of benefits in case of injury. U is the worker's utility of income with no accident and V is the utility function in the disabled state. U' and V' are positive and U'' and V'' are negative, implying risk aversion.

The worker chooses C to maximize his expected utility and the first-order condition for a maximum, derived from the equation above, is

$$E_c = V'(C) - ek(1 - p)(1 + h)U'[W - ek(1 + h)pC] = 0.$$

Using the first-order condition we can derive the representative worker's optimal choice of benefits

$$C^w = C(e, k, p, h, W).$$

The comparative statics from the maximization problem imply that the worker would seek higher benefits at higher wages (W), when the wage offset (k) was lower, when the insurance load factor (h) was lower, and when workers' compensation premiums were less experience rated (e). The impact of changes in accident risk on the worker's benefit choice is uncertain. On the one hand, higher accident risk raises the worker's demand for higher benefits because the accident state of the world is more likely; on the other hand, if there is a wage offset the cost of the insurance to the worker also rises with the increase in accident risk. For a description of how these results were derived, see Fishback and Kantor (1998b, app. A).

12. In situations where workers were lobbying not for levels but for replacement

percentages, a higher wage did not necessarily cause workers to demand higher benefit percentages because their benefit levels were already tied directly to the wage rate by the replacement percentage.

13. Danzon (1988) used a median voter model to examine modern workers' compensation benefit levels. While offering some useful insights, it is only one model that can be used to explain legislative behavior. There is a variety of qualitative and quantitative evidence that state legislators paid attention to the pressures from interest groups and to political coalitions within the legislature. Employers, insurance companies, and organized labor had a much greater influence within state legislatures than their voting numbers would suggest. Many of these interest groups offered funds or personnel for reelection campaigns, framed the legislative debates for legislators, flooded hearings with lobbyists, and often served as key sources of information in an era when legislators did not have large staffs to conduct research or write legislation.

14. See also Fishback and Kantor (1998b).

15. Another factor that potentially influenced the mining coefficient was the size of the wage offset. As argued in chapter 3, nonunion coal miners experienced a full wage offset, but unionized miners experienced close to no wage offset. Since the mining variable includes both union and nonunion workers, the workers aggregated in the measure did not experience a full wage offset. Under this condition, employers in mining would demand lower benefits because workers were paying less of the benefits through lower wages (see table 7.2).

16. The employer's choice of benefit levels was unaffected by the wage in the theoretical model. This does not imply that the employer was indifferent to changes in benefit levels that were caused by wage changes. Instead, his optimal benefit choice was the same whether the wage was high or low; therefore, the employer would have been opposed to changes in the benefit level that were driven only by wage changes, holding other relevant determinants constant. When the focus was on benefit percentages as opposed to levels, employers tended to want lower benefit percentages as wages rose.

17. Ohio State Federation of Labor (1915a, 25–27). Cox charged that Willis was hostile to workers' compensation. Willis always strongly denied this. While running for reelection in 1916, Willis stated that not one line of the law had been changed during his administration, and that he had sought higher benefits but both labor and capital stated that the time was not yet right (Ridinger 1957, 103–5).

18. Wyoming administered the law through the courts but had a monopoly state insurance fund, so we have treated it in the regression analyses as having an administrative body.

19. See the analysis in Fishback and Kantor (1997, 15–17) of roll-call votes in the Ohio House of Representatives on 26 April 1911 on an amendment to raise the workers' insurance cost burden to 20 percent from 10 percent, on a House Speaker ruling that an amendment requiring employers to pay 100 percent of insurance premiums was out of order, and then a direct vote on an amendment to force employers to pay 100 percent of insurance premiums. For Minnesota see the discussion in Kantor and Fishback (1998) of the battle in the House over a series of amendments proposed by Representative Lundeen in April 1913 and of House votes on a reduction in the waiting period in 1915. For Missouri, see the analysis in Kantor and Fishback (1994a, 282–90) of four referenda and of a 1919 House amendment to raise the weekly maximum to twenty-one dollars.

20. The labor group voted unanimously against the speaker and for Kilpatrick's amendment. Among progressives 68.4 percent voted against the speaker, while only 27 percent of nonprogressives voted against him. We gathered information

on the amount awarded in workers' compensation claims in Ohio from 1 January 1914 to 30 June 1915, as reported by the Ohio Industrial Commission (1916, 64–118), and divided by the adult male population in 1910 to get a sense of the extent of workplace injury problems in each county. Of representatives from counties where per capita injury payments were higher than the mean, 61 percent voted against the speaker in favor of Kilpatrick, while only 33.2 percent of the representatives from counties below the mean voted against the speaker.

21. See also Ohio House of Representatives *Journal* (1911, 846–52); *Cleveland Plain Dealer*, 28 April 1911; *Ohio State Journal*, 28 April 1911; *Toledo News-Bee*, 28 April 1911.

22. Although organized labor supported the amendment, the earlier support of progressives, Democrats, and representatives from high-injury areas evaporated. It is clear that their earlier support was based on the procedural issue involved, not the desire to force employers to pay a greater share of the de jure costs of workers' compensation insurance. A regression analysis of the voting revealed no sign of statistically significant support from progressives, Democrats, or representatives from counties that had relatively high accident risk. A one-standard-deviation increase in the probability of being a labor representative raised the probability of voting in favor of the amendment by a statistically significant 12.6 percentage points. Legislators who were farmers also supported labor's amendment. A one-standard-deviation increase in the probability of being a farmer raised support by a statistically significant 11 percentage points. The results from this roll-call analysis are available from the authors. See also Ohio House of Representatives *Journal* (1911, 846–52); *Cleveland Plain Dealer*, 28 April 1911; *Ohio State Journal*, 28 April 1911; and *Toledo News-Bee*, 28 April 1911.

23. The roll-call analysis involved estimating a probit of the legislators' vote on the issue while controlling for membership in key legislative committees, whether the legislator was a Democrat, the legislator's occupation, the percentage of the population in unions, the percentage in manufacturing, and agricultural output per person in the district. The roll-call votes were from the Minnesota House of Representatives *Journal* (1913, 1623–29). Committee memberships and occupations are from Minnesota Secretary of State (1913, 146–47, 151–53). Union membership is from Minnesota Department of Labor and Industries (1913–1914, 229). Agricultural output, population, and manufacturing employment data were obtained from the Inter-University Consortium for Political and Social Research (ICPSR) census tapes for 1910 and 1920.

24. See *Minneapolis Labor Review*, 14 March 1913; Lawson (1955, 217); *Labor World*, 19 April 1913; and MnSFL (1913, 36–37). The *Minneapolis Journal*, 10 April 1913, made the same plea to its readers: "[P]ass the bill and get the system started. It can be perfected better after it is in operation than by laying aside the whole matter for another two years, while the extremists on both sides quarrel about terms."

25. See MEA, 14 March 1913; *Labor World*, 15 March 1915; and *Minneapolis Labor Review*, 11 and 18 April 1913. The railroad brotherhoods were concerned that the new law would preempt their rights under the Federal Employers' Liability Acts of 1906 and 1908.

26. In 1913 the Senate and the House also chose different maximums for medical expenses, one hundred and two hundred dollars, respectively. They struck a compromise in conference committee that imposed an initial maximum of one hundred dollars but allowed the courts to order an additional one hundred dollars of benefits.

8

Epilogue
Lessons from the Origins of Workers' Compensation

Workers' compensation was the first of the social insurance programs to be widely enacted in the United States. A number of states in the 1920s and 1930s tentatively expanded workers' compensation to cover a limited range of occupational diseases. The states considered introducing unemployment insurance, health insurance, and old-age insurance during the 1910s and 1920s, but it was not until the 1930s that the federal government established unemployment insurance and old-age pensions for nonveterans. Government health insurance for the elderly followed in the 1960s, while broader government programs for health insurance have been the source of controversy in the 1990s.

Because workers' compensation was adopted during the Progressive Era, there has been a tendency to consider it as just one of the many reforms that the progressives initiated. In the political arena the progressives proposed and enacted the ballot initiative, referenda, popular election of senators, and recall elections for judges across the United States. In the economic realm, reformers sought a variety of labor market regulations and social insurance programs to protect workers against the risks associated with an industrializing society. One might argue that market competition for workers would have provided them with an implicit payment in the form of a compensating wage premium for accepting the risks of unemployment, illness, or accident. Moreover, by understanding that such events could occur, workers could plan their financial affairs in anticipation of experiencing a drop in income.

Social reformers of the early twentieth century understood the logic of the market, however, they rejected such thinking. As prominent economist and social reformer Richard T. Ely (1908, 13–14) argued: "The eighteenth century economic philosophy was . . . based on a now discredited and discarded belief in the beneficent code of nature, ruling the economic life as all other social life spheres, and which, if not interfered with, would bring to all classes and especially the workers, the maximum amount of economic well-being. . . . But experience has shown conclusively that . . . unregulated contract does not always conduce to freedom and fair opportunity—"the square deal"—but frequently means bondage and degradation." Further, according to some reformers, not only did market competition fail to protect workers, but individual workers failed to protect themselves. Reformer Henry Seager (1908, 91) of the American Association for Labor Legislation reasoned that since "the development of saving habits among wage-earners is painfully slow . . . [i]t is my contention that these evils [unemployment, accidents, illness] that are not in practice provided against by individual thrift and forethought can be and should be provided against by collective action." Thus, if the market supposedly could not help workers or if they could not help themselves, then government could.

Of the ambitious plans of reformers during the Progressive Era for a social safety net to protect workers from the potentially deleterious effects of modern industrialism, only workers' compensation was enacted almost universally across the United States. Such limited success, despite their ambitious plans, raises questions about the true strength progressives wielded in the early twentieth century. If workers' compensation was adopted because reformers overwhelmed conservative opposition to the expansion of government, why were the reformers so much less successful in establishing unemployment insurance, health insurance, and many of their other favored programs? Progressives, although they may have raised the public's awareness of the private and social problems that industrial accidents wrought, have probably received more credit for the success of workers' compensation than they deserve.

We offer an alternative interpretation of the success of workers' compensation that builds on and enhances the analyses of earlier scholars. Each of the major interest groups—workers, employers, and insurance companies—anticipated gains from the legislation. Employers were dissatisfied with an increasingly uncertain negligence liability system that engendered substantial frictions and court costs. Further, they were able to pass on to workers a substantial portion of the costs of workers' compensation insurance through wage reductions. Workers received on average much larger payments for workplace accidents than under the old system. Even if workers "bought" most of this increase in average benefits, their welfare improved. They had faced problems in obtaining their desired level of accident insurance before workers' compensation, and the higher average benefits left them better insured. Finally, insurance companies anticipated gains from workers' compensation, as long as they could avoid the introduction of state insurance. Insurers had faced information problems in writing individual accident insurance. The shift to workers' compensation allowed commercial insurers to sell more coverage for workplace accidents than before as employers ended up purchasing more workers' compensation insurance than the combined amount of accident and employer liability insurance than they had sold before. Thus, instead of revolutionary change, workers' compensation was in fact an evolutionary change. The legislation evolved from the mutual desires of workers, employers, and insurers to resolve problems with workplace accident liability that had developed in the first decade of the twentieth century.

In contrast, employers in the various states showed little interest in supporting state government programs for unemployment insurance, old-age insurance, or sickness and health insurance. They had not been liable to workers in these areas before, and few employers saw much reason to expand their liability during the 1910s and 1920s. In addition, doctors actively opposed government-based health insurance once they had fully considered the implications of the program for their control of patient care. In sum, workers' compensation was the only workplace-based social insurance system that received strong support from all of the major interest groups involved in the issue.

To the extent that progressive reformers were trying to make government more responsive to the everyday needs of ordinary Americans, perhaps workers' compensation can be considered "progressive." Compensation legislation sprang from the shared interest of employers and workers to correct a market and legal imperfection. Both parties would have liked to have written a contract whereby workers, before any accident occurred, waived their rights to negligence suits in return for a fixed and guaranteed set of benefits. Yet, the common law and legislation in a number of states prevented employers and workers from individually negotiating preaccident contracts. Workers, reformers, and judges seem to have decided that individual workers could too easily have been persuaded to sign away their rights to negligence suits for an inadequate set of benefits, and thus the lot of the typical worker would be improved by having the benefits negotiated through the political process. The workers' compensation laws therefore both allowed these preaccident contracts and completed the contract by establishing the set of benefits to be paid.

Our interpretation of the origins of workers' compensation turns the analysis of the Progressive Era in a new direction. Progressive legislation has been seen by some as either top-down or bottom-up, that is, imposed by employers or won by workers and reformers. Yet reformers typically succeeded only when a variety of interest groups anticipated gains from their proposals. Therefore, future research into this episode of American economic and political history must address why such common ground could not be struck on other plans such as unemployment insurance, old-age pensions, and health insurance. Because progressives failed to rally support for their other plans, it was workers' compensation that served as a prelude to the welfare state, setting the stage for the dramatic expansion of the government's role during the New Deal and Great Society.

Placing our research into the broader context of the literature on institutional change, our results are consistent with an optimistic view of institutional development. While some recent research shows that expected net gains are neither a necessary nor sufficient condition for institutional change to occur, workers' compensation seems to be a case where legislation popular with large segments of the each of the major interest groups was passed.[1] Early research on the economics of institutional development offered only limited discussion of the actual process of change. Our study has uncovered in detail the important hurdles that must be overcome before a new legal regime is implemented. The realization that the major players could gain from the legislation is only a starting point. The interest groups still have to complete the tedious and often frustrating task of building the political coalition that ensures legislative success.

In the case of workers' compensation, although the majority in each group with a stake in the legislation supported the general idea of a no-fault accident compensation scheme, establishing a consensus on the specific details of the law within each group and across the interest groups often proved quite contentious. The legislation was very complex, consisting of multiple attributes that required multidimensional negotiations and trade-offs. In some cases when a consensus could not be reached, the passage of the income-improving policy was delayed. Thus, although groups may see benefits from a new institutional arrangement, how they resolve the distributional conflicts that naturally arise when the rules of the game are changed is what will determine whether profitable institutions displace the unprofitable. Specifically, because workers' compensation was so widely supported and offered critical relief from the worsening negligence liability system, workers' or employers' groups were willing to settle for less desirable features of the legislation but with the full expectation of amending the system later. In many states, for example, unions accepted relatively low benefit levels in the beginning, despite some internal squabbles, in order to establish the basic law. In many of these states they later succeeded in ratcheting these benefits upward.

Finally, a natural question to ask of any historical study concerns what we can learn from the past. One lesson we might learn is that state-level liability legislation is more likely to become widespread when the major interest groups all favor it. During the 1970s there was a series of attempts to limit negligence liability and introduce no-fault liability for automobile accident insurance, which seems like a move similar to the adoption of workers' compensation. Yet, only sixteen states adopted no-fault laws and several have since repealed them.[2] There were some similarities in the adoption processes. The states where consumers had the greatest rise in auto insurance premiums were more likely to adopt the no-fault auto insurance laws, just as states that faced the greatest problems with employers' liability adopted workers' compensation earlier in the 1910s. The contrast between the no-fault laws may lie in two areas. First, the expectations for gain might not have been as great for automobile liability. There is only weak evidence that limiting tort liability reduces accident rates and severity. Consumers sought lower insurance premiums, but the evidence that no-fault laws lowered insurance premiums is mixed (Harrington 1994, 277). Second, there is a difference in the extent to which key interest groups were in agreement on the benefits of the liability change. Workers' compensation was favored by most workers, employers, and insurers, all represented by significant lobbying groups. Many attorneys also supported the legislation. On the other hand, no-fault automobile insurance laws, while favored by high-income drivers and the medical community, were vehemently opposed by tort lawyers. The success of the no-fault auto insurance laws in each state therefore was determined more by the strength of opposing lobbies. The limited passage of no-fault auto insurance laws reminds us more of the battles over state insurance waged by insurers and organized labor. In that case the stiff opposition of insurance companies prevented a majority of states from establishing state funds.

We might also ask how the insights gleaned from the history of the adoption of workers' compensation might guide efforts to reform the system today. A central reason why workers' compensation received widespread support in the 1910s was that it helped resolve legal and information problems associated with insuring individual workers' accident risk. The escalation of workers' compensation costs over the past twenty years has led to increasing dissatisfaction with the program. Ironically, a major reason why costs rose so rapidly stems from increasing problems with insuring workers' compensation risk associated with moral hazard.

The increase in moral hazard problems may stem from the expansion in benefit levels and injury coverage from the beginning of workers' compensation to the modern setting. The workers' compensation laws in the early 1900s explicitly limited problems with moral hazard. Workers bore a significant share of the burden of the injury because they received at most two-thirds (and often less) of their income in replacement. Medical costs were covered, but only up to a maximum level typically ranging from one hundred to two hundred dollars. Finally, the types of accidents arising at the time were relatively easy to monitor. Workers at the time were sustaining severe sprains, breaking bones, or losing limbs.

Since that time the level of benefits has been determined in the political arena. Into the 1970s, wage replacement rates were relatively low, in part because legislatures in a number of states were slow to raise weekly maximums. But in the 1970s legislatures finally responded to the demands of workers by raising the weekly maximums paid for benefits. Changes in the extent of taxation also played a substantial role in making benefits more lucrative because workers' compensation benefits are not subject to income taxes. Prior to World War II, less than 7 percent of American households paid income tax and prior to 1935 there was no social security tax. Thus, very few workers were subject to income taxes and there was almost no gap between after-tax income and pretax income. As tax rates have increased and the income levels at which taxes are paid have been lowered, the gap between after-tax income and regular income has grown. In consequence, workers' compensation benefits today replace from 80 to 100 percent of after-tax income, even though they may only replace 45 to 67 percent of pretax income. In addition, the costs of medical care for compensation injuries have risen sharply and in many states there is no deductible nor is there a limit on insurance payments. Finally, the most common types of injuries now are ones where detection is more problematic, particularly back injuries, and in some states coverage has been expanded to include job-related stress.

All three of these trends have contributed to increased problems with moral hazard.[3] In response, employers and insurers have proposed reforms designed to reduce problems with moral hazard by limiting benefits, introducing medical copayments and narrowing the range of compensable injuries. For the reforms to succeed, employers and insurers likely will have to persuade workers to join in a coalition favoring reform. In return for their support, workers must anticipate some benefit. They might be willing to participate in such a reform coalition if they expected their wages to rise in response to diminished postaccident benefits, as most empirical studies of compensating differences predict. However, would risk-averse workers be able to use the wage premiums to purchase private insurance to replace the reduction in their benefits? Certainly the disability and health insurance markets have broadened and deepened since the early 1900s. On the other hand, workers would be trying to replace the segment of the benefits that may have been the primary source of the modern increase in moral hazard problems. In fact, Moore and Viscusi (1990, 62) found that workers valued the increase in benefits in the 1970s so highly that they were willing to accept wage reductions that were nearly triple the increase in expected benefits.

Studying the origins of workers' compensation convinces us that the success of uniting workers, employers, and insurers to reform the modern workers' compensation system turns on workers' ability to privately insure some aspects of their own workplace accident risk. Because the moral hazard and adverse selection problems of insuring an individual's accident risk are great, especially for hard-to-detect injuries, it is not clear that workers will be able to find private insurance for the greater coverage that they received from the reforms of the 1970s. By raising benefit levels and expanding coverage, a move that workers valued greatly and that generally seemed humane, the states have created a situation in which insurance problems have contributed to escalating workers' compensation costs.

To resolve the insurance issues may require reducing the benefits and coverage from levels highly valued by workers. Employers would experience a reduction in their workers' compensation premiums that reflects both the lower benefits and reduced moral hazard problems. Yet, for workers to be made whole in this setting, if Moore and Viscusi's estimates of workers' valuations for the 1970s are correct, wages would have to rise by triple the decline in expected benefits. It is not clear that employers would be willing to pay such an increase in wage rates and, given the general distrust of markets as protectors of workers' interests, it might be harder still to convince workers that they would receive such a large increase. Thus, a modern reform would likely mean making one group better off at the expense of the other. The introduction of workers' compensation was relatively easy because so many interest groups gained. In contrast, reforming the modern problems with workers' compensation might be far more vexing because there may not be a simple reform that allows both workers and employers to gain relative to their positions under the current system.

Notes

1. See, for instance, Libecap (1989a) and Kantor (1998) for historical case studies showing the complex process of institutional change.

2. Our description of the adoption of automobile no-fault insurance laws is drawn from Harrington (1994).

3. Studies of the impact of higher benefit levels suggest that the number of reported temporary total disability accidents rises when benefit levels increase, while fatal and severe accident rates do not rise and in some cases fall. Kniesner and Leeth (1991) and Viscusi (1992) claim that this may be a sign that the problems with moral hazard may be less a function of workers' reducing the care that they exercise in the workplace and more a problem with increased reporting of accidents and possible fraud. Results also suggest that extending the waiting period reduces the number of reported accidents.

Appendixes

Appendix A
Accident Reporting under the Negligence System

It is extremely difficult to get comparable estimates of workers' losses due to nonfatal accidents because of substantial differences in the reporting of such accidents under negligence liability and workers' compensation. Comparisons of the number of nonfatal accidents reported to bureaus of labor before and after workers' compensation show that two to ten times as many serious nonfatal accidents were reported after workers' compensation was introduced. By contrast, fatal accident reporting did not spike upward after workers' compensation was adopted.

The differences in reporting under the two systems may have been caused by the disparate benefits the injured expected to receive under the two regimes. Under negligence liability workers had little incentive to report accidents to employers if they felt that there was little chance of receiving compensation. By reporting such an accident, the worker would be signaling to the employer that he was "accident prone," or worse yet that he was a "troublesome" employee. Either label might lead to negative repercussions. Similarly, employers had little incentive to reveal accidents to bureaus of labor unless they knew that the worker was going to press the issue with a suit or a request for compensation. By reporting relatively more accidents, the employer would have raised the factory inspectors' awareness of problems at his workplace, thus raising the risk of inspections and possible fines. Under workers' compensation, however, all workplace accidents were potentially compensable, so workers had far more incentive to report them and pursue their entitled benefits.[1]

In the course of examining the accident reporting issue, we have collected evidence from a variety of sources. This information is summarized below.

Accident Reporting at the Stonega Coke and Coal Company

One sign of the accident reporting problem within a single firm can be seen by studying the records of the Stonega Coke and Coal Company, which was primarily located in Virginia. The *Annual Reports of the Operations Department* reported a doubling in the rate of serious and slight accidents once workers' compensation was enacted. The number of serious accidents reported rose from 29 per million tons of coal produced during the period 1912 to 1918 (before workers' compensation in Virginia) to 61 per million tons in the period 1919 to 1925 (when workers' compensation was in effect). The number of slight accidents rose from 111 per million tons in 1912–1918 to 232 per million tons in 1919–1925. The reporting of fatal accidents was not nearly as different under the two legal systems. The number of fatalities per million tons held roughly constant at 0.005 per million tons in 1912–1918 and 0.004 per million tons in 1919–1925.[2]

Illinois Coal Mines

Between 1897 and 1906 the *Annual Coal Reports* of the Illinois Bureau of Labor Statistics reported an average of 118.7 fatal accidents per year and 492.4 nonfatal accidents during a period when the average number of employees rose from 33,788 to 61,988 men. In the report of the Illinois Industrial Commission for the calendar year 1919, by which time workers' compensation had been in effect for several years, coal mining experienced 145 deaths and 7,652 compensable injuries while employing approximately 87,000 men.[3]

Iowa Coal Mines

From 1906 to 1910, Iowa coal mines reported an average of 35.4 fatal accidents per year and 108.2 nonfatal accidents per year, while employing an average of 17,491 workers.[4] During the two-year period ending 30 June 1914, when workers' compensation was in effect in the state, the Iowa Industrial Commissioner (1914, 48–49) reported an average of 33 fatal accidents per year, 2 permanent total disability accidents, 22.5 permanent partial disability accidents, 216 temporary disability accidents lasting longer than two weeks, and 684 minor injuries.

Minnesota

In 1909 the Minnesota legislature required employers to report their accidents to the Minnesota Department of Labor and Industries. Extant letters between the department and Minnesota employers show that the department took its responsibility of investigating accidents in the state very seriously. A clipping department within the department scoured the state's newspapers looking for evidence of industrial accidents. If it found a mention of an accident, without receiving notification from the company, a letter of inquiry was generated. In general, the department believed that large numbers of firms were underreporting accidents. In quite a few cases the department sent out incredulous letters to firms that did not send any information about accidents. The archives of the department at the Minnesota State Historical Society in St. Paul contain many letters like the one of 29 September 1911, in which Labor Commissioner Houk sent a letter to the Parker and Topping Foundry asking, "Can it be possible that no accidents have occurred in that length of time [year ending 31 July 1911] to the people in the employ of said company?"

Ohio

Ohio is a valuable state to study the differences in reporting because it was quick to establish an industrial commission to oversee workers' compensation and it had a strong factory inspection law prior to the legislation. The same dramatic increase in the reporting of serious and minor injuries occurred. Just prior to the passage of the state's workers' compensation law, Ohio in 1910 tightened the rules for reporting accidents. As a result there was a substantial increase in the reporting of nonfatal accidents from 1910 to 1911: the number of serious nonfatal accidents rose from 795 to 1,481. Once workers' compensation was established and firmly in place, the number of serious accidents took another sharp turn upward from 1,481 to 7,344. When we compare the figures from 1910 to 1912, the number of fatal accidents in each industry changed very little, from 163 to 195. On the other hand, the number of serious accidents (disability lasting more than seven days) rose nearly tenfold from 795 to 7,344, while the number of minor accidents (disability of seven days or less) rose from 1,499 to 5,161.[5] The accident statistics from the factory inspection reports pale in comparison with the annualized number of industrial accidents reported under workers' compensation for the eighteen-month period from 1 January 1914 to 30 June 1915 (we annualized the report by dividing the number of accidents by 1.5). Because the workers' compensation report included a number of industries not listed in the factory inspection reports, we compare the situations where we believe the industrial categories matched up in the two reports. Typically, the number of fatal accidents reported is similar in both reports. There are, however, dramatic differences in the number of serious and minor accidents reported. The rise in reported accidents is at least double in every category and in some cases there is a tenfold increase. The sheer difference in accident reporting under the two systems suggests that it is extremely difficult to compare the compensation of nonfatal accidents before and after workers' compensation. In appendix C, however, we attempt such a comparison using two different methods. One method uses workers' reports of their accident compensation, which is surely to be plagued with the underreporting problem, and the other uses data from employers' reports of their accident compensation.

Appendix B

Workers' Compensation Benefits and the Construction of the Expected Benefits Variable

Workers' compensation laws established parameters for the payment of benefits to workers injured on the job and the families of workers who were killed in workplace accidents. Injured workers typically received payments of up to two-thirds of their weekly wage each week for the period of the disability, while the families of fatalities typically received weekly payments for a period of up to eight years. The parameters for compensation varied across states and by type of accident. In this appendix we describe the various payment parameters and show how we construct the expected benefits variable that is discussed in chapters 3 and 7.

Fatal Accident Payments

Table B.1 summarizes the provisions related to fatal accidents at the end of the first year of operation of each state's workers' compensation law.[6] In many states the percentage of the wage replaced varied in proportion to the number of family members. To aid comparability, the calculations in all of the benefit calculations are based on the assumption that the deceased's family consisted of a widow age thirty-five, a child age ten, and a second child age eight. We also assumed that the deceased's widow did not remarry and lived another thirty years. The New Jersey law of 1911, which established a pattern followed by many states, offered this family weekly payments equal to 45 percent of the worker's wage for up to three hundred weeks. Weekly benefits could not be lower than five dollars a week or higher than ten dollars a week, and the sum of the payments could not exceed three thousand dollars or be lower than fifteen hundred dollars. In addition, New Jersey offered the family one hundred dollars

Table B.1 Fatal Accident Compensation in the First Year of Operation for States Adopting Workers' Compensation before 1930

State	First Year in Effect[a]	National Weekly Wage	Present Value of Stream of Fatal Benefits	Ratio of Present Value of Fatal Benefits to Annual Earnings	Funeral Expenses	Weekly Payment Replaced This Percent of Weekly Wage	Maximum Number of Weeks	Minimum Weekly Payment	Maximum Weekly Payment	Maximum Total Payout	Minimum Total Payout
Cal.	1911	14.83	2,149	2.9	0	—	156	6.41	32.05	5,000	1,000
N.J.	1911	14.83	1,840	2.48	100	0.45	300	5	10	3,000	1,500
Nev.	1911	14.83	2,314	3.12	0	—	—	—	—	3,000	2,000
Wash.	1911	14.83	4,511	6.08	75	—	—	6.9	6.9	—	0
Wis.	1911	14.83	2,719	3.67	0	—	—	7.21	14.42	3,000	1,500
Ill.	1912	15.34	2,548	3.32	0	0.5	—	0	200	3,500	1,500
Kan.	1912	15.34	2,068	2.7	0	0.5	—	6	15	3,600	1,200
Mass.	1912	15.34	1,999	2.61	0	0.5	300	4	10	3,000	1,200
Md.	1912	15.34	2,548	3.32	0	—	—	—	—	—	1,000
Mich.	1912	15.34	1,999	2.61	0	0.5	300	4	10	3,000	1,200
Ohio	1912	15.34	2,771	3.61	0	0.67	312	0	200	3,400	1,500
R.I.	1912	15.34	1,999	2.61	0	0.5	300	4	10	3,000	1,200
N.Y.	1912	15.34	2,302	3	0	—	150	0	200	3,000	0
Ariz.	1913	15.82	2,626	3.32	0	0.5	400	0	200	4,000	0
Minn.	1913	15.82	2,161	2.73	100	0.5	300	6	10	3,000	1,800
Neb.	1913	15.82	2,450	3.1	100	0.5	350	5	10	3,500	1,750
Tex.	1913	15.82	2,888	3.65	0	0.6	360	5	15	5,400	1,800
W. Va.	1913	15.82	3,981	5.03	75	—	—	6.9	6.9	—	0
Conn.	1914	15.84	2,235	2.82	100	0.5	312	5	10	3,120	1,560
Iowa	1914	15.84	2,164	2.73	100	0.5	300	5	10	3,000	1,500
N.Y.	1914	15.84	5,131	6.48	100	0.5	—	0	11.5	—	0
Or.	1914	15.84	6,541	8.26	100	—	—	9.67	9.67	—	—
Colo.	1915	15.79	2,127	2.69	0	0.5	312	0	8	2,500	1,000
Ind.	1915	15.79	2,363	2.99	100	0.55	300	5.5	13.2	5,000	1,500
La.	1915	15.79	2,157	2.73	100	0.5	300	3	10	3,000	900
Mont.	1915	15.79	2,696	3.41	75	0.5	400	6	10	4,000	2,400
Okla.	1915	15.79	—	—	—	—	—	—	—	—	—
Vt.	1915	15.79	1,528	1.94	75	0.4	260	2	10	3,500	520
Wyo.	1915	15.79	1,890	2.39	50	—	—	—	—	2,000	—

(*continued*)

Table B.1 (continued)

State	First Year in Effect[a]	National Weekly Wage	Present Value of Stream of Fatal Benefits	Ratio of Present Value of Fatal Benefits to Annual Earnings	Funeral Expenses	Weekly Payment Replaced This Percent of Weekly Wage	Maximum Number of Weeks	Minimum Weekly Payment	Maximum Weekly Payment	Maximum Total Payout	Minimum Total Payout
Ky.	1916	17.57	3,345	3.81	75	0.65	335	5	12	4,000	1,675
Me.	1916	17.57	2,289	2.61	0	0.5	300	4	10	3,000	1,200
Pa.	1916	17.57	2,389	2.72	100	0.5	300	5	10	3,000	1,500
N.M.	1917	19.87	2,640	2.66	50	0.5	300	5	15	4,500	1,500
S.D.	1917	19.87	2,604	2.62	0	0.5	—	—	200	3,000	1,650
Utah	1917	19.87	3,096	3.12	150	0.55	312	0	15	4,500	2,000
Del.	1918	24.01	2,670	2.22	100	0.45	270	4.5	13.5	3,645	1,215
Idaho	1918	24.01	4,085	3.4	100	0.55	400	6	12	4,800	2,400
N.D.	1919	27.67	10,004	7.23	100	0.55	—	9.9	16.5	—	—
Tenn.	1919	27.67	3,753	2.71	100	0.5	400	5	11	4,400	2,000
Va.	1919	27.67	2,706	1.96	100	0.5	300	5	10	4,000	1,500
Ala.	1920	33.81	3,749	2.22	100	0.6	300	5	14	5,000	1,500
Ga.	1921	30.77	2,706	1.76	100	0.5	300	5	10	4,000	1,500
Mo.	1927	33.23	5,362	3.23	150	0.67	300	6	20	6,000	1,800
N.C.	1929	34.08	5,333	3.13	200	0.6	333	7	18	6,000	2,450

Notes: The details of the laws come from Clark and Frincke (1921), Hookstadt (1918, 1919, 1920, 1922), Jones (1927), and U.S. Bureau of Labor Statistics Bulletin Nos. 126 (1913b), 203 (1917), 243 (1918), 332 (1923), 423 (1926b), and 496 (1929), with supplementation from the session laws for the individual states. The information comes from the first year that the law was in effect. The present value of fatal accident benefits as a percentage of annual earnings is calculated based on the national average weekly wage in manufacturing. For the years prior to 1927, the average weekly wage was calculated as average weekly hours times hourly earnings from Paul Douglas's series (series D-765 times series D-766 in U.S. Bureau of the Census 1975, 168). We then interpolated values for the years 1927 through 1930 by running a regression of the weekly wage measure on Stanley Lebergott's measure of average annual earnings per full-time employee for manufacturing (series D-740 in U.S. Bureau of the Census 1975, 166) divided by fifty-two. The interpolated values for 1927 through 1930 are equal to 2.021638 + 1.080317 times the Lebergott measure of weekly wages. For years after 1927, the average weekly wage is from the U.S. BLS series (series D-802, U.S. Bureau of the Census 1975, 169–70). Given the weekly earnings, we calculated the present value of the stream of payments allowed by the workers' compenstaion statute using continuous discounting and a discount rate of 5 percent. The worker was assumed to have had a wife age thirty-five and two children age eight and ten. In some states there was an overall maximum payment that was binding. We assumed the families were paid the weekly amount until the time that the maximum total payment (not discounted) was reached; therefore, time in the discounting formula in those states was equal to the maximum total payment divided by the weekly payment. In Nevada, New York, Oregon, Washington, and West Virginia the payments were for the life of the spouse or until remarriage. We assumed that the spouse lived thirty more years without remarrying. Payments to dependents were stopped when they reached the state's defined age of adulthood. Annual earnings were defined as the average manufacturing weekly wage times fifty weeks.

[a] In quite a few states the first year of operation was the year after the law was adopted. Maryland (for miners in 1902), New York (1910), Montana (for miners in 1909), and Kentucky (1914) passed earlier laws that were declared unconstitutional. Maryland also passed a law specific to miners in 1910, while New York passed a voluntary compensation law and a compulsory compensation law in 1910. The compulsory law was declared unconstitutional, and the voluntary law was little used. New York passed a new compulsory law in 1913 after the state constitution was amended.

for funeral expenses. Several states deviated from the New Jersey pattern. Washington, West Virginia, and Oregon established fixed weekly payments. Oklahoma did not pay workers' compensation benefits for fatal accidents. Nevada, California, Maryland, and Kansas chose the total payment level based on three times annual earnings, while Wisconsin, Illinois, and South Dakota based it on four times annual earnings. Wyoming paid a fixed lump sum for fatal accidents based on the number of survivors. Some states chose not to limit either the number of weeks of payment or the maximum total payout.

Nearly all states focused on paying the money weekly over an extended period of time. Most states legally allowed for accident victims to be paid a lump sum after an appeal, usually using a discount rate between 3 and 6 percent to determine the size of the lump sum. Our impression, however, is that the administrators of workers' compensation discouraged the payment of a lump sum.[7] To allow easier comparisons of the fatal accident parameters in each of the states, we have calculated the present value of the stream of weekly payments prescribed by the workers' compensation acts using a discount rate of 5 percent. We assumed that the worker was paid the national average weekly wage at the time of the accident. As an example, the present value of the stream of payments for the New Jersey family in 1911 was $1,840.

The present values for the states adopting later in the period appear artificially high in comparison with those for states adopting earlier because the national average weekly wage more than doubled over the time period. Therefore, we have also calculated a ratio of the present value of fatal benefits to annual earnings, which were calculated as fifty weeks times the national weekly wage. In terms of fatal accident payments, the least generous states were Georgia, Vermont, and Virginia, each with present values that replaced less than two years' income. Generally, these states had relatively low maximum weekly payments. The states with present values that replaced more than five times annual incomes—Washington, New York, Oregon, West Virginia, and South Dakota—generally did not limit the length of time for fatal accident payments or impose maximum total payments. The relative generosity of these high-benefit states is affected more by the discount rate than in the rest of the states. For example, raising the discount rate from 5 percent to 10 percent lowered the ratio from 6.08 to 4 in Washington in 1911, while lowering the ratio in New Jersey from 2.48 to 2.19.

Nonfatal Accident Payments

Another major component of workers' compensation was the benefits paid for nonfatal accidents, which were far more common than fatal accidents. Nonfatal accidents were separated into three major categories: permanent total disability (e.g., full paralysis), permanent partial disability (e.g., loss of a hand), and temporary disability (e.g., broken leg). In most states, the compensation for nonfatal accidents followed the general pattern of that for fatal accidents. During his disability the worker was paid a percentage of his weekly wage, subject to statutory minimum and maximum payments, for a maximum number of weeks. Each state established a waiting period, ranging from three days to two weeks from the date of the accident, during which time no accident compensation was paid. Injured workers who were out of work for a period less than the waiting period received no compensation. In some states at the time of introduction (and later in most states), workers with more serious injuries that lasted beyond four to eight weeks were able to collect compensation forgone during the waiting period, retroactively. The rules for permanent total disability payments, say for full paralysis, were similar to the rules for fatal accident payments (without the funeral expense payments) in nearly every state.

To show how the various states compensated temporary total disability, table B.2 shows the waiting period, the retroactive pay feature, the percentage of the wage replaced, and the minimum and maximum weekly payments. For example, a worker injured for five weeks in New Jersey in 1911 would have started receiving payments for his injury after two weeks. For the remaining three weeks of his injury he was paid half of his weekly wage, and the payment could not be lower than $5 or higher than $10. A worker receiving the national weekly wage of $14.83 would have been paid $7.415 per week for three weeks for a total of $22.245. The present value of this stream of income using continuous discounting and a discount rate of 5 percent was $22.11, which was 1.49 times the national weekly wage. Comparison of all the states in table B.2 in their first year of operation shows that North Dakota in 1919 was the most generous for temporary total disability at 3.31 times the weekly wage, while Missouri and Oregon had ratios of almost 3 times the weekly wage. The three states combined relatively generous maximums with either no waiting period or the payment of retroactive benefits after a relatively short period of time. It is important to note, however, that states starting operation later generally were adopting benefit parameters that were similar to the parameters in other states at that time.

Permanent partial disabilities ranged from the loss of a finger to the loss of a leg. It was anticipated that someone with a permanent partial disability might be able to continue to work, although the type of work depended on the disability. Table B.3 shows the rules for compensating people who lost a hand. Among the states that adopted workers' compensation earlier, the typical pattern was to pay the worker as if he were totally disabled for a period of time and then begin paying the worker a partial disability payment. In New Jersey in 1911, the worker was paid as if he were totally disabled for 15 weeks, which appeared to be common in many states, and

Table B.2 Workers' Compensation for a Five-Week Spell of Disability in the First Year of Operation

State	Year	National Weekly Wage	Present Value of Five-Week Disability Pay	Ratio of Present Value of Disability Pay to Weekly Wage	Waiting Period in Days	Retroactive Pay for Waiting Period after This Number of Weeks	Weekly Payment Replaced This Percent of Weekly Wage	Minimum Weekly Payment	Maximum Weekly Payment
Cal.	1911	14.83	38.35	2.59	7	—	0.65	4.17	20.83
N.J.	1911	14.83	22.11	1.49	14	—	0.5	5	10
Nev.	1911	14.83	31.6	2.13	10	—	0.6	0	—
Wash.	1911	14.83	38.34	2.59	1.5	—	0.6	8.05	8.05
Wis.	1911	14.83	37.29	2.51	7	—	0.65	4.69	9.38
Ill.	1912	15.34	30.52	1.99	7	—	0.5	5	12
Kan.	1912	15.34	22.88	1.49	14	—	0.5	6	15
Mass.	1912	15.34	22.88	1.49	14	—	0.5	4	10
Md.	1912	15.34	15.26	0.99	7	—	0.5	0	—
Mich.	1912	15.34	22.88	1.49	14	8	0.5	4	10
Ohio	1912	15.34	36.58	2.38	7	—	0.67	5	12
R.I.	1912	15.34	22.88	1.49	14	—	0.5	4	10
N.H.	1912	15.34	22.88	1.49	14	—	0.5	0	10
Ariz.	1913	15.82	23.58	1.49	14	—	0.5	0	—
Minn.	1913	15.82	23.58	1.49	14	—	0.5	6	10
Neb.	1913	15.82	23.58	1.49	14	8	0.5	5	10
Tex.	1913	15.82	37.75	2.39	7	—	0.6	5	15
W. Va.	1913	15.82	28.31	1.79	7	—	0.5	4	8
Conn.	1914	15.84	23.62	1.49	14	—	0.5	0	10
Iowa	1914	15.84	23.62	1.49	14	—	0.5	5	10
N.Y.	1914	15.84	31.46	1.99	14	—	0.67	5	15
Or.	1914	15.84	47.28	2.98	0	—	0.6	10.81	10.81
Colo.	1915	15.79	15.68	0.99	21	—	0.5	5	8
Ind.	1915	15.79	25.89	1.64	14	—	0.55	5.5	13.2
La.	1915	15.79	23.53	1.49	14	—	0.5	3	10

(continued)

Table B.2 (continued)

State	Year	National Weekly Wage	Present Value of Five-Week Disability Pay	Ratio of Present Value of Disability Pay to Weekly Wage	Waiting Period in Days	Retroactive Pay for Waiting Period after This Number of Weeks	Weekly Payment Replaced This Percent of Weekly Wage	Minimum Weekly Payment	Maximum Weekly Payment
Mont.	1915	15.79	23.53	1.49	14	—	0.5	6	10
Okla.	1915	15.79	23.53	1.49	14	—	0.5	6	10
Vt.	1915	15.79	23.53	1.49	14	—	0.5	3	12.5
Wyo.	1915	15.79	24.64	1.56	10	—	1	6.94	6.94
Ky.	1916	17.57	34.05	1.94	14	—	0.65	5	12
Me.	1916	17.57	26.19	1.49	14	—	0.5	4	10
Pa.	1916	17.57	26.19	1.49	14	—	0.5	5	10
N.M.	1917	19.87	19.74	0.99	21	—	0.5	5	10
S.D.	1917	19.87	29.63	1.49	14	8	0.5	6	12
Utah	1917	19.87	38.81	1.95	10	—	0.55	7	12
Del.	1918	24.01	29.82	1.24	14	—	0.5	4	10
Idaho	1918	24.01	47.73	1.99	7	—	0.55	6	12
N.D.	1919	27.67	91.7	3.31	7	1	0.67	6	20
Tenn.	1919	27.67	32.8	1.19	14	6	0.5	5	11
Va.	1919	27.67	29.82	1.08	14	—	0.5	5	10
Ala.	1920	33.81	59.69	1.77	14	4	0.5	5	12
Ga.	1921	30.77	35.78	1.16	14	7	0.5	6	12
Mo.	1927	33.23	99.48	2.99	3	4	0.67	6	20
N.C.	1929	34.08	89.53	2.63	7	4	0.6	7	18

Notes: See table B.1 for the sources to the workers' compensation laws. The information comes from the first year that the law was in effect. The national weekly wage is the same as in table B.1. The present value of the weekly payments was calculated using continuous discounting at a rate of 5 percent. The retroactive pay feature worked as in the case of Alabama in 1920. The waiting period in Alabama was two weeks, which meant that a worker had to be injured for more than two weeks to receive any benefits. If he was injured for three weeks, then the worker would receive a payment only for the third week of the injury. If he was disabled longer than four weeks, however, he received a retroactive payment that paid him benefits for the first two weeks of the injury. For further details see the sources to table B.1 and the text of appendix B.

Table B.3 Workers' Compensation for the Loss of a Hand in the First Year of Operation

State	First Year	Present Value of Hand Disability Pay	Ratio of Present Value to Annual Earnings	Weekly Payment Replaced This Percent of Weekly Wage	Weeks of Payment	Minimum Weekly Payment	Maximum Weekly Payment	Standard Payment Method	Hand Payments Start after Period of Total Disability Payments
Cal.	1911	1,936.53	2.61	0.65	200	4.16	20.83	Weekly	Yes
N.J.	1911	1,116.56	1.51	0.5	150	5	10	Weekly	Yes
Nev.	1911	631.36	0.85	0.15	260	0	No max	Weekly	Yes
Wash.	1911	1,263.16	1.7	—	—	—	—	Lump sum	No
Wis.	1911	2,283.19	3.08	0.65	—	—	—	Weekly	Yes
Ill.	1912	1,364.56	1.78	0.5	—	0	12	Weekly	Yes
Kan.	1912	1,312.72	1.71	0.5	—	3	12	Weekly	Yes
Mass.	1912	2,925.56	3.81	0.5	50	4	10	Weekly	Yes
Md.	1912	1,456.05	1.9	0.5	—	0	No max	Weekly	Yes
Mich.	1912	1,069.61	1.39	0.5	150	4	10	Weekly	No
Ohio	1912	1,298.68	1.69	0.666	—	5	12	Weekly	Yes
R.I.	1912	1,415.06	1.84	0.5	50	4	10	Weekly	Yes
N.H.	1912	1,041.26	1.36	0.5	—	—	—	Weekly	Yes
Ariz.	1913	2,584.03	3.27	0.5	—	—	—	Weekly	Yes
Minn.	1913	1,102.61	1.39	0.5	150	6	10	Weekly	No
Neb.	1913	1,271.41	1.61	0.5	175	5	10	Weekly	No
Tex.	1913	2,180.24	2.76	0.6	50	5	15	Weekly	Yes
W. Va.	1913	1,030.13	1.3	0.5	156	4	8	Weekly	No
Conn.	1914	1,145.3	1.45	0.5	156	0	No max	Weekly	No
Iowa	1914	1,104.35	1.39	0.5	150	5	10	Weekly	No
N.Y.	1914	2,290.35	2.89	0.666	244	5	20	Weekly	No
Or.	1914	1,744.71	2.2	0.6	330	5.75	5.753	Weekly	Yes
Colo.	1915	778.87	0.99	0.5	104	0	8	Weekly	No
Ind.	1915	1,210.38	1.53	0.55	150	5.5	13.2	Weekly	No
La.	1915	1,100.35	1.39	0.5	150	3	10	Weekly	No

(continued)

Table B.3 (continued)

State	First Year	Present Value of Hand Disability Pay	Ratio of Present Value to Annual Earnings	Weekly Payment Replaced This Percent of Weekly Wage	Weeks of Payment	Minimum Weekly Payment	Maximum Weekly Payment	Standard Payment Method	Hand Payments Start after Period of Total Disability Payments
Mont.	1915	1,100.35	1.39	0.5	150	6	10	Weekly	No
Okla.	1915	1,433.25	1.82	0.5	200	6	10	Weekly	No
Vt.	1915	1,120.53	1.42	0.5	140	0	10	Weekly	Yes
Wyo.	1915	800	1.01	—	—	—	—	Lump sum	No
Ky.	1916	1,592.03	1.81	0.65	150	5	12	Weekly	No
Me.	1916	1,658.69	1.89	0.5	125	4	10	Weekly	Yes
Pa.	1916	1,412.12	1.61	0.5	175	5	10	Weekly	No
N.M.	1917	1,140.36	1.15	0.5	110	5	10	Weekly	Yes
S.D.	1917	1,515.76	1.53	0.5	150	6	10	Weekly	Yes
Utah	1917	1,524.79	1.53	0.55	150	0	12	Weekly	No
Del.	1918	1,463.03	1.22	0.5	158	4	12	Weekly	No
Idaho	1918	1,674.61	1.39	0.55	150	0	10	Weekly	No
N.D.	1919	4,234.79	3.06	0.666	260	0	20	Weekly	No
Tenn.	1919	1,533.59	1.11	0.5	150	5	11	Weekly	No
Va.	1919	1,394.17	1.01	0.5	150	5	10	Weekly	No
Ala.	1920	1,673	0.99	0.5	150	5	12	Weekly	No
Ga.	1921	1,673	1.09	0.5	150	6	12	Weekly	No
Mo.	1927	3,220.05	1.94	0.666	175	6	20	Weekly	No
N.C.	1929	2,511.91	1.47	0.6	150	7	18	Weekly	No

Notes: See tables B.1 and B.2. The payments are based on the national weekly wage reported in tables B.1 and B.2. In the first year of operation for many of the states adopting workers' compensation early (the states with Yes in the far-right column), the hand payments began after a period of paying the worker for temporary total disability, typically for a period of fifteen weeks. Thus the initial payments for the fifteen weeks followed the rules described in table B.2. In other states (the states with No in the far-right column), there was no period of temporary total disability pay. Nearly all states set up the payments on a weekly basis with an option for the worker to petition for a lump-sum payment. Most workers' compensation administrations discouraged the payment of lump sums. Washington and Wyoming, however, used lump-sum payments as their standard practice.

then he began receiving payments of half his wage for 150 weeks. The weekly payments could not exceed $10 or be lower than $5. For a worker receiving the national weekly wage at the time of the accident, the present value of this stream of payments, discounted at 5 percent, would have been $1,117, which was roughly 1.5 times his average annual earnings (50 weeks times the national weekly wage). In most of the rest of the states, like Michigan in 1912, the injured worker received just the hand payments without any period of receiving temporary total disability payments. The Michigan payment stream for a worker earning the national weekly wage of $15.34 a week led to a present value of $1,070, which was 1.39 times average annual earnings. In Washington and Wyoming the hand payment was typically paid as a lump sum. Most other states allowed the worker to receive a lump sum under appeal, but they generally did not encourage the practice.

Calculating Expected Benefits

The relative generosity of the states sometimes varied for different types of accidents. Table B.4 combines the present values of the accident payments into a measure of expected benefits to develop a summary measure of workers' compensation benefits. For each type of accident we calculated the gross benefit as the present value of the stream of payments for that type of accident. We then converted these gross benefit estimates into an expected benefit measure ($E(B)$) by weighting each of the four types of accident benefits by the probability that each type of accident would occur and then summing the four expected compensation estimates, as in the following equation:

$$E(B) = p_f B_f + p_{pt} B_{pt} + p_{pp} B_{pp} + p_{tt} B_{tt},$$

where B is the benefit paid and p is the probability that the accident will occur. The subscript f denotes fatal accidents, pt permanent total disability, pp permanent partial disability, and tt represents temporary total disability. In essence, the expected benefit shows what an insurance company might expect to pay to the families of workplace accident victims earning the national weekly wage during the course of a year.

The accident probabilities for the expected benefits calculations in tables B.4 and 7.1 are based on the manufacturing average for Oregon and represent the average accident experiences of all Oregon industries (Oregon Industrial Accident Commission 1919, 28–42). The probability of a fatal accident over the course of a year was 0.001895, for permanent total disability 0.000136, for permanent partial disability 0.0099, and for temporary total disability 0.1199. After multiplying these probabilities by the present value of the benefits and scaling down the hand benefits to reflect

Table B.4   **Expected Workers' Compensation Benefits in the First Year of Operation**

State	First Year	National Weekly Wage	Expected Benefit	Expected Benefit as Percentage of Annual Earnings	Present Value of Fatal Accident Payments	Present Value of Five-Week Disability Payments	Present Value of Hand Disability Payments
Cal.	1911	14.83	13.17	1.78	2,149	38.35	1,936.53
N.J.	1911	14.83	8.81	1.19	1,840	22.11	1,116.56
Nev.	1911	14.83	9.86	1.33	2,314	31.6	631.36
Wash.	1911	14.83	16.5	2.23	4,511	38.34	1,263.16
Wis.	1911	14.83	14.95	2.02	2,719	37.29	2,283.19
Ill.	1912	15.34	11.8	1.54	2,548	30.52	1,364.56
Kan.	1912	15.34	9.79	1.28	2,068	22.88	1,312.72
Mass.	1912	15.34	13.15	1.72	1,999	22.88	2,925.56
Md.	1912	15.34	10.16	1.33	2,548	15.26	1,456.05
Mich.	1912	15.34	9.13	1.19	1,999	22.88	1,069.61
Ohio	1912	15.34	12.83	1.67	2,771	36.58	1,298.68
R.I.	1912	15.34	9.88	1.29	1,999	22.88	1,415.06
N.H.	1912	15.34	9.68	1.26	2,302	22.88	1,041.26
Ariz.	1913	15.82	13.77	1.74	2,626	23.58	2,584.03
Minn.	1913	15.82	9.61	1.21	2,161	23.58	1,102.61
Neb.	1913	15.82	10.56	1.34	2,450	23.58	1,271.41
Tex.	1913	15.82	15.13	1.91	2,888	37.75	2,180.24
W. Va.	1913	15.82	13.72	1.73	3,981	28.31	1,030.13
Conn.	1914	15.84	9.86	1.24	2,235	23.62	1,145.3
Iowa	1914	15.84	9.63	1.22	2,164	23.62	1,104.35
N.Y.	1914	15.84	19.17	2.42	5,131	31.46	2,290.35
Or.	1914	15.84	19.74	2.49	6,541	47.28	1,744.71
Colo.	1915	15.79	7.89	1.00	2,127	15.68	778.87

Ind.	1915	15.79	10.53	1.33	2,363	25.89	1,210.38
La.	1915	15.79	9.59	1.21	2,157	23.53	1,100.35
Mont.	1915	15.79	10.69	1.35	2,696	23.53	1,100.35
Okla.	1915	15.79	6.73	0.85	395	23.53	1,433.25
Vt.	1915	15.79	8.36	1.06	1,528	23.53	1,120.53
Wyo.	1915	15.79	8.53	1.08	1,890	24.64	800
Ky.	1916	17.57	14.33	1.63	3,345	34.05	1,592.03
Me.	1916	17.57	11.39	1.30	2,289	26.19	1,658.69
Pa.	1916	17.57	11.06	1.26	2,389	26.19	1,412.12
N.M.	1917	19.87	10.2	1.03	2,640	19.74	1,140.36
S.D.	1917	19.87	12.13	1.22	2,604	29.63	1,515.76
Utah	1917	19.87	14.25	1.43	3,096	38.81	1,524.79
Del.	1918	24.01	12.17	1.01	2,670	29.82	1,463.03
Idaho	1918	24.01	17.66	1.47	4,085	47.73	1,674.61
N.D.	1919	27.67	40.51	2.93	10,004	91.7	4,234.79
Tenn.	1919	27.67	14.88	1.08	3,753	32.8	1,553.59
Va.	1919	27.67	12.1	0.87	2,706	29.82	1,394.17
Ala.	1920	33.81	18.4	1.09	3,749	59.69	1,673
Ga.	1921	30.77	13.42	0.87	2,706	35.78	1,673
Mo.	1927	33.23	29.81	1.79	5,362	99.48	3,220.05
N.C.	1929	34.08	27.02	1.59	5,333	89.53	2,511.91

Sources: See sources to table B.1 and appendix B. The expected benefit is the weighted sum of the present value of fatal accident payments, the present value of hand payments, and the present value of the five-week disability payment. The weights are the probability of this type of accident. The same probabilities were used for all states and are based on averages for manufacturing in Oregon (Oregon Industrial Accident Commission 1919, 28–42). The probability of a fatal accident over the course of a year was 0.001895, for a permanent total disability 0.000136, for permanent partial disability 0.0099, and for temporary total disability 0.1199. We used the fatal accident present value as a measure for the permanent total disability benefits because they were so similar in nearly all the states. We scaled the hand present value down to 21.8 percent of the level listed above because the average value paid for permanent partial disabilities was about 21.8 percent of the hand value (see accident statistics reported in Wisconsin Industrial Commission [1915, 41; 1916, 44; 1917, 6–7] for 1914 to 1917).

that a permanent partial disability typically was about 21.8 percent of the hand benefits, table B.4 reports the expected workers' compensation benefit in each state during the first year of operation. For workers earning the national weekly wage in New Jersey in 1911, an insurer might have anticipated paying out $8.81 per worker, or approximately 1.19 percent of the workers' annual earnings, in workers' compensation benefits. In chapter 7 we discuss the factors determining the choice of benefit levels and table 7.1 compares the expected benefits in each state from the first year of operation through 1930.

In calculating the expected benefits we merged the fatal accident and permanent total disability accident categories together because permanent total disability accidents, like full paralysis, were relatively rare and the payments were very close to the fatal accident payouts. Workers' compensation benefits and the expected benefit measure are based on the workers' weekly wage. We used different weekly wages for expected benefits calculations in different settings. When comparing the workers' compensation benefits across states and time in tables B.1 through B.4 and when analyzing the determinants of expected benefits in chapter 7 and table 7.1, we used the national average weekly wage in manufacturing. In the wage offset regressions discussed in chapter 3 and appendix D, we used the national average weekly wage for each occupation in the sample. In the analysis of household savings in chapter 3, table 3.4, and appendix F, we used the weekly wage for the head of the household, which was reported in the Bureau of Labor Statistics (BLS) cost-of-living sample.

We obtained the statutory descriptions from various bulletins of the U.S. Bureau of Labor Statistics in the Workmen's Compensation and Insurance Series (U.S. Bureau of Labor Statistics 1914, 1917, 1918, 1923, 1926b), Hookstadt (1920, 1922), and Clark and Frincke (1921). We also consulted Jones (1927). When questions arose about the timing of changes in the law, the state's statutes were consulted directly.

For fatal accidents, the typical law allowed weekly payments to be a percentage (up to two-thirds) of the weekly wage for a specified period of time. We calculated the present value (using continuous discounting) of the stream of benefits using a discount rate of 5 percent, which was the typical return on stocks and bonds for the period. The rate of 5 percent also was in the range of statutory rates used when the stream of workers' compensation benefits were converted to lump sums. The calculations were sometimes complicated because states usually imposed maximums on the weekly payment or maximums on the sum total of all the weekly payments. If the percentage times the weekly wage exceeded the maximum weekly payment, we inserted the maximum weekly payment into the present value calculations. In cases where there was a maximum total payment, we assumed the family received the regular weekly payment until the total undiscounted stream of payments reached the maximum total. Thus, we determined the number of weekly payments by taking the maximum total divided by the weekly payment (states did not worry about discounting issues when deciding when a family reached its maximum total benefit).

For the loss of a hand, the typical state paid a percentage of the weekly wage for a fixed amount of time, subject to minimum and maximum weekly amounts. Some states commenced the hand payments after the worker collected a statutory amount of temporary disability pay. Following the recommendations of the International Association of Industrial Accident Boards and Commissions in 1920 (Hookstadt 1920, 77), we assumed that the loss of a hand temporarily disabled the worker fully for fifteen weeks before he could return to work. We calculated the present value of the stream of payments using continuous discounting. It was important to calculate the present value because some states would pay a relatively small amount per week for the rest of the worker's life. Without discounting, the total amount paid would look quite large when, in fact, the present value of the stream of payments was in the range of other states' benefits. In the few cases where a hand payment was not mentioned specifically, we followed the BLS in describing it as a 50 percent disability.

For the permanent partial disability category, we used the loss of a hand as a typical accident because the payment structure for the amputation of a hand was defined in almost all of the states' laws. The typical accident in the permanent partial category, however, was actually much less serious. Based on accident statistics reported by the Wisconsin Industrial Commission (1915, 41; 1916, 44; 1917, 6–7) for 1914 to 1917, we found that the average payment for a permanent partial disability was 21.9 percent of that for the loss of a hand. Thus, in the expected benefits calculations, we scaled down the present value of the hand payment by multiplying the figure by 21.9 percent. We treated the typical temporary disability accident as one in which the injured worker was out of work for five weeks.

For temporary disabilities, workers were paid a percentage of their weekly wage during the period of the disability, which we assumed to be five weeks. These payments were usually subject to minimum and maximum weekly amounts. Nearly all states had waiting periods. In many cases a worker injured for five weeks would receive no payment for the first three to fourteen days of the disability, such that he might receive as few as three weekly payments. In a number of states, the worker would receive nothing during the waiting period, but if the disability lasted beyond four weeks (up to eight weeks in some states) the worker would eventually receive a retroactive payment for the first week or two of the disability. We have made our calculations sensitive to these nuances across states.

In a number of years the statutory parameters of the law changed. For the purposes of the wage regression analysis in chapter 3 and in appendix D, we determined from the states' session laws when the new workers' compensation provisions went into effect. We then used a weighted average of the benefits calculated under the old and new laws, with the weight being the percentage of time during the year that each law was in effect. In the wage regressions we wanted the benefits throughout the year because the wages were typically averages of the wages throughout the years. When we calculated the expected benefit values in tables B.1 through B.4 and in table 7.1, we focused instead on the benefits as they existed at the end of the year. In these situations our focus is on the decisions made by legislatures as to the benefits that they wanted to establish, which was best represented by what was in place after the legislature had met.

In the years prior to the introduction of workers' compensation, the courts and settlements with employers determined the payments to injured workers. We need to come up with measures of the generosity of negligence liability for states without workers' compensation for the wage regressions and the savings analysis in chapter 3 and appendixes D and F. Based on the material presented in table 2.1, we assumed that the family of a worker killed in a workplace accident could expect to receive about half a year's income on average (which takes into account the probability of getting nothing). We then calculated the payment for a hand to be 54.02 percent of the fatal accident benefit and for the five-week disability to be 1.557 percent of the fatal accident benefit. These percentages were based on national averages of the ratios of hand-to-death benefits and disability-to-death benefits from all workers' compensation states during the year 1923. It is clear that the generosity of the liability systems varied across states because insurance companies established state differentials for employers' liability premiums in their ratebooks. The state differentials would typically reflect differences in the liability rules and differences in the court treatments of accident compensation. The differentials are reported in DeLeon (1907, 26–27). To make this calculation we multiplied the benefits above by the state's reported liability differential and then divided by 0.64333, which was the average liability differential reported for the forty-six states plus Arizona and New Mexico (still territories in 1909) in the sample.

It is clear that our estimates of the negligence liability payments suffer from measurement error because we cannot make the calculations with as much certainty as we did for workers' compensation because there were no statutory proscriptions under the negligence system. We have experimented with a variety of measures of the benefits under negligence liability and generally have obtained similar results to the ones reported in chapter 3, appendix D, and appendix F. In both the wage analyses and the savings and insurance analyses, we ran tests in which we assumed that families received nothing under the non–workers' compensation regime and we tried using the benefits without adjusting for the liability differential. The fundamental results remain the same.

The probabilities of each type of accident were derived from different sources for each of the analyses. In the wage regression analysis in chapter 3 and appendix D for the coal industry we started with an average fatal accident rate of 2.043 per million man hours from the sample of coal states used to estimate the wage equation (Fishback 1992, 87). To translate that into a fatal accident rate per full-year worked of 3.37 per one thousand men, we assumed that the men worked 206.4 eight-hour days (from the sample means). The remaining coal accident rates were determined by comparing the relative number of fatal cases (61), permanent total disability cases (3), permanent partial disability cases (82), and temporary disability cases (1,971) receiving compensation in coal mining from the Ohio State Insurance Fund during the eighteen months ending 30 June 1915. For example, the permanent total disability probability is calculated as the probability of a fatal accident in coal mining (0.00337) multiplied by the ratio of the number of permanent total disability cases to the number of fatal cases in Ohio (three to sixty-one). Using the Ohio workers' compensation information to estimate the probability of nonfatal accidents understates the actual probability of an accident because some injured workers were not compensated and, thus, were not included in the official accident statistics. The lumber and building trades accident rates in the wage regressions in chapter 3 and appendix D were obtained from the Oregon Industrial Accident Commission (1919, 28–42). The commission reported the total number of accidents in each accident category and the number of full-time workers covered under the workers' compensation system.

Expected benefits in the wage regression analyses discussed in chapter 3 and appendix D were based on the national average wage for each occupation in each year. We did not use the wage corresponding to each observation because the expected benefits would have been a function of the wage, thus imparting a positive bias to the estimated coefficients of the expected benefits index. Similarly, we could not use the ratio of expected benefits to wages because in some cases maximum allowable benefits became binding and the ratio of expected benefits to wages would have imparted a spurious negative bias. To eliminate these problems, we used the national average wage for each occupation in each year, which allowed the expected benefits index to rise in response to rising wages during the period as well as reflect differences in expected benefits driven by differences in wages at each skill level. Thus, the expected benefits variable becomes an instrumental variable for the actual expected benefits the worker would receive. For a particular occupation, even though our calculation assumed a constant wage across all states, each state's expected calculation measure in a particular year was different because each state's law was unique. In addition, because a state's law might have changed over the period of study, the expected benefits measure for an occupation class would have changed over time (holding state and average occupational wages constant). Further, if we were to hold a state's law constant over time, nominal expected benefits would change because average occupational wages fluctuated over the course of the sample. Thus, the factors that caused each observation to take a unique value were occupational differences, changes in average occupational wages over time, differences in each state's workers' compensation law, and changes in states' laws over time.

In the calculations for tables B.1 to B.4 and 7.1, the national average manufacturing weekly wage was constructed using Paul Douglas's measures of weekly hours and hourly earnings (series D-765 and D-766 in U.S. Bureau of the Census 1975, 168) for the years 1890 to 1926. We then interpolated values for the years 1927 through 1930 by running a regression of the weekly wage measure on Stanley Lebergott's measure of average annual earnings per full-time employee for manufacturing (series D-740 in U.S. Bureau of the Census 1975, 166), divided by fifty-two. The interpolated values for 1927 through 1930 are equal to 2.021638 + 1.080317 times the Lebergott measure of weekly wages.

Appendix C

Measuring the Change in Accident Benefits from Negligence Liability to Workers' Compensation

To show the relative generosity of the nonfatal accident benefits under the two systems, we compare the expected benefits, $E(B)$, that were paid as a share of income, holding accident rates constant. Let

$$E(B) = p_f B_f + p_n B_n,$$

where p is the probability of an accident and B is the average payment for fatal (f) and nonfatal (n) accidents. To make comparisons across time, we divided the expected benefits by average annual income to compare expected benefits as a percentage of workers' annual income or employers' payrolls. Since the number of reported nonfatal accidents rose sharply with the introduction of workers' compensation (see app. A), the nonfatal portion of the expected benefits measure may have risen either because a higher percentage of actual accidents received compensation or because the average percentage of wages paid as benefits increased.

We have tried to make comparisons of the generosity of workers' compensation benefits in two ways. First, we tried comparing the expected payment of wage benefits (ignoring medical payments) by fixing the probability of compensation and then calculating the payments that injured workers reportedly received for different types of accidents under negligence liability. We then compared these amounts to the statutory payments that workers' compensation guaranteed. Second, we examined employers' reports on the amounts of wage benefits, settlements, and medical payments that they and their insurance companies paid to the families of accident victims under the negligence system. We then compared these figures to similar reports generated by workers' compensation commissions on the amounts of wages and medical benefits that workers received. The comparisons were made in terms of employers' total payments relative to their payroll expenditures.

The employer-based technique has one major advantage over the worker-based technique. When employers' liability commissions sought a sample of accident victims, they usually started with accidents reported to the state bureau of labor. Since the reporting of nonfatal accidents (lasting longer than a week) rose substantially with the introduction of workers' compensation, it is likely that our estimates of the change in payments per nonfatal accident are overstated when we rely on injured workers' reports. By contrast, from the employers' reports, we are likely to get a better picture of their expenditures under negligence liability because the employer did not have to reveal the total number of accidents, only how much was paid in the aggregate. Our measure of employers' expenditures under both legal regimes combines both the probability of the accident and the payout per accident. Therefore, even if the underlying accident probabilities remained the same, the total payments per dollar on the payroll might have risen because of an increase in reported accidents that received compensation and/or an increase in compensation per accident. The total payments might also have risen because of an increase in the underlying probability of accidents resulting from moral hazard. We do not believe that the rise in the underlying probability of accidents is nearly as great as the rise in the reporting of accidents.

Comparisons Based on Injured Workers' Reports

In table B.4 we report a measure of expected benefits under workers' compensation in New York in 1914 as 2.42 percent of annual earnings. This calculation was based on inserting values into the following equation:

$$(C1) \qquad E(B) = p_f B_f + p_{pt} B_{pt} + p_{pp} B_{pp} + p_{tt} B_{tt},$$

where B is the benefit paid and p is the probability of an accident. The subscript f denotes fatal accidents, pt represents accidents causing permanent total disability, pp is permanent partial disability, and tt is temporary total disability. We then divided the expected benefits by annual earnings. See appendix B for further details.

In our calculation for the negligence system we focus on wage replacement. We believe that medical coverage was better under workers' compensation, but it is much harder to document the extent of medical coverage than it is to document wages. By eliminating medical payments, however, we believe that we are biasing the calculations against finding that workers' compensation was more generous. As a starting point, we use accident probabilities based on workers' compensation experience to calculate the expected payouts under both negligence liability and workers' compensation. The biases that result from this assumption are discussed below. The expected benefits under each system are calculated as:

$$(C2) \qquad E(B) = 0.001895 B_f + 0.000136 B_{pt} + 0.009932 B_{pp}$$
$$+ 0.119916 B_{tt}.$$

The accident probabilities represent the experience in Oregon from 1917 to 1919 across all industries, as reported in Oregon Industrial Accident Commission (1919). We calculated the accident probabilities as the number of compensable accidents divided by the number of workers covered.

The New York Commission on Employers' Liability (1910, 210–11, 246–50) conducted a series of direct interviews of a random sample of workers who had been injured and whose accidents had been reported to the New York Bureau of Factory Inspection. The average annual earnings for workers in New York at the time was $536 (p. 223), which translates into weekly earnings of $10.31.[8] The workers experiencing temporary disability received $10,623 in wage payments on lost earnings of $66,854. In addition they received $11,663 in other receipts (we believe these include settlements). Eleven workers had suits pending. We assume that workers won half the cases and received $200 in each case for an additional $1,100. Thus, employers were replacing 34.98 percent of the lost earnings. For comparative purposes we assumed the typical temporary disability involved five weeks of lost wages. Therefore, if the average wage replacement for five weeks of lost earnings was about 35 percent, then the average replacement per accident was $18.

In forty-eight fatal accident cases in the survey (p. 249), employers paid a total of $22,343 in settlements plus $2,274 in medical or funeral expenses, and eight suits were pending. We assume that funeral expenses were half of the $2,274 and that workers' heirs won or settled half of the pending cases, receiving an average payment of $2,000 for an additional payout of $8,000. If we include all other receipts of $1,840 as coming from employers, then total fatal accident payments were $33,320, or $694.17 per case.

There were ten permanent complete disability cases, where employers paid settlements of $965 (p. 247). One case was pending and we assume that it paid $2,000. The total payout was therefore $2,965, or an average of $296.50 per case. If we include all other receipts of $656, the payout was $3,621, or $362.10 per case.

There were sixty permanent partial disability cases, with settlements equal to $7,950. Ten cases were pending. Assuming that workers won half the cases and received $2,000 each, the total payout was $17,950, or $299.16 per case. If we add in other receipts of $4,196, the total is $22,146, or $369.10 per case.

Inserting these payment values across the different types of accidents into equation C2, the calculation becomes

$$E(B) = 0.001895*694 + 0.000136*362 + 0.009932*369$$
$$+ 0.119916*18.03 = \$7.19,$$

which is 1.34 percent of the $536 annual wage.

Using the same accident rates and the weekly wage of $10.31, we calculated the present value of the benefits that would have been paid for a typical accident in each category under New York's workers' compensation law that went into effect in 1914. We gave the same payment for permanent total disability as we did for a fatal accident. As reported above we treated the typical temporary disability accident as one in which the injured worker was out of work for five weeks. For the permanent partial disability category, we calculated the benefits for the loss of a hand as a typical accident and then adjusted the payment downward by multiplying by 0.219 because the typical accident in the permanent partial category was actually much less serious than a hand amputation. The 0.219 figure is based on actual accident statistics reported by the Wisconsin Industrial Commission (1915, 41; 1916, 44; 1917, 6–7) for 1914 to 1917. For more details about the precise procedure, see appendix B on the construction of the expected benefits variable.

For a worker earning $10.31 a week or $536 per year, the New York workers' compensation law promised expected benefits equal to $12.54, which was 2.34 percent of annual wages and roughly 75 percent more than what was paid under negligence liability.[9]

The rise in expected benefits received by workers when workers' compensation was introduced in New York is probably *understated* in this analysis. First, the estimate of expected benefits per nonfatal accident are probably substantially overstated in the negligence liability case because of problems faced in the reporting of accidents to the New York Bureau of Labor Statistics. We fixed the probability of an accident in the equations based on accident probabilities under workers' compensation. However, as we have suggested above, there was a significant rise in the reporting of nonfatal accidents when workers' compensation was introduced. This suggests that there was substantial underreporting of accidents by employers under negligence liability, and it is likely they would not report injuries where they paid no compensation. Since the sample of injured workers collected by the New York Commission on Employers' Liability was drawn from reports to the New York Bureau of Labor, it is likely that it is missing a large number of nonfatal accidents for which no payment was made to workers. The biggest effect this reporting might have on our calculation is on the payments to temporarily totally disabled workers and permanently partial disabled workers. If we base calculations on the idea that reported accidents for temporary total disablement doubled, we should cut the average payment for temporarily totally disabled workers from $18 to $9 per accident, which would cut the expected benefits to $6.13, or 1.14 percent of annual earnings. If we assume that reported accidents went up 1.5 times for the accidents causing permanent partial disability, the expected benefits fall further to $4.91, or 0.92 percent of expected earnings. Thus the expected benefits might have risen 2.54 times with the introduction of workers' compensation.[10]

The near doubling in benefits also understates the rise in the net amount received by workers after they paid legal fees. Evidence from various sources suggests that workers paid lawyers' contingency fees under the negligence system ranging from 20 to 50 percent. Evidence from Kansas and Minnesota suggests that of payments made to workers, lawyers received about 13 to 23 percent, which is lower than the contingency fees because a number of workers did not hire lawyers. It is likely that some workers hired lawyers to contest workers' compensation payments as well. At most, 5 percent of the total amount that workers received went to lawyers under workers' compensation. Thus, the expected net benefits after paying legal fees rose from 0.75 percent of annual earnings under negligence liability to 2.22 percent of annual earnings under workers' compensation. The expected net benefits under workers' compensation might have been as large as three times the levels received under negligence liability.

Comparisons Based on Employers' Reports

Our second method for making the benefits comparison is to start from reports made by employers about their total accident expenditures that injured workers received. The Wisconsin Bureau of Labor and Industrial Statistics (WBLIS) conducted a survey of employers regarding their accident expenses in 1906 (see WBLIS 1909, 34–35). They received responses from 540 establishments that reported both accident expenses and total wages paid.[11] The total accident expenses include all expenditures on insurance premiums, medical expenses not paid by the insurer, wages paid during disablement, settlements, and payments to insurance companies for workers' collective benefits. The study found that employers spent $164,696 on accident expenses while paying $30,534 million in wages, which translates into a rate of $0.53 for every $100 in wages paid for accident expenses. The WBLIS (p. 31) also found that the percentage of the employers' expenditures on accidents that eventually reached the worker (including compensation and aid before the worker paid attorney fees) was only 45.5 percent.[12] Therefore, workers would have received only about $75,000 of the employers' expenditures (before legal fees) which is $0.245 in accident payments for every $100 in wages paid by the employer. The estimate for Wisconsin is very similar to estimates calculated from information provided by the employers' liability commissions in New York at $0.298 per $100 on the payroll, Michigan at $0.34, and Massachusetts at $0.29.[13] Under workers' compensation in 1913, by contrast, the Wisconsin Industrial Commission (1915, 32–38) calculated that workers received wage and medical benefits of $0.82 for every $100 of payroll. This Wisconsin comparison suggests that workers' compensation was 3.35 times more generous than the negligence liability system.

As mentioned in chapter 3, we were concerned that the Wisconsin comparison may be biased because the industries surveyed in 1906 and 1913 differed. To examine this issue more carefully, we matched industries from the 1906 and 1913 listings and found that in all but one of the twenty-three comparisons workers' compensation benefits exceeded those under negligence liability. These comparisons are presented in table C.1.

We made another comparison based on the experience of the Stonega Coke and Coal Company, largely based in Virginia, before and after workers' compensation. The comparison is based on information reported in the *Annual Reports of the Operating Department* for the years 1916–25. We estimate the percentage of the payroll that went to compensation of workers, excluding medical expenses.[14] For the period 1916 to 1918, the reports of the legal department show the compensation paid to workers through settlements and court suits. We believe that these reports give full coverage of the payments, because numerous situations mention that there was consultation with the liability insurance company. In no other place in the annual operating reports could we find mention of expenditures for payments to workers. We followed the legal reports for years after 1916 to 1918 to see the final results of pending cases in those years. Therefore, we believe that we have a good understanding of what Stonega paid to accident victims in the form of damages for accidents occurring between 1916 and 1918. Stonega spent roughly $52,225 on settlements and court awards for accidents occurring during this period.[15] Stonega's payroll for coal mining during this period was approximately $5,685,506; therefore Stonega spent roughly $0.975 per $100 on the payroll on compensating workers.[16] During the period 1919 to 1923, after workers' compensation was established, we have information on the number of compensable weeks associated with accidents at the Stonega mines. We translated this into workers' compensation payments using the rule that Virginia paid 50 percent of weekly earnings, with a minimum of $5 per week and a maximum of $10 per week in compensation payments in 1919. The minimum rose to $6 per week and the maximum to $12 per week in the 1920 session of the legislature. Motormen during this period typically earned about $5 to $6

| Table C.1 | | Generosity of Wage and Medical Benefits in Wisconsin before and after Workers' Compensation, by Industry, 1906 and 1913 | | | |

| | | Benefits Workers Received per $100 on Payroll in | | | |
| | | 1913 for Employers | | Ratio 1913 to 1906 | |
Industry	1906	With Insurance	Without Insurance	With Insurance	Without Insurance
Agricultural implements	.13	.59		4.5	
Boots and shoes	.08	.33		4.2	
Chairs	.06	.58	.30	9.2	4.7
Clothing	.08	.16	.26	2.1	3.4
Furniture	.14	.58	.30	4.1	2.1
Knit goods	.05	.16	.26	3.2	5.2
Leather tanning	.13	.12	.37	.95	2.9
Lumber	.38	.58	.78	1.5	2.0
Machinery	.25	.48	.49	1.95	2.0
Malt liquors	.33	.52	.36	1.6	1.1
Paper and pulp	.43	.93	.56	2.2	1.3
Sheet metal	.41	.74	.58	1.8	1.4
Iron		.12	.84		7.1

Sources: Wisconsin Bureau of Labor and Industrial Statistics (1909, 31–35) and Wisconsin Industrial Commission (1915).

Notes: The compensation amount in 1906 represents a gross figure, before attorneys fees are subtracted. It is calculated by multiplying employers' total expenditures on accidents in 1906 by 45.6 percent, which is the percentage of the employers' expenditures that workers actually received after all of the employers' expenses were subtracted, including employers' liability insurance and collective accident insurance premiums. The amount that workers received would have included compensation and medical aid not paid by insurers, and perhaps wages paid during the disability. The benefits received by workers in 1913 from employers with insurance is the "pure premium" listed by insurance companies with policies that had been terminated. The pure premiums reflect the actual amounts insurance companies paid out to the families of killed and injured workers. The expenditures by noninsured employers shows the compensation and medical payments paid out during the year ending 31 December 1913.

Possible biases in the data: The Wisconsin Bureau of Labor and Industrial Statistics (WBLIS) claimed that the entire amount of compensation paid in 1906 may not reflect the amounts actually reported for 1906. However, the survey asked for all expenditures employers had in the year 1906 on account of accidents. Many firms probably reported all expenditures on accounts, including payouts for accidents from prior years, thus the typical annual amount they paid would not be understated.

In 1913, the same questions arise for uninsured employers carrying their own risk. We do not believe this is a problem for the insurance information in 1913 because it focuses on completed policies, where some measure of the total payouts for which the insurer is liable on accidents is included in the totals.

Matching industries: The industry titles in the 1906 and 1913 studies matched precisely for agricultural implements, boots and shoes, furniture, machinery, and paper and pulp. We matched chairs in 1906 with furniture for the insurance spending in 1913 and with woodworking for the uninsured spending in 1913. We matched clothing and knit goods in 1906 with textiles in 1913; iron in 1906 with iron for insured in 1913, and iron and steel for uninsured in 1913; leather tanning in 1906 with other leather for insured in 1913, leather and leather products for uninsured in 1913; lumber in 1906 with logging and lumbering in 1913; malt liquors in 1906 with breweries in 1913; sheet metal in 1906 with metal working for insured in 1913 and stamping works for uninsured in 1913.

per day, or $20 to $24 for a four-day week. Thus coal miners were probably receiving at least $9 per week in compensation for accidents, which would imply payouts of $255,326 on a payroll of $14,983,930, or $1.70 per $100 on the payroll, which is about 74 percent higher than the payouts under negligence liability.[17] We should note that the rise in payouts is smaller than what we see in Wisconsin and in New York in part because Virginia during 1919 was one of the least generous workers' compensation states. Comparisons of the generosity of workers' compensation in table B.4 show that Virginia's expected benefits in 1919 were about 0.87 percent of annual earnings, compared with Wisconsin's index of 2.02 in 1911 and New York's index of 2.42 in 1914. Further, the rise in benefits received by workers may be understated for two reasons. The benefits under workers' compensation do not include medical payments or funeral expenses, whereas it is likely that the payments listed under negligence liability in part covered medical and funeral expenses. As in other settings, we have not yet subtracted the legal fees that workers paid under the two systems, and legal fees were a higher percentage of negligence liability payments than of workers' compensation payments.

Appendix D
Econometric Analysis Used to Estimate Wage Offsets

In chapter 3 we present several estimates of the wage offsets that workers experienced when workers' compensation was introduced. This appendix discusses the techniques used to estimate these wage offsets in more detail (see also Fishback and Kantor 1995). To estimate how the wages of workers adjusted in response to the introduction of workers' compensation, we constructed three separate panel data sets for relatively dangerous industries in the early 1900s. The first sample covers hourly wage rates from payrolls collected by the U.S. Bituminous Coal Commission. The sample contains state averages for ten jobs from the twenty-three leading coal producing states at the end of each year from 1911 to 1922. The second sample is hourly earnings collected from payrolls by the U.S. Bureau of Labor Statistics for ten different jobs in the lumber industry for the years 1910 to 1913, 1915, 1921, and 1923 in the twenty-three major lumber producing states. The third sample is the wage scales listed in union contracts in the building trades for thirteen occupations in seventy-seven cities for each year between 1907 and 1913.[18] All three data sets allow examination of differences across states and over time during the period when nearly all the workers' compensation laws were adopted.

For each of the three industries, we estimate reduced-form, weighted least squares wage regressions with the real hourly wage (in constant 1890–99 dollars) of occupation i in state j in year t (W_{ijt}) as the dependent variable.[19] The reduced-form equation that we estimate can be written as

$$W_{ijt} = (D_{ijt}, \; B_{ijt}, \; WT_{ijt}, \; A_{ijt}, \; U_{ijt}, \; O_i, \; S_j, \; Y_t, \; e_{ijt}).$$

The reduced-form equation contains variables affecting the employers' wage offer function and the workers' wage acceptance function. The employers' offers were influenced by fluctuations in the product market and in worker productivity (D_{ijt}). Variables affecting the workers' wage acceptance function include the extent of postaccident benefits (B_{ijt}), measures of restrictions on working time (WT_{ijt}), and the accident rate (A_{ijt} which was available at the state level only for the coal sample). Workers seek higher wages as compensation for lower accident benefits, greater restrictions on working time, and higher accident rates. For the coal industry analysis we were also able to include a vector of information on strikes and union strength (U_{ijt}), which also might have affected the wages that workers sought. A vector of state dummy variables (S_j, city dummies for the building trades) controls for geographic differences in labor market conditions, such as differences in the cost of living and other labor laws specific to individual states. A vector of year dummies (Y_t) controls for labor market differences specific to each year, like the government's greater control of markets during World War I. A vector of occupation dummy variables (O_i) in all of the regressions controls for skill differences and other differences in the supply and demand conditions for those particular jobs.

The regression coefficients presented in table D.1 are generally consistent with the findings of other wage studies. Wage rates were positively related to product prices in the coal and lumber samples, whereas increases in building activity (measured by the real value of building permits per capita) were associated with higher wages in the building trades.[20] Output per man hour was positively associated with wages in both the coal and lumber industries. In all of the estimations, the coefficients of the occupation dummy variables suggest that higher skilled workers earned relatively higher wages. Limitations on working time, as measured by full-time hours, were offset by higher wages in the lumber sample.[21] Unions and strike activity were associated with higher wages in the coal industry, although the union coefficient was statistically insignificant.

Columns (1), (3), and (5) in the table show the regression results when the impact of workers' compensation is measured by a zero-one dummy variable that takes the value one for states and years in which the law was in effect, and zero otherwise. In coal mining the presence of a workers' compensation law was associated with a statistically significant 2.16 percent decline in hourly earnings when evaluated at the mean hourly earnings. Similarly, the lumber industry wage offset was 1.60 percent and statistically significant. In the building trades, however, the decline was smaller at 0.33 percent, and not statistically different from zero.[22]

Columns (2), (4), and (6) of the table show the full regression results when we use the expected benefits measure described in the text and in appendix B to measure the impact of workers' compensation. The expected benefits measure is an index that corresponds better to the generosity of employer-provided accident compensation both before and after workers' compensation. It is calculated using the national average wage for each occupation in each year. We did not use the wage corresponding to each observation because the expected benefits would have been a function of the wage, thus imparting a positive bias to the estimated coefficients of the expected benefits index. Similarly, we could not use the ratio of expected benefits to wages because in some cases maximum allowable benefits became binding and the ratio of expected benefits to wages would have imparted a spurious negative bias. To eliminate these problems, we used the national average wage for each occupation in each year, which allowed the expected benefits index to rise in response to rising wages during the period as well as reflect differences in expected benefits driven by differences in wages at each skill level.[23]

The expected benefits variable is therefore an instrumental variable that measures the monetary value that a risk-neutral worker would place on his expected accident compensation. If workers were risk-averse, however, our measure of expected compensation actually provides a lower-bound estimate of the value that workers would have placed on these postaccident benefits. A coefficient of −1 implies that workers fully paid for increases in the expected benefits that they received, although the worker would not have fully paid for the employer's cost of purchasing insurance to provide those benefits. Coefficients of roughly −1.67 imply that employers were able to pass on their full insurance costs to workers.

We have also estimated the various wage equations using a semilog specification often used in wage studies. Table D.2 gives a summary of the accident benefit coefficients from a variety of different empirical specifications. Column (1) of the table corresponds to the second column for each sample in table D.1. Column (2) of table D.2 shows the change in the wage associated with a one-dollar increase in expected benefits under the semilog specification, evaluated at the sample mean of average annual earnings for each industry. The absolute values of *t*-statistics are listed in parentheses below the estimates of the wage offsets. The estimates based on the semilog specification are similar to the results reported in the level specification.[24]

These results are generally robust to the inclusion or exclusion of the

Table D.1   Fixed-Effects Weighted Least Squares Wage Regressions

Variable	Coal Mining Hourly Wage Workers		Lumber Mill Workers		Unionized Building Trades	
	(1)	(2)	(3)	(4)	(5)	(6)
Workers' compensation dummy	−0.603 (3.67)		−0.335 (2.62)		−0.124 (0.604)	
Expected present value of accident compensation[a]		−1.72 (4.14)		−1.04 (2.11)		0.020 (0.031)
Limits on working time[b]	0.053 (0.138)	0.264 (0.704)	−0.359 (18.5)	−0.362 (18.6)	−0.843 (22.7)	−0.843 (22.7)
Product price or other product demand index[c]	8.46 (17.7)	8.35 (17.5)	0.277 (6.68)	0.286 (6.95)	0.044 (5.02)	0.044 (5.01)
Productivity measure[d]	6.43 (3.46)	7.66 (4.12)	0.387 (2.44)	0.386 (2.43)		
Fatal accidents per million man-hours	−0.029 (0.505)	−0.005 (0.086)				
Paid-up membership in the United Mine Workers of America as a percentage of employment	0.111 (0.161)	0.317 (0.469)				
Strike days per employee	0.010 (2.56)	0.012 (3.16)				
Strike days per employee lagged one year	−0.006 (2.28)	−0.005 (2.20)				
Strike days per employee in states other than state i	0.072 (4.00)	0.079 (4.42)				
Intercept	3.40 (2.52)	2.57 (1.91)	37.4 (30.5)	37.6 (29.5)	77.1 (45.7)	77.0 (45.5)

	9 of 10	9 of 10	9 of 10	9 of 10	12 of 13	12 of 13
Occupation dummies	22 of 23	22 of 23	22 of 23	22 of 23	76 of 77	76 of 77
Geography dummies	states	states	states	states	cities	cities
Year dummies	Included	Included	Included	Included	Included	Included
N	2,690	2,690	1,236	1,236	6,563	6,563

Sources: Fishback and Kantor (1995, 727–28). Average hourly earnings in the coal industry are from Fisher and Bezanson (1932, 254–89, 296–325). The union variable is the percentage of workers with paid-up membership in the UMWA reported in U.S. Coal Commission (1925, 1052), with straight-line interpolations to fill years not reported. The remaining coal data were compiled from U.S. Bureau of Mines Bulletins titled, "Coal-Mine Fatalities in the year . . .," and U.S. Geological Survey (after 1922 Bureau of Mines) publications titled, *Mineral Resources of the United States, Part II, Nonmetals,* various years. For further details on the coal sample, see appendix B of Fishback (1992, 234–41). Wage and hours-worked data for each of the lumber occupations were collected from U.S. Bureau of Labor Statistics Bulletin Numbers 129, 153, 225, 317, and 363. Lumber price and output data are reported in U.S. Department of Agriculture (1948). The total number of lumber workers in each state was derived using a straight-line interpolation of data reported in U.S. Bureau of the Census (1913, 504–5; 1923, 466–71). Wage and hours-worked data for each of the building occupations were collected from the following U.S. Bureau of Labor Statistics "Union Scale of Wages and Hours of Labor" Bulletins (year(s) of coverage in parentheses): No. 131 (1907–1912), No. 143 (1913), No. 171 (1914), No. 194 (1915), No. 214 (1916), No. 245 (1917), No. 259 (1918), No. 274 (1919), No. 286 (1920), No. 302 (1921), No. 325 (1922), and No. 354 (1923). Building permit data were collected from Riggleman (1934, 263–76). All dollar values have been deflated using Paul Douglas's cost-of-living index (1890–1899 = 100), series E185 in U.S. Bureau of the Census (1975, 212).

Notes: Dependent variable is hourly wage in 1890–99 cents. Absolute value of *t*-statistics in parentheses below coefficient estimates. *F*-tests reject the hypothesis that the coefficients of occupation, year, and geography dummy variables are simultaneously zero. The mean of the wage is 27.7 (standard deviation of 28) in the coal sample, 20.4 (10.4) in the lumber sample, and 37.3 (9.4) in the building trades sample. Since the data use information based on means from states with different sample sizes, we used weighted least squares. In the coal estimation the square root of the number of coal workers in the state is used as the weight. In the lumber sample, the square root of the number of sampled workers is used as the weight. The building trades data did not report sample size, so White's (1980) method is used to adjust the standard errors. Using White's standard error correction for the coal and lumber regressions does not change the basic results reported above.

[a]The expected value of accident compensation is scaled to correspond to the hourly measurement of the dependent variable. We divided the expected benefits measures by estimates of hours worked per year. For the coal sample, we assumed that miners worked an average of 206.4 eight-hour days (derived from the sample). We assumed that lumber workers worked a total of 3,000 hours per year and building tradesmen worked 2,250 hours. The latter two estimates were calculated as the average number of hours worked per week given in the sample multiplied by fifty weeks.

[b]Limits on working time in the coal industry is measured as the mean number ($\times 10^{-2}$) of days the state's mines were open in that year and the number of hours in a full-time week in the lumber and building trades industries.

[c]The product price is the average price of coal at the mine mouth adjusted for inflation. The lumber price index is a weighted average (by output) of the real prices of individual species of lumber produced in each state. Product demand in the building trades is measured as the per capita value of building permits. Since these data were reported at the regional level, we matched each city observation to its particular region for the given year.

[d]The productivity variable in the coal industry is total coal output divided by total man-days (number of workers multiplied by average days worked multiplied by average hours per day). Lumber productivity is calculated as the total quantity of lumber cut per lumber worker in each state ($\times 10^{-2}$).

Table D.2   Wage Offsets Associated with Different Specifications

Specification	1907 to 1923		Only Compensation and Dummies Included		1907 to 1915		Only Workers' Compensation States and Years	
Sample	Linear (1)	Semilog (2)	Linear (3)	Semilog (4)	Linear (5)	Semilog (6)	Linear (7)	Semilog (8)
Coal	-1.72	-2.50	-1.55	-2.35	-1.56	-2.28	-2.38	-3.48
	(4.14)	(5.07)	(3.53)	(4.38)	(3.64)	(3.78)	(2.85)	(3.63)
Lumber	-1.04	-0.69	-0.68	-0.41	-0.95	-0.67	-1.64	0.70
	(2.11)	(1.18)	(1.21)	(0.58)	(1.94)	(1.43)	(1.48)	(0.57)
Unionized building trades	0.02	-0.17	-0.39	-0.61	0.14	-0.52	4.12	4.09
	(0.03)	(0.27)	(0.56)	(0.91)	(0.19)	(0.75)	(3.83)	(4.15)

Sources: Fishback and Kantor (1995, 732). See table D.1.

Notes: Absolute value of *t*-statistics in parentheses. The entries for the linear specifications are the actual coefficients from the regression. The entries for the semilog specifications are evaluated at the mean wage rate for each sample. A −1 entry would imply a dollar-for-dollar wage offset. Each regression contained the variables listed in table D.1, although the list of year and state dummies was adjusted to include only years and states included in the samples.

various labor demand and supply variables in the equations. For example, columns (3) and (4) of table D.2 report the wage offsets for the level and semilog specifications when only the expected accident compensation variable, along with the dummies for occupations, years, and geography, are included in the estimation. The same patterns are detected. Coal and lumber experienced near or greater than dollar-for-dollar offsets, although the lumber estimates are imprecise. Unionized building tradesmen experienced no offsets.[25]

The samples cover a period of substantial change in American labor markets. During World War I the federal government played a much larger role in labor and product markets and the war led to substantial shocks to labor and product markets. Nominal wages and the price level rose sharply between 1916 and 1920 and both experienced sharp declines in 1921. Within labor markets the gap between skilled and unskilled wages narrowed and the wages of southern and nonsouthern workers began to converge. While the year, skill, and location dummy variables attempt to control for these effects, another method is to limit the samples to the period prior to 1916. The restricted sample captures the substantial change in postaccident benefits associated with the adoption of workers' compensation but avoids the large wage inflation and wage squeeze associated with U.S. participation in World War I. Comparisons of columns (5) and (6) with columns (1) and (2) in table D.2 show that limiting the sample to the early years does not substantially change the results. The coal wage offset ranges between -1.56 and -2.28, while the lumber offset ranges between -0.67 and -0.95. As before, the contractual wages in the building trades are generally unaffected by the expected benefits variable. These results suggest that the wage offsets in the full samples are not driven by the narrowing of regional or skilled-unskilled wage differentials during World War I.[26]

To further test the robustness of our central results, we limited the sample to states and years when workers' compensation was in effect. This test serves a dual purpose. First, because our estimates of postaccident compensation under negligence liability are less accurate than our measures for workers' compensation, focusing solely on the workers' compensation observations is a way to reduce measurement error.[27] Second, since recent studies using modern data find wage offsets associated with more generous workers' compensation benefits, we would expect to find a similar effect for labor markets in the early twentieth century. We can test the reliability of our data by restricting our attention to the wage adjustment associated with the variations in benefit levels under workers' compensation, ignoring the effect of the big change in expected compensation when the laws were first introduced. As shown in columns (7) and (8) of table D.2, the restricted samples produce the same general patterns found in the full samples. Coal wages in fact show an offset that is larger than the one from the full sample. The lumber offset in the linear case is larger than the one from the full sample but not precisely estimated. The building trades coefficients remain positive and are larger in magnitude and are statistically different from zero.

Appendix E
A Model of Insurance Consumption and Saving Behavior

How did the rise in postaccident benefits associated with workers' compensation influence a household's decision to save for and insure against a workplace accident? The answer to this question largely depends on whether the worker's access to insurance was rationed or not. If a worker's access to workplace accident insurance was not rationed, such that he could freely buy his desired amount of insurance at a price below the opportunity cost of savings, he would have bought less insurance and saved more when postaccident benefits increased. If, on the other hand, access to insurance was limited, such that the worker faced a binding constraint on the amount of insurance he could purchase, then increases in postaccident benefits would have led him to reduce his saving.[28] Increases in postaccident benefits would have affected accident insurance purchases only if the worker's new optimal level of insurance purchases fell below the original binding constraint.

Modeling the Unconstrained Case

We capture the essential elements of the household's demand for saving and insurance using a two-period, expected-utility framework. In the first period total household income includes the earnings of the household head, y, and other household income, denoted n, which might include other family members' earnings and nonwage income, such as rent from boarders. At the beginning of the second period, the household head might have a workplace accident with probability q ($0 \leq q \leq 1$). If the primary wage earner has no accident, then the family again receives y and n in period 2. If the head of the household is killed on the job, the family still earns n from other family members plus a postaccident payment of C. The family can adjust its income stream across time periods by saving an amount s in period 1, which earns an interest rate r. The family can also insure against the income loss from an accident by paying a premium p that insures a payment of I if the household head is killed. We have parameterized the model to treat the consumption goods as the numeraire.

The household's budget constraints can be written as follows:

$$n + y = x_1 + pI + s \quad \text{in period 1,}$$

$$n + y + (1 + r)s = x_{2n} \quad \text{in period 2 if no accident occurs, and}$$

$$n + (1 + r)s + C + I = x_{2a} \quad \text{in period 2 if an accident occurs.}$$

Consumption in the first period is denoted x_1, x_{2n} is consumption in the second period with no accident, and x_{2a} is consumption in the second period with an accident. The household's expected utility over the two periods can be written as

$$Z(x_1, x_{2n}, x_{2a}) = U(x_1) + (1 - q)V(x_{2n}) + qW(x_{2a}).$$

The use of different nonaccident utility functions (U and V) for the two time periods implicitly reflects the household's discount rate. Different second-period utility functions for the nonaccident (V) and accident (W) states reflect lower utility for the same income when the family loses a loved one to an accident (see Viscusi and Evans 1992). All three utility functions are assumed to rise at a diminishing rate with increasing consumption (i.e., $U' > 0$, $V' > 0$, $W' > 0$, $U'' < 0$, $V'' < 0$, and $W'' < 0$).

After solving the budget constraints for x_1, x_{2n}, and x_{2a} and substituting them into the utility function, we can derive the comparative statics in the case when insurance is not rationed. In this unconstrained setting, the household chooses a saving level s and insurance purchases I to maximize the following objective function:

$$Z(s,I) = U(n + y - pI - s) + (1 - q)V(n + y + (1 + r)s)$$
$$+ qW(n + C + I + (1 + r)s).$$

The first-order conditions for a maximum are

$$Z_s = -U'(x_1) + (1 + r)(1 - q)V'(x_{2n}) + q(1 + r)W'(x_{2a}) = 0,$$

$$Z_I = -pU'(x_1) + qW'(x_{2a}) = 0,$$

where Z_s and Z_I are the first derivatives of Z with respect to saving and insurance, respectively. The first-order conditions imply that the household chooses saving and insurance levels such that the ratio of the marginal utility in the first period to the expected marginal utility in the second period $\{U'(x_1)/[(1 - q)V'(x_{2n}) + qW'(x_{2a})]\}$ is equal to $(1 + r)$ and the ratio of the marginal utility in the first period to the marginal utility if an accident occurs in the second period $[U'(x_1)/W'(x_{2a})]$ is equal to the ratio of the probability of an accident to the insurance premium (q/p).

The second-order conditions for a maximum are

$$Z_{ss} = U''(x_1) + (1 - q)V''(x_{2n}) + q(1 + r)^2 W''(x_{2a}) < 0$$

and

$$Z_{II} = p^2 U''(x_1) + q W''(x_{2a}) < 0.$$

$$Z_{ss} Z_{II} - Z_{Is}^2 > 0,$$

where

$$Z_{Is} = p U''(x_1) + q(1 + r) W''(x_{2a}) < 0$$

because $U'' < 0$ and $V'' < 0$.

Denote the demand functions for insurance and saving derived from these first-order conditions as $s^* = s^*(y, n, r, p, q, C)$ and $I^* = I^*(y, n, r, p, q, C)$, respectively. The saving and insurance decisions become functions of the income of the household head (y), the nonwage income and income of other family members (n), the interest rate on saving (r), the probability of a workplace accident (q), the premium paid for accident insurance (p), and postaccident payments (C). Of course, these decisions will also be influenced by differences in household preferences (particularly rates of time preference), which might be based on the age of the household head, the number and ages of children in the family, and the skill levels of the workers in the household or their union status.

The comparative statics for changes in savings and insurance when postaccident compensation changes (ds^*/dC and dI^*/dC) are

$$ds^*/dC = (-Z_{sC} Z_{II} + Z_{IC} Z_{Is})/(Z_{ss} Z_{II} - Z_{Is}^2)$$

and

$$dI^*/dC = (-Z_{ss} Z_{IC} + Z_{sC} Z_{Is})/(Z_{ss} Z_{II} - Z_{Is}^2).$$

From the definition of a maximum and from the assumptions that U'', V'', and W'' are negative, the denominator of both equations is positive. Therefore, the sign of the numerator determines the results.

$$Z_{sC} = q(1 + r) W''(x_{2a}) < 0$$

because $W'' < 0$, and

$$Z_{IC} = q W''(x_{2a}) < 0$$

for the same reason.

Given this information, $-Z_{sC} Z_{II} + Z_{IC} Z_{Is}$ and $-Z_{ss} Z_{IC} + Z_{sC} Z_{Is}$ are both ambiguous in sign at first glance. If we substitute in the values of the derivatives, however, the signs of the above functions become clearer. The sign of ds^*/dC is determined by the sign of $-Z_{sC} Z_{II} + Z_{IC} Z_{Is} = W''(x_{2a}) U''(x_1) q p [1 - (1 + r)p]$, which is determined by the sign of $[1 - (1 + r) p]$. This expression is positive as long as p is less than $1/(1 + r)$.

The sign of dI^*/dC is similarly affected by the relationship between p

and $1/(1 + r)$. Its sign is determined by the sign of $-Z_{ss}Z_{IC} + Z_{sC}Z_{Is} = W''(x_{2a})U'' q[p (1 + r) - 1] - q(1 - q) (1 + r)^2 W''(x_{2a})V''(x_{2n})$. Since the second term is negative, the whole term will be negative if $p(1 + r) - 1 < 0$. When p is less than $1/(1 + r)$, the model predicts that dI^*/ds is negative. Thus, if the insurance premium p is less than $1/(1 + r)$, we should expect that increases in postaccident compensation would lead to increases in savings and reductions in insurance purchases in the unrationed model.

Historically, $1/(1 + r)$ was probably no smaller than 0.9 because interest rates on saving rarely reached as high as 10 percent. Given that the probability of an accident was at most 0.2, and generally more like 0.02, the insurance premium p would have been much lower than 0.9 if insurance was actuarially fair. For the insurance premium p to exceed $1/(1 + r)$ the load factor on insurance had to have been enormous or the insurance was unavailable or rationed (in other words the premium at the margin was infinite). In fact, if p exceeded $1/(1 + r)$, the worker could not achieve a maximum because the first-order conditions would never hold. From the first-order condition $Z_1 = 0$, $p/q\ U''(x_1) = W''(x_{2a})$. Substitute this into the first-order condition $Z_s = 0$ and simplify, then $U'(x_1)[1 - (1 + r)p] = (1 + r)(1 - q)V'(x_{2n})$. By assumption U', V', $(1 + r)$, and $(1 - q)$ must be positive; therefore, $[1 - (1 + r)p]$ must be positive for the first-order conditions to hold.

Comparative Statics in the Constrained Model

The comparative statical results change markedly when we assume that insurance purchases were rationed. Insurance companies, in response to problems with adverse selection, often establish maximums for the amount of insurance people can buy and in some cases sell no insurance at all. If this constraint is binding, the worker faces a maximization problem with the extra constraint that insurance purchases I equal the maximum M. The maximization problem then becomes a Lagrangian with an objective function,

$$X(s, I, u) = U(n + y - pI - s) + (1 - q)V(n + y + (1 + r)s)$$
$$+ qW(n + C + I + (1 + r)s) + u(M - I),$$

where M is the maximum amount of insurance allowed by the insurance companies and u is a LaGrangian multiplier.

The first-order conditions for a maximum are

$$X_s = -U'(x_1) + (1 + r)(1 - q)V'(x_{2n}) + q(1 + r)W'(x_{2a}) = 0,$$

$$X_I = -pU'(x_1) + qW'(x_{2a}) - u = 0,$$

$$X_u = (M - I).$$

The choice functions for insurance and saving derived from these first-order conditions are now $s^c = s^c(y, n, r, p, q, C, M)$ and $I^c = I^c(y, n, r, p, q, C, M)$, and $u^c = u^c(y, n, r, p, q, C, M)$. X_{ss}, X_{II}, and X_{sI} are all negative (they are the same as the expressions Z_{ss}, Z_{II}, and Z_{sI} above). Also, $X_{su} = 0$, $X_{Iu} = -1$, and $X_{uu} = 0$.

The comparative statics show that increases in postaccident benefits (C) cause workers to save less. The sign of ds^*/dC is determined by the sign of

$$X_{sC} = q(1 + r)W''(x_{2a}),$$

which is less than zero because W'' is negative. The binding constraint on insurance purchases also leads to the result that insurance purchases are unaffected by changes in postaccident compensation ($dI^*/dC = 0$). However, this presumes that the insurance constraint remains binding. It is possible that the optimal level of insurance could fall below the constraint, in which case the impact of higher postaccident compensation would be to lower insurance purchases again.

We can also derive comparative statics for the impact on savings and insurance when insurance companies raise the maximum amount of insurance allowed. The impact on insurance (dI^*/dM) is determined by the sign of $-X_{ss}$, which is greater than zero; therefore, increases in the maximums lead workers to purchase more insurance. The impact on savings (ds^*/dM) is determined by the sign of X_{sI}, which is negative; therefore, increases in the insurance maximum lead workers to save less.

The intuition underlying the differences in the saving response in the unconstrained and rationed cases is relatively simple. If insurance were not rationed and priced near actuarial fairness, the worker would have found it much less costly to buy accident insurance than to use saving for insurance purchases. An increase in postaccident benefits would allow him to purchase lower amounts of insurance, freeing funds for more saving and consumption. If accident insurance, on the other hand, were constrained at the maximum, then saving would have been a more reasonable means of insuring against the risk of an accident, and increases in postaccident compensation would have led to reductions in saving.

Recasting the Models Incorporating Compensating Wage Differentials in Response to a Rise in Expected Benefits

We have also reformulated the model to include the presence of compensating differentials in wages in response to the change in the postaccident payment C. In that case, income y can become a function of C, $y(C)$, where $y'(C) < 0$. When insurance is unconstrained and relatively inexpensive [$p < 1/(1 + r)$], the more complicated model predicts that saving would rise whenever postaccident payments rise. When insurance is rationed, the model predicts that saving could either fall or rise when post-accident payments rise. Thus, even under compensating differentials, the only setting in which saving would be expected to fall with a rise in postaccident compensation is when there are limitations on the availability of insurance.

Appendix F

An Econometric Analysis of the Effect of Increased Expected Benefits on Saving and Insurance Behavior

This appendix reports the results of a regression analysis of how variations in expected postaccident benefits on the part of working-class families influenced precautionary saving and private insurance coverage (see Kantor and Fishback 1996). We use cross-sectional data on families' financial decisions in both workers' compensation states and negligence liability states. Between late 1917 and early 1919 the U.S. Bureau of Labor Statistics (BLS) conducted an intricate analysis of the consumption patterns of working-class families in industrial centers of the United States. The study established the budget weights for the consumer price index (U.S. Bureau of Labor Statistics 1924). Agents interviewed 12,817 families of wage earners or salaried workers in ninety-nine cities in forty-two states. Although the BLS believed that the survey families fairly represented the urban population at the time, the investigation was limited in a number of important ways. The interviewers surveyed only households of wage and salary earners where both spouses and one or more children were present. The salaried workers were not to earn more than two thousand dollars a year and the families had to reside in the same community for a year prior to the survey. Further, the BLS excluded families with more than three boarders, "slum" families, charity families, and non-English-speaking families who had been in the United States less than five years. As a result, craft workers and other high-wage workers were oversampled relative to factory operatives and laborers.

We imposed some additional limits on the sample, restricting it to laborers, operatives, and craft workers for several reasons. First, domestic service workers and farm workers were excluded because workers' compensation laws usually exempted these occupations from coverage. Second, we eliminated managers, professionals and semiprofessionals, salesmen, and clerical workers because our measure of accident risk largely pertains to the workers directly involved in the defining activities of that industry.[29] The exclusions reduce measurement error because the managerial, sales, and clerical workers were typically not exposed to the same accident risk as manufacturing workers. Third, men working in the maritime industry were eliminated from the sample because the nature of their postaccident compensation was in a state of flux at the time of the survey.[30] Fourth, railroad workers were eliminated because of inadequate information on their postaccident compensation. Railroad workers typically fared better than nonrailroad workers under negligence liability because employers could not invoke the fellow servant and contributory negligence defenses after 1908. However, because interstate railroad workers were not covered under workers' compensation, we are uncertain how they fared relative to nonrailroad workers when the laws were enacted. Fifth, government workers were eliminated because the status of postaccident compensation for these workers was poorly defined in many states.[31] After all of these restrictions to the original sample, we were left with a total of 7,475 observations.

The cost-of-living survey contains information on household purchases of accident and life insurance and household saving. "Saving" is defined as the household's total income minus its total expenditures. The BLS survey asked the family how many people in the household had accident insurance. In the sample 90 percent responded that no one had accident insurance, 9.4 percent responded that at least one person had accident insurance, and only 0.6 percent responded that more than one person had insurance. Presumably, most households with just one accident insurance policy were insuring the household head, the primary wage earner. We used this information to create a dummy variable taking the value of one if the household held one or more accident insurance policies, and zero otherwise.

The BLS also asked about the number of household members with five different types of life insurance: old-line (whole life), fraternal, industrial, establishment, and other types. Because life insurance covered so many more people within the household than accident insurance, the life insurance variable by necessity focuses on the purchases of life insurance for all members of the household. We used the information to create a dummy variable valued at one if the household claimed at least one life insurance policy, and zero otherwise. Given the zero-one nature of the variables we estimated probit equations.

The insurance and saving functions that we estimate can be derived from the first-order conditions in appendix E or from extensions of the models that Leland (1968) and Kotlikoff (1989) developed. In such a model the demands for insurance and precautionary saving would be affected by the expected postaccident benefit, accident risk, the interest rate, and income. We included other demand variables pertaining more specifically to the household's financial status. Thus, the regressions include the wife's annual earnings, the children's earnings, income from boarding and lodging, net income from rent and interest, and the number of children between ages zero and four, five and nine, ten and fourteen, and older than fourteen. Moreover, following Haines (1985), our empirical models include a number of variables designed to capture differences in the utility functions across households. We control for possible life-cycle effects by including the age and age squared of the household head, and we include dummy variables controlling for his occupational skill level and whether he contributed to a labor organization. To capture differences in the cost of living that households faced, we included an index of the average cost of living in urban areas in each state for the period 1919 to 1921. We also included regional dummy variables to capture geographic differences in interest rates caused by differences in banking regulations and differences in insurance premiums caused by state-specific regulations or varying costs of selling and monitoring policies across the country.

To measure the workplace accident risk that each worker in the sample faced, we matched each worker's industry with the premium paid per one hundred dollars on the payroll that *employers* in that industry were required to pay into the Ohio State Workmen's Compensation Fund in 1923. Note that this premium is not the one that workers paid for personal life or accident insurance. We chose the Ohio information because Ohio had a wider range of industries than any other state where premiums were available. The premiums that employers paid should be correlated with fatal and nonfatal accident risk in the workplace because the Ohio Industrial Commission sought to price the insurance so that industries paid for the accident costs they generated. To some extent, this accident risk measure should be correlated with the accident insurance premium that a worker would have paid for private accident insurance, which was priced according to his particular industry and occupation.

To calculate a worker's expected postaccident compensation, we followed the procedures described in appendix B. In this case we used the worker's actual wage to calculate the expected benefits.

Coefficient estimates and t-statistics from the probit estimations of life and accident insurance coverage and ordinary least squares estimation of the saving equation are presented in table F.1. To calculate the impact of a one-standard-deviation change in each of the independent variables on the life insurance and accident insurance probabilities, we followed the standard procedure of translating probit coefficients into marginal effects. That is, we calculated a baseline probability of purchasing insurance by setting the independent variables at their sample means and the dummy variables equal to zero. We then computed the change in the baseline probability caused by a one-standard-deviation change in each independent variable, holding all others constant at their sample means. The marginal effects of the dummy variables represent shifts from zero to one.

The coefficient of the expected-benefits variable in the life insurance probit is negative, but it is not statistically significant. A one-standard-deviation change in the expected postaccident benefits ($7.15) would have

Table F.1   Coefficients from Probit Analyses of Accident and Life Insurance Coverage and OLS Estimation of Saving

Variable	Means (1)	Life Insurance Purchased {0,1} (2)	Accident Insurance Purchased {0,1} (3)	Saving (4)	Saving (5)
Intercept		0.320	−6.491[a]	−330.7[a]	−48.78
		(0.184)	(2.394)	(1.995)	(1.055)
Present value of expected benefits	14.67	−0.0061	−0.0165[a]	−1.624[a]	−1.156[a]
	(7.149)	(1.578)	(3.634)	(4.544)	(4.501)
Accident risk	1.203	0.00098	−0.0196	2.016	1.639
	(1.054)	(0.056)	(0.957)	(1.187)	(0.966)
Age of husband	36.93	0.0169	−0.0067	2.148	2.301
	(8.463)	(1.075)	(0.367)	(1.368)	(1.467)
Age squared	1,435	−0.00019	0.00017	−0.004	−0.005
	(679.6)	(0.956)	(0.752)	(0.201)	(0.283)
Husband's annual earnings	1,301	0.00012[a]	0.00040[a]	0.202[a]	0.202[a]
	(363.6)	(2.050)	(6.274)	(35.45)	(35.71)
Wife's annual earnings	18.53	−0.00017	0.00055	0.143[a]	0.138[a]
	(73.99)	(0.686)	(1.911)	(5.733)	(5.580)
Net income from rent and interest	6.003	−0.0015[a]	0.00062	0.456[a]	0.451[a]
	(32.23)	(3.012)	(1.058)	(8.200)	(8.106)
Children's annual earnings	87.93	0.00015	−0.00001	0.194[a]	0.194[a]
	(272.7)	(1.330)	(0.057)	(17.80)	(17.86)
Income from board and lodging	5.165	−0.00006	−0.0011	−0.154[a]	−0.153[a]
	(29.47)	(0.089)	(1.306)	(2.542)	(2.537)
State cost-of-living index	101.5	−0.0024	0.052[a]	1.264	−1.613[a]
	(5.139)	(0.147)	(2.033)	(0.817)	(4.547)
Contributes to union organization	0.320	−0.067	−0.090	−13.93[a]	−13.39[a]
	(0.467)	(1.698)	(1.944)	(3.542)	(3.457)

Craft occupation	0.489	0.151[a]	0.030	4.695	4.374
	(0.500)	(3.054)	(0.492)	(0.954)	(0.889)
Operative occupation	0.301	0.111[a]	0.181[a]	−0.027	−0.569
	(0.459)	(2.167)	(2.942)	(0.005)	(0.111)
Number of children ages	0.917	−0.025	−0.009	−16.94[a]	−17.42[a]
0 to 4	(0.871)	(1.076)	(0.349)	(7.467)	(7.691)
Number of children ages	0.802	0.062[a]	−0.041	−20.05[a]	−20.51[a]
5 to 9	(0.847)	(2.702)	(1.557)	(9.080)	(9.291)
Number of children ages	0.567	0.004	0.030	−26.48[a]	−26.74[a]
10 to 14	(0.804)	(0.156)	(1.045)	(10.45)	(10.52)
Number of children ages	0.312	−0.026	−0.044	−37.07[a]	−37.33[a]
15 and up	(0.711)	(0.584)	(0.843)	(8.34)	(8.409)
Regional Dummy Variables					
New England	0.119	0.643[a]	−0.539[a]	−6.827	
	(0.324)	(6.222)	(3.759)	(0.668)	
Mid-Atlantic	0.189	0.735[a]	−0.644[a]	3.743	
	(0.391)	(8.774)	(5.876)	(0.446)	
East North Central	0.220	0.509[a]	−0.841	14.56	
	(0.415)	(3.693)	(0.414)	(1.081)	
West North Central	0.086	0.406[a]	−0.265	−10.47	
	(0.281)	(3.602)	(1.839)	(0.931)	
South Atlantic	0.119	0.555[a]	−0.996[a]	−11.80	
	(0.324)	(5.021)	(6.877)	(1.085)	
East South Central	0.059	0.466[a]	−0.628[a]	4.121	
	(0.236)	(3.636)	(3.753)	(0.329)	
West South Central	0.048	0.273	−0.120	−1.458	
	(0.213)	(1.830)	(0.933)	(0.098)	

(continued)

Table F.1   (continued)

Variable	Means (1)	Life Insurance Purchased {0,1} (2)	Accident Insurance Purchased {0,1} (3)	Saving (4)	Saving (5)
Mountain	0.055 (0.228)	0.013 (0.051)	−0.578 (1.436)	−63.92[a] (2.478)	
N	7,475	7,475	7,475	7,475	7,475
Adj. R^2		0.852	0.100	0.214	0.212
Mean of dependent variable				71.71 (173.1)	71.71 (173.1)

Sources: Kantor and Fishback (1996, 434–35). "Cost-of-Living in the United States, 1917–1919," available through the Inter-University Consortium for Political and Social Research, No. 8299. The accident risk measure matches each worker's industry with the workers' compensation premium paid per one hundred dollars on the payroll by Ohio employers in 1923. The premiums are reported in Ohio Industrial Commission (1923). The expected benefits are calculated based on the procedure described in appendix B. The cost-of-living index is calculated from Williamson and Lindert (1980, 323–25). They report a Koffsky-adjusted cost of living for the entire state including rural and urban areas, which was originally derived from urban cost-of-living indices. We reversed the formula to calculate the urban cost of living, by dividing the cost of living they report on pages 323–24 by $(1 - a \times 0.065)$, where a is the percentage of farm workers in the labor force and 0.065 is the percentage difference between the urban and rural cost of living.

Notes: Absolute values of t-statistics are in parentheses. Standard deviations are reported in parentheses below all means. The craft dummy variable has a value of one for all workers listed as craftsmen, foremen, or kindred workers (code numbers 300–398 in the 1940 census occupation codes, see note 29). The operatives dummy has a value of one for all workers listed as operatives and kindred workers (codes 400–496). The category left out of the regressions is laborers (codes 900–988). The BLS survey was taken during the period from August 1917 through February 1919, a period of substantial inflation. We also ran the regressions with the monetary values adjusted to constant dollars using Douglas's cost-of-living index (1890–1899 = 100) as the deflator (U.S. Bureau of the Census 1975, 212). The central results reported in the table remain the same when the monetary variables are deflated.

[a]Statistically significant at the 5 percent level.

lowered the probability of purchasing life insurance by only 0.1 percentage point—from 86.1 percent to 86.2 percent—when evaluated at the independent variables' sample means.[32] Changes in expected accident benefits had more influence on the probability of purchasing accident insurance, as a one-standard-deviation change in the benefits would have lowered the probability of purchasing accident insurance by a statistically significant 1.9 percentage points.

The coefficient on expected benefits in the saving regression in column (4) of the table indicates that each dollar increase in expected benefits was associated with a reduction in saving of $1.62, which is statistically significantly different from zero.[33] To get a sense of the general magnitude of a switch from negligence liability to workers' compensation, consider a worker who moved from Virginia, where negligence liability was still in force, to the neighboring workers' compensation state of Maryland. All else equal, his expected postaccident benefits would have risen by approximately eleven dollars. Such an increase would have allowed him to reduce his precautionary saving by $17.82, or about 25 percent of the mean level of saving in the sample.

The $1.62 estimate may understate the full macroeconomic effect of introducing workers' compensation because income is held constant in the saving regression. If, as we argue in chapter 3, workers paid for increases in postaccident benefits in the form of lower wages, then the reduction in earnings associated with the adoption of workers' compensation itself probably led to reduced saving. Consider a situation in which the household head experienced a wage offset that lowered his annual earnings by the full increase in his expected postaccident benefits. The coefficient on the household head's income in the table implies that saving would have fallen an additional $0.202 for each dollar increase in expected postaccident benefits, thus raising the overall impact on saving to $1.82.

We have performed several tests to ensure that the estimated impact of changes in postaccident benefits on saving behavior is not spurious. There may be worries that the regional dummy variables are capturing some of the impact of workers' compensation, so we have estimated the equation without the regional dummies. The coefficient of the expected-benefits variable is slightly smaller at -1.16 and remains statistically significant. It should be noted, however, that F-tests reject the hypothesis that the coefficients of the regional dummy variables are simultaneously zero.

Another potential criticism is that states without workers' compensation in 1918 tended to be southern states, where saving might have been lower. Further, there may be questions about measurement error in the non–workers' compensation states because we could not rely on explicit laws to estimate the expected accident benefits in such states. Such concerns are unfounded, however. The saving regression includes income and regional dummies that should control for this effect. Further, we estimated the saving equation on a sample that eliminated the non–workers' compensation states and the expected-benefits coefficient was actually somewhat larger at -2.24, with a t-statistic of -5.48.

Another more serious concern is that the BLS survey was taken during World War I, which was a period of substantial upheaval in the economy. The government became heavily involved in labor markets and the economy experienced substantial demand and supply shocks that were probably unevenly distributed geographically. The saving result potentially could be spurious if these shocks were correlated in some way with the generosity of workers' compensation benefits across states. We have tested for this possibility by estimating the saving regression on an alternative sample of households from the BLS survey that would have been largely unaffected by the expected benefits under workers' compensation. In this sample we included professional and clerical workers who did not face the risks that operatives, workers, and craftsmen faced, domestic service workers who were not covered by workers' compensation, federal government workers who were covered under federal workers' compensation law, and railroad workers who were involved in interstate commerce and were covered under an entirely different set of liability rules. For each worker in this alternative sample we calculated his expected benefits as if he were covered under his state's workers' compensation law and faced the same accident risk as that of manufacturing operatives and skilled workers in his particular industry. Given that these households' saving decisions were not in actuality affected by the generosity of their states' workers' compensation programs, we would expect to find that the expected-benefits variable would have a small and statistically insignificant effect on saving. That is exactly what we find. The expected-benefits coefficient when regional dummies are included is small at -0.56, roughly one-third the size of the coefficient in the table, and we cannot reject the hypothesis that the coefficient is zero (t-statistic of -0.76). In an equation with the regional dummies excluded, the coefficient is 0.21, and again statistically insignificant (t-statistic of 0.42).

Most of the other variables in the table tended to affect saving and insurance as expected. The age variables indicate that saving and insurance purchases increased at a diminishing rate with age, but the coefficients are not statistically significant. A husband's higher earnings were associated with more saving and insurance coverage, while the earnings of other household members had a positive effect on saving, but varied effects on accident insurance purchases. Households also saved less as they had more older children. For example, an additional child between the ages of zero and four lowered saving by seventeen dollars, but one more child older than fifteen years reduced saving by thirty-seven dollars. This result may be driven by the fact that saving is measured as a residual (household income minus expenditures), and older children may have consumed more in terms of food and clothing. Alternatively, the result might be interpreted as evidence that families used children as substitutes for precautionary saving. Having children in the household who could be sent to work in case of financial hardship meant that families did not have to rely so heavily on saving as a means of insurance.

Appendix G
Employers' Liability Laws

Employers' liability laws were a group of statutes that outlined the liability of employers for workplace accidents. Because of the wide range of such laws (Clark 1908) we have classified them into several types: laws that had an impact on employers' liability for most nonrailroad workers in the state (these are the laws summarized in table 4.1), laws that restated the common law for all workers, laws that influenced the liability of railroad employers, laws that assigned liability to mineowners for willful violations of the mine safety laws, laws that specified employers' liability in mining, and laws that outlawed contracts in which workers' waived their liability.

In determining the classification of laws we began with Clark (1908) to get a picture of the situation as of 1907. We went backward in time and examined the laws as of 1900, as reported by Fessenden (1900, 1157–210). We then went forward in time and reexamined the laws again as of 1913, using U.S. Bureau of Labor Statistics (1914) and then once again reexamined the laws as of 1925 using U.S. Bureau of Labor Statistics (1925a). For states where there were changes in the law, we examined when the changes were made (often the date of the change was listed in these sources). These laws are complex and in some cases interpreting them requires a heavy reliance on court interpretations; other scholars might choose to reclassify some of our designations.

Laws That Affected Employers' Liability for Nonrailroad Workers

Often employers' liability laws are lumped into one category. In a number of states the employers' liability law referred specifically to railroading or mining, while in other states the law was more general. Railroad workers were covered by the Federal Employers' Liability Acts of 1906 and 1908 if they were involved in interstate commerce. Given that workers' compensation was focused more on nonrailroad workers, we feel it important to identify a separate class of laws that were general or focused on manufacturing. In this grouping of laws, for which annual totals are given in table 4.1, we have tried to focus on those laws that we felt increased the liability of employers. There was a class of laws that restated the common law and thus probably had no impact on the liability of employers, and we have grouped those in a separate category.

The states with laws that appear to have affected employer liability for nonrailroad workers include Alabama (pre-1900), Arizona (1912), Arkansas (1913), California (1907), Colorado (pre-1900, 1901), Indiana (pre-1900, 1911), Idaho (1909), Iowa (1907), Kansas (1903 and 1909), Louisiana (pre-1900), Maine (1909), Massachusetts (1902, 1909), Mississippi (1896 ending in 1903, 1910), Nebraska (1913), Nevada (1905), New Jersey (1910), New York (1902), Ohio (1902, 1904, 1910), Oklahoma (1907), Oregon (1907), Pennsylvania (1907), Utah (pre-1900), Vermont (1910), Washington (1903), Wisconsin (1906), and Wyoming (pre-1900).

Alabama, Colorado, Massachusetts, and New York had detailed employers' liability laws that described contributory negligence, the fellow servant defense, and assumption of risk in detail and seemed to be more than just a restatement of the common law. Colorado in 1901 limited the fellow servant defense. Massachusetts in 1909 further altered the employers' defenses by establishing comparative negligence and limits on liability. The Arizona Constitution of 1912 and consequent legislation in 1912 abrogated the fellow servant defense and established comparative negligence. Utah specified in detail who was considered a fellow servant. Indiana established that the burden of proof for contributory negligence was on the defendant prior to 1900 and then in 1911 set up a more-detailed employers' liability law. Iowa in 1907 established an assumption of risk law that ensured that if an employee notified the employer of a defect in machinery, the employee had not assumed the risk if he continued to work on the machine. Louisiana had a very broad statement that seemed to limit the fellow servant defense because it was based on the Napoleonic Code. In 1912 Louisiana further limited the assumption of risk defense. Mississippi established comparative negligence in 1910. In 1896 Mississippi enacted a law that tried to expand its railroad employers' liability law to apply to all corporations but it was struck down as unconstitutional in 1903 (Clark 1908, 114). Oklahoma's Constitution of 1907 stated that the fellow servant defense was not applicable in mining and railroading. Oklahoma also established that a jury was to decide as a question of fact whether the assumption of risk and/or contributory negligence defenses applied; therefore, we classified it as having an impact on liability. Alabama, Indiana, and Pennsylvania imposed limits on the fellow servant defense. Wyoming's constitution disallowed laws that would limit the amount of damages to be recovered by an injured person. Idaho in 1909 established a general employers' liability bill, as did Vermont in 1910. Maine's 1909 law seemed to cover both nonrailroad and railroad employers. Nevada had a statute similar to Connecticut, which restated the common law, although it was stated differently enough that we have classified it as having an impact on employers' liability.

Ohio established a statute making the employer liable for accidents that resulted from their failure to follow the inspection statutes; in 1904 the state limited assumption of risk; and in 1910 Ohio established comparative negligence and limited the fellow servant defense. Oregon, Washington, and Wisconsin as part of their factory inspection laws made the employer liable for failure to comply with the factory inspection. In Kansas, the statute requiring the installation of fire escapes and safety devices in manufacturing establishments authorized an action for injuries or death from the employer's disregard of the act. Kansas in 1909 later established a factory act like the ones in Washington and Oregon. Nebraska passed a 1913 statute that was similar to the ones in Oregon, Washington, and Wisconsin. Although Rhode Island and New Jersey (in the 1890s) had statutes for fire escapes and elevators, we did not treat them as a main employers' liability law because of their limited focus. New Jersey in 1910 established a general employers' liability act. Arkansas set up comparative negligence and limited assumption of risk in 1913. Colorado in 1911 imposed a liability maximum of five thousand dollars and added a factory inspection clause that imposed liability for noncompliance. Florida in 1913 passed a law establishing comparative negligence and disallowing contracts whereby workers waived their right to sue in the railroad, street railway, telephone and telegraph, boating, and blasting industries. However, we treated this Florida law as primarily a railroad law.

Laws That Restated the Common Law

Clark (1908) claimed that Arizona, California, Connecticut (1902), Georgia, Minnesota, Montana, North Dakota, Oklahoma, and South Dakota (pre-1900) all had statutes or constitutional provisions that simply restated the common law, without expanding employers' liability.

Employers' Liability for Willful Failure to Follow Mining Statutes

The following states included in their mining regulations a statement that willful violation of the mining statute could lead to a rightful claim for damages: Arkansas, California, Colorado, Illinois, Indiana, Iowa, Maryland (1902), Michigan, Missouri, New Mexico, North Carolina, Ohio, Oklahoma, Pennsylvania, Utah (1905), Washington, and Wyoming. We treat this type of employers' liability law as a separate category specific to mining. All of the laws were enacted prior to 1900 unless another year is noted in parentheses.

General Employers' Liability Laws Specific to Mines

Maryland (1902), Missouri (1907), Nevada (1907), and Oklahoma (1907) all had general liability laws for the mining industry.

**Laws Preventing Workers from Signing Contracts
Waiving Rights to Negligence Suit Prior to Injury**

States with laws preventing such ex ante contracts in railroading included Arkansas, Florida, Iowa, Minnesota, Mississippi, Missouri, Nebraska, Nevada (1907), New Mexico, New York, North Carolina, North
Dakota, Ohio, Oregon, South Carolina, South Dakota, Texas, Virginia,
and Wisconsin. States with general laws were Alabama (1907), Arkansas
(1913), California, Colorado, Georgia, Idaho (1909), Indiana, Massachusetts, Missouri (mining only), Montana, Nevada (1907 for railroading,
mining, and milling), Ohio (1910), and Wyoming (constitution).

Employers' Liability Laws for Railroads

The states with employers' liability laws for the railroad industry included Arkansas (pre-1900), Colorado (pre-1900), Delaware (1903), Florida (pre-1900), Georgia (pre-1900), Illinois (pre-1900), Indiana (1901),
Iowa (pre-1900), Kansas (pre-1900), Kentucky (1903), Maine (1905), Massachusetts (pre-1900), Michigan (1909), Minnesota (pre-1900), Mississippi
(pre-1900), Missouri (pre-1900), Montana (pre-1900), Nebraska (pre-
1900), Nevada (1907), New Mexico (pre-1900), New York (1906), North
Carolina (pre-1900), North Dakota (pre-1900), Ohio (pre-1900), Oklahoma (1907), Oregon (1903), South Carolina (pre-1900), South Dakota
(1907), Texas (pre-1900), Vermont (pre-1900), Virginia (1902), Washington (pre-1900), Wisconsin (pre-1900), and Wyoming (1913).

Appendix H

*Discrete-Time Hazard Analysis of the Timing
of Adoption across the United States*

In chapter 4 we discuss how the timing of adoption across states was influenced by interest group pressure, changes in the climate of employers'
liability, and political reform movements. In the text we show comparisons
of mean values of various factors that influenced adoption for states
adopting prior to 1913, between 1913 and 1916, and after 1916. It is important to remember, however, that all of these factors are influencing the
adoption process at the same time. Thus, we must look at the impact of
these factors on adoption from a multivariate perspective. This section
provides the statistical background for the statements made in chapter
4, section 4.3. The analysis was first reported in Fishback and Kantor
(1998a).

To examine the marginal impact of each factor on the probability of adoption, we estimated an equation summarizing the first-time adoption decisions by state legislatures between 1909 and 1930 using a discrete-time hazard model with time-varying covariates (Allison 1984, 16–22; Yamaguchi 1991, 16–24):

$$\ln(p(t;\mathbf{X})/[1 - p(t;\mathbf{X})]) = a + b\mathbf{X} + e,$$

where $p(t; \mathbf{X})$ is the conditional probability of adoption at a discrete point in time t given that the event did not occur prior to time t and given the covariate vector $\mathbf{X}$ (which includes variables measuring the liability environment, interest group strength, and the political climate); b is a $1 \times k$ vector of coefficients for the $k \times 1$ covariate vector $\mathbf{X}$; a is the log-odds of a baseline group where the vector $\mathbf{X}$ is all zeroes; and e is an error term.[34] We chose the discrete-time hazard model because there were significant discontinuities in the opportunities for legislatures to adopt the legislation. The legislatures could only adopt the law when they met, and most legislatures met every other year.

Table H.1 presents the variables' economic impacts on the probability of adopting workers' compensation, based on the coefficients from the discrete-time hazard model.[35] For the continuous variables the impact represents the marginal effect on the probability of adopting workers' compensation (in year t, given that the state had not already adopted the law) caused by a one-standard-deviation (OSD) increase in each independent variable, holding all others constant at their sample means. The marginal effects of the dummy variables show the change in the probability when the dummy variables switch from zero to one. Note that a positive effect implies that an increase in the variable leads to a higher probability of enacting the legislation. The absolute value of t-statistics of the coefficients from the hazard model are reported in parentheses to allow the reader to assess the statistical significance of the original hypothesis tests on the coefficients from the model. In the discussion below we focus on the results in column (1).

Changes in the Legal Environment Governing Accident Compensation

There are several signs that changes in the employers' liability climate influenced the timing of first adoption by state legislatures. The presence of an employers' liability law for nonrailroad workers that altered one or more of the three common law defenses raised the probability of adopting workers' compensation by a statistically significant 7.9 percentage points. In contrast, the presence of a law that restated the common law without truly expanding the employers' liability law had only a small and statistically insignificant effect on the probability of adoption.

Table H.1   **Economic Impact of Changes in Variables on the Probability of Adopting Workers' Compensation, 1909–30, Derived from Parameters Estimated in Discrete-Time Hazard Model**

Variables	Mean (std. dev.)	Impact of Changes on the Probability of Enacting Workers' Compensation (absolute value of t-statistic of underlying regression coefficient)[a]	
		(1)	(2)
Baseline probability		0.043	0.043
Changes in workplace accident liability			
Employers' liability law limiting	0.430	0.079	0.078
common law defenses	(0.496)	(2.27)	(2.21)
Employers' liability law	0.157	0.002	−0.0001
restating the common law	(0.365)	(0.05)	(0.004)
Ratio of employers' liability	0.113	0.036	0.039
and accident insurance	(0.048)	(2.39)	(2.49)
premiums to life insurance			
premiums			
Index of workplace accident	1.897	0.023	0.020
supreme court cases	(2.63)	(1.97)	(1.71)
(1904–6 = 1) lagged one year			
Manufacturing accident risk	1.789	0.013	0.006
index	(0.659)	(0.60)	(0.29)
Interest group influence			
Percentage of workers in	7.44	−0.016	−0.015
manufacturing establishments	(6.37)	(0.89)	(0.77)
with less than 5 workers			
Percentage of workers in	23.7	0.047	0.044
manufacturing establishments	(11.0)	(1.92)	(1.77)
with more than 500 workers			
Manufacturing value added per	4.451	0.049	0.054
worker (thousands; constant	(1.39)	(1.96)	(2.06)
1967 dollars)			
Percentage of labor force	22.12	0.076	0.086
employed in manufacturing	(11.08)	(1.78)	(1.89)
Percentage of labor force	2.32	0.002	0.001
employed in mining	(3.61)	(0.12)	(0.06)
Manufacturing unionization	9.484	0.110	0.102
index	(4.604)	(3.03)	(2.84)
Life insurance premiums per	45.76	−0.008	−0.013
worker (constant 1967	(18.48)	(0.49)	(0.81)
dollars)			
State spending on labor-related	0.159	−0.016	−0.014
bureaucracy per worker	(0.177)	(1.25)	(1.02)
(constant 1967 dollars)			

Table H.1   (continued)

Variables	Mean (std. dev.)	Impact of Changes on the Probability of Enacting Workers' Compensation (absolute value of t-statistic of underlying regression coefficient)[a]	
		(1)	(2)
Political climate			
Power shift in at least one	0.132	0.078	0.071
branch of legislature	(0.339)	(1.59)	(1.48)
Power shift in both branches	0.083	0.009	0.013
of legislature	(0.399)	(0.17)	(0.25)
Progressive law index	4.65	0.019	0.012
	(1.82)	(1.13)	(0.70)
Progressive vote for Roosevelt	15.60	0.093	0.083
in 1912 presidential election	(10.37)	(3.77)	(3.37)
Percent of presidential vote for	3.673	0.010	0.012
socialist	(3.296)	(0.55)	(0.64)
Southern state dummy variable	0.541	0.074	0.069
	(0.499)	(1.82)	(1.66)
"Contagion effect"			
Percentage of nearby states			
that had adopted workers'	0.277		0.016
compensation $t - 1$	(0.316)		(1.03)

Sources: Fishback and Kantor (1998a, 322–23). See appendix I.

Note: The information covers the forty-eight states for the period 1909 to 1930 when the state legislatures met up until the year of adoption by the legislature in each state, with a total of 242 state-years.

[a]The impact of changes for continuous variables is based on a one-standard-deviation increase in each of the continuous variables, holding the other variables constant at their sample means. The marginals of the dummy variables are based on switches from 0 to 1, centered at the mean for the variable, holding all else constant. The baseline probability was computed at the sample means of all the variables. The t-statistics in parentheses are the ones from the estimated coefficients of the discrete-time hazard model; they cannot be used to construct confidence intervals for the measures of the impact of the variables.

A rise in the supreme court case index, our measure of increased legal uncertainty, was associated with a statistically significant increase in the probability of adopting workers' compensation. An OSD increase in the index increased a state's probability of enacting the legislation by 2.3 percentage points.

To capture the expansion in employers' liability insurance premiums and greater interest in insurance purchases, we included the ratio of employers' liability insurance premiums to life insurance premiums that were collected by commercial insurance companies in each state. Consistent with the view that expanding employers' liability led to the adoption of workers' compensation, an OSD increase in the insurance ratio raised the adoption probability by a statistically significant 3.6 percentage points.[36]

To examine the impact of the shift in manufacturing employment toward more dangerous jobs, we created an accident risk index based on the manufacturing industrial mix in each state. Shifts of manufacturing employment into more dangerous industries did not appear to stimulate earlier adoption of the law. The risk index had a small and statistically insignificant impact on the probability of adopting workers' compensation. This result may imply that greater public awareness of accident risk was not nearly as important as changes in the employers' liability climate.

Interest Group Influence

Greater strength of the manufacturing lobby raised the probability of adoption. In states where the manufacturing share of employment was OSD higher than the mean, the probability of adoption was a statistically significant 7.6 percentage points higher. A greater presence of large firms and more productive firms also increased the probability of adopting workers' compensation. Within the manufacturing lobby, an OSD increase in the percentage of establishments with over five hundred workers raised the likelihood of adoption by 4.7 percentage points, while an OSD increase in manufacturing value added raised the probability of adoption by 4.9 percentage points. Meanwhile, an OSD increase in the percentage of workers in firms with less than five workers, the types of firms typically exempted from the law, had a small negative but statistically insignificant impact on the probability of adoption.

Organized labor joined manufacturing interests in strongly supporting the passage of workers' compensation. We developed a union index in each state, which reflects the degree to which the industries represented in the state were unionized at the national level. An OSD increase in the union percentage increased the probability of adopting the law by 11.0 percentage points, and the effect is statistically significant.

To measure the general strength of the insurance lobby, we included the total life insurance premiums paid (in 1967 dollars) divided by the number of workers in the state. The life insurance premiums per worker had virtually no impact on the probability of adopting workers' compensation. Finally, an OSD increase in state spending on labor issues had a small (−1.6 percentage point) and statistically insignificant impact on the probability of adoption.

Political Climate

We examine the impact of the Progressive Movement with four measures: the electorate's support for socialist presidential candidates, the support for Theodore Roosevelt's progressive presidential candidacy in 1912, variables that measure shifts in party control of state legislatures, and an index of progressive laws that each state had adopted to date.

The percentage of the vote won by Theodore Roosevelt's progressive presidential campaign offers a rough measure of the extent to which voters in each state supported the nationwide progressive platform in 1912. An OSD increase in the percent voting for Roosevelt raised the probability of adopting workers' compensation in any one year by 9.3 percentage points.[37] It should be noted, however, that the support for socialist candidates had only a very small effect on the probability of adoption, and we cannot reject the hypothesis of no effect.

One way to capture the effect of reform movements at the state level is to measure their success in adopting other forms of progressive legislation. Therefore, we developed an index of progressive legislation that each state had in place at any point in time. The index measures the number of laws from the following list of progressive proposals that the state had passed: ballot initiatives, referenda, direct primaries, a mothers' pension law, a state tax commission, compulsory school attendance legislation, a state welfare agency, a merit system for state employees, a minimum age for child labor, and a state commission to regulate electricity rates. An OSD increase in the progressive law index raised the probability of adoption by 1.9 percentage points, but the effect was not statistically significant.

Another way to capture the effect of reform movements is to create dummy variables that track the major political party shifts occurring within each state's legislature. The first legislative power shift variable takes a value of one if in at least one branch of state i's legislature, the majority party of the previous session lost its majority coming into year t's session.[38] When only one branch changed parties, it typically produced a situation in which different parties controlled each of the state's two legislative chambers.[39] The second dummy variable has a value of one if both branches of the legislature experienced a political power shift. For every double-chamber power shift in the sample, both chambers always shifted to the same party. We would expect that the probability of enacting workers' compensation would have increased if both branches of a state's legislature experienced a power shift, because otherwise each branch would have had veto power over the decisions of the other.[40] A single-chamber power shift increased the probability of adoption by 7.8 percentage points, but we cannot reject the hypothesis of no effect. A double-chamber shift had a very small influence on the probability of adoption.

The analysis also includes a southern dummy variable to control for any "southern" effect that is not already captured by the other independent variables. States in the South were more likely to adopt workers' compensation, holding the other factors constant.[41]

"Contagion" Effect

When workers' compensation was first being considered, employers raised concerns that the legislation would put them at a cost disadvantage relative to their competitors in neighboring states. Given this attitude, employers may have been more willing to endorse workers' compensation when they were assured that their rivals in other states had similar labor costs. In an attempt to measure such a "contagion" effect, we reestimated the hazard equation including a variable that measures the proportion of nearby states that had adopted workers' compensation by the end of year $t - 1$.[42] The results, reported in column (2) of table H.1, suggest that states were more likely to enact workers' compensation if nearby states had adopted before them. An OSD change in the contagion variable raised the probability of adopting the law by only 1.6 percentage points, however, and the coefficient from the hazard analysis is not statistically significant.[43] Comparisons of the two columns of results in the table show that inclusion of the contagion effect has relatively little impact on the other findings.

Appendix I
Data Sources and Descriptions of Quantitative Variables

This appendix describes the sources of the variables used in the state panel that underlies the comparisons of means in chapter 4 and the hazard model analysis reported in appendix H.

Workers' Compensation Laws

The years in which states enacted their workers' compensation laws and the details of the laws described in various chapters throughout the book come from Clark and Frincke (1921), Hookstadt (1918, 1919, 1920, 1922), Jones (1927), U.S. Bureau of Labor Statistics Bulletins 126 (1913b), 203 (1917), 243 (1918), 332 (1923), 423 (1926b), and 496 (1929), and from closer inspection of the state statutes for the timing of changes in the various parameters of the law.

Variables Characterizing Employers' Liability Laws

Information on the status of each state's employers' liability laws was collected from a variety of sources: Fessenden (1900, 1157–210), U.S. Department of Labor (1903, 1363–64), Clark (1908 and 1911, 904–11), and U.S. Bureau of Labor Statistics Bulletins 111 (1913a), 148 (1914), and 370 (1925a). See also appendix G.

Insurance Measures

The employers' liability and accident insurance premiums that were collected in each state are reported in the Spectator Company's *Insurance Year Book,* 1900 through 1930. For many states there were not separate listings for accident and employers' liability insurance, which is why we have combined the two types of insurance. Although the *Year Book* was published each year, the volumes sometimes did not contain information for the current year, but repeated data from an earlier year. When data were missing in the years before workers' compensation was introduced, we filled the gaps using a straight-line interpolation of the years surrounding the missing year. In some cases the employers' liability and accident insurance data were missing for the year of adoption. In that case we estimated the data using an extrapolation procedure in which we multiplied the ratio of accident and employers' liability insurance to life insurance from the previous year and multiplied that ratio by the amount of life insurance sold during the year of adoption. We could not use straight-line interpolation to estimate the value for the adoption year because workers' compensation dramatically changed the nature of the employers' liability insurance market.

The life insurance premiums are the sum of ordinary and industrial life insurance premiums, also from the *Year Book.* For years with missing insurance premium data, we multiplied the reported life-insurance-in-force measure by the ratio of premiums to insurance-in-force over the period for which we had data. In some cases we still had missing data, because insurance-in-force was not reported, so we filled those years with straight-line interpolations between adjacent years. We deflated the life insurance premiums using the CPI (1967 = 100).

Index of Workplace Accident Supreme Court Cases

The index of state supreme court cases dealing with workplace accidents is based on counting all nonrailroad, street railroad, and railroad nontrain cases in each state's supreme court reporter. In searching for cases, we began with the following headings in the reporters indexes: master-servant liability, negligence, employer liability, assumption of risk, fellow servant, contributory negligence, personal injuries, and other headings referenced in those. We read each case to ensure that it dealt with a workplace accident and not, for example, a dispute over wages. For each state, we then created an index that used the average number of cases from 1904–6 as the base. We use an index of the cases, instead of the actual number of cases adjudicated in our adoption regression equation, because there were differences in the structure of court systems across states that might have led to differences in the number of cases reaching the state supreme court level.

We eliminated railroad train cases because railroad workers who were injured in the course of interstate commerce after 1908 were covered under the Federal Employers' Liability Act. Workers' compensation laws covered nonrailroad cases, street railroad cases, and some railroad cases if the person was not involved in interstate commerce. Typically, railroad workers in the nontrain category were ones who were not likely to be involved in interstate commerce and probably were covered by a workers' compensation law.

Index of Accident Risk

The index of manufacturing accident risk is based on the workers' compensation premiums that Ohio employers paid into the Ohio State Insurance Fund in 1923, and the distribution of manufacturing employment in 1899, 1909, 1919, and 1929. The index is a weighted average of the accident risk in each state's manufacturing industries, where the relative danger in each industry is held fixed over time. The only reason a state's index would change over time is because of changes in the relative employment in each industry. Our measure of the accident risk in each industry is workers' compensation premiums that employers in a wide range of industries paid per one hundred dollars of payroll into Ohio's state-run compensation fund in 1923. The premiums were reported in Ohio Industrial Commission (1923). The workers' compensation premiums are a reasonable measure of the relative danger across industries because the Ohio Industrial Commission experience rated the premiums such that industries paid higher premiums if they generated relatively more accident costs. We chose Ohio premiums because the state had a broader set of industries than most other states for which data were available. The employment data for each industry in each state, which are used as the weights in the weighted average calculation, represent the average number of wage earners in the industry. The data are from U.S. Bureau of the Census (1902, vol. 7; 1913, vol. 9; 1923, vol. 8; 1933, vol. 3). The risk index for the intervening years was calculated using a straight-line interpolation.

Manufacturing Firm Size and Value Added

The percentage of manufacturing establishments employing less than five workers and more than five hundred workers were reported by the census for the years 1899, 1909, 1914, 1919, 1929, and 1939. We used straight-line interpolations to fill the intervening years. The data were collected from the U.S. Bureau of the Census (1902, vol. 7, 336–67; 1913, vol. 8, 469; 1917, 422–25; 1923, vol. 8, 90; 1933, vol. 1, 72–73; 1943, vol. 1, 169).

Manufacturing value added per manufacturing worker was reported in the manufacturing censuses of 1899, 1904, 1909, 1919, 1921, 1923, 1925,

1927, 1929, and 1931. The values were deflated using the CPI (1967 = 100, series E135 in U.S. Bureau of the Census 1975, 211). Values for the intervening years were determined using straight-line interpolation. Hand trades were excluded. Data from 1899, 1904, and 1909 are from U.S. Bureau of the Census (1913, vol. 8, 542–44); 1914 data are from U.S. Bureau of the Census (1917, 171–73); data for 1921, 1923, and 1925 are from U.S. Bureau of the Census (1928, 1283–87); 1919, 1927, and 1929 are from U.S. Bureau of the Census (1933, vol. 1, 17–20); and 1931 data are from U.S. Bureau of the Census (1935, 21).

Employment Shares in Agriculture, Manufacturing, and Mining

The percentages of gainfully employed workers in agriculture, manufacturing, and mining were reported in the population censuses for the years 1900, 1910, 1920, and 1930. See U.S. Bureau of the Census (1902, vol. 2, 508; 1913, vol. 4, 44–45; 1923, vol. 4, 48; 1933, vol. 5, 54). Straight-line interpolation was used to fill the intervening years.

Unionization Index

The union index implicitly assumes that the national unionization rates for each industry in 1899, 1909, 1919, and 1929 were the same across states. For each of the four manufacturing census years, we calculated a weighted average of the unionization rates across each state's manufacturing industries. The weights are the shares of the manufacturing wage earners in each industry. We used Whaples's (1990, 434–47) estimates of the unionization rates in each manufacturing industry from 1909. We then followed Whaples's procedure to recalculate his 1919 unionization rates across industries and to derive estimates for 1899 and 1929 using information on union membership from Wolman (1936). The average number of wage earners was reported by the U.S. Bureau of the Census (see the earlier section on accident risk for sources).

To fill in the years between 1899, 1909, 1919, and 1929 for each state, we interpolated based on movements in the ratio of U.S. trade union membership (Wolman 1936, 16) to nonagricultural employment (series D-127 in U.S. Bureau of the Census 1975, 137).

State Government Spending on Labor Programs

The costs to state government of labor programs include spending for factory inspection, labor bureaus, mining inspection, bureaus of labor statistics, boards of arbitration, boiler inspector, and free employment bureaus. The data were collected from appropriations to state labor departments reported in the states' statutes. For each state-year observation we collected the appropriations for factory inspection, boards of conciliation and arbitration, bureaus of labor, bureaus of labor or industrial statistics, free employment bureaus, boiler inspection (but not ship boiler inspection), mining inspection, industrial welfare commissions, and industrial commissions from the states' session laws. In many states appropriations were given for all labor spending without separating out what share went to each division. In a few states, Iowa for example, the statute volumes offered the exact amounts spent by the state treasurer. Some states were either missing appropriations volumes or the appropriations were unnecessarily obtuse. In those states we used interpolations to fill any gaps. In interpolating we tried to be sensitive to the fact that many states were on a two-year cycle and often gave the same amount of appropriations in both years of the cycle. Maryland and Michigan offered extremely uninformative appropriations information. For Michigan we collected the appropriations data from the Michigan Auditor General's *Annual Report* for years between 1900 and 1920. For Maryland we collected information from the Maryland Bureau of Statistics and Information, *Annual Reports.*

We deflated the expenditures using the CPI (1967 = 100) and then divided the real expenditures by an estimate of the number of workers gainfully employed in the state. The employment estimate was determined by calculating the share of total U.S. citizens gainfully employed in each state for the years 1900, 1910, 1920, 1930, and 1940 from series D-26 in U.S. Bureau of Census (1975, 129–31). The shares between the census years were calculated using straight-line interpolations. We then multiplied the shares for each state and year by total employment in the United States in each year (series D-5 in U.S. Bureau of Census 1975, 126) to create an estimate of employment in each state.

The Political Composition of State Legislatures

The variables indicating political power shifts in each state legislature are based on the number of Republicans, Democrats, and other party members in each chamber of the state's legislature at each legislative session. For each state we sought information on the political structure of the state legislature from legislative manuals, state bluebooks, House and Senate journals, newspapers, and historical listings. In many of the southern states the legislatures were overwhelmingly Democratic and many of the bluebooks did not bother to list party affiliations.

To fill in any gaps we encountered, we used information from the New York Secretary of State *Manual* for the years 1925 to 1940. The data there seem reasonably accurate when matched up against information we collected from states' bluebooks. For the earlier years we collected information from the *Chicago Daily News Almanac and Yearbook,* 1918–30, *Tribune Almanac,* 1900–1909, and *World Almanac and Encyclopedia,* 1910–18.

There is still probably some measurement error in the data. This is due to some disagreement among the sources as to the exact party splits of the legislatures either because some legislators may have changed parties midcourse or because people died and vacancies were filled.

We determined whether the legislature was in session by examining the frequency of each state's legislative sessions, as reported in U.S. Bureau of the Census (1918, 62–63). However, because some states held special sessions during the period under investigation, we examined the statute volumes for each state to determine all of the years that the legislatures met.

Presidential Voting Information

The percentage of votes for Republican and socialist presidential candidates are from Congressional Quarterly (1975, 281–91). Socialist votes include votes for socialist candidates and in 1924 votes for LaFollette. The values for years between presidential elections are based on straight-line interpolations between election years. The progressive voting measure in 1912 is the percent voting for Roosevelt for president in 1912. For years between 1908 and 1912 values were derived from a straight-line interpolation between zero in 1908 and the value in 1912. After 1912 the values are assumed to be the 1912 value on the grounds that the progressive ideas espoused by Roosevelt in 1912 were subsumed under other parties.

Southern States

The dummy for southern states gives a value of one to Alabama, Arkansas, Florida, Georgia, Kentucky, Louisiana, Maryland, Mississippi, North Carolina, South Carolina, Tennessee, Texas, and Virginia.

Labor Laws in the Various States

We created a series of dummy variables that took on a value of one if the state had enacted various labor laws, and zero otherwise. The index includes the following laws that were supported by organized labor: minimum wage laws, union trademark laws, laws protecting labor organizations, mothers' pension laws, antiblacklisting laws, armed guard laws, laws stating that labor agreements were not conspiracies, laws preventing the false use of labor membership cards, laws limiting injunctions, laws exempting labor organizations from antitrust laws, laws against employers not telling incoming workers about the existence of a strike, laws allowing the incorporation of labor unions, and laws prohibiting contracts that restrain workers from joining labor unions. The index also considers laws that unions opposed: antiboycotting laws, laws preventing conspiracies against workers, laws preventing the enticement of workers, laws preventing interference for workers in all industries, laws preventing interferences for workers only in railroad industries, laws against the intimidation of workers, and laws against picketing. We also created a dummy variable indicating whether the state had a general women's-hours law, which took on a value of one if there was a women's-hours law covering manufacturing, mercantile, or other types of occupations. The information regarding the status of these labor laws in each state was obtained from the Department of Labor's series "Labor Laws of the United States and Decisions of the Courts Related Thereto." The volumes include U.S. Commissioner of Labor (1892, 1904, 1908) and U.S. Bureau of Labor Statistics Bulletins 148 (1914), 370 (1925a), 552 (1931), and 590 (1933). The women's-hours laws were collected from Smith (1929). Data for intervening years and the years that the laws were adopted were obtained from the states' statutes.

To compute the overall labor law index we vector-added the dummy variables that represent the prolabor laws described above and the women's-hours law and subtracted those dummy variables that indicate laws that were inimical to labor's interests. Finally, to this measure we added an estimate of the share of men covered by men's-hours laws. For each state we calculated the number of men working in industries and occupations—such as public employment, railroads, street railroads, and mining—that were covered by an hours law and divided this number by the total male employment in 1910. Although some states had a general law declaring men's-hours restrictions, the vast majority of these laws were passed in the 1800s and were rarely enforced. In order to give some weight to the fact that a state had a general men's-hours law, even though it was rarely enforced, we added 0.1 to our estimated percentage of men covered by an hours law. We used 1910 gainful employment as the basis for our calculation because we wanted the labor law index to capture changes in the laws and not changes in employment. The men's-hours law data are from Brandeis (1966, 540–63). The number of males age ten and over gainfully employed in each industry by state in 1910 was collected from U.S. Bureau of the Census (1913, vol. 4, 96–151).

Progressive Law Index

To create the progressive law index, we created a series of dummy variables that took on a value of one if the state had enacted the law and zero otherwise. The index is the sum of the dummies for the following laws: compulsory attendance at school, establishing a state tax commission, establishing a state welfare agency, establishing a merit system, initiative and referendum, direct primary, minimum age for child labor, mothers' pension, and a state commission to regulate electricity rates. The information on commissions regulating electric rates is from Stigler and Friedland (1962). The remaining variables were collected from Jack Walker's ICPSR

Data Set Number 0066, "Diffusion of Public Policy Innovation Among the American States." The information on the mothers' pension laws was obtained from the U.S. Commissioner of Labor (1892, 1904, and 1908). Information for later years was obtained from U.S. Bureau of Labor Statistics Bulletins 148 (1914), 370 (1925a), 552 (1931), and 590 (1933).

Appendix J

State versus Private Insurance: An Ordered-Probit Analysis of the State's Choice

To examine the impact that interest groups and political reformers had on the state's involvement in writing workers' compensation insurance, we added further to the analysis reported in Fishback and Kantor (1996). We estimated an ordered probit. The dependent variable is an ordinal ranking depending on which form of insurance the state had in effect in 1930— either private insurance (coded 0), a state fund that was designed to compete with private carriers (1), or a monopoly state fund (2). In the majority of states, the ultimate state fund decision was made in the year workers' compensation was first adopted. In a handful of states, however, workers' compensation was first enacted without a state fund for political expediency, but was subsequently amended to include state insurance.[44] For those states our analysis considers the year in which the legislature adopted the state fund (or lack thereof) because it represented their long-term choice. The analysis is based on a sample of the forty-four states that had enacted a workers' compensation law by 1930.[45] The data for each observation are drawn from the year in which each of the forty-four states made its decision relating to the form of state insurance it had in place in 1930. For example, Washington had a monopoly state fund in 1930 that was enacted in 1911. Therefore, the independent variables reflect Washington's political economic environment in 1911.

Since state insurance represented such a radical change in public policy, we anticipate that it would have taken a major change in a state's political environment to enact the legislation. To test this hypothesis, we include two dummy variables that indicate whether the state insurance question was decided by a legislature that had experienced a power shift since its last meeting. The first legislative power shift variable takes a value of one if in at least one branch of the state's legislature, the majority party of the previous session lost its majority. The second dummy variable has a value of one if both branches of the legislature experienced a party shift in the year the state insurance decision was made. In our sample it is always the case that if both legislative chambers switched parties, they changed to the same party. We speculate that the probability of enacting a state fund was much more likely if both branches of a state's legislature experienced a power shift, otherwise each branch would have had veto power over the decisions of the other.

We also include two other ways to test the impact of progressive reformers. The first is the percentage of the electorate that voted for Theodore Roosevelt in 1912 when he ran on the progressive platform. This method is imperfect because it measures the support for the national progressive platform in 1912, even though many states made the state insurance choice in other years. We also included an index of progressive legislation that had been passed in the state at any point in time. The index measures the number of laws from the following list of progressive proposals that the state had passed: ballot initiatives, referenda, direct primaries, a mothers' pension law, a state tax commission, compulsory school attendance legislation, a state welfare agency, a merit system for state employees, a minimum age for child labor, and a state commission to regulate electricity rates.

The impact of special interests is captured by several variables. Unions, who ardently supported state funds, are represented by a manufacturing union index, which combines the national percentage of each industry that was unionized with the distribution of employment across industries within each state. The strength of insurance interests, who strongly opposed state intervention in the insurance industry, is measured as the ratio of life insurance premiums collected in the state to the state's employment. The percentage of gainfully employed workers in agriculture captures the relative strength of farming interests within each state. The percentage of manufacturing workers employed in plants with more than five hundred workers is used to capture the influence of large firms. We have also included a dummy variable for southern states to see if there was a separate southern region effect.

The results of an ordered probit estimation are reported in table J.1. The results suggest that both political coalitions and narrowly defined economic interest groups played important, and statistically significant, roles in the adoption of state funds. As predicted, and holding political shifts constant, states that had a greater union presence were more likely to adopt a state fund, while in states that had relatively strong insurance and agricultural interests, employers were more likely to retain their freedom to insure through private firms. As a measure of the impact that these interest groups had on the probability of enacting state insurance, we calculated the marginal effect that a one-standard-deviation (OSD) change in each of the independent variables had on the baseline probability of adopting a monopoly state insurance fund. The baseline probability is a prediction of the probability that the state imposed a monopoly fund, based on the sample means for the independent variables. An OSD

Table J.1 **Ordered-Probit Results of States' Choices between No State Fund, Competitive State Insurance, and Monopolistic State Insurance**

Variables	Means (std. dev.)	Coefficient (*t*-stat.)	Change in Variable	Marginal Effect on Probability of Choosing Monopoly State Fund, Assuming Changes in Variables[a]
Intercept		6.47 (2.015)		
Union index	12.52 (4.76)	0.206 (3.05)	4.76 increase in union index	0.086
Percentage of gainfully employed in agriculture	32.24 (15.37)	−0.182 (−3.30)	15.37 decrease in agriculture variable	0.689
Ratio of life insurance premiums in 1967 dollars to employment	0.56 (0.20)	−11.39 (−2.62)	0.20 decrease in life insurance variable	0.485
Percentage of workers in manufacturing plants with over 500 workers	27.07 (12.1)	−0.068 (2.22)	12.1 percent decrease in workers in large plants	0.062
Percentage of voters voting for Roosevelt in the 1912 presidential election	25.96 (9.35)	0.0639 (1.36)	9.35 percent increase in the percent voting for Roosevelt	0.034
Index of progressive laws	5.93 (1.55)	0.313 (1.38)	1.55 increase in progressive law index	0.025
Power shift in at least one branch of legislature	0.34 (0.49)	0.891 (1.20)	Power shift in only one legislative branch	0.053
Power shift in both branches	0.091 (0.29)	2.175 (2.72)	Power shift in both legislative branches	0.429
Southern state	0.273 (0.45)	1.26 (1.06)	Southern state	0.083
N	44	44		

Sources: Information on state funds came from Clark (1911, 906–9) and the following Bulletins from the Bureau of Labor Statistics series on Workmen's Compensation and Insurance: 126, 185, 203, 240, 243, 272, 275, 301, 332, 379, 423, 496. Where these sources left confusion, we examined the states' statutes directly. For details on the sources of the independent variables, see appendix I.

Notes: Standard deviations are in parentheses below the means. Value of *t*-statistics are reported under the coefficients. The estimated ordered-probit threshold coefficient is 1.63, with a *t*-ratio of 2.33.

[a]The impact for each interest group variable and the Roosevelt progressive vote variable is the change in the baseline probability associated with a one-standard-deviation change in each variable, holding the other variables constant. The marginals of the power-shift variables are switches from 0 to 1, holding all else constant. The baseline probability of 0.011 was computed at the sample means of the variables.

increase in the union index increased the chances of choosing state insurance by 8.6 percentage points. A decrease in the life insurance variable, on the other hand, increased the probability of choosing a monopoly state fund by 48.5 percentage points. Farm interests had a strong influence over the state insurance decision. An OSD fall in the percent of the gainfully employed in agriculture increased the chances of enacting monopoly state insurance by 68.9 percentage points. Finally, large firms also appear to have reduced the probability of choosing a state fund in a statistically significant fashion. An OSD decrease in the percentage of workers in plants with over five hundred workers led to a 6.2 percent increase in the probability of choosing the state fund.

Thus, with the right combination of strong unions and weaker than average agricultural and insurance interests, it was theoretically possible to obtain the passage of state insurance even without a political power shift in the legislature. This set of circumstances occurred in two states—Nevada and Wyoming. Nevada adopted a state fund in 1913 without a measured power shift. Nevada's predicted probability of adopting monopoly state insurance in 1913 was 0.57, which was driven by a unionization rate that was 1.6 standard deviations above the sample mean for all the states, an insurance value 0.51 standard deviation below, and an agriculture value 0.76 standard deviation below the mean. Similarly, Wyoming adopted a monopoly state fund in 1915 in part because the union variable was 1.36 standard deviations above the mean and the insurance variable was 0.79 standard deviation below.

Progressive reform movements also played an important role in the choice of a state fund. In several states power shifts in both chambers of the legislature played a significant role in the decision to adopt a monopoly state fund. If only one branch of the legislature experienced a power shift, the effect was small and statistically insignificant. It appears that the presence of an entrenched political party in one branch limited whatever ambitions the new political coalition espoused in the other branch. On the other hand, if both branches shifted, the probability of choosing a monopoly state fund changed in a dramatic and statistically significant manner. By adding a power shift in both branches of the hypothetical baseline state, the probability of enacting a monopoly state insurance fund increases by 42.9 percentage points. Of the four states in our sample that experienced a power shift in both branches of the legislature, Ohio adopted a monopoly state fund, and Colorado, Idaho and Utah adopted competitive state funds.

The other measures of progressive reform have a positive relationship with the choice of a state fund, although the effects are not statistically significant. An increase in the percentage of people voting for Roosevelt gives an indication of the general interest in national progressive platform as of 1912. In states where the percentage voting for Roosevelt was a standard deviation higher than the mean, the probability of adopting a monopoly state fund rose by 3.4 percentage points, although the ordered-probit coefficient was not statistically significant. A larger index of progressive legislation was also associated with a higher probability of adopting a state fund, although again the coefficient was not statistically significant.[46]

Finally, there does not appear to have been a southern regional bias against the adoption of state insurance funds. The coefficient of the southern variable is not negative and we cannot reject the hypothesis of no effect.

The ordered-probit analysis results, taken as a whole, indicate that the adoption of monopoly state insurance was relatively unlikely. In Nevada and Wyoming it came about because of an unusual combination of strong unions and relatively weak insurance interests. If the proper combination of narrow economic interest groups did not exist, then monopoly state insurance was unlikely to be enacted unless union leaders melded their demands with the broader socioeconomic agenda of a strong political reform movement, as discussed in chapter 6.

Appendix K

A Quantitative Analysis of Workers' Compensation Benefit Levels

In chapter 7 we describe the results of a quantitative analysis of workers' compensation benefit levels. This work was originally reported in Fishback and Kantor (1998b). Our quantitative analysis examines both the initial benefit parameters that states established as well as changes in those benefits through 1930. We have collected information on the extent of union strength, the extent of accident risk, potential differences in the degree of the wage offset across states, firm size, and a measure of manufacturing productivity. In addition, as in our other empirical analyses, we have included variables that capture the influence of broad-based political coalitions and the impact of the workers' compensation bureaucracy after it was in place.

It is worth commenting briefly on two parameters of the model for which empirical information is not easily obtained: the extent of experience rating and the extent of wage offsets. We discuss the role of experience rating in influencing employers' and workers' choices of benefit levels in chapter 7. We may be able to test what influence the less-complete experience rating of smaller firms had on the determinants of benefit levels. Given that insurers actively sought to adjust premiums across industries,

our crude measures of accident risks across industries are unlikely to capture fully the subsidies that sometimes arose from temporary mismatches
between the insurance rates that industries paid and their actual accident
experiences.

Another important consideration, but not easily measurable, is the extent to which workers paid for higher benefits through market adjustments
in their wages. Chapter 3 shows that wage offsets varied across industries
and by union status. Nonunion miners experienced wage reductions that
fully offset the insurance costs of providing workers' compensation benefits; lumber workers experienced wage offsets that covered the value of
their expected benefits, but did not fully cover the employer's insurance
costs of providing the benefits; while unionized coal workers and building
tradesmen experienced much smaller wage offsets. We do not have enough
direct information on the extent of wage offsets in each state, although we
may be able to gain some insights by examining the relationships between
benefit levels and the union index, the percentage of workers in mining,
and the productivity variable.

The dependent variable is the natural log of each state's expected workers' compensation benefit index (in 1967 dollars), which is shown in table
7.1.[47] The regression equations are estimated in semilog form, controlling
for year and state fixed-effects. The year effects control for unmeasured
influences, such as World War I, that were common to all states during a
particular year. In addition, they play an important role in controlling
for changes over time in the weekly wage used to calculate the workers'
compensation benefits. The benefits for each state are calculated using the
national average weekly manufacturing wage, which rose substantially
over time. Failing to control for year effects might lead to a spurious positive relationship between the average manufacturing wage in a state, which
was typically correlated with changes in the national average manufacturing wage, and our measure of the benefit levels in that state. The state
dummy variables control for unmeasured characteristics of a state that did
not change over time. These might include the rules governing the state
legislature, the underlying political strength of employers and workers,
and political attitudes that remained unchanged during the period under
consideration. To the extent that some of our independent variables did
not vary over time within a particular state or did not vary across states
during a particular year, then the state and year fixed-effects, respectively,
will diminish the importance of these variables in explaining the benefit
levels. Thus, after controlling for the state and year effects, the coefficients
of the remaining variables capture the relationship between the benefit
parameters and the components of the right-hand-side variables that were
not state or year specific. F-tests reject the hypothesis that the coefficients
of the year and state effects are jointly equal to zero.[48]

Our sample is an unbalanced panel because states are only included in the analysis after they had adopted workers' compensation. The determinants of benefits, therefore, are estimated conditional upon the state's enactment of a workers' compensation law. To control for any selectivity bias that might arise from the conditional nature of the analysis, we used the following procedure. First, we estimated a reduced-form probit equation where the dependent variable reflects the presence of a workers' compensation law for the sample of forty-eight states in each year from 1910 to 1930. From this equation we calculated the inverse Mill's ratio, which was then used as a sample-correction variable in the fixed-effects benefits regression. We report the results in table K.1 both with and without the selectivity correction, but we focus the discussion on the results with the selectivity correction because the *t*-test for the coefficient of the inverse Mill's ratio suggests the presence of selectivity bias when estimating the benefits equation (see the last column of the table).[49]

The results are consistent with the suggestion that legislators chose benefit levels by weighing the demands of both employers and workers. Even though workers were more politically numerous and thus a worker was likely to be the median voter, it appears that legislatures also heeded the demands of employers. Meanwhile, in the states where workers had more political clout through unionization, they were successful in shifting the benefit levels upward. Benefit levels were higher, ceteris paribus, in states with greater unionization, where political upheaval led to shifts in party control of the state legislature, and where bureaucracies, as opposed to the courts, administered the workers' compensation system.

One sign that state legislatures responded to the demands of high-accident-risk employers is that benefits were lower in states where more workers were employed in dangerous industries. The comparative statics predict that employers in more dangerous industries would prefer lower benefit levels, while the impact of higher risk on the workers' demands for benefit levels is theoretically unclear. The analysis includes two measures of accident risk: one that proxies accident risk in manufacturing, which is based on the industrial mix in each state, and the other that is the percentage of workers in mining, one of the most dangerous forms of employment during this time period. The coefficients of both the manufacturing accident risk index and the percentage of workers in mining are negative and statistically significant. A one-standard-deviation (OSD) increase in the risk index (0.57) from its sample mean (1.48) would have reduced benefits by about 19.1 percent. Similarly, an OSD increase (4.4) in the percentage of workers in the dangerous mining industry was associated with a 10.6 percent reduction in benefit levels.

Another sign that legislators were attentive to the demands of employers is the absence of a statistically significant effect of wages on benefit levels. Theoretically, higher wages would have caused workers to seek higher benefit levels. On the other hand, the employer's choice of benefit levels was

Table K.1　　**Coefficients from Regression Analyses of Expected Workers' Compensation Benefits, 1910–30**

Variables	Means (std. dev.)	No Correction for Selectivity Bias	Correction for Selectivity Bias
		Coefficients	
Constant		3.84	3.74
		(21.46)	(14.50)
Instrument for average manufacturing wage in the state (1967 dollars)[a]	59.8 (10.1)	0.0047 (1.14)	0.0038 (0.64)
Manufacturing accident risk index	1.48 (0.57)	−0.259 (5.36)	−0.335 (4.98)
Percentage of labor force employed in mining	3.3 (4.4)	−0.026 (5.97)	−0.024 (3.71)
Manufacturing value added per worker (thousands; constant 1967 dollars)	5.65 (1.43)	−0.0133 (0.81)	−0.002 (0.08)
Percentage of workers in manufacturing establishments with more than 500 workers	32.0 (11.7)	−0.0017 (1.44)	0.0006 (0.32)
Percentage of workers in manufacturing establishments with less than 5 workers	5.3 (4.1)	0.0042 (0.99)	−0.0075 (1.14)
Manufacturing unionization index	14.5 (7.7)	0.0048 (2.83)	0.0067 (2.58)
Political climate			
Power shift in at least one branch of legislature	0.130 (0.34)	0.0384 (2.49)	0.051 (1.89)
Power shift in both branches of legislature	0.037 (0.19)	−0.0048 (0.19)	−0.026 (0.58)
Percentage of presidential vote for Republican	52.7 (11.2)	−0.0004 (0.43)	0.0002 (0.17)
Percentage of presidential vote for socialist	6.5 (8.2)	−0.00006 (0.08)	0.0004 (0.34)
Workers' compensation administered by commission or state fund in prior year	0.741 (.439)	0.075 (4.61)	0.073 (3.40)
Lambda (inverse Mill's ratio)[b]			0.249 (3.81)
Year dummies (all except 1930)		Included	Included
State dummy variables (all except Connecticut)		Included	Included
R^2		0.87	0.88
N	702	702	702

Sources: Fishback and Kantor (1998b, 124). See appendix I.

Notes: The dependent variable is natural log of expected benefits in constant 1967 dollars (see table 7.1). Use of deflators besides the CPI with a 1967 base does not change the results. Absolute value of *t*-statistics are in parentheses below the coefficients and standard deviations are below the means.

Table K.1   (continued)

[a]The instruments for the wage are predicted values from a wage regression equation using the accident risk, union, mining, productivity, firm size, power shift, and presidential vote variables listed above, plus percent black, percent foreign born, percent illiterate, percent urban, strike activity, percent of the gainfully employed in agriculture, and percent of the gainfully employed in mining. We have also experimented with using a five-year lagged value of wages as an instrument. We chose a five-year lag because the wage information was interpolated over five-year periods prior to 1919 and two-year periods after 1919. The coefficients and t-tests using the five-year lagged wage were similar to those reported in the table above.

[b]The selection equation based on whether states had adopted workers' compensation or not was run on a sample of 1,002 observations with the following variables: presence of an employers' liability law that substantively affected the common law, presence of an employers' liability law that simply restated the common law, and all of the variables above, except the state and year dummies, the wage instrument, and the dummy for the presence of the commission. We did not include the state and year dummies because of multicollinearity problems when they are included.

unaffected by the wage in the theoretical model. This does not imply that the employer was indifferent to changes in benefit levels that were caused by wage changes. Instead, his optimal benefit choice was the same whether the wage was high or low; therefore, the employer would have been opposed to changes in the benefit level that were driven only by wage changes, holding other relevant determinants constant. To examine the impact of wages on benefit levels, the regression includes an instrument for the current year's wage in each state to avoid potential simultaneity problems.[50] The wage coefficients in the table show that an OSD increase leads to a 3.8 percent increase in benefits, but we cannot reject the hypothesis that there was no relationship. Thus, in states where wages were higher, employers appear to have been successful in limiting the benefit increases that workers sought because their wages rose.

Our theoretical prediction is that employers with higher product prices and/or labor productivity would likely seek higher benefits. The combined impact of product prices and labor productivity in manufacturing is captured by the measure of manufacturing value added per worker. In the table the coefficient of the value-added variable is positive, but very small and statistically insignificant. The weakness of this relationship might be the result of wage offsets that would dampen the impact that higher benefits had on a worker's overall remuneration package and, thus, productivity. Employers at high productivity firms might have had more inelastic demands for labor, which might have reduced the size of the wage offset that workers experienced. If so, employers with higher value-added may have balanced the productivity benefits from higher workers' compensation benefits against the fact that they were likely to pay a higher percentage of those benefits, thus weakening their support for higher benefits.

To test the impact of firm size on benefit levels, we also included measures of the percentage of manufacturing workers working in establishments with one to five workers and in those with more than five hundred workers.[51] In the theoretical model, the sign of this effect is uncertain. The size variables might also be influenced by incomplete experience rating within industries, since larger firms paid premiums that were more fully experience rated than smaller firms. Employers and workers in the smaller firms therefore might have pressed for higher benefits. On the other hand, workers' compensation laws allowed small firms to avoid joining the workers' compensation system, which may have left them largely indifferent in the benefits debate. The effects of both measures of firm size on benefit levels are small and statistically insignificant.

The political strength of workers generally was greater in areas with more unionization. We developed an index of unionization in manufacturing that combines the national percentage of each industry that was unionized with the distribution of employment across industries within each state. In essence, the variable captures the extent to which industries that were strongly unionized at the national level were represented in each state. Greater unionization was not only associated with greater political strength, but unionized workers also had relatively strong incentives to push for higher benefit levels because they were more effective at preventing wage offsets. On the other hand, the lower wage offset meant that employers had an incentive to lobby for lower benefit levels. The regression results indicate that in states dominated by industries where organized labor had a greater national presence, organized labor was successful in overcoming the pressure from employers for lower benefit levels. An OSD increase in the unionization index (7.7) led to a statistically significant 5.2 percent increase in expected benefits.

Legislators may have had broader agendas than simply pleasing narrowly focused economic interest groups. To ensure reelection they also had to pay at least some attention to the demands of the electorate, which may have meant balancing workers' compensation issues with other social, political, or economic issues. We have tried to measure the impact of broader political agendas within each state in several ways. One way to measure the political attitudes of voters is to include voting results from presidential elections. The results suggest, however, that changes in voter support for national Republican, Democratic, or more socialist views had little impact on the benefit levels at the state level. After controlling for the state and year effects, the effect of changes across states and time in the percentage of the electorate voting for Republican candidates and socialist candidates were small and statistically insignificant.[52]

Since workers' compensation legislation was state-based, we also have tried to measure the influence of legislative upheavals at the state level. Strong political reform movements during the Progressive Era often caused the party composition of state legislatures to shift dramatically around the time of the introduction of workers' compensation. Thus, during these initial upheavals, we might expect to see higher benefits in settings where political control of the legislature shifted from one party to the other. Further, when the reformers' opponents attempted to retake the legislature, they may have competed to obtain the support of the reform-minded sectors of the electorate by proposing even higher benefits. For example, in the 1914 gubernatorial race in Ohio, conservative Republicans campaigned for higher benefits in their efforts to unseat a progressive Democrat (Fishback and Kantor 1996).

We have included dummy variables that measure situations in which the political dominance of one party shifted in at least one branch of the legislature and in which it shifted in both legislative chambers. The debate over accident benefits was certainly a controversial one, although perhaps not as rancorous as the state insurance debate, and the empirical analysis suggests that political party shifts also played an important role in helping workers secure higher benefits. If one branch of a state legislature shifted parties in a particular year, expected benefits rose by a statistically significant 5.1 percent. There was no additional effect on the benefit levels to have both branches shift simultaneously. These results contrast with our findings for the same variables in examining the overall adoption of workers' compensation laws. It is also important to note that our measures of shifts in political coalitions are incomplete and offer only a lower-bound estimate of the importance of progressive political groups that sought significant socioeconomic reforms in the early twentieth century.

Once workers' compensation was adopted, workers appear to have been joined in the struggle for higher benefits by the bureaucratic agents that administered the new system. States typically chose to administer their workers' compensation programs in one of two ways. By 1930, ten states administered the laws through the courts, with employers and workers establishing agreements regarding accident compensation subject to the statutory guidelines and the courts settling disputes. Thirty-eight states administered workers' compensation with a bureaucratic commission, which directly oversaw the disbursement of accident compensation.[53] The state commissions had the potential to act as advocates for changes in the workers' compensation laws because they were often a key source of information for legislators, although their attitudes could have been influenced by either employers or workers. We examine the bureaucrats' impact on benefit levels by including a dummy variable that takes a value of one if the state had a workers' compensation commission in operation at the end of year $t - 1$, and zero otherwise. The dummy variable indicates the presence of a commission in the previous year because the bureaucracy could lobby the legislature in the current year only if it was already in existence. The coefficient of the commission dummy implies that the presence of an administrative body led legislatures to establish benefits that were 7.3 percent higher, which is statistically significant.[54] Thus, it appears that workers benefited disproportionately from the administrative agencies' lobbying.

Notes

1. The one caveat to this statement would be that if the worker's accident was relatively minor, and he was only expected to lose a few days of work, then the accident would probably go unreported. Because all states imposed waiting periods before accident benefits would commence, those accidents that were relatively minor would still go unremunerated because the injured workers would be back at work before the waiting period was over.

2. These data are from the Stonega Coke and Coal Company Records, *Annual Report of Operations Department* (1925, 155).

3. For earlier information see Hoffman (1908, 461) and Fay (1916, 12–13). For later information see Illinois Industrial Commission (1920) and Adams (1923, 41). The nonfatal injuries for 1919 were arrayed as follows: 11 permanent total injuries, 1,275 specific losses, 297 disfigurements, 66 permanent partial disablements, 5,983 temporary total disablements, and 20 temporary partial disablements.

4. Iowa Employers' Liability Commission (1912, 106).

5. See Ohio Department of Inspection of Workshops, Factories, and Public Buildings (1906–1913). The coverage of industries is the same in all of these comparisons.

6. The year of adoption may differ from the first year of operation because quite a few states made their workers' compensation laws effective in the year after the law was adopted.

7. A lump-sum settlement typically required a paternalistic hearing before a state board to determine whether a lump-sum payment was in the best interest of the family. Conyngton (1917, 119–21, 137–44) found that less than 13 percent of the families of fatal accident victims in Ohio and Connecticut received their benefits as lump-sum amounts.

8. The commission reported that they had some problems in 1909 locating the families of workers injured in 1907. They originally sought 3,264 cases, but there were 1,777 for whom information could not be obtained. The information was based on the memories of the families in direct interviews. The distribution of accidents investigated and reported across industries were similar.

9. Note that this replacement percentage is different from the one reported for New York in tables 3.1 and B.4. Although the method of calculating the expected workers' compensation benefits is the same here and in the table, the assumed wage rates are different.

10. A second way in which the rise in benefits is understated stems from discounting, but the effect is very small. We discounted the stream of benefits paid out under workers' compensation using a 5 percent interest rate. We did not discount any of the negligence liability benefits because we assumed they were lump-sum payments. However, there typically were delays in the payment of the benefits under negligence liability. Some of the delay was similar to what we see for workers' compensation given the waiting period. On the other hand, at least one-third of the death and permanent disability cases involved delays of at least a year in payments being made, and at least 20 percent of the death and disability cases involved delays of over two years. This would lower the expected benefits by about four to five cents, which is a very small percentage of annual income.

11. The sample size of survey respondents and nonrespondents appears to have been about the same. Some companies did not fully state wages paid during disablement (but there is some question about this).

12. The 45.5 percent figure is similar to those reported in other states. Over the

period from 1902 to 1911, insurance companies doing employers' liability business in Iowa paid out 51.1 percent of the premiums they collected in the form of losses, or direct payments to workers. See Iowa Employers' Liability Commission (1912, 103).

13. The New York Commission on Employers' Liability (1910, 254–55) also reported information on what 327 employers employing 125,995 workers paid for accidents under negligence liability. The total amount they paid was $254,636, which is $0.374 per $100 on the payroll. Of that amount, after eliminating legal fees and conservatively estimating the insurance companies' expense ratio at 33 percent, the amount received by workers was approximately $202,580 or $0.298 per $100 on the payroll.

We have used the following reasoning to deflate the $254,636 total to the $202,580 amount eventually received by workers. Firms with liability insurance only spent $45,925 and had total wages of $22,438,829. Given an expense ratio of 0.33, workers at these firms would have received about $30,770 in medical expenses and wage payments, which is $0.137 per $100 on the payroll. For firms having both liability insurance and other expenditures, their total wages were $22,896,808. They spent $69,277.72 on liability insurance and $48,700 on other expenditures. Of the liability insurance expenditures using an expense ratio of 0.33, $46,416 would have gone to compensating workers. Of the $48,700 in other expenditures, $11,725 were contributions to benefit associations (which may not count as required, although it may have reduced the probability of lawsuits), $5,274 went to payments of claims, $6,180 went to legal expenses, $9,194 went to medical expenses, $12,363 went to wages, $2,157 went to pensions, $1,449 went to funeral expenses, and $358 went to other expenses. Summing the claims, wages, pensions, funeral expenses, payments to benefit associations, medical expenses, and other payments yields a total of $42,520. So the maximum amount received by workers from employers for wage replacement and medical expenses would have been $88,936, which is $0.39 per $100 on the payroll.

Firms without liability insurance had total wages of $22,748,898. Of the $91,251 they spent on accidents, $1,640 was contributions to employee benefit associations, $57,504 was paid in claims, $8,377 went to legal fees, $10,252 went to medical expenses, $12,196 went to wage payments, $241 went to funeral expenses, and $1,040 went to other expenses. Eliminating legal fees, the maximum amount going to workers was $82,814.

The total amount that workers received for wage replacement and medical expenses papers was $202,580. The total amount paid in wages was $68.0845 million, which is about $0.298 per $100 on the payroll.

The Michigan Employers' Liability and Workmen's Compensation Commission (1911, 10–11, 75–100) conducted a survey of 466 industrial employers, employing 99,134 workers, and asked them information on their costs of accidents. The amount of money that they spent that went to workers was in the range of $0.353 per $100 on the payroll. A collection of mining companies employing 21,080 workers spent less than $0.34 per $100 on the payroll on compensating workers (see Michigan Employers' Liability and Workmen's Compensation Commission 1911, 10–11, 14, 84, 86–89, 98, 108–11). The employers paid $20,159 in wages during the workers' disabilities, $43,225 in settlements, and $14,229 in other aid, first aid expenses of $4,831, medical costs of $14,127, hospital costs of $9,574, and legal costs of $2,707. The total, eliminating legal costs, is $106,145. They paid $120,111 for insurance. Assuming an expense ratio of 0.33, the workers would have received $80,074 from employers.

14. Medical expenses are excluded because we have no good measure of medical

expenses under workers' compensation or under negligence liability. To the extent that the payments made to workers under negligence liability also covered the workers' medical expenses, the payouts overstate the wage replacement that the workers received.

15. Of the $52,225, we are certain that $48,075 was paid for accidents occurring during the time frame. In several cases in the report of 1916, the date of the accident was not reported, but we could tell pretty well from context if it occurred in 1916, thus the additional $3,250 in payments are for accidents we are reasonably certain occurred in 1916.

16. For 1916–18 we have the costs of coal production from the operating statements of the company. We assumed that 74.1 percent of the operating costs went to paying workers, based on evidence on the labor share of operating costs in 1921, where we have information on both operating costs and wages paid.

17. For all years we have operating costs and for some years we also have direct measures of labor costs. In the years when we have both, the labor costs are 74.1 percent of operating costs. Thus, we calculated labor costs in years where only operating costs were available as 74.1 percent of operating costs. The 1916–18 percentages may be biased upward because they include coking accidents in the numerator, while payments to coke workers are not reported in the denominator. On the other hand, we cannot be certain that we have captured all of the information on payments to workers, although the coverage seems fairly complete. The 1919–23 weeks of compensable accidents may overstate the amounts actually paid, because it is the company's estimate of the severity of accident losses. Total weeks of compensation for the period 1919–23 is from the *Annual Report of the Operating Department Stonega Coke and Coal Company Records* (1925, 160). Information on labor costs and operating costs comes from operating statements for the years 1912–19, 1920, 1921–29. Information on payouts to workers during the period 1916–18 come from the lawyer reports in the *Annual Report of the Operating Department,* for the years 1916–21. The wage scales are in the *Annual Report of the Operating Department* for 1929. All are in the records of the Stonega Coke and Coal Company, at the Hagley Museum and Library, Wilmington, Delaware.

18. We have focused the analysis on thirteen occupational classes from the forty specific occupations for which the U.S. Bureau of Labor Statistics reported wage scales by 1923. The occupations chosen reflect a wide and representative characterization of the important building trades in the early twentieth century.

19. All the equations are estimated with weighted least squares because each observation is a state (or city) average from samples of different sizes, which implies that the variance of the error terms is inversely related to the number of workers in each state. In the coal and lumber samples we used the square root of the number of workers sampled for each observation as the weight. In the building sample, the data sources did not provide information on the number of workers sampled. Therefore, we used White's 1980 correction for heteroskedasticity. We have also estimated the lumber and coal equations using the White correction and the main results are roughly the same as those reported below.

20. The prices for lumber and coal are the prices at the mill and the mine. Even though both lumber and coal were competitive, national markets, prices at individual mines and mills varied substantially due to differences in the transport costs of sending the product to market and variations in the quality and type of the product.

21. The full-time hours per week in the lumber and building trades are not measures of labor supply. They reflect the constraints on working time offered by the employer, such that workers might demand higher wages if full-time hours were

shortened. Similarly, in the coal industry the days variable is the number of days the tipples operated, representing a measure of the maximum amount of working time available to workers. Workers therefore made their labor-supply decisions subject to the constraints on full-time hours.

22. All calculations are based on the mean earnings in the sample. When the equations are run in semilog form, the wage reductions in response to workers' compensation are similar, coal at 1.51 percent, lumber at 1.91 percent, and the building trades at 0.35 percent.

23. We have also experimented with using the maximum allowable benefits as an instrument for the expected benefits for all observations, and the results suggest a negative and statistically significant wage offset in all cases. We did not focus on these results because the wages in many occupations were not high enough to hit the legal maximums.

24. We have also tried a specification for the coal sample that interacts the fatal accident rate and expected benefits variable. The wage offsets are close to the ones reported in the text. We cannot do the same interactions in the lumber and building trades samples because we have no information on differences in accident rates across states and years.

We have experimented by including lagged benefits in the various equations. In every sample when we included a lagged benefits term (up to three-year lag) along with the contemporaneous benefits, the coefficient on the lagged term was consistently small and not statistically different from zero.

25. To further investigate whether the dramatic changes in the American labor market during the period under consideration has generated spuriously measured wage offsets, we collected wage data for a relatively safe industry in an attempt to determine whether these workers experienced a wage offset, even though they stood to benefit very little from the change in expected postaccident benefits. If we detected a strong wage offset, then this finding may imply that there is a spurious inverse relationship between benefits and wages during this time period. Cotton textile work was much less risky than the others we have considered. Workers' compensation insurance premiums for cotton mills, for example, were approximately one-tenth of the premiums of coal and one-fifth the premiums for lumber and the building trades (these comparisons are based on the average workers' compensation premiums that employers in each industry would have paid in Ohio, New Jersey, Illinois, and Wisconsin in 1912, as reported in Washington Industrial Insurance Department 1912, 277). We estimated regressions for a cotton textile sample covering eight states with twenty-nine occupations for the years 1910–14, 1916, 1918, 1920, and 1922. The results revealed a large positive coefficient on the benefits variable, which suggests that we should have few worries that the time period analyzed here has imparted a spurious negative bias to the relationship between wages and benefits. We are reluctant to draw definitive conclusions from the cotton sample because the small number of states considered sharply limits the effectiveness of our empirical tests.

26. We have investigated the variation further by running separate regressions for each occupation in each industry. As Gruber and Krueger (1991, 128–29) also found, the wage-offset coefficients for individual occupations vary widely around the estimates from the pooled sample of all occupations. The wage offsets for each occupation in the coal and lumber industries are typically -1 (or more in absolute value), although some are not precisely estimated. In the building trades, there was a mixture of positive and negative coefficients, but we could detect no consistent pattern of differences in the offsets for skilled, semiskilled, or unskilled workers. As another test, we reestimated the full sample with interaction terms between the

state dummy variables and the occupation dummy variables. Inclusion of these interaction terms does not change our main conclusions.

27. We have tried several methods of calculating benefits under negligence liability, including inserting a value of zero for benefits under negligence liability and assuming benefits based on death benefits of 50 percent of annual earnings, without an adjustment for liability differentials. The results show the same pattern as reported in the text.

28. Finding that workers' access to insurance was rationed prior to workers' compensation does not necessarily imply that the new regime was a more efficient legal system than negligence liability, as far as workplace accidents are concerned. A worker consuming his desired level of insurance might not hold a socially optimal amount. Viscusi (1991, 82) notes that as workers reach their optimal levels of insurance, there may be increases in moral hazard, which raise the accident costs of insurers and employers. In fact, studies of accident rates and modern problems with fraudulent claims suggest that moral hazard problems have increased with the passage of workers' compensation (Fishback 1987; Moore and Viscusi 1990). A comparison of the relative efficiency of the two systems would require, at a minimum, a complete examination of the employers' and workers' costs of accident prevention, the damages incurred by injured workers, the administrative costs of the two systems, and other transaction and information costs.

29. We thank Martha Olney for making Claudia Goldin's occupation codes for these data available to us. Goldin matched the listed occupation in the cost-of-living survey with the occupation codes developed for the 1940 Census Public Use Sample. In restricting the sample we eliminated professional and semiprofessional workers (codes under 98), farmers and farm managers (98–99), proprietors, managers, and officials (100–156), clerical and kindred workers (200–266), salespeople (270–98), domestic service workers (500–520), protective service workers (600–614), service workers (700–798), farm laborers and foremen (844–88), and non-classifiable occupations (998–99).

30. Originally, most maritime states with workers' compensation laws claimed jurisdiction over maritime industries, but the U.S. Supreme Court in *Southern Pacific Co. v. Jensen,* 244 U.S. 205 (1917), claimed that U.S. admiralty and maritime law made state compensation laws inapplicable to maritime injuries. On 6 October 1917, Congress enacted the Johnson amendment which allowed state workers' compensation laws to include maritime industries, but the law was declared unconstitutional by the Supreme Court in *Knickerbocker Ice Co. v. Stewart,* 40 S. Ct. 438, 485 (1920). See French (1920).

31. For example, Arizona, Delaware, and Texas did not include public employment under workers' compensation; New Hampshire and New Mexico did not mention public employees in the compensation act; Iowa exempted firemen and policemen; Kentucky, Maine, Massachusetts, Oregon, and Rhode Island allowed individual municipalities to choose whether their public employees would be covered by the compensation law; Minnesota public employees were covered, except for employees of the state and employees of cities whose charters provided their own compensation schemes; Ohio exempted policemen and firemen in places where pensions were established; and, finally, Oklahoma and Washington limited coverage to public employees who were engaged in hazardous work. For further discussion of these intricate rules, see Clark and Frincke (1921, 21–68).

32. We experimented with estimating separate probits for old-line life insurance, industrial life insurance, and fraternal insurance. The coefficient of expected benefits in each equation was small and statistically insignificant, just as we see when we aggregated all life insurance policies in table F.1.

33. We have also experimented with other specifications in the saving regression by adding an interaction term between the accident-rate measure and the expected-benefits variable. The magnitudes and t-tests of the expected benefits and accident risk coefficients are similar to the ones reported in table F.1.

34. This technique was used in Pavalko's (1989) and Buffum's (1992) earlier studies of the adoption of workers' compensation and is widely used in tests of search models. We focus on the period from 1909 to 1930 because of the substantial changes in the attitudes of employers and labor unions during the course of the period 1900 to 1908. As noted in the text, organized labor's attitude toward workers' compensation reversed in 1909, thus the measure for organized labor would have a different impact before and after 1909. When we estimate the hazard equation including information from the 1900 to 1930 period, we obtain largely the same set of results, but not surprisingly, the effects are muted relative to those reported in table H.1.

35. We also ran a cross-sectional ordinary least squares regression with years since 1910 to adoption on the left-hand side of the regression and all but the legislative change variables on the right-hand side. We got very similar results to the ones we report in table H.1. The variables that significantly reduce the time to adoption are the presence of an employers' liability law limiting the common law defenses, the ratio of employers' liability premiums to life insurance premiums, manufacturing value added per worker, the percentage of workers in manufacturing, the union index, and the presidential votes for Roosevelt in 1912. In this analysis the effect of the state supreme court cases is no longer statistically significant. We believe that the reason for this difference is that this variable in the various states changed substantially over time, a feature missed by a cross-sectional analysis.

36. Recall that total employers' liability premiums may have increased either because rates increased or because more employers chose to insure their accident liability risks. Since the empirical analysis controls for changes in manufacturing accident risk and for the change in employers' liability laws, the measured impact of the insurance ratio might suggest that employers saw workers' compensation as a means to control their insurance costs.

37. The general impression of the development of progressivism at the national level is that it rose to a peak in the 1912 presidential election. After 1912 many of the progressive ideas were incorporated in both the Republican and Democratic party platforms. To capture this rise and leveling off in each state, we constructed the Roosevelt voting variable to start at zero in each state in 1908 and then to rise through straight-line interpolation to the value in 1912. From 1912 onward the variable retains its 1912 level. We have also run the analysis using the 1912 values throughout with very little change in the results reported. We also reran the analysis allowing the progressive variable to fall back to zero by 1916. In those cases the progressive variable has very little impact.

38. Buffum (1992, 48) found that a power shift in either legislature enhanced the probability of adopting a workers' compensation law.

39. There was one exception to this observation. In 1919 the Non-Partisan League gained control of the upper house of the North Dakota legislature, while the lower house had been captured by the Non-Partisans in 1917.

40. We chose a general power shift measure, as opposed to a party shift measure, because there was substantial variation across states in the attitudes of Republicans and Democrats. In many settings both the Republican and Democratic parties established support for a workers' compensation measure in their state platforms. Out of seventeen power shifts identified in our sample, ten were shifts from

Republican to Democrat, five were shifts in the other direction, one was a shift from Republican to an even split, and there was one shift from Republican to Non-Partisan League in North Dakota.

41. We were sensitive to the issue of unmeasured heterogeneity across states in the sample, so we experimented with dummy variables representing much smaller geographical groupings. Estimation of the model with dummy variables for eight of the nine census regions led to results similar to those reported in table H.1. We also estimated the model using dummy variables for groupings of two and three states, and the results were qualitatively similar to those reported here. We are unable to estimate the model with a dummy variable for all but one of the states due to problems of perfect collinearity with the remaining variables in the analysis.

42. Nearby states include states in the same census region (of nine regions) and other contiguous states. We have experimented with other measures of contagion, such as the total number of states in the United States that have adopted and a time counter. The basic results remain the same.

43. When we experimented with other variables that may capture the contagion effect, such as a time trend or the number of other states within the entire United States that had adopted the legislation, the results were nearly identical. When a time trend and the neighborhood adoption variable were included together, the impact of the neighborhood adoption variable remained strong and statistically significant, while the coefficient of the time trend was small and statistically insignificant. The results of the remaining variables were very similar to those reported in column (2) of table H.1.

44. New York adopted workers' compensation without a state fund in 1910 and later added a competitive state fund in 1913. Similar processes occurred in California (no fund 1911, competitive fund 1913), Arizona (no fund 1912, competitive fund 1925), and Nevada (no fund 1911, monopoly fund 1913). In no case did a state create a state fund and then revert to competitive insurance. In Kentucky the workers' compensation law of 1914 was declared unconstitutional, and another law was passed in 1916. We chose 1914 for the sample, although estimates with 1916 are very similar. The Missouri legislature passed several laws that were struck down in referenda between 1919 and 1925, some with state insurance and some without. We chose the 1925 law because that was the law that made it through the referendum. We have also estimated an ordered probit equation where we added observations representing each of the earlier decisions described above, and the results changed very little. In addition, we have re-estimated the equation with corrections for possible selection bias related to the year of the decision and found essentially the same results.

45. By stopping in 1930, Florida (which adopted in 1935), South Carolina (1935), Arkansas (1939), and Mississippi (1948) are left out of the sample. None of these states adopted a state fund. Since these states were notably nonunion, agricultural, probably low in insurance coverage, and had almost no change in the party power in the legislature, we expect the results reported in table J.1 to be largely unchanged if these states were included in the sample.

46. We have also experimented with including a measure of spending on state labor issues. It turns out that this variable is strongly related to the progressive measures in part because it was a policy decision that progressives and labor leaders pressed, like the state insurance fund. When we include the state labor spending, the coefficients for the progressive, state spending, power shift, and labor index measures are all positive, as expected, but the coefficients are not statistically significant individually; however, we can reject the hypothesis that they are all zero.

47. We have also estimated the equations using the expected benefits as a per-

centage of the annual wage as the dependent variable, and the results are very similar to the ones reported here.

48. Comparisons of the coefficients from estimations with and without the state and year effects show that the basic results are unchanged for the accident risk, mining percentage, unionization, power shift, and state commission variables. When the state and year effects are excluded, the coefficients of the value-added, plant size, and Republican presidential voting variables are negative and statistically significant, and the presidential vote for the socialists has a positive and statistically significant effect on benefits. Given the construction of the benefits variable, it is not surprising that the exclusion of the state and year effects leads to a strong positive relationship between the benefit level and the wage variable.

49. Although the identification of the benefits equation in the two-stage process is satisfied because of the nonlinearity of the probit, we have included dummy variables for employers' liability laws in the selection equation and not in the benefits equation. The presence of an employers' liability law was likely to influence the initial adoption of the law, but not necessarily the level of benefits.

50. We wanted to eliminate the negative bias that arises when wages adjust downward in the labor market to offset higher benefits. Inclusion of the contemporary wage does lead to a smaller coefficient on the wage than those reported in table K.1. We have experimented with several other instruments for the wage and the results are essentially the same as those reported in the table.

51. It should be noted that this is not a measure of firm size because the manufacturing census reported the number of workers in an establishment. That is, if workers for a firm were divided into two plants of four hundred workers each, then these workers would not be included in the over-five-hundred measure.

52. Part of the impact of political sentiment, as measured by votes for presidential candidates, might be captured by the state effects if voter attitudes did not change over time. When we estimate the equations without the fixed effects, the Republican voting measure is negative and statistically significant and the socialist measure is positive and statistically significant. The socialist measure includes votes for candidates to the left of the Democrats, including LaFollette progressives in 1924. In the analyses reported in table K.1, we have treated votes for Theodore Roosevelt as Republican votes in 1912. We treat the two types of progressives differently because Roosevelt progressives tended to be far more conservative than the later LaFollette progressives. In our analysis of the overall adoption of workers' compensation and the choice of state insurance (see appendixes H and J), we have experimented with using the vote for Roosevelt in 1912 as a separate measure of underlying progressive attitudes. In this model the measure would be collinear with the vector of state dummies, so we cannot use it separately. We have also rerun the equations including the state and year effects and separating the Republican votes and the Roosevelt progressive votes. The progressive votes are interpolated upward from zero in 1908 and back down to zero by 1916, following the fortunes of progressive candidates at the national level. The socialist and Republican votes have small and statistically significant effects, while the progressive vote has a negative effect.

53. Wyoming administered the law through the courts but had a monopoly state insurance fund, so we have treated it as having an administrative body in the regression analyses.

54. There is potentially a simultaneity bias in this variable to the extent that legislatures that created commissions when they first enacted a workers' compensation law might have also favored higher benefit levels if legislatures chose a package favorable to organized labor. On the other hand, legislatures may have chosen

a compromise piece of legislation in which workers traded a commission for higher benefits, or vice versa. We tried developing an instrument for this variable but we could find no variables that belonged in an instrument equation for the commission that would not also be in the selectivity equation. Thus, the coefficient of the commission variable might be overstated if the commission and high wages were packaged together to appease unions, or understated if the commission was a compromise that unions accepted in return for lower benefits.

References

Abraham, Katharine G., and Henry S. Farber. 1987. Job duration, seniority and earnings. *American Economic Review* 77 (June): 278–97.

Ackerman, S. B. 1926. *Industrial life insurance.* New York: Spectator Company.

Adams, William W. 1923. *Coal-mine fatalities in the United States, 1923.* U.S. Bureau of Mines Bulletin no. 241. Washington, D.C.: Government Printing Office.

Aetna Insurance Company. 1919. *Classification of risks for accident insurance.* Hartford, Conn.: Aetna Insurance Company.

Alchian, Armen A., and Harold Demsetz. 1973. The property rights paradigm. *Journal of Economic History* 33 (March): 16–27.

Aldrich, Mark. 1997. *Safety first: Technology, labor, and business in the building of American work safety, 1870–1939.* Baltimore: Johns Hopkins University Press.

Allison, Paul D. 1984. *Event history analysis: Regression for longitudinal data.* Beverly Hills, Cal.: Sage Publications.

Alston, Lee J. 1996. Empirical work in institutional economics: An overview. In *Empirical studies in institutional change,* ed. Lee J. Alston, Thráinn Eggertsson, and Douglass C. North, 25–33. New York: Cambridge University Press.

Alston, Lee J., and Joseph P. Ferrie. 1985. Labor costs, paternalism, and loyalty in southern agriculture: A constraint on the growth of the welfare state. *Journal of Economic History* 45 (March): 95–117.

———. 1993. Paternalism in agricultural labor contracts in the U.S. south: Implications for the growth of the welfare state. *American Economic Review* 83 (September): 852–76.

Altonji, Joseph G., and Robert A. Shakotko. 1987. Do wages rise with job seniority? *Review of Economic Studies* 54 (July): 437–59.

Annual Cyclopedia of Insurance in the United States, 1921, 1921. New York: R. B. Caverly, Publisher.

Asher, Robert. 1969. Business and workers' welfare in the Progressive Era: Workmen's compensation reform in Massachusetts, 1880–1911. *Business History Review* 43 (winter): 452–75.

———. 1971. Workmen's compensation in the United States, 1880–1935. Ph.D. diss., University of Minnesota.

————. 1973. Radicalism and reform: State insurance of workmen's compensation in Minnesota, 1910–1933. *Labor History* 14 (winter): 19–41.

————. 1983. Failure and fulfillment: Agitation for employers' liability legislation and the origins of workmen's compensation in New York state, 1876–1910. *Labor History* 24 (spring): 198–222.

Associated Industries of Missouri. Various years. *Bulletin.* Various issues. State Historical Society of Missouri, Columbia, Mo.

Aumann, Francis. 1942. Ohio government in the twentieth century, from Nash to White (1900–1931). In *The history of the state of Ohio. Vol. 6, Ohio in the twentieth century, 1900–1938,* ed. Harlow Lindley, 3–54. Columbus: Ohio State Archaeological and Historical Society.

Baicker, Katherine, Claudia Goldin, and Lawrence F. Katz. 1998. A distinctive system: Origins and impact of U.S. unemployment compensation. In *The defining moment: The great depression and the American economy in the twentieth century,* ed. Michael D. Bordo, Claudia Goldin, and Eugene N. White, 227–63. Chicago: University of Chicago Press.

Bale, Anthony. 1987. America's first compensation crisis: Conflict over the value and meaning of workplace injuries under the employers' liability system. In *Dying for work: Workers' safety in twentieth-century America,* ed. David Rosner and Gerald E. Markowitz, 34–52. Bloomington: University of Indiana Press.

Bartel, Ann P., and Lacy Glenn Thomas. 1985. Direct and indirect effects of regulation: A new look at OSHA's impact. *Journal of Law and Economics* 28 (April): 1–25.

Bartrip, P. W. J. 1985. Beveridge, workmen's compensation and the alternative remedy. *Journal of Social Policy* 14 (October): 491–511.

Bebchuk, Lucian Arye. 1984. Litigation and settlement under imperfect information. *Rand Journal of Economics* 15 (autumn): 404–15.

Becker, Gary S. 1983. A theory of competition among pressure groups for political influence. *Quarterly Journal of Economics* 98 (August): 371–400.

Blanchard, Ralph Harrub. 1917. *Industrial accidents and workmen's compensation.* New York: D. Appleton and Company.

Boyd, James H. 1912. The economic and legal basis of compulsory industrial insurance for workmen. *Michigan Law Review* 10 (March): 345–69.

Brandeis, Elizabeth. 1966. Labor legislation. In *History of labor in the United States, 1896–1932,* ed. John R. Commons, 399–697. New York: Augustus M. Kelley. Reprint.

Brown, Charles, and James Medoff. 1989. The employer size-wage effect. *Journal of Political Economy* 97 (October): 1027–59.

Brown, James N. 1989. Why do wages increase with tenure? *American Economic Review* 79 (December): 971–91.

Brown, John Prather. 1973. Toward an economic theory of liability. *Journal of Legal Studies* 2 (June): 323–49.

Buffum, David. 1992. Workmen's compensation: Passage and impact. Ph.D. diss., University of Pennsylvania.

Byrum, Ike, and Ohio State Federation of Labor. *Report of legislative agent Ike S. Byrum and executive board of the Ohio State Federation of Labor on the 79th General Assembly of Ohio, 1911 and record of labor laws enacted since 1907.* Located at Ohio Historical Society, Columbus, Ohio.

Caballero, Ricardo J. 1991. Earnings uncertainty and aggregate wealth accumulation. *American Economic Review* 81 (September): 859–71.

Cantor, Richard. 1985. The consumption function and the precautionary demand for savings. *Economics Letters* 17, no. 3:207–10.

Carroll, Christopher D. 1992. The buffer-stock theory of saving: Some macro-economic evidence. *Brookings Papers on Economic Activity* 2:61–135.

Castrovinci, Joseph L. 1976. Prelude to welfare capitalism: The role of business in the enactment of workmen's compensation legislation in Illinois, 1905–12. *Social Service Review* 50 (March): 80–102.

Chancellor, H. C. 1919. *Letters in favor of state insurance from managers of state funds.* St. Louis: Labor Publishing Company.

Chelius, James R. 1976. Liability for industrial accidents: A comparison of negligence and strict liability systems. *Journal of Legal Studies* 5 (June): 293–309.

Chelius, James R., and John F. Burton Jr. 1994. Who actually pays for workers' compensation? The empirical evidence. *Workers' Compensation Monitor* 7 (November/December): 20–27.

Chicago Daily News Almanac and Yearbook. Various years, 1918–1930. Chicago: Chicago Daily News Company.

Chrislock, Carl H. 1971. *The Progressive Era in Minnesota 1899–1918.* St. Paul: Minnesota Historical Society.

Clark, Lindley D. 1908. *The legal liability of employers for injuries to their employees, in the United States.* U.S. Bureau of Labor Bulletin No. 74. Washington, D.C.: Government Printing Office.

———. 1911. *Review of labor legislation of 1911.* U.S. Bureau of Labor Bulletin No. 97, 904–11. Washington, D.C.: Government Printing Office.

———. 1914. *Workmen's compensation laws of the United States.* Bureau of Labor Statistics Bulletin No. 126. Washington, D.C.: Government Printing Office.

———. 1925. Referendum on Missouri workmen's compensation law. *Monthly Labor Review* 21 (September): 602–4.

Clark, Lindley D., and Martin C. Frincke Jr. 1921. *Workmen's compensation legislation of the United States and Canada.* U.S. Bureau of Labor Statistics Bulletin No. 272. Washington, D.C.: Government Printing Office.

Coase, Ronald. 1960. The problem of social cost. *Journal of Law and Economics* 3 (October): 1–44.

Congressional Quarterly. 1975. *Guide to U.S. elections.* Washington, D.C.: Congressional Quarterly Inc.

Conyngton, Mary K. 1917. *Effect of workmen's compensation laws in diminishing the necessity of industrial employment of women and children.* Bureau of Labor Statistics Bulletin No. 217. Washington, D.C.: Government Printing Office.

Cooter, Robert D., and Daniel L. Rubinfeld. 1989. Economic analysis of legal disputes and their resolution. *Journal of Economic Literature* 27 (September): 1067–97.

Cornelius, Martin P. 1920. *Accidental means: A brief on the insuring clause of personal accident policies.* New York: Thomas A. Hine.

Croyle, James L. 1978. Industrial accident liability policy of the early twentieth century. *Journal of Legal Studies* 7 (June): 279–97.

Cutler, David M., and Jonathan Gruber. 1996. Does public insurance crowd out private insurance? *Quarterly Journal of Economics* 111 (May): 391–430.

Danzon, Patricia M. 1988. The political economy of workers' compensation: Lessons for product liability. *AmericanEconomic Review Papers and Proceedings* 78 (May): 305–10.

Daughety, Andrew F., and Jennifer F. Reinganum. 1993. Endogenous sequencing in models of settlement and litigation. *Journal of Law, Economics, and Organization* 9 (October): 314–48.

Davis, Lance E., and Douglass C. North. 1971. *Institutional change and American economic growth.* Cambridge: Cambridge University Press.

Deaton, Angus. 1991. Saving and liquidity constraints. *Econometrica* 59 (September): 1221–48.

DeLeon, Edwin W. 1907. *Manual of liability insurance.* New York: Spectator Company.

Demsetz, Harold. 1966. Some aspects of property rights. *Journal of Law and Economics* 9 (October): 61–70.

———. 1967. Toward a theory of property rights. *American Economic Review* 57 (May): 347–59.

Denzau, Arthur T., and Robert J. Mackay. 1983. Gatekeeping and monopoly power of committees: An analysis of sophisticated and sincere behavior. *American Journal of Political Science* 27 (November): 740–61.

Dickens, William T. 1984. Differences between risk premiums in union and nonunion wages and the case of occupational safety regulation. *American Economic Review Papers and Proceedings* 74 (May): 320–23.

Dodd, Walter. 1936. *Administration of workmen's compensation.* New York: Commonwealth Fund.

Donnelly, Thomas J. 1915. History of Ohio's workmen's compensation law. *National* 1 (September): 41–42.

Downs, Anthony. 1957. *An economic theory of democracy.* New York: Harper & Row.

Drescher, Nuala McGann. 1970. The workmen's compensation and pension proposal in the brewing industry, 1910–1912: A case study in conflicting self-interest. *Industrial and Labor Relations Review* 24 (October): 32–46.

Driggers, G. H. 1913. *The true situation in Washington with regard to the state managed workmen's compensation fund.* New York: Market World and Chronicle Print.

Dryden, John F. 1914. Burial (or "industrial") insurance. In *Personal insurance: Life and accident,* ed. Lester W. Zartman and William H. Price, 384–99. New Haven, Conn.: Yale University Press.

Eastman, Crystal. 1910. *Work-accidents and the law.* New York: Charities Publication.

Ely, Richard T. 1908. Economic theory and labor legislation. In *Proceedings of the first annual meeting of the American Association for Labor Legislation,* 10–39. Madison, Wis.: American Association for Labor Legislation.

Epstein, Richard A. 1973. A theory of strict liability. *Journal of Legal Studies* 2 (January): 151–204.

———. 1982. The historical origins and economic structure of workers' compensation law. *Georgia Law Review* 16 (summer): 775–819.

Faulkner, Edwin J. 1940. *Accident-and-health insurance.* New York: McGraw-Hill.

Fay, Albert H. 1916. *Coal mine fatalities in the United States, 1870–1914.* U.S. Bureau of Mines Bulletin No. 115. Washington, D.C.: Government Printing Office.

Feldstein, Martin. 1974. Social security, induced retirement, and aggregate capital accumulation. *Journal of Political Economy* 82 (September/October): 905–26.

———. 1980. International differences in social security and saving. *Journal of Public Economics* 14 (October): 225–44.

———. 1982. Social security and private saving: Reply. *Journal of Political Economy* 90 (June): 630–42.

Fessenden, Stephen. 1900. *Present status of employers' liability in the United States.* Department of Labor Bulletin No. 29, 1157–210. Washington, D.C.: Government Printing Office.

Fiorina, Morris P. 1977. *Congress: Keystone of the Washington establishment.* New Haven, Conn.: Yale University Press.

Fishback, Price V. 1987. Liability rules and accident prevention in the workplace:

Empirical evidence from the early twentieth century. *Journal of Legal Studies* 16 (June): 305–28.

———. 1992. *Soft coal, hard choices: The economic welfare of bituminous coal miners, 1890 to 1930.* New York: Oxford University Press.

———. 1998. Operations of "unfettered" labor markets: Exit and voice in American labor markets at the turn of the century. *Journal of Economic Literature* 36 (June): 722–65.

Fishback, Price V., and Shawn Everett Kantor. 1992. "Square deal" or raw deal? Market compensation for workplace disamenities, 1884–1903. *Journal of Economic History* 52 (December): 826–48.

———. 1995. Did workers pay for the passage of workers' compensation laws? *Quarterly Journal of Economics* 110 (August): 713–42.

———. 1996. The durable experiment: State insurance of workers' compensation risk in the early twentieth century. *Journal of Economic History* 56 (December): 809–36.

———. 1997. The origins of workers' compensation in Ohio. University of Arizona working paper.

———. 1998a. The adoption of workers' compensation in the United States, 1900–1930. *Journal of Law and Economics* 61 (October): 305–42.

———. 1998b. The political economy of workers' compensation benefits, 1910–1930. *Explorations in Economic History* 35 (April): 109–39.

Fisher, Waldo, and Anne Bezanson. 1932. *Wage rates and working time in the bituminous coal industry, 1912–1922.* Philadelphia: University of Pennsylvania Press.

Fisher, Willard C. 1920. American experience with workmen's compensation. *American Economic Review* 10 (March): 18–47.

Foote, Allen Ripley. 1910. *Report on legislative work for 1910 to members of the Ohio State Board of Commerce.* Columbus: Ohio State Board of Commerce.

———. 1912. *Government by the initiative and referendum will destroy representative government.* Columbus: Ohio Journal of Commerce.

French, Will J. 1920. The trend of workmen's compensation—A glance at compensation history, past and present. *Monthly Labor Review* 11 (November): 881–82.

Friedman, Lawrence M. 1985. *A history of American law.* 2d ed. New York: Simon and Schuster.

Gillette, George M. 1911a. A bill for an act. In *Papers and proceedings of the fourth annual meeting of the Minnesota Academy of Social Sciences,* ed. William A. Schaper, 226–32. Minneapolis: Minnesota Academy of Social Sciences.

———. 1911b. Comment on the principal differences between the Gillette Code and the McEwen-Mercer Code. In *Papers and proceedings of the fourth annual meeting of the Minnesota Academy of Social Sciences,* ed. William A. Schaper, 233–41. Minneapolis: Minnesota Academy of Social Sciences.

———. 1911c. Employer's Liability and Workmen's Compensation Acts. In *Papers and proceedings of the fourth annual meeting of the Minnesota Academy of Social Sciences,* ed. William A. Schaper, 172–89. Minneapolis: Minnesota Academy of Social Sciences.

Gilligan, Thomas W., William J. Marshall, and Barry R. Weingast. 1989. Regulation and the theory of legislative choice: The Interstate Commerce Act of 1887. *Journal of Law and Economics* 32 (April): 35–61.

Goldberg, Victor P. 1976. Regulation and administered contracts. *Bell Journal of Economics* 7 (autumn): 426–48.

Goldin, Claudia. 1981. Family strategies and the family economy in the late nineteenth century: The role of secondary workers. In *Philadelphia: Work, space, and group experience in the nineteenth century,* ed. Theodore Hershberg, 277–310. New York: Oxford University Press.

————. Forthcoming. Labor markets in the twentieth century. In *Cambridge economic history of the United States,* ed. Stanley Engerman and Robert Gallman. New York: Cambridge University Press.

Graebner, William. 1976. *Coal-mining safety in the Progressive Era.* Lexington: University of Kentucky Press.

Gruber, Jonathan. 1994. The incidence of mandated maternity benefits. *American Economic Review* 84 (June): 622–41.

Gruber, Jonathan, and Alan B. Krueger. 1991. The incidence of mandated employer-provided insurance: Lessons from workers' compensation insurance. In *Tax policy and the economy,* ed. David Bradford, 111–43. Cambridge, Mass.: MIT Press.

Haines, Michael R. 1985. The life cycle, savings, and demographic adaptation: Some historical evidence for the United States and Europe. In *Gender and the life course,* ed. Alice S. Rossi, 43–63. New York: Aldine Publishing.

Harrington, Scott E. 1994. State decisions to limit tort liability: An empirical analysis of no-fault automobile insurance laws. *Journal of Risk and Uncertainty* 61:276–94.

Hayden's Annual Cyclopedia of Insurance in the United States, 1905–1906. 1906. Hartford, Conn.: The Insurance Journal Company.

Hayden's Annual Cyclopedia of Insurance in the United States, 1911–1913. 1913. Hartford, Conn.: The Insurance Journal Company.

Hersch, Joni, and Patricia Reagan. 1990. Job match, tenure and wages paid by firms. *Economic Inquiry* 28 (July): 488–507.

Higgs, Robert. 1987. *Crisis and leviathan: Critical episodes in the growth of American government.* New York: Oxford University Press.

Hoffman, Frederick. 1908. *Industrial accidents.* Bureau of Labor Bulletin No. 78. Washington, D.C.: Government Printing Office.

Hookstadt, Carl. 1918. *Comparison of workmen's compensation laws of the United States up to December 17, 1917.* U.S. Bureau of Labor Statistics Bulletin No. 240. Washington, D.C.: Government Printing Office.

————. 1919. Comparison of experience under workmen's compensation and employers' liability systems. *Monthly Labor Review* 8 (March): 230–48.

————. 1920. *Comparison of workmen's compensation laws of the United States and Canada up to January 1, 1920.* U.S. Bureau of Labor Statistics Bulletin No. 275. Washington, D.C.: Government Printing Office.

————. 1922. *Comparison of workmen's compensation laws and administration, April 1922.* U.S. Bureau of Labor Statistics Bulletin No. 301. Washington, D.C.: Government Printing Office.

Howitt, Peter, and Ronald Wintrobe. 1995. The political economy of inaction. *Journal of Public Economics* 56 (March): 329–53.

Hubbard, R. Glenn, Jonathan Skinner, and Stephen P. Zeldes. 1994. The importance of precautionary motives in explaining individual and aggregate saving. *Carnegie-Rochester Conference Series on Public Policy* 40 (June): 59–125.

————. 1995. Precautionary saving and social insurance. *Journal of Political Economy* 103 (April): 360–99.

Huber, Peter W. 1988. *Liability: The legal revolution and its consequences.* New York: Basic Books.

Hughes, Jonathan. 1977. *The governmental habit.* New York: Basic Books.

Hutchens, Robert. 1987. A test of Lazear's theory of delayed payment contracts. *Journal of Labor Economics* 5 (October): S153–S170.

Hylton, Keith. 1993. Asymmetric information and the selection of disputes for litigation. *Journal of Legal Studies* 22 (January): 187–210.

Illinois Employers' Liability Commission. 1910. *Report of the Employers' Liability Commission.* Chicago: Stromberg, Allen & Co.

Illinois Industrial Commission. Various years. *Annual report.*

Insurance Federation of Minnesota (IFM). 1989[?]. *History: Insurance Federation of Minnesota, 1914–1989.* In IFM Papers, location 152.K.3.4F, box 1, Minnesota State Historical Society, St. Paul, Minn.

———. Report of the Secretary. Various years. In IFM Papers, location 152.K.3.4F, box 1, Minnesota State Historical Society, St. Paul, Minn.

Insurance Research and Review Service. 1938. *Fraternal life insurance.* Indianapolis: IRRS.

Insurance Year Book. Various years. New York: Spectator Company.

Iowa Employers' Liability Commission. 1912. *Report.* Des Moines, Iowa: Emory H. English, State Printer.

Iowa Industrial Commissioner. 1914. *First biennial report for the period ending June 30, 1914.* Des Moines, Iowa: Robert Henderson, State Printer.

Johnson, Ronald N., and Gary D. Libecap. 1994. *The federal civil service system and the problem of bureaucracy: The economics and politics of institutional change.* Chicago: University of Chicago Press.

Jones, F. Robertson. 1927. *Digest of workmen's compensation laws in the United States and territories, with annotations, revised to December 1, 1927.* New York: Workmen's Compensation Publicity Bureau.

Jovanovic, Boyan. 1979. Job matching and the theory of turnover. *Journal of Political Economy* 87 (October): 972–90.

Kansas City (Missouri) Board of Public Welfare. 1912. *Report of investigations of 100 industrial accidents in Kansas City during the year of 1912 by the Factory Inspection Department of the Board of Public Welfare of Kansas City, Missouri.* Kansas City, Mo.: Kansas City Department of Factory Inspection and Labor Statistics.

———. 1916. *Report of investigations of 300 industrial accidents in Kansas City during the year of 1916 by the Factory Inspection Department of the Board of Public Welfare of Kansas City, Missouri.* Kansas City, Mo.: Kansas City Department of Factory Inspection and Labor Statistics.

Kantor, Shawn Everett. 1998. *Politics and property rights: The closing of the open range in the postbellum south.* Chicago: University of Chicago Press.

Kantor, Shawn Everett, and Price V. Fishback. 1994a. Coalition formation and the adoption of workers' compensation: The case of Missouri, 1911 to 1926. In *The regulated economy: A historical approach to political economy,* ed. Claudia Goldin and Gary D. Libecap, 259–97. Chicago: University of Chicago Press.

———. 1994b. Fatal accident compensation under the negligence liability system. In *Hours of work and means of payment: Proceedings of 11th International Economic History Congress,* 37–45. Milan: Universita Bocconi.

———. 1995. Non-fatal accident compensation under the negligence liability system at the turn of the century. *Journal of Law, Economics, and Organization* 11 (April): 406–33.

———. 1996. Precautionary saving, insurance, and the origins of workers' compensation. *Journal of Political Economy* 104 (April): 419–42.

———. 1998. How Minnesota adopted workers' compensation. *Independent Review* 2 (spring): 557–78.

Katz, Lawrence F. 1986. Efficiency wage theories: A partial evaluation. In *NBER macroeconomics annual, 1986,* ed. Stanley Fischer. Cambridge, Mass.: MIT Press.

Kent, Marthe Beckett. 1983. A history of occupational safety and health in the United States. Office of Technology Assessment, Contract 333–4260.1 (April).

Kerr, William T. 1963. The progressives of Washington (1910–1912). Senior thesis, University of Washington.

Keyssar, Alexander. 1986. *Out of work: The first century of unemployment in Massachusetts.* New York: Cambridge University Press.

Kim, Seung-Wook. 1988. Accident risk and railroad worker compensation: An historical study, 1880–1945. Ph.D. diss., University of Georgia.

Kim, Seung-Wook, and Price V. Fishback. 1993. Institutional change, compensating differentials, and accident risk in railroading, 1892–1945. *Journal of Economic History* 53 (December): 796–823.

Kimball, Miles S. 1990. Precautionary saving in the small and in the large. *Econometrica* 58 (January): 53–73.

Kip, Richard De Raismes. 1953. *Fraternal life insurance in America.* Philadelphia: College Offset Press.

Kniesner, Thomas J., and John D. Leeth. 1991. Improving workplace safety: Standards or insurance? *Regulation* 14 (fall): 64–70.

Kotlikoff, Laurence J. 1989. *What determines savings?* Cambridge, Mass.: MIT Press.

Kotlikoff, Laurence J., and Avia Spivak. 1981. The family as an incomplete annuities market. *Journal of Political Economy* 89 (April): 372–91.

Krueger, Alan B., and Lawrence H. Summers. 1988. Efficiency wages and the interindustry wage structure. *Econometrica* 56 (March): 259–93.

Kulp, C. A. 1928. *Casualty insurance.* New York: Ronald Press.

Landes, William M., and Richard A. Posner. 1987. *The economic structure of tort law.* Cambridge, Mass.: Harvard University Press.

Lawson, George W. 1955. *History of labor in Minnesota.* St. Paul: Minnesota State Federation of Labor.

Lazear, Edward. 1979. Why is there mandatory retirement? *Journal of Political Economy* 87 (December): 1261–84.

Leimer, Dean R., and Selig D. Lesnoy. 1982. Social security and private saving: New time-series evidence. *Journal of Political Economy* 90 (June): 606–29.

Leland, Hayne E. 1968. Saving and uncertainty: The precautionary demand for saving. *Quarterly Journal of Economics* 82 (August): 465–73.

Libecap, Gary D. 1989a. *Contracting for property rights.* Cambridge: Cambridge University Press.

———. 1989b. Distributional issues in contracting for property rights. *Journal of Institutional and Theoretical Economics* 145 (March): 6–31.

Lubove, Roy. 1967. Workmen's compensation and the prerogatives of voluntarism. *Labor History* 8 (fall): 254–27.

Maryland Bureau of Statistics and Information. Various years. *Annual report.*

Massachusetts Commission for the Compensation for Industrial Accidents. 1912. *Report.* Boston: State Printers.

Mayhew, David R. 1974. *Congress: The electoral connection.* New Haven, Conn.: Yale University Press.

McCahan, David. 1929. *State insurance in the United States.* Philadelphia: University of Pennsylvania Press.

McEwen, William E. 1911. The evils of the present system of employer's liability. In *Papers and proceedings of the fourth annual meeting of the Minnesota Academy of Social Sciences,* ed. William A. Schaper, 154–71. Minneapolis: Minnesota Academy of Social Sciences.

McGouldrick, Paul F., and Michael B. Tannen. 1977. Did American manufacturers discriminate against immigrants before 1914? *Journal of Economic History* 37 (September): 723–46.

Mengert, H. R. 1920. The Ohio Workmen's compensation law. *Ohio Archaeological and Historical Publications* 29:1–48.

Michelbacher, G. F. 1942. *Casualty insurance principles.* McGraw-Hill Insurance Series. New York: McGraw-Hill.

Michigan Auditor General. Various years. *Annual report of the Auditor General.* Lansing: Michigan State Printer.

Michigan Bureau of Labor and Industrial Statistics. 1898–1904. *Annual report.* Lansing: Michigan State Printer.

Michigan Employers' Liability and Workmen's Compensation Commission. 1911. *Report of the Employers' Liability and Workmen's Compensation Commission.* Lansing: Michigan State Printer.

Minnesota Bureau of Labor, Industries, and Commerce. 1909–1910. *Twelfth annual report, 1909–1910.*

Minnesota Bureau of Labor Statistics. 1893. *Third biennial report, 1891–1892.* Minneapolis.

Minnesota Commissioner of Insurance. Various years. *Annual report.* Minneapolis: Syndicate Printing.

Minnesota Department of Labor and Industries (MDLI). Various years. *Biennial report.* Minneapolis: Syndicate Printing.

———. Insurance Compensation Correspondence. Location 115.H.17.3B. St. Paul: Minnesota Historical Society.

———. Workmen's Compensation Commission Hearings. Location 115.H.17.8F. 24 February 1920 file, pp. 2–3. St. Paul: Minnesota State Historical Society.

Minnesota Employers' Association (MEA). Various years. *Minute book.* In MEA Papers, location 152.K.16.1B, box 13. Minnesota State Historical Society, St. Paul, Minn.

Minnesota House of Representatives. 1909. Public hearing on the Employers' Liability Act, February 10, 1909. In Minnesota Association of Commerce and Industry Papers. Location 152.K.16.2F, box 14, Minnesota Historical Society, St. Paul, Minn.

———. Special Interim Committee. 1921. Workmen's compensation: Majority and minority report. In Minnesota House of Representatives *Journal,* 1921, 1832–48.

Minnesota Secretary of State. Various years. *Legislative manual.*

Minnesota Senate. Interim Commission on Industrial Accident Compensation and State Industrial Insurance. 1921. *Report to the legislature of Minnesota.* Senate document no. 1. St. Paul, Minn.: McGill-Warner.

Minnesota State Federation of Labor (MnSFL). 1909. *Proceedings of the twenty-seventh convention of the Minnesota State Federation of Labor held at Red Wing, Minnesota, June 14–16, 1909.*

———. 1910. *Proceedings of the twenty-eighth convention of the Minnesota State Federation of Labor held at Fargo, N.D., June 20–22, 1910.*

———. 1911. *Proceedings of the twenty-ninth convention of the Minnesota State Federation of Labor held at Mankato, Minnesota, June 19–21, 1911.*

———. 1913. *Proceedings of the thirty-first convention of the Minnesota State Federation of Labor held at St. Cloud, Minnesota, June 16–18, 1913.*

———. 1914. *Proceedings of the thirty-second convention of the Minnesota Federation of Labor held at Duluth, Minnesota, June 20–22, 1914.*

———. 1919. *Proceedings of the thirty-seventh convention of the Minnesota State Federation of Labor held at New Ulm, Minnesota, July 21–23, 1919.*

Missouri Bureau of Labor Statistics (MBLS). 1918–1920. *A wartime industrial history of Missouri, part II, fortieth and forty-first annual reports.*

———. 1921–1922. *An industrial history of Missouri, 1922, 1921, 1920, forty-second and forty-third annual reports.*

Missouri State Federation of Labor (MoSFL). 1918. *Reasons for state managed insurance for workmen's compensation.* St. Louis: Labor Publishing Company.

Modell, John. 1979. Changing risks, changing adaptations: American families in the nineteenth and twentieth centuries. In *Kin and communities: Families in America,* ed. Allan J. Lichtman and Joan R. Challinor, 119–44. Washington, D.C.: Smithsonian Institution Press.

Moore, Michael J., and W. Kip Viscusi. 1990. *Compensation mechanisms for job risks: Wages, workers' compensation, and product liability.* Princeton, N.J.: Princeton University Press.

Moss, David A. 1996. *Socializing security: Progressive-Era economists and the origins of American social policy.* Cambridge, Mass.: Harvard University Press.

Nash, Gerald D. 1963. The influence of labor on state policy 1860–1920. *California Historical Quarterly* 42 (September): 241–57.

National Industrial Conference Board. 1927. *The workmen's compensation problem in New York state.* New York: National Industrial Conference Board.

New York Commission on Employers' Liability (NYCEL). 1910. *Report to the legislature of the state of New York by the commission appointed under Chapter 518 of the laws of 1909 to inquire into the question of employers' liability and other matters, first report.* Albany, N.Y.: J. B. Lyon Company.

New York Secretary of State. 1925–1940. *Manual of the legislature of the state of New York.*

Nichols, Hugh L. 1932. Judson Harmon. *Ohio State Archaeological and Historical Quarterly* 41:145.

Nichols, Walter S. 1914. Fraternal life insurance. In *Personal insurance: Life and accident,* ed. Lester W. Zartman and William H. Price, 351–83. New Haven, Conn.: Yale University Press.

Noble, Charles. 1997. *Welfare as we knew it: A political history of the American welfare state.* New York: Oxford University Press.

North, Douglass C. 1981. *Structure and change in economic history.* New York: Norton.

———. 1987. Institutions, transaction costs and economic growth. *Economic Inquiry* 25 (July): 419–28.

Ohio Department of Inspection of Workshops, Factories, and Public Buildings. Various years. *Annual report.* Columbus, Ohio.

Ohio Employers' Liability Commission. 1911. *Report to the legislature of the state of Ohio of the commission appointed under Senate Bill No. 250 of the laws of 1910.* 2 vols. Columbus, Ohio: F. J. Heer, State Printer.

Ohio Industrial Commission. 1916. *Industrial accidents in Ohio, January 1, 1914 to June 30, 1915.* Columbus, Ohio.

———. 1923. *The Ohio state insurance manual, rules and rates effective July 1, 1923.* Columbus, Ohio.

Ohio Manufacturers' Association. *Records, 1910–1950.* Microfilm No. 148. Ohio Historical Society, Columbus, Ohio.

Ohio State Board of Commerce. 1910. *Proceedings of the seventeenth annual meeting, Columbus, November 16–17, 1910.* Columbus, Ohio: Chamber of Commerce.

Ohio State Board of Liability Awards. 1912. *Does the workmen's compensation law of Ohio protect the employers of Ohio?* Columbus, Ohio: F. J. Heer Printing Co.

Ohio State Federation of Labor. 1910. *Report of proceedings of the twenty-seventh annual convention.*

———. 1912. *Proceedings of the twenty-ninth annual convention.*

————. 1913a. *Proceedings of the thirtieth annual convention.*

————. 1913b. *Report of the legislative board of the Ohio State Federation of Labor, Brotherhood of Railway Trainmen, and Brotherhood of Locomotive Firemen and Enginemen.*

————. 1915a. *Proceedings of the thirty-second annual convention.*

————. 1915b. *Report of the joint legislative committee of the Ohio State Federation of Labor, Brotherhood of Railway Trainmen, and Brotherhood of Locomotive Firemen and Enginemen.*

————. 1917. *Report of the legislative agent of the Ohio State Federation of Labor.*

Olson, Mancur. 1965. *The logic of collective action: Public goods and the theory of groups.* Cambridge, Mass.: Harvard University Press.

————. 1982. *The rise and decline of nations.* New Haven, Conn.: Yale University Press.

Oregon Industrial Accident Commission. 1919. *Second report for the two year period ending June 30, 1917.* Salem, Or.: State Printing Department.

Orloff, Ann Shola. 1993. *The politics of pensions: A comparative analysis of Britain, Canada, and the United States, 1880–1940.* Madison, Wis.: University of Wisconsin Press.

Pacific Coast Lumber Manufacturers' Association. 1911. *Proceedings and addresses, annual meeting of the Pacific Coals Lumber Manufacturers' Association, Inc. at Seattle, Wash., January 28, 1911.*

Paterson, J. V. 1913. *Workmen's compulsory compensation system, state of Washington, a proved failure and a business menace.* Pamphlet. U.S. Department of Labor Library, Washington, D.C.

Pavalko, Eliza K. 1989. State timing of policy adoption: Workmen's compensation in the United States, 1909–1929. *American Journal of Sociology* 95 (November): 592–615.

Peltzman, Samuel. 1976. Toward a more general theory of regulation. *Journal of Law and Economics* 19 (August): 211–48.

Petition suggesting plans for legislation looking toward compensation of employees for injuries received in the course of their employment ("Petition"). 21 January 1909. Department of Labor Library, Washington, D.C.

Poole, Keith T., and Howard Rosenthal. 1993. The enduring battle for economic regulation: The Interstate Commerce Act revisited. *Journal of Law and Economics* 36 (October): 837–60.

————. 1994. Congress and railroad regulation: 1874 to 1887. In *The regulated economy: A historical approach to political economy,* ed. Claudia Goldin and Gary D. Libecap, 81–120. Chicago: University of Chicago Press.

————. 1997. *Congress: A political-economic history of roll call voting.* New York: Oxford University Press.

Posner, Richard A. 1972. A theory of negligence. *Journal of Legal Studies* 1 (January): 29–96.

Priest, George L., and Benjamin Klein. 1984. The selection of disputes for litigation. *Journal of Legal Studies* 13 (January): 1–55.

Quadagno, Jill S. 1988. The transformation of old age security: Class and politics in the American welfare state. Chicago: University of Chicago Press.

Railroad Brotherhoods State Legislative Board of the State of Minnesota. Various years. *Biennial report.*

Ransom, Roger L., and Richard Sutch. 1989. Codebook and user's manual: A survey of 1,165 workers in Kansas, 1884–1887. Reported in *First, second, and third annual reports of the Kansas Bureau of Labor and Industrial Statistics.* Berkeley, Cal.

————. 1990. Codebook and user's manual: A survey of 1,085 workers in Maine,

1890. Reported in *Fifth annual report of the Maine Bureau of Industrial and Labor Statistics.* Berkeley, Cal.

Reagan, Patrick D. 1981. The ideology of social harmony and efficiency: Workmen's compensation in Ohio, 1904–1919. *Ohio History* 90 (autumn): 317–31.

Ridinger, Gerald Erwin. 1957. *The political career of Frank B. Willis.* Ph.D. diss., Ohio State University.

Riggleman, John Randolph. 1934. Variations in building activity in United States cities. Ph.D. diss., Johns Hopkins University.

Rohr, W. J. 1910. Proposed workmen's compensation law. *Ohio Journal of Commerce* 12 (November): 307.

Rotella, Elyce, and George Alter. 1993. Working class debt in the late nineteenth century United States. *Journal of Family History* 18 (spring): 111–34.

Rowe, J. Scofield. 1912[?]. *Compensation for accidents to work-people: Should it be administered by the state?* Pamphlet. Department of Labor Library, Washington, D.C.

Rubinow, Isaac. 1913. *Social insurance: With special reference to American conditions.* New York: Henry Holt.

Sandmo, Agnar. 1970. The effect of uncertainty on saving decisions. *Review of Economic Studies* 37 (July): 353–60.

Schwantes, Carlos. 1979. *Radical heritage: Labor, socialism, and reform in Washington and British Columbia, 1885–1917.* Seattle: University of Washington Press.

Seager, Henry R. 1908. Outline of a program of social legislation with special reference to wage-earners. In *Proceedings of the first annual meeting of the American Association for Labor Legislation,* 91–92. Madison, Wis.: American Association for Labor Legislation.

———. 1910. *Social insurance: A program of reform.* New York: Macmillan.

Shavell, Steven. 1980. Strict liability versus negligence. *Journal of Legal Studies* 9 (January): 1–25.

———. 1987. *Economic analysis of accident law.* Cambridge, Mass.: Harvard University Press.

Shepsle, Kenneth A., and Barry R. Weingast. 1981. Structure-induced equilibrium and legislative choice. *Public Choice* 37, no. 3:503–19.

———. 1984. When do rules of procedure matter? *Journal of Politics* 46 (February): 206–21.

Skinner, Jonathan. 1988. Risky income, life cycle consumption, and precautionary savings. *Journal of Monetary Economics* 22 (September): 237–55.

Skocpol, Theda. 1992. *Protecting soldiers and mothers: The political origins of social policy in the United States.* Cambridge, Mass.: Harvard University Press, Belknap Press.

Smith, Florence P. 1929. *Chronological development of labor legislation for women in the United States.* U.S. Women's Bureau Bulletin No. 66, Part II. Washington, D.C.: Government Printing Office.

Somers, Herman Miles, and Anne Ramsay Somers. 1954. *Workmen's compensation: Prevention, insurance, and rehabilitation of occupational disability.* New York: John Wiley & Sons.

Spier, Kathryn E. 1994. Settlement bargaining and the design of damage awards. *Journal of Law, Economics, and Organization* 10 (April): 84–95.

Stigler, George J. 1971. The theory of economic regulation. *Bell Journal of Economics and Management Science* 2 (spring): 3–21.

Stigler, George J., and Claire Friedland. 1962. What can regulators regulate? The case of electricity. *Journal of Law and Economics* 5 (October): 1–16.

Stiglitz, Joseph E. 1987. The causes and consequences of the dependence of quality on price. *Journal of Economic Literature* 25 (March): 1–48.

Stonega Coke and Coal Company Records. Various years. *Annual report of Operations Department.* Boxes 210–212. In Stonega Collection at Hagley Museum and Library, Wilmington, Del.

Taft, Philip. 1964. *Organized labor in American history.* New York: Harper & Row.

Tone, Andrea. 1997. *The business of benevolence: Industrial paternalism in progressive America.* Ithaca, N.Y.: Cornell University Press.

Topel, Robert. 1991. Specific capital, mobility, and wages: Wages rise with job seniority. *Journal of Political Economy* 99 (February): 145–76.

Tribune Almanac. 1900–1909.

Tripp, Joseph. 1976. An instance of labor and business cooperation: Workmen's compensation in Washington state, 1911. *Labor History* 17 (fall): 530–50.

Tullock, Gordon. 1967. The welfare costs of tariffs, monopolies, and theft. *Western Economic Journal* 5 (June): 224–32.

U.S. Bureau of the Census. 1902. *Twelfth census of the United States: 1900, manufactures, vol. 7.* Washington, D.C.: Government Printing Office.

———. 1903. *Twelfth census of the United States: 1900, population, part 1, vol. 1.* Washington, D.C.: Government Printing Office.

———. 1904. *Twelfth census of the United States: 1900, special report—occupations.* Washington, D.C.: Government Printing Office.

———. 1913. *Thirteenth census of the United States: 1910, population, vol. 1; occupations, vol. 4; manufactures, vols. 8 and 9.* Washington, D.C.: Government Printing Office.

———. 1917. *Abstract of the census of manufactures, 1914.* Washington, D.C.: Government Printing Office.

———. 1917–1922. *Mortality statistics.* Washington, D.C.: Government Printing Office.

———. 1918. *Financial statistics of states, 1917.* Washington, D.C.: Government Printing Office.

———. 1923. *Fourteenth census of the United States: 1920, population, vols. 1 and 4; manufactures, vol. 8.* Washington, D.C.: Government Printing Office.

———. 1928. *Biennial census of manufactures, 1925.* Washington, D.C.: Government Printing Office.

———. 1933. *Fifteenth census of the United States: 1930, manufactures, vols. 1 and 3; population, vols. 2 and 5.* Washington, D.C.: Government Printing Office.

———. 1935. *Biennial census of manufactures, 1931.* Washington, D.C.: Government Printing Office.

———. 1943. *Sixteenth census of the United States: 1940, manufactures, vols. 1 and 3; population, vols. 2 and 5.* Washington, D.C.: Government Printing Office.

———. 1975. *Historical statistics of the United States, colonial times to 1970.* Washington, D.C.: Government Printing Office.

U.S. Bureau of Labor. 1911. *Bulletin of the Bureau of Labor.* U.S. Bureau of Labor Bulletin No. 92. Washington, D.C.: Government Printing Office.

U.S. Bureau of Labor Statistics. 1913a. *Labor legislation of 1912.* Bureau of Labor Statistics Bulletin No. 111. Washington, D.C.: Government Printing Office.

———. 1913b. *Workmen's compensation laws of the United States and foreign countries.* Bureau of Labor Statistics Bulletin No. 126. Washington, D.C.: Government Printing Office.

———. 1914. *Labor laws of the United States with decision of courts relating thereto.* Bureau of Labor Statistics Bulletin No. 148, parts 1 and 2. Washington, D.C.: Government Printing Office.

———. 1917. *Workmen's compensation laws of the United States and foreign countries.* Bureau of Labor Statistics Bulletin No. 203. Washington, D.C.: Government Printing Office.

————. 1918. *Workmen's compensation legislation in the United States and foreign countries, 1917 and 1918.* Bureau of Labor Statistics Bulletin No. 243. Washington, D.C.: Government Printing Office.

————. 1923. *Workmen's compensation legislation of the United States and Canada, 1920 to 1922.* Bureau of Labor Statistics Bulletin No. 332. Washington, D.C.: Government Printing Office.

————. 1924. *Cost of living in the United States.* Bureau of Labor Statistics Bulletin No. 357. Washington, D.C.: Government Printing Office.

————. 1925a. *Labor laws of the United States with decision of courts relating thereto.* Bureau of Labor Statistics Bulletin No. 370. Washington, D.C.: Government Printing Office.

————. 1925b. New compensation law of Missouri. *Monthly Labor Review* 20 (June): 1329–31.

————. 1926a. Missouri workmen's compensation law adopted by referendum. *Monthly Labor Review* 23 (December): 1224–25.

————. 1926b. *Workmen's compensation legislation of the United States and Canada as of July 1, 1926.* Bureau of Labor Statistics Bulletin No. 423. Washington, D.C.: Government Printing Office.

————. 1929. *Workmen's compensation legislation of the United States and Canada as of January 1, 1929.* Bureau of Labor Statistics Bulletin No. 496. Washington, D.C.: Government Printing Office.

————. 1931. *Labor legislation, 1930.* Bureau of Labor Statistics Bulletin No. 552. Washington, D.C.: Government Printing Office.

————. 1933. *Labor legislation, 1931 and 1932.* Bureau of Labor Statistics Bulletin No. 590. Washington, D.C.: Government Printing Office.

————. 1986. Cost of living in the United States, 1917–1919. ICPSR 8299 Data Tape. Ann Arbor: Inter-University Consortium for Political and Social Research.

U.S. Coal Commission. 1925. *Report, part III.* Washington, D.C.: Government Printing Office.

U.S. Commissioner of Labor. 1892. *Labor laws of the various states and territories and the District of Columbia, second special report of the U.S. Commissioner of Labor.* House of Representatives Report No. 1960, 52d Congress, 1st session. Washington, D.C.: Government Printing Office.

————. 1904. *Tenth special report of the Commissioner of Labor: Labor laws of the United States, 1904.* Washington, D.C.: Government Printing Office.

————. 1908. *Twenty-second annual report of the Commissioner of Labor: Labor laws of the United States, 1907.* Washington, D.C.: Government Printing Office.

————. 1909. *Twenty-third annual report of the Commissioner of Labor: Workmen's insurance and benefit funds in the United States, 1908.* Washington, D.C.: Government Printing Office.

U.S. Department of Agriculture. 1948. *Lumber productions in the United States, 1799–1946.* Miscellaneous Publication No. 669. Washington, D.C.: Government Printing Office.

U.S. Department of Labor. 1903. *Decisions of courts affecting labor.* Department of Labor Bulletin No. 47. Washington, D.C.: Government Printing Office.

U.S. Social Security Administration. 1996. *Social Security bulletin, annual statistical supplement, 1996, to the Social Security bulletin.* Washington, D.C.: Government Printing Office.

Veljanovski, Cento G. 1982. The employment and safety effects of employers' liability. *Scottish Journal of Political Economy* 29 (November): 256–71.

Viscusi, W. Kip. 1986. The determinants of the disposition of product liability claims and compensation for bodily injury. *Journal of Legal Studies* 15 (June): 321–46.

————. 1991. Product and occupational liability. *Journal of Economic Perspectives* 5 (summer): 71–91.

————. 1992. *Fatal tradeoffs: Public and private responsibilities for risk.* New York: Oxford University Press.

Viscusi, W. Kip, and William Evans. 1992. Utility functions that depend on health status: Estimates and economic implications. *American Economic Review* 80 (June): 353–74.

Vorys, Arthur I. 1914. State insurance: An address delivered at the banquet of the Insurance Federation of Ohio, February 26, 1914. Pamphlet. U.S. Department of Labor Library, Washington, D.C.

Wang, Gyu Ho, Jeong-Yoo Kim, and Jong-Goo Yi. 1994. Litigation and pretrial negotiation under incomplete information. *Journal of Law, Economics, and Organization* 10 (April): 187–200.

Warner, Hoyt Landon. 1964. *Progressivism in Ohio, 1897–1917.* Columbus: Ohio State University Press.

Washington Industrial Insurance Department. 1912. *First annual report for the twelve months ending September 30, 1912.* Olympia, Wash.: Public Printer.

Washington Insurance Commissioner. Various years. *Report of the Insurance Commissioner.*

Weingast, Barry R., and William R. Marshall. 1988. The industrial organization of Congress; or, why legislatures, like firms, are not organized as markets. *Journal of Political Economy* 96 (February): 132–63.

Weinstein, James. 1967. Big business and the origins of workmen's compensation. *Labor History* 8 (spring): 156–74.

Weiss, Harry. 1966. Employers' liability and workmen's compensation. In *History of labor in the United States, 1896–1932,* ed. John R. Commons, 564–610. New York: Augustus M. Kelley. Reprint.

Wesser, Robert F. 1971. Conflict and compromise: The workmen's compensation movement in New York, 1890s-1913. *Labor History* 12 (summer): 345–72.

Whaples, Robert. 1990. The shortening of the American work week: An economic and historical analysis of its context, causes, and consequences. Ph.D. diss., University of Pennsylvania.

Whaples, Robert, and David Buffum. 1991. Fraternalism, paternalism, the family, and the market: Insurance a century ago. *Social Science History* 41 (April): 97–122.

White, Halbert. 1980. A heteroskedasticity-consistent covariance matrix estimation and a direct test for heteroskedasticity. *Econometrica* 48 (May): 817–38.

Williamson, Jeffrey G., and Peter H. Lindert. 1980. *American inequality: A macroeconomic history.* New York: Academic Press.

Williamson, Oliver E. 1976. Franchise bidding for natural monopolies—In general and with respect to CATV. *Bell Journal of Economics* 7 (spring): 73–104.

Winans, W. J. 1910. New workmen's compensation law is necessary. *Ohio Journal of Commerce* 5 (November): 291–92.

Wisconsin Bureau of Labor and Industrial Statistics (WBLIS). 1909. *Thirteenth biennial report, 1907–1908.* Madison, Wis.: State Printer.

Wisconsin Industrial Commission. 1915–1917. *Annual report.* Madison, Wis.

Wolman, Leo. 1936. *The ebb and flow of trade unionism.* New York: National Bureau of Economic Research.

Workmen's Compensation Publicity Bureau. 1927. *Digest of workmen's compensation laws in the United States and territories.* New York: WCPB.

World Almanac and Encyclopedia. Various years. New York: Press Publishing.

Worrall, John D., and Richard J. Butler. 1988. Experience rating matters. In *Workers' compensation insurance pricing: Current programs and proposed reforms,* ed. Philip S. Borba and David Appel, 81–94. Boston: Kluwer Academic Publishers.

Wright, Gavin. 1986. *Old South, new South: Revolutions in the southern economy since the Civil War.* New York: Basic Books.

Yamaguchi, Kazuo. 1991. *Event history analysis.* Newbury Park, Cal.: Sage Publications.

Zeldes, Stephen P. 1989. Optimal consumption with stochastic income: Deviations from certainty equivalence. *Quarterly Journal of Economics* 104 (May): 275–98.

Index

Abraham, Katharine, 52n9, 53n16
accident prevention, 17, 18, 59, 77–82, 85n17, 108, 144n25, 201
accident prevention incentives, 5, 11, 12, 16, 27n6, 31, 54–56, 77–83, 86n24
accident rates, 83, 85n19, 203n3
accident risk, 23, 56, 57–58, 72, 79–80, 84n17, 86–87n28, 87nn29–32, 88, 99, 100t, 102, 106t, 107, 117–18n28, 173, 178, 180–81, 183, 191, 193n6, 194n10, 194n11, 196n22, 217, 223, 225, 227, 232–35, 256t, 258, 262, 273–74, 278n3; determinants of, 51n3, 79–80; impact on benefits, 183, 191, 193n6, 194nn10–11, 196n22, 273–74; trends, 23, 88, 99, 100t, 117–18n28. *See also* reporting of accidents
Ackerman, S. B., 71
actuarial fairness, 193n7, 193n11, 241–42
Adams, William W., 278n3
administration, 59, 125, 103–4t, 183–85, 195n18, 277, 285n53, 285–86n54
administrative costs, 11, 16, 26n3, 31, 125, 140, 153, 154, 170n37
administrators: impact on benefits, 173, 182–86, 191
adoption: committee structure impact on, 121, 124, 127–29, 135, 137, 140; determinants, 88–89, 102–13, 254–60, 283n35; multivariate analysis of, 254–60; political process of, 120–47; support by multiple groups, 4, 5, 11–

14, 19–20, 89, 101–2, 111–13, 128, 131–32, 140, 198–200; timing, 3, 23, 54, 88–89, 102–13
adverse selection, 17, 73, 90, 112, 193n7, 202, 241
Aetna Life Insurance Company, 72, 73, 98, 151, 153, 170n37
age, impact on savings, 250
Aid to Families with Dependent Children, 6n1
Alabama, 58t, 95t, 103t, 114n6, 172, 175t, 210t, 214t, 216t, 219t, 252, 254, 265
Alabama Manufacturers and Operators Association, 172
Alchian, Armen A., 15, 19
Aldrich, Mark, 100t
Alexander, Magnus, 128
Allegheny County, Pennsylvania, 35t
Allison, Paul D., 255
Alston, Lee J., 27n8, 112
Alter, George, 74
Altonji, Joseph G., 52n9, 53n16
amendments, strategies, 127, 133, 134, 136, 139, 142, 145n39, 159, 161–62, 173, 189, 190–91, 196n24, 200
American Association for Labor Legislation (AALL), 26n2, 28, 29, 100, 118n29, 197, 198
American Federation of Labor (AFL), 101, 106t, 108, 124
analytical framework, 15–21
Annual Coal Reports, 206